Contents

Discover Austin, San Antonio, and the Hill Country

When Austin is mentioned in casual conversation, all eyes light up. Those who have been to Austin can't help but chime in with enthusiasm, and those who have never been have heard only amazing things about this alluring city in the heart of Texas. What makes Austin so memorable and so liked? Austin is perhaps the most diverse city in Texas, and probably all of the American South. It is the land where John Wayne meets Andy Warhol. Here cowboys drive pickup trucks with abstract murals painted on the side, Christmas lights are on year-round, bizarre landmark art is everywhere, and hip youngsters and old country folk two-step together in honky-tonks.

Absolutely anyone can come here and feel right at home. The closet cowboys can safely pretend they are real cowboys without fear of looking out of place. Messy-haired hipsters can stagger down urban streets lined with clubs, diners, and music stores, while fans of folk art and Americana pillage countless boutiques and curiosity shops. The voices of passionate politicos boom throughout grand halls, while sports fans hoot 'n' holler at UT Longhorn games in jam-packed stadiums. Music lovers of all genres fall in love with countless musicians and venues in a wildly eclectic music scene that never shuts off its amps.

The capital city dances to the beat of many tunes, but the fun doesn't stop at the Austin city limits. This colorful town is the porch

overlooking the gorgeous Texas Hill Country. This lush region at the center of the state is lined with vast rolling hills spotted with fields of wildflowers, grazing cattle, and little historic towns founded by German pioneers who brought their accordions and schnitzels to the Wild West. Folks from all over come to the region's sleepy hamlets to hunt for antiques, ride horses, explore caves, go wine-tasting, and hide out in bed-and-breakfasts.

At the southern reaches of the Hill Country is the Graceland of Texas history – San Antonio. Here pilgrims from all over venerate the legendary Alamo, stroll down the beautiful and romantic River Walk, and spend the day at massive theme parks and world-class museums.

Given half a chance, Austin, San Antonio, and the Hill Country are guaranteed to suck you in and take you for a spin, like a cow in a twister on the plains. Where else can you see Willie Nelson perform, go wine-tasting, explore underground caves, visit the Alamo, see ancient dinosaur bones, dance to German polka music, and catch a Mexican rodeo all in one weekend? Nowhere else but deep in the heart of Texas.

Planning Your Trip

Austin can make your head spin with the amount of things to see, hear, smell, taste, and touch. On top of this there's all that the Hill Country and San Antonio has to offer. When planning your trip to this region, no matter how much time you plan on staying, it's best to know what exactly you want out of your travel experience. However, relying too heavily on schedules and planning isn't the best way to get the most out of Austin and the Hill Country. Instead, I highly recommend the "research and meander" approach. This consists of flipping through the book in hand, flagging the pages and listings that catch your attention, and then when you arrive, let yourself get lost in the destination. In Austin and the Hill Country it takes no effort to get sidetracked and find yourself in a situation or a place that

is most unique. Whatever your plans might be, you will most likely end up straying, roaming, swerving, and meandering off course. Follow your curiosity and sense of adventure.

On a more practical note, Austin and San Antonio are easy places to get to, with all major airlines flying in and out of Austin-Bergstrom International Airport and San Antonio International Airport. Booking your flight or getting a spot on a bus is easy from anywhere in the United States. If you want an urban experience filled with live music, tall buildings, late-night escapades, and socializing, stick to the Austin metropolitan area. If you want to explore the great outdoors, the many hiking and biking trails, the lakes and streams, the fields of wildflowers, and maybe visit some wineries, you can find all this in the

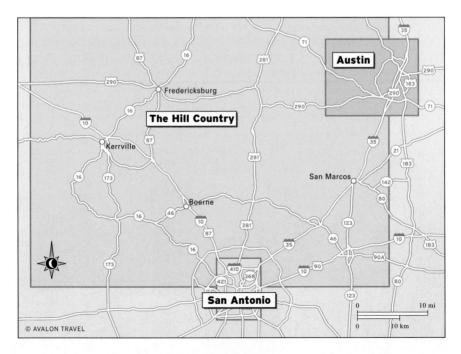

surrounding Hill Country. If you want a family vacation filled with museums and theme parks, you'll probably stick to Austin and San Antonio. Or, you may opt for the very best way to experience it all—a road trip through the whole Hill Country, from Austin to San Antonio. All this requires is an operable automobile (with air-conditioning), a Wilco CD (or Son Volt if you prefer), some gasoline, and the will to meander.

▶ WHERE TO GO

Texas is big, and the south-central Texas area commonly referred to as the Hill Country is nothing to shake a stick at either. This guidebook starts with Austin, then moves south through the beautiful stretch of the Hill Country just west of Austin and down to San Antonio.

Austin

Although Austin is geographically south of the center of Texas, it's definitely the heart of the state. The Austin metropolitan area is situated at the eastern edge of the Hill Country on the I-35 corridor. The Colorado River winds its way through town and has been dammed off, making a lush and beautiful lake the focal point of downtown. Austin is the state capital and the commercial heart of several established industries such as ranching, dairy, and cotton, and in the last decade a thriving tech industry has taken root. To the surprise of visitors, Austin is not in a flat and arid Texas setting as one might imagine. Austin is hilly, and these hills are blanketed with a wide variety of deciduous and evergreen trees and an astounding amount of wildflowers. Rivers, streams, and lakes abound, and all the regional and state parks serve to protect and keep this area beautiful.

The Hill Country

The remarkably beautiful region called the Hill Country, to the west of Austin and north of San Antonio, is the Napa Valley of Texas. This

IF YOU HAVE...

- **A WEEKEND:** Explore Austin and make a trip to the Salt Lick in Driftwood.

- **FIVE DAYS:** Add a tour of the Hill Country.

- **ONE WEEK:** Head south and visit the Alamo while exploring San Antonio.

picturesque Boerne in the Hill Country

slow-paced, wildly beautiful, sprawling region is filled with small towns—some have been frozen in time and others are catching up. Nearly all these wide spots in the road have the signature Hill Country feature at the center of town—a beautiful, historic, ornate limestone courthouse. Between many of these towns there are pristine parks, wineries, antique shops, and roadside fruit stands. The industry in these parts is farming, ranching, wine-making, and tourism. As you drive around the Hill Country you may notice exotic animals such as zebra, bison, and antelope grazing in fields. Many ranches in the Hill Country have become home to these rare animals.

San Antonio

The age-old city of San Antonio is just to the south of the Hill Country, southwest from Austin. If you look at a map of this vibrant, historic city you will notice that all roads lead to San Antonio. This river town is one of the top 10 largest cities in the United States. It's also home to Texas's most visited tourist attraction—the Alamo—as well as the famous River Walk, which cuts its way through downtown, and several Spanish missions. The Mexican border is only 175 miles away; this proximity has given San Antonio an incredibly rich Latino heritage.

▶ WHEN TO GO

Many locals say that south-central Texas has only two seasons: winter and summer. For the sake of simplicity, we'll do like the locals and lump fall and spring in with summer since they're so short. The best time to come to Austin, San Antonio, and the Hill Country is during this long summer season, which starts in March and wraps up by the end of October. Although June, July, and August are hellishly hot, these are the peak months for tourism. Central Texas is overflowing with people. The warm, laid-back climate and the uncanny amount of festivals and music events draw thousands to the area from all over the country. Everyone is kept alive during the summer months by drinking lots of

Barton Springs Pool in Austin

water and by air-conditioning. Anywhere you go indoors the air is a cool 78°F, and outdoors there are many swimming holes, lakes, rivers, and pools to keep cool in.

Besides the long summer heat the only other thing to keep in mind when planning to visit south-central Texas is allergies. The Hill Country is rife with wildflowers and trees that come to life in the spring. Sure, it's beautiful, but for the person who suffers from seasonal allergies, it can be hard to enjoy. The peak allergy times are December–January (mountain cedar), March–April (oak), and September–October (ragweed). If you plan to come during these months, be prepared to buy an antihistamine.

Although folks visit the region year-round, winter is definitely the quiet season. In Austin you can always find fun things to do, however San Antonio and the Hill Country are pretty sleepy this time of year.

► BEFORE YOU GO

The first thing one must consider before heading to Austin, San Antonio and the Hill Country is lodging. Because of the many festivals and events that happen, and due to the large crowds that descend on Austin and San Antonio, hotels are often booked months in advance. The earlier you book your hotel the better chance you have of staying in the hotel of your choice, or having a place to stay at all.

Getting to Austin and San Antonio is easy as both destinations have international airports with flights offered by most of the larger carriers. However getting to the Hill Country isn't as easy. Due to the lack of public transportation in the rural areas you will need to either rent or borrow a car for your Hill Country road trip. As for getting around in Austin, a great metro system, pedi cabs, and taxi cabs make navigating the signs pretty easy. However, getting around San Antonio is much more complicated. There is a metro system, however everything is so spread out you will have more fun and waste less time by renting a car.

When visiting during the warmer months bring lots of casual clothes. It is imperative to bring lots of shorts, comfortable shirts, and sandals or flip-flops. Why lots of these you may ask? Everything gets sweaty in a matter of minutes. In one day you can easily go

the Driskill Hotel in Austin

through four changes of clothes: one for the morning, one for swimming, one for after swimming, and one for dinner out. If you'll be visiting the region anytime between June and September don't waste any room in your luggage with jackets, sweaters, or anything with long sleeves. Believe me, you won't get chilly, except for the kind that comes in a bowl. However, during the winter months temperatures are sometimes near freezing, so be sure to bring warm clothes.

Explore Austin, San Antonio & the Hill Country

► AUSTIN IN A LONG WEEKEND

Austin is a city that can easily be explored in a weekend. It's so alive and accessible that it takes little effort to be completely submerged in its life and culture.

Day 1
This is the only day you will probably wake up early. First thing on the agenda is a hearty breakfast at the Magnolia Cafe. To walk off all the calories you just consumed, head straight out the door of Magnolia Café and down the street to Town Lake. Enjoy walking the overgrown trails, watch the turtles and ducks putter in the lake, and take in the stunning view of Austin's skyline.

Just as a Catholic must first visit the Vatican upon arriving in Italy, a first day in Austin must include a visit to the Texas State Capitol. Walk the grounds, stand beneath the dome, and take in the gubernatorial history. If it's between 10 A.M. and noon make your way over to the Governor's Mansion for a tour of the historic home that some think is haunted.

By this point you may be burnt out on politics. The solution to this is South Congress

South Congress Avenue

Uncommon Objects

Avenue. Take your time walking the popular strip lined with funky shops, trendy boutiques, and restaurants. If you get hungry order shrimp fajitas at popular Güero's Taco Bar. Be sure to check out the oddity shop, Uncommon Objects, and marvel at the $3,000 cowgirl boots at Allen's Boots.

Before evening descends, be sure to get a copy of the *Austin Chronicle* and look at the entertainment section. Pick a show—any show—and plan to have your socks blown off by a great night on the town. For an authentic Austin night out, catch an authentic country band at the Broken Spoke. If you have the guts and gumption, try your hand at two-stepping.

Day 2

The first half of Day 2 is devoted to an education in Texas pride by visiting the Bob Bullock Texas State History Museum. Mull over the exhibits, experience the multimedia show in the Spirit Theatre, and buy some souvenirs in the gift shop. After you're all Texased out, have lunch at nearby Texas Chili Parlor, then walk over to Austin's world-class repository for art, the Blanton Museum of Art. After admiring Picasso's art, make your way to one of the most popular record stores in the United States, Waterloo Records. Be sure to check out their extensive collection of Texas music. After buying a Willie Nelson CD, walk across the street to Whole Foods world headquarters and buy some granola, energy bars, or dried fruit to consume the following day on a hike.

Walk up West 6th Street to Z'Tejas Southwestern Grill for an amazing dining experience. The blackened catfish enchiladas are a hit. To work off some of the calories, walk to Baylor Street to marvel at the famous poison survivor, the Treaty Oak. Walk to the

TEXAS PRIDE

Texans have lot of reasons to be proud. Much of this pride stems from the state's history. Texas was created in a revolution against a brutal dictator, and stood alone for almost ten years as an independent nation. Eventually Texas joined the United States as a result of a treaty between two sovereign nations, not because it was a conquered territory or constituted land purchased from a European power. It's understandable that the original Texans were proud of what they created and have passed on that pride to later generations and new arrivals. Most of Texas pride finds its roots in Austin and San Antonio.

AUSTIN

Since Austin is the capital of the Lone Star State, much of Texas pride has been generated, legislated, and spurned here. The **Texas State Capitol** alone is a testament to Texas self-adulation. After all, it's taller than the nation's capitol. Here you can gaze into the portraits of all the state's governors and peer into Texas politics. Not too far from the capitol building is the **Old State Capitol Building Ruins,** which tell ghost tales of the founding of the State of Texas. And one can't forget the **Governor's Mansion,** which is an original Abner Cook design that is still inhabited by presiding governors and their families.

Just a stone's throw from the state capitol is the most grand testament to Texas in all the world, the **Bob Bullock Texas State History Museum.** Inside this enormous and opulent shrine are historical exhibits, dioramas, and a multi-media experience – all promoting the richness of Texas pride.

From Austin all the way out into the Hill Country is what's known as LBJ land. Lyndon B. Johnson, the 36th president of the United States, was a proud native son of Texas. Austin is home to the **LBJ Library and Museum,** the nation's most visited presidential library. Texans are proud of LBJ, and his library/museum is a sort of mecca for them. The exhibits follow LBJ's story, from a small-town Texas upbringing to carrying the presidential torch through the civil rights movement.

LBJ

All of the above are passive ways to experience Texas pride. The best way to actively experience it is by dancing two-step at Austin's premier honky-tonk, the **Broken Spoke.** Dance to live country bands and drink Texas longneck beers (Lone Star or Shiner) in a friendly environment.

THE HILL COUNTRY

Just west of Austin, in a wide spot in the road called Driftwood, is one of Texas's most famous BBQ joints, the **Salt Lick.** People drive from miles around to eat ribs, brisket, and smoked turkey in this ancient converted ranch house. Just up the road, in the town of Johnson City, is **LBJ's boyhood home** and **LBJ State Park and Historic Site,** which is the sight of LBJ's ranch and his **Texas White House.**

Texas German heritage is ushered in each October with the sounds of accordions for **Oktoberfest.** This three-day bratwurst, schnitzel, and German beer extravaganza draws big crowds to Fredericksburg. Two stages, two

the Salt Lick

tents, great food, polka and waltz contests, and music with an oompah make this a great Texas Hill Country celebration.

Texas is where the art of ranching was invented and perfected. One of the state's most famous and historic ranches is **Y. O. Ranch,** with longhorn cattle drives, a classy lodge-style resort, cowboys, and zebras. Whether you stay here or just take a wildlife tour, your experience will be exclusively Texan.

SAN ANTONIO

Out of all points of interest related to Texas pride, the one that is most revered, most iconic, and embodies the most legend is **The Alamo.** This is where the revolution went down, the independent spirit was ignited, and the pride was grafted. Ponder where and how Davy Crockett may have died, and marvel at the bravery of those men who faced certain slaughter.

Also in San Antonio is the **Institute of Texan Cultures,** which features exhibits on all the peoples that have lived in Texas and occupied prominent places in the state's history. For Texas dinosaur history there's the **Witte Museum.** Lastly, a visit to Texas wouldn't be complete without seeing the **Texas Pioneer and Ranger Museum.**

You can't talk about Texas pride without talking about Mexico and Latino heritage. The experience of Mexican food is best had at **Mi Tierra.** The old building is festively decorated with stings of lights, tinsel, and a mariachi band often strolls around the tables. Be sure to sit in the dining room with masterfully executed murals telling the story of Mexico and Texas.

The most spectacular festival in all of Texas is **Fiesta San Antonio.** For 10 days in April San Antonio has a citywide celebration in honor of the heroes of Texas history that includes carnivals, sports, fireworks, entertainment, feasts, art exhibits, and parades that float down the San Antonio River.

Lastly, Texas history can't be more enjoyable that experienced through a simulated helicopter experience in the **Tower of the Americas** 4D theater ride **Skies Over Texas.**

Stubb's

Alamo Drafthouse

corner of Lamar and 6th Street and watch someone beat the hell out of a scoop of ice cream at famous Amy's Ice Cream.

By this time the music scene is getting revved up. Check out music listings in the *Austin Chronicle* and catch some live music at any of the venues on 6th Street or Red River Street, such as Stubb's, Emo's, Antone's, or anywhere for that matter.

Day 3

Day 3 is kicked off with a visit to the most visited presidential library in the United States, the LBJ Library and Museum. You're sure to be moved by the exhibit about the president's life, and may well up with tears when you walk into the JFK assassination exhibit, or feel a sense of pride at seeing the pen LBJ used in signing the Civil Rights Act. Follow up the LBJ experience with lunch at the Rudy's Country Store and BBQ for some smokey beef brisket. If it's not over 100°, make your way to Wild Basin Wilderness Preserve, which is close by. Walk the hills and learn

about central Texas flora and fauna through interpretive trails. At the end of the trail be sure to sit on the bench and enjoy the view for as long as you can. Once you've acquired peace of mind take a walk through Zilker Botanical Garden. Consider how this area was the stomping grounds of dinosaurs in the Prehistoric Garden, then get a bite to eat at nearby Shady Grove. Once you've filled up on great Tex-Mex, head downtown to famous Alamo Drafthouse. Order a pitcher of beer and either watch a random movie or attend a Michael Jackson sing-along.

Day 4

Your final day in Austin will start with a trip to Zilker Park where you'll take a ride on the Zilker Zephyr. This mini-train takes both mini and full-size passengers throughout the park. Assuming it's a hot summer day, get off at the Barton Springs stop and jump in Barton Springs Pool. Plan to splash around in the constantly 68° water and people-watch for a couple of hours.

the Zilker Zephyr

Before evening sets in, make your way to Town Lake and watch the Bats of Congress Avenue Bridge, which take flight just before sundown. A great way to view them is by taking a ride on Lone Star Riverboat, a genuine double-decker paddle-wheel riverboat. Follow this up with a visit to Austin's burgeoning Warehouse District. First stop off at the popular pub The Gingerman and drink a pint of beer produced by local brewhouse Live Oak Brewery. It's your last night, so if you still have ears for music, check out some more bands and musicians. Or if you prefer a calm evening, walk over to Halcyon Coffeehouse to roast marshmallows and make s'mores at your table.

► AUSTIN'S MUSIC SCENE

Austin is the undisputed Live Music Capital of the World. With an unprecedented number of live music performances happening every night of the week throughout the year, it has earned the title. Touring national acts, local favorites, and unknowns perpetually fill Austin's venues, clubs, and bars as well as unusual places such as clothing stores, supermarkets, and even the airport. Music fans take full advantage of all this live music and are out supporting the music scene year-round, rain or shine.

The Quintessential Austin Music Experience

Music style and tastes vary greatly, making it difficult to suggest one quintessential music experience, but here's a start. The proper accommodations are crucial for the live music fan. They need to be cheap, centrally located, and near a restaurant that serves breakfast all day. Musicians and fans alike love to stay at The Austin Motel on South Congress Avenue because it meets all these criteria. Once you arrive in town, immediately consult the music section of the Austin Chronicle. All venue listings and festival and event information are found in the pages of this weekly rag. Chances are that at least one band or musician of interest to you will be performing while you're in town.

After a night of live music followed by a visit to one of Austin's many dive bars, you'll probably wake up after noon. If you stay at The Austin Motel, saunter up the street to Home Slice Pizza or Güero's Taco Bar for great grub. If you want to continue with a music-themed visit to Austin, be sure to check out one of the most popular music stores in the country, Waterloo Records, or Cheapo Discs, which is lesser known but has a bigger selection of used discs. If you're a vinyl collector, head over to Guadalupe Avenue and check out Antone's Records. While in town it's imperative that you

Cheapo Discs

MUSIC NOT TO MISS

Out of all the **music festivals** that happen in and around Austin there are a few you simply can't miss if you happen to be in town.

SXSW

In March one of the biggest music festivals in the nation takes over Austin – SXSW, also known as **South by Southwest.** For one week the city is completely overrun by hundreds of musicians and celebrities and thousands of music fans. Restaurants, clubs, music stores, and BBQ joints are teeming with greasy-haired, tattooed, ripped-jean-wearing rock stars and rock star wannabes. The festival features literally hundreds of big names and up-and-coming artists in alternative, indie rock, and even pop. This isn't your typical music convention held in a convention center. Shows happen in all Austin venues from midday to the wee hours. You have to purchase pricy wristbands to get into venues, but it's well worth it. Oh, and good luck getting a hotel if you haven't booked it months in advance.

ACL

The biggest festival on Austin's calendar is **Austin City Limits Music Festival.** For three days in September nearly 200,000 people fill Zilker Park and overdose on music and sun. Spun out of the famous public television show, ACL Fest features top acts, bands, performers, and musical legends in nearly all genres of music. Passes are available for all three days or for single days. Be sure to bring sunscreen and be prepared to sit in the Texas summer heat for this one.

FUN FUN FUN FEST

In the fall, Waterloo Park becomes the site of Fun Fun Fun Fest which features neo-punk, indie pop, electronic, metal and random icons from punk's bygone era. Along with a messy hairdo, be sure to bring sunscreen and a penchant for FUN.

OLD SETTLERS MUSIC FESTIVAL

To kick off spring with some two-steppin', the Old Settlers Music Festival is held in April. For a four-day weekend banjos will be plinkin' and fiddles will be fiddlin' at the Salt Lick BBQ Pavilion in Driftwood just outside of Austin. The festival features over two dozen of the top performers of bluegrass and Americana music on four stages.

KERRVILLE FOLK FESTIVAL

One of the biggest folk festivals in the nation, the Kerrville Folk Festival happens out in the Hill Country every May. This 18-day folk implosion draws the biggest names in Americana, folk, bluegrass, acoustic rock, blues, and country. Fans mull around in fields all day long listening to folk legends past and present. Most festivalgoers camp on site.

pay your respects to local music legend Stevie Ray Vaughn on the south-shore trail of Town Lake. On the banks of the Colorado stands a life-size bronze statue of the guitar god.

While in Austin all music lovers invariably ask themselves, "I wonder how to get tickets to a taping of Austin City Limits?" You have a better chance at sprouting wings than acquiring tickets to a taping of this famous PBS program. The closest most of us can get to that legendary stage is by taking the tour of the studio during the day.

Venues

Austin has over a hundred places that offer live music for both regional and national acts, and nearly all of them are worth checking out. Most are in the downtown area on 6th Street, Red River Street, and South Congress Avenue. Venues generally come alive after dark, except during special benefit shows and during SXSW (more on this later). Most venues have something going on every night of the week, so don't expect the good shows to be only on weekends. You're sure to catch something interesting virtually any time doors are open at the following venues.

Antone's has been Texas's outlet for the blues for decades. In recent years they've expanded their repertoire to include pop, rock, and indie, bringing in some major national acts. If you want to see Willie Nelson perform in a backyard, The Backyard is where it will happen. Austin's premier open-air venue features big-name national acts in pop, country, folk, and rock. Stubb's serves up both great barbecue brisket and superb big-name rock and indie bands. Housed in a historic limestone building, this is where the hip parties go down during SXSW. There's a small indoor stage for smaller acts, while the big outdoor stage features national acts such as Death Cab for Cutie and Queens of the Stone Age. For traditional country and two-step dancing, there's the legendary Broken Spoke. This real honky-tonk will blow your Stetson off when you walk through the door. The crowd is a perfect mix of country folk, young hipsters, and everyone in between, which makes it all-inviting. The premier intimate venue for all things unplugged is the Cactus Café. Big-name acoustic, singer-songwriter, country, and folk acts have graced the small corner stage for over 70 years. The space is small, upscale, and outfitted with a full bar in the back. For those who like it loud and grungy, Emo's is Austin's outlet for punk, metal, and indie rock. To give an idea what is to be expected at Emo's, Trail of Dead got their start here and Johnny Cash has graced the stage. Need I say more?

► HILL COUNTRY ROAD TRIP

A road trip in the Hill Country is an adventure into both beautiful parks with natural wonders and tiny towns that meticulously preserve remnants of Americana and the Wild West. Get ready to do some serious wine-tasting, antique hunting, horseback riding, and hiking. Before setting out, be sure to do some planning. It may be wise to arrange for accommodations ahead of time as well as prearrange activities such as horseback riding.

Day 1

Start your road trip off with a splash by taking a dip in Hamilton Pool Preserve. From Austin drive west on Highway 290, and then go north on Highway 71. If it's hot take a dip; if it's cold gawk for a while at the beauty. Afterwards, head south on Highway 12 to Dripping Springs and eat some great Texas barbecue at Riley's. Once you enter Johnson City stop off at Whittington's Jerky,

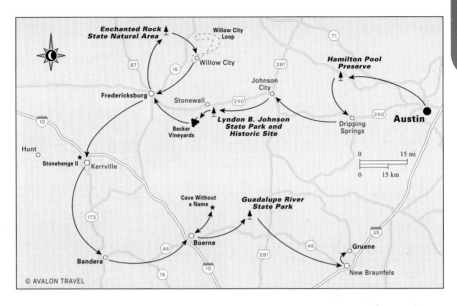

because no road trip is complete without some beef to gnaw on. Swing by the old limestone jail, which was built back in 1894 and is still in use, then proceed westward on Highway 290 towards Stonewall to LBJ State Park and Historic Site. This ranch was President Lyndon B. Johnson's retreat from the world. While here see the Texas White House and watch an old movie about the 36th president. Once you're back on Highway 290 be sure to

stop off at Becker Vineyards to do some wine-tasting. After buying a bottle, continue westward on Highway 290, but make sure the poor sap that didn't drink drives.

Fourteen miles down the road you'll come to the German hamlet of Fredericksburg. For dinner there's schnitzel, beer, and German polka music at Auslander Biergarten. If there's a jazz band playing at the Hangar Hotel head out to the airport for a swinging time. You can also stay at this WWII-style hangar for the night.

Day 2

Be sure to walk Main Street Fredericksburg and check out the various shops and boutiques, and pay a visit to the Pioneer Museum and funky Gish's Old West Museum. If you're a WWII buff check out the National Museum of the Pacific War, where you can see artillery used in the war. Then head north on RR 965 to one of the Hill Country's most precious natural wonders, Enchanted Rock State Natural Area. Take the time to hike

Hamilton Pool Preserve

FAMILY FUN

Central Texas has a wide variety of activities, events, and sights that are sure to keep the kids stimulated and the adults fascinated. From theme parks and curiosity shops to museums with interactive exhibits and mysterious caves, it would take a family two weeks to soak up all the fun. Caution to adults – leave your inner adult at the hotel before embarking on family fun in Central Texas.

SAN ANTONIO

San Antonio is known the world over as a family town. The imaginations of both parents and children are sparked when visiting **The Alamo**, along with the other historic Spanish missions on the **Mission Trail**. A boat ride on the **River Walk** is another great experience for the whole family. The Alamo and River Walk aside, San Antonio is known by kids the world round for its internationally recognized **San Antonio Zoo and Aquarium.** All the animals kids have read about and imagined are here ready to be explored up close. While at the zoo be sure to climb aboard the **Brackenridge Eagle,** a miniature train that travels over two miles around Brackenridge Park.

River Walk

San Antonio also has two gigantic theme parks. First there's **Six Flags,** which has over 200 acres of fun for the whole family. Older thrill-seekers will enjoy the wild rides, and for the younger bunch there are less-scary kiddie rides. Six Flags also puts on campy shows that kids will clamor to see. The other mega-theme park is **SeaWorld San Antonio.** The main attraction here is the killer whale Shamu, who performs in front of an audience. Be prepared to be soaked if you sit in the first rows.

San Antonio also has some popular indoor family hot spots such as the **San Antonio Children's Museum.** The museum has over 80 hands-on exhibits, where children can pretend to be a plumber, an H.E.B employee, an airplane pilot, or a construction worker, and learn about the hardships of being an adult while at play.

There's also the popular **Witte Museum.** Inside the grand halls of the Witte the whole family will marvel at Triceratops and Tyrannosaurus Rex bones, mummies, dioramas, and history and natural science exhibits. There's even a big tree house.

One of the more obscure things in town for the family is the **Texas Transportation Museum.** Here the whole family will marvel at miniature-scale model train sets meticulously built, painted, and erected with a frightening attention to detail. The scale models and their detailed environments are a must-see for the train geek and the curious.

Although your kids may not jump for joy at the idea of an evening of dancing, I guarantee if you drag them to **Leon Springs Dancehall** they will have the time of their life. Here families dance two-step to a live country band along with hundreds of other folks. This family-friendly dance hall has a massive 18,000 square feet of wooden floor that's packed Friday and Saturday nights.

Every January the San Antonio River is drained, and the **River Walk Mud Festival** begins. All weekend this mud-based festival puts smiles on faces. A king and queen of mud are elected to preside over events that include music, games, and all sorts of festivities.

After a long day of fun, make sure to enjoy a meal at **Liberty Bar.** Parents can enjoy a great lunch or dinner with upscale food, while the kids will enjoy eating in a unique two-story house. Think Alice in Wonderland. Another popular place to eat with kids is **Mi Tierra.** Mexican food and ambience reach a zenith here.

AUSTIN

Family fun in Austin begins with watching the flight of the **Bats of Congress Avenue Bridge.** This is a sure-fire way to get the kids excited on a summer evening. Indoor fun is to be had at the **Bob Bullock Texas State History Museum,** where families can have a multimedia sensory overload. Also indoors is the **Austin Children's Museum.** Here kids can come completely unglued in a safe environment. Also inside is **Toy Joy,** the toy store for adults as well as kids.

Kids are crazy about dinosaurs. There are three great places that you can explore their secret past. First there's the **Texas Memorial Museum,** which has an entire room filled with dino bones as well as pickled critters. A good way to get the kids interested in a walk through a botanical garden is by bringing them to the **Dinosaur Walk** in **Zilker Botanical Garden.** Lastly in the dino field, there's the **Austin Nature and Science Center,** where kids can become mini-paleontologists and dig for prehistoric bones.

A train ride can do a family a lot of good. You can't help but smile ear to ear while riding the **Zilker Zepher,** a mini-train that runs through Zilker Park. If mini doesn't satisfy, there's the real deal, the **Austin Steam Train.** This old locomotive takes passengers into the Hill Country for a chugging ride to remember.

A fun place to take the whole family for lunch or dinner is Tex-Mex **Chuy's.** Kids can marvel at the junk hanging from the ceiling and color with crayons while parents can sip margaritas.

THE HILL COUNTRY

The primary sights in the Hill Country for both kids and adults are the various caves and caverns. Everyone will be interested in walking through the **Natural Bridge Caverns** or the **Cave without a Name.** For more of a theme park spin on a natural-cave experience there's **Wonder World Caverns** in San Marcos. If you prefer being high up in the trees, there's **Cypress Valley Canopy Tours.** Here the whole family can travel on cables, up in the tree tops, for thrilling views along with adventure.

The historic German pioneer town of New Braunfels is home to Texas's largest water park, **Schlitterbahn.** A good way for a family to cool down in the summer is to ride chutes and tubes of water, and to splash in pools for a day. West from New Braunfels, in the art town of Wimberley, everyone loves to visit **Wimberley Glass Works.** Watch the world-renowned glass artists blow melted glass into beautiful shapes in a matter of minutes. In Fredericksburg, be sure to take the family to eat at the **Airport Diner.** It's located at the county airport, right on the airstrip. Watch planes come and go while eating a burger.

A fun place for the whole family to stay in the Hill Country is at the **Mayan Dude Ranch.** Families can take horseback rides in the country, eat in Wild West–style mess halls, go on hay-bail rides, and hear ghost stories told around a campfire.

Out in the far reaches of the Hill Country is a replica of Stonehenge.

the face of the enormous granite-domed rock to check out the view and ponder the myths and legends that were born here. If it's not past noon, take a drive on the most scenic country road in Texas, Willow City Loop.

From Fredericksburg your journey will continue south on Highway 16 to Kerrville and on to RR 1340 towards Hunt. Out here you'll be looking for Stonehenge II, a small version of the mysterious rock formation in Salisbury, England. After pondering this head back to Kerrville where you'll head south on RR 173 to get to your final destination, the "cowboy capital of the world" known as Bandera. Once in Bandera be sure to eat at O.S.T. Restaurant. The food is down-home country cooking in the presence of John Wayne memorabilia. One of the area's many dude ranches, such as the Mayan Dude Ranch, is where you'll want to stay.

Day 3

Start the day off with a big cowboy-style breakfast at the dude ranch mess hall, followed by a horseback ride. A guide will take you into the backcountry on trails that have been trodden under hoof for eons. After lunch in the mess hall and a siesta, head downtown and explore the strange Western shops that line Bandera's dirt sidewalks. Also pay a visit to the Frontier Times Museum.

Once you've seen Bandera, leave town by way of Highway 46, towards the historic German pioneer town of Boerne. This lovely spot on Cibolo Creek is a great place to hunker down for the rest of the day. The main activity here is walking Main Street, known to locals as Hauptstrasse. Here you'll find dozens of antique shops, boutiques, and eateries, all in historic limestone buildings built by the German pioneers. When you get hungry, walk over to the river, turn left, and walk down to the Dodging Duck Brew Haus. Dinner with a beer on the outdoor patio is the only way to go. Most folks who come to Boerne stay in a bed-and-breakfast. A reservation service can help you find the right lodgings for your budget.

Day 4

First thing you'll want to do in the morning is drive north on RR 474, where you'll explore the Cave Without a Name. The cave is full of intriguing rock formations, stalagmites, and stalactites. After this head back to Boerne, then head east on Highway 46. Along the way you'll encounter Guadalupe River State Park. Stop off here for some incredible scenery, then make your way to New Braunfels. The main attraction in this area is the charming town of Gruene. Explore Gruene's quaint buildings full of antiques and a few restaurants overlooking beautiful Guadalupe River. At the base of the old town is the Gristmill Restaurant, situated in the ruins of an old cotton gin.

A grand finale to your road trip should be famous Gruene Hall. This old structure with chicken-wire windows is Texas's oldest dance hall. Country music legends still fill this hall with great foot-stomping music.

AUSTIN

At the end of the 19th century, in one of his short stories, the great American author O. Henry referred to the then small municipality of Austin as the "city of the violet crown." In a single phrase he captured the striking violet sunsets that often surrounded Austin in the evenings. Today this colorful evening show is the backdrop to Texas's most alluring city.

The core of Austin's life revolves around a few things: the Capitol, the university, the high-tech industry, and the music. The most prominent of these is its role as the capital of Texas. If Texas were a nation, its economy would rank as the eighth largest in the world. Austin provides the stage for this powerful political and economic evolution and has hosted politicians and their ideas for well over a century. The second most important driving force of the city is the University of Texas, which has always functioned as its main repository of knowledge and disseminator of progressive ideas. Consistently ranked as one of the top universities in the nation and the 15th-best university in the world, UT draws people from all walks of life to Austin, adding to the city's diverse character. Third is the high-tech industry that was first planted here by IBM, and later exploded with UT graduate Michael Dell's founding of Dell Computers. For the past few decades the tech industry has grown to such proportions that Austin has been dubbed "the silicon hills." Lastly is everybody's favorite, the music. Austin is proud to crank up the volume and loudly proclaim itself as the Live Music Capital of the World. With thousands of musicians, hundreds of clubs and venues, and an

© JUSTIN MARLER

HIGHLIGHTS

◖ Texas State Capitol: The stately pink granite building that houses Austin's politics is impressive both historically and visually. Texas is proud to have a capitol building that's taller than the nation's capitol building (page 35).

◖ Barton Springs Pool: The quintessential Austin experience is swimming at Barton Springs in the summer. The town's most popular way to cool down when it's over 100° is splashing, diving, and swimming in the perpetually 68° water (page 37).

◖ South Congress Avenue: Strolling down this popular avenue lined with unique stores, boutiques, curiosity shops, and restaurants is the best way to experience Austin at its zenith (page 38).

◖ 6th Street: Catch a wide variety of live music, meet uninhibited partiers and lonely folks in bars, and gawk at Austin's itinerant homeless, bearded, cross dresser, Leslie Cochran (page 38).

◖ The Bats of Congress Avenue Bridge: Austin is probably most known for the bats that live under Congress Avenue Bridge in the summer. Before dusk, pack a picnic dinner, head downtown to the bridge, find a spot on the grass, and watch the cloud of flying mammals swoop off into the night (page 40).

◖ LBJ Library and Museum: No one has impacted recent Texas history as did President Lyndon B. Johnson. Here you can explore his life, his presidency, and even hear a mechanical LBJ tell some jokes (page 40).

◖ Blanton Museum of Art: The biggest art repository in town is at the newly erected Blanton. Check out the largest public collection of Latin American art in the country, along with works by notable artists including Pablo Picasso and Peter Paul Rubens (page 40).

◖ Bob Bullock Texas State History Museum: The Bob Bullock Museum will change your perspective of the Lone Star State. Texas's vibrant history is captured in dioramas, historical artifacts, and educational exhibits that dazzle the imagination (page 41).

◖ Alamo Drafthouse Cinema: Sip pints of beer, eat burgers and screen independent films and long forgotten B-movies introduced by the stars and directors themselves (page 66).

◖ Lady Bird Lake: One of Austin's best attractions is a natural one. Walk the many trails around the lake, paddle out in a kayak, or take a ride on the lake in a genuine paddle-wheel riverboat (page 75).

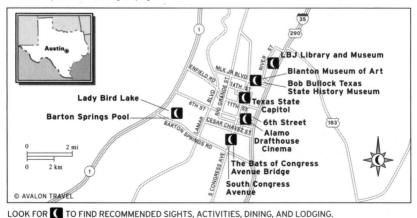

LOOK FOR ◖ TO FIND RECOMMENDED SIGHTS, ACTIVITIES, DINING, AND LODGING.

entire population of devout music lovers, the title is well deserved.

Austin has proven that when you combine politics, education, high tech, and music you get an extraordinary concoction. With these elements Austin has successfully forged its own unique identity and stands in stark contrast to the rest of the state. It's a city that was built with spare parts from the Wild West, pop culture, and Americana. It's urban, and it's rural; it's a big city but somehow retains a small-town vibe; it's rich in history, but forward-looking; it's progressive but laid-back. All the above makes this central Texas town a thrill to visit. Exploring Austin is like being the steel ball in a Rube Goldberg invention. You simply slide down the chute and go for the ride, not fretting about what is around each twist and turn.

PLANNING YOUR TIME

If a long three- to four-day weekend is all you have to explore the town, it can help to plan your time a little. However, the best way to experience Austin is to let yourself meander. For the weekend traveler you can plan to spend most of your time right in the downtown area because all that you could ever want is within arm's reach. Most attractions are within walking distance, such as the State Capitol, 6th Street, and the museums, and everything else is accessible by an inexpensive cab ride. On foot or by cab, in a weekend you can check out some of the galleries and museums, walk around Lady Bird Lake, poke your head into some of the great curiosity shops on South Congress Avenue, and eat some great Tex-Mex. Above all plan on staying up late, walking down 6th Street, and catching some live music at the many varied venues downtown. Music is absolutely everywhere, and is usually good, often great.

If you plan to be in Austin for a couple weeks or longer, I would suggest a whole different approach to planning your time. Figure out where you would like to stay and settle in. Make a home base where you can leave your things and not worry too much about anything. Immediately upon checking in and

unloading your luggage grab a free copy of the *Austin Chronicle* and look through the music and events pages. There's so much going on that there's bound to be something of interest for everyone. Once you've made some mental notes on events to catch, take your time exploring the town and scouring the surrounding area. Catch one of the creepy Ghost Tours downtown, hike in the Green Belt, relax at Barton Springs, take a ride on Lady Bird Lake in an authentic double-decker paddle-wheel riverboat, and spend half a day out at the Lady Bird Johnson Wildflower Center. After all this, if you still have a day to spare take a road trip out into the Hill Country.

ORIENTATION

Austin has several distinct areas where most of the attractions, restaurants, and accommodations are found. These areas are defined by neighborhoods and their streets—some of these streets being sights in their own right. Although Austin has several highways fanning out into the surrounding country the two main highways that box in the city are I-35 and Highway 1. I-35 is on the east side of downtown, and is notorious for traffic accidents and congestion, and Highway 1, known to locals as Mo-Pac (Missouri-Pacific Railroad), is to the west. Most of Austin's sights, great restaurants, hotels, and live music are somewhere between these two freeways.

Since there's no definitive way to explain the geographical areas that comprise Austin, it's broken up here in a way that should make it easy for the newcomer to get around.

Downtown

The first and foremost area is downtown, which encompasses the area north of Lady Bird Lake between I-35 and Lamar Boulevard. Downtown hot spots includes **Congress Avenue,** which rolls down from the State Capitol into town. Then there's the historic and infamous bar-studded **6th Street,** which is Austin's version of New Orleans's Bourbon Street. 6th Street features bars, live-music venues, and some tourist shops that sell junk that doesn't reflect

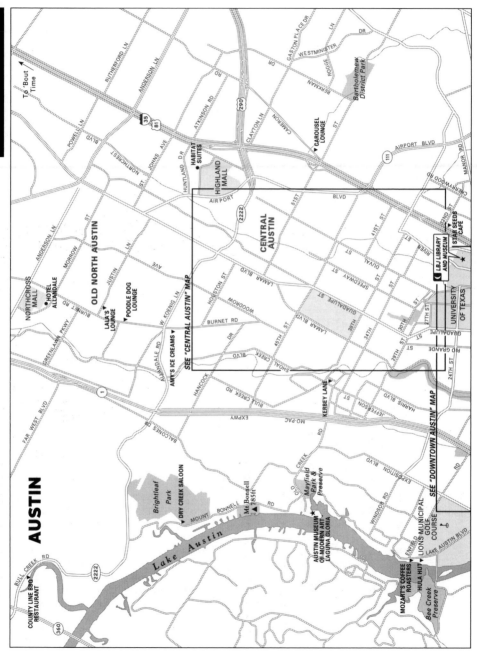

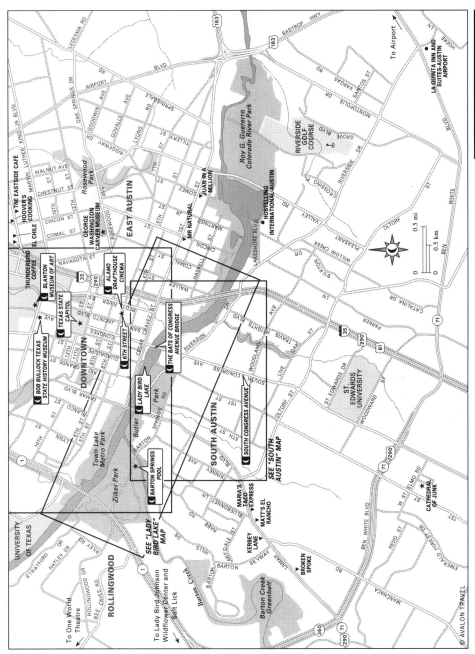

© AVALON TRAVEL

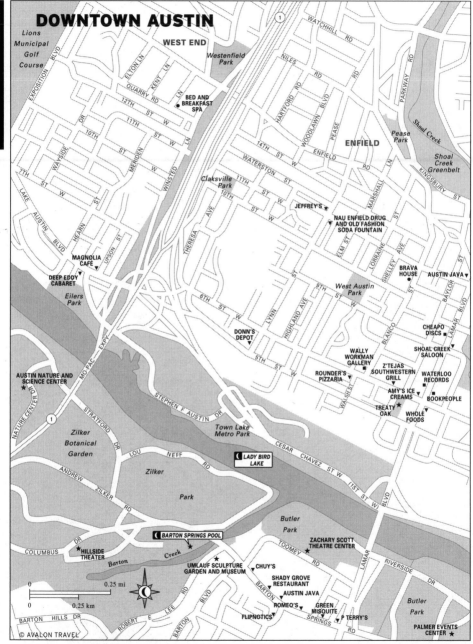

DOWNTOWN AUSTIN

Lions Municipal Golf Course

WEST END

Westenfield Park

ENFIELD

Pease Park

Shoal Creek

Shoal Creek Greenbelt

BED AND BREAKFAST SPA

Clarksville Park

JEFFREY'S

NAU ENFIELD DRUG AND OLD FASHION SODA FOUNTAIN

MAGNOLIA CAFÉ

DEEP EDDY CABARET

Eilers Park

West Austin Park

BRAVA HOUSE

AUSTIN JAVA

DONN'S DEPOT

CHEAPO DISCS

WALLY WORKMAN GALLERY

SHOAL CREEK SALOON

AUSTIN NATURE AND SCIENCE CENTER

ROUNDER'S PIZZARIA

Z'TEJAS SOUTHWESTERN GRILL

WATERLOO RECORDS

AMY'S ICE CREAMS

BOOKPEOPLE

TREATY OAK

WHOLE FOODS

Zilker Botanical Garden

Town Lake Metro Park

LADY BIRD LAKE

Zilker

Park

Butler Park

ZACHARY SCOTT THEATRE CENTER

HILLSIDE THEATER

Barton

Creek

BARTON SPRINGS POOL

UMLAUF SCULPTURE GARDEN AND MUSEUM

CHUY'S

SHADY GROVE RESTAURANT

AUSTIN JAVA

ROMEO'S

GREEN MISQUITE

Butler Park

FLIPNOTICS

P TERRY'S

PALMER EVENTS CENTER

0   0.25 mi
0   0.25 km

© AVALON TRAVEL

COLUMBUS

BARTON HILLS DR

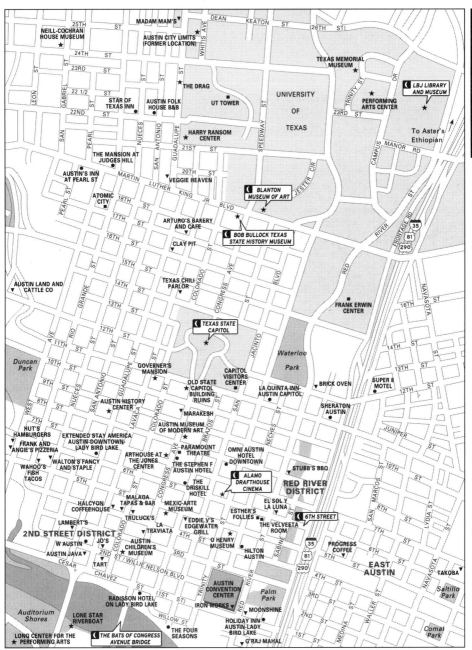

AUSTIN

NEILL-COCHRAN HOUSE MUSEUM
25TH ST
MADAM MAM'S
DEAN
KEATON ST
26TH ST
24TH ST
AUSTIN CITY LIMITS (FORMER LOCATION)
WHITIS AVE
23RD ST
TEXAS MEMORIAL MUSEUM
22 1/2 ST
THE DRAG
LBJ LIBRARY AND MUSEUM
STAR OF TEXAS INN
AUSTIN FOLK HOUSE B&B
UT TOWER
UNIVERSITY
PERFORMING ARTS CENTER
22ND
OF
23RD
LEON
GABRIEL
SAN
PEARL
NUECES
HARRY RANSOM CENTER
TEXAS
To Aster's Ethiopian
MANOR RD
CAMPUS
TRINITY ST
DR
THE MANSION AT JUDGES HILL
21ST ST
GUADALUPE
SAN ANTONIO
AUSTIN'S INN AT PEARL ST
MARTIN
20TH ST
VEGGIE HEAVEN
JESTER CIR
ATOMIC CITY
18TH ST
LUTHER
KING
JR
BLANTON MUSEUM OF ART
PEARL ST
17TH ST
ARTURO'S BAKERY AND CAFE
BLVD
RIVER
FRONTAGE RD
35
16TH ST
CLAY PIT
BOB BULLOCK TEXAS STATE HISTORY MUSEUM
81
290
15TH ST
AUSTIN LAND AND CATTLE CO
14TH ST
TEXAS CHILI PARLOR
COLORADO
CONGRESS AVE
BLVD
RED
FRANK ERWIN CENTER
16TH ST
NAVASOTA ST
GRANDE
13TH ST
RIO
12TH ST
TEXAS STATE CAPITOL
JACINTO
14TH ST
11TH ST
Duncan Park
10TH
GOVERNOR'S MANSION
Waterloo Park
13TH ST
9TH ST
CAPITOL VISITORS CENTER
WEST
8TH ST
SAN ANTONIO
GUADALUPE
NUECES
OLD STATE CAPITOL BUILDING RUINS
LA QUINTA INN-AUSTIN CAPITOL
SAN
BRICK OVEN
SUPER 8 MOTEL
12TH ST
7TH ST
AUSTIN HISTORY CENTER
LAVACA
COLORADO
SHERATON AUSTIN
HUT'S HAMBURGERS
MARAKESH
AUSTIN MUSEUM OF MODERN ART
BRAZOS
JUNIPER ST
FRANK AND ANGIE'S PIZZERIA
EXTENDED STAY AMERICA AUSTIN-DOWNTOWN-LADY BIRD LAKE
PARAMOUNT THEATRE
OMNI AUSTIN HOTEL DOWNTOWN
WALTON'S FANCY AND STAPLE
ARTHOUSE AT THE JONES CENTER
NECHES
STUBB'S BBQ
10TH ST
WAHOO'S FISH TACOS
6TH
THE STEPHEN F AUSTIN HOTEL
RED RIVER DISTRICT
5TH
THE DRISKILL HOTEL
ALAMO DRAFTHOUSE CINEMA
SAN MARCOS ST
8TH ST
HALCYON COFFEEHOUSE
MALAGA TAPAS & BAR
MEXIC-ARTE MUSEUM
EL SOL Y LA LUNA
6TH STREET
LAMBERT'S
TRULUCK'S
ESTHER'S FOLLIES
THE VELVEETA ROOM
LYDIA ST
7TH ST
2ND STREET DISTRICT
LA TRAVIATA
EDDIE V'S EDGEWATER GRILL
SABINE
W AUSTIN
JO'S
4TH
O HENRY MUSEUM
35
PROGRESS COFFEE
EAST AUSTIN
AUSTIN JAVA
2ND
AUSTIN CHILDREN'S MUSEUM
3RD
HILTON AUSTIN
81
6TH
5TH
TART
CESAR
CHAVEZ
WILLIE NELSON BLVD
ST
290
4TH ST
NAVASOTA ST
TAKOBA
RADISSON HOTEL ON LADY BIRD LAKE
1ST
AUSTIN CONVENTION CENTER
TRINITY ST
RED RIVER
Palm Park
3RD ST
Saltillo Park
Auditorium Shores
LONE STAR RIVERBOAT
IRON WORKS
MOONSHINE
2ND ST
MEDINA
WALLER ST
LONG CENTER FOR THE PERFORMING ARTS
THE BATS OF CONGRESS AVENUE BRIDGE
WILLOW ST
HOLIDAY INN AUSTIN-LADY BIRD LAKE
THE FOUR SEASONS
G'RAJ MAHAL
Comal Park

AUSTIN QUICK FACTS

- Founded in 1838

- Population: 790,309 (2010 U.S. Census Bureau data)

- Land area: 266 square miles

- Time zone: GMT/UTC -6 (Central Time)

- Fourth-largest city in Texas

- 16th most populous city in the United States

- County: Travis

- Ethnicity: 49 percent white, 35 percent Hispanic, 7.8 percent African American, 8 percent other

- Sunshine: Austin averages 300 days of sun every year

- Average temperatures: 42-62° F in winter, 75-95° F in summer

- Average rainfall: 32.49 inches annually

- Major employers: City of Austin, Dell, Federal Government, Motorola, IBM Corp., State of Texas, University of Texas at Austin

- Area colleges and universities: The University of Texas at Austin, Huston-Tillotson College, St. Edward's University, Concordia University at Austin, Southwest Texas State University, Austin Community College, Southwestern University

- Median home price in 2009: $214,600

- Sales tax: 8.25 percent

Austin at all. For some reason tourists love 6th Street while locals are way "over it."

Bordered by West 7th, West 8th, Guadalupe, and San Antonio Streets is the **Bremond Historic District,** a rich, middle-class neighborhood of old Victorian homes situated under ancient oak trees. Under the glow of the Frost Building, the most noticeable building on Austin's skyline, there's the **Warehouse District,** also known as 4th Street. In the late 1800s this was the brothel district, then it was turned into an industrial area, and in recent years reverted to the spirit of its origins and is now lined with upscale bars and pubs.

Just west of downtown is **West End,** which includes **Enfield** and restaurants on **West Lynn Street.** Lastly, there's the burgeoning **Red River District** on Red River Street. Just a few years ago this area was the quietest part of downtown, but today it's a bustling street of clubs, bars, and live music in the alternative/punk/metal/hipster vein.

South Austin

The cherished favorite for locals is South Austin. Here you have the ever-popular **South**

Congress Avenue, which has some great curiosity shops, restaurants, clothing boutiques, and music clubs. A few streets west there's **South Lamar Boulevard,** where you can find some of Austin's many vintage and retro shops. South Austin is also popular for outdoor activities, with the gigantic grassy fields of **Zilker Park,** as well as trail heads to the beautiful hiking and biking area called **The Green Belt.** Also in this area is Austin's premiere feature, **Barton Springs.**

Central Austin

Central Austin is largely dominated by the **University of Texas** campus. The UT campus features some excellent museums, the LBJ presidential library, sports stadiums, and performing-arts theaters. The street that connects the UT campus area to downtown is **Guadalupe Street,** known to locals as **the Drag.** This used to be a main artery of action but in recent years has little pulse. Here you'll find some chain clothes stores, freak and chic shops, some cheap eats, and some bars. Also in Central Austin is the **Hyde Park** area, which is home to beautifully restored Victorians and some of Austin's great restaurants on **Duval Street.**

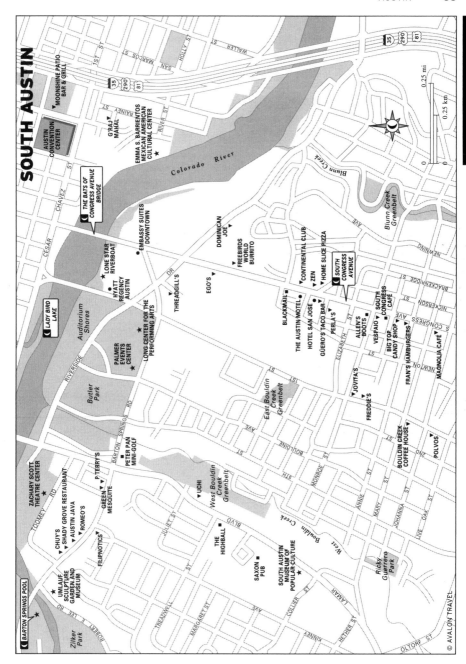

SOUTH AUSTIN

MOONSHINE PATIO BAR & GRILL

G'RAJ MAHAL

EMMA S. BARRIENTOS MEXICAN AMERICAN CULTURAL CENTER ★

THE BATS OF CONGRESS AVENUE BRIDGE

AUSTIN CONVENTION CENTER

Colorado River

Blunn Creek

DOMINICAN JOE

EMBASSY SUITES DOWNTOWN

LONE STAR RIVERBOAT

LADY BIRD LAKE

HYATT REGENCY AUSTIN

Auditorium Shores

FREEBIRDS WORLD BURRITO

CONTINENTAL CLUB
ZEN
HOME SLICE PIZZA

SOUTH CONGRESS AVENUE

Blunn Creek Greenbelt

THREADGILL'S

EGO'S

LONG CENTER FOR THE PERFORMING ARTS

PALMER EVENTS CENTER

BLACKMAIL

THE AUSTIN MOTEL

HOTEL SAN JOSE

GÜERO'S TACO BAR

PERLA'S

VESPAIO

SOUTH CONGRESS CAFE

ALLEN'S BOOTS

BIG TOP CANDY SHOP

FRAN'S HAMBURGERS

MAGNOLIA CAFE

Butler Park

East Bouldin Creek Greenbelt

JOVITA'S

FREDDIE'S

PETER PAN MINI-GOLF

ZACHARY SCOTT THEATRE CENTER

P. TERRY'S

GREEN MESQUITE

UCHI

West Bouldin Creek Greenbelt

BOULDIN CREEK COFFEE HOUSE

POLVOS

CHUY'S
SHADY GROVE RESTAURANT
AUSTIN JAVA
ROMEO'S

FILIPINOTICS

THE HIGHBALL

SAXON PUB

SOUTH AUSTIN MUSEUM OF POPULAR CULTURE ★

Ricky Guerrero Park

BARTON SPRINGS POOL ★

UMLAUF SCULPTURE GARDEN AND MUSEUM

Zilker Park

0 0.25 mi

0 0.25 km

© AVALON TRAVEL

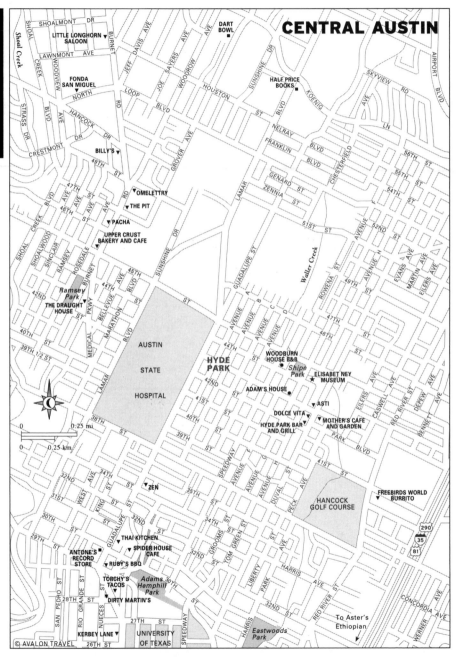

CENTRAL AUSTIN

East Austin

Also referred to as the East Side, East Austin is the area in town that's experiencing growing pains. This is the "sketchy" part of town that's getting gentrified with the help of chic restaurants and city development. What Austinites consider sketchy is tame compared to similar areas in other cities. The East Side has some fine restaurants, a few boutique shops, some art spaces, a few bars and music clubs, and is home to many of Austin's artists.

Old North Austin

Burgeoning Old North Austin is just starting to realize its potential. Visitors to Austin probably won't find themselves up in this area without special effort. It's just north of the UT campus area, and only five miles from downtown. Although there are no sights to speak of, there are some interesting shops, boutiques, antique stores, and "old time" eateries. The area is popular among locals because it has a weird 70s time warp appeal. In Old North Austin there's **Old Burnet Road** (pronounced BURN-it), which has some of Austin's more unusual businesses, and the area's best dive bars. There's also **East North loop,** which is a small bend in the road. This tiny area of shops doesn't look like much, but give it a chance and your sense of curiosity and adventure is sure to be piqued.

Sights

Austin has an eclectic and multifarious array of sights and attractions that include all of what one might expect from a large U.S. city, such as museums, grand architecture, botanical gardens, and monuments to historic figures. These are all what I would call the "typical" sights. Then there are the "atypical" sights, such as the ghostly bronze statue of Angelina Eberly firing her cannon and single-handedly saving Austin, the Cathedral of Junk, the Umlauf Sculpture Garden, the 500-year-old Treaty Oak tree (chainsaw and poison survivor), and the famous bat colony of Congress Avenue Bridge. From typical, to unique, to downright bizarre, all Austin's attractions singularly and collectively perk the imagination, summon the bizarre, and foster new curiosities.

Austin's main attraction is simply nature. The parks and gardens, the lakes and streams, the hiking and biking trails, and the wildflowers and oaks are most worthy to behold, especially at twilight when Mother Nature's coronation ceremony fills the city skyline with the violet crown.

◖ TEXAS STATE CAPITOL

The Texas State Capitol is the nucleus of Austin, both historically and visually. When you see the massive statehouse on the skyline, consider that it almost never was. Over a hundred years ago a tug of war between the cities Houston and Waterloo (Austin was initially named Waterloo) went on for years and every so often the seat of the state capitol would shift between the cities. Austin eventually won the title of state capital and this decision has since shaped the city's development.

When the capitol building was first erected back in 1888 it was believed to be the seventh-tallest building in the world. Today it supposedly stands taller than the U.S. Capitol, a detail Texans are proud to point out. The interior of the Capitol exudes a hushed dignity. Each component, from the grand marble pillars down to the door hinges, is an example of the fine craftsmanship of a bygone era. Old battle flags, sculptures, and portraits of historical figures and significant events in Texas history grace the entryways, walls, and legislative chambers, leaving visitors with strong visual images of Texas's story. A large, colorful marble terrazzo covers the floor of the capitol rotunda, depicting the six sovereign flags that have flown over Texas and 12 battles significant in the history of the state. The rotunda is also home to portraits of all the Texas governors.

© JUSTIN MARLER

Texas State Capitol Building

During the 20th century, as the state of Texas grew, so did its government, and the Capitol became increasingly hard-pressed for space. Over the years quick fixes were made to accommodate the demands placed on the century-old building. Successive additions of new technologies like telephones, air conditioners, and computers, and the need for more offices, led to a maze of false walls and generations of wiring. No one was surprised when a fire broke out in 1983. The event highlighted the need for renovation and expansion. After 10 years of bureaucracy, funding woes, and architectural debate, excavation and construction finally started. In 1993, the underground expansion of the Capitol was dedicated. The results of this project are truly a sight to behold. To build the 620,000-square-foot subterranean extension, nearly 700,000 tons of rock had to be removed, and a 130-foot-long, 32-foot-deep trench had to be dug through solid limestone to connect the original building to the new extension without harming the original foundation or structure.

Today, the opulent Capitol and the beautiful surrounding 22-acre grounds are well worth a visit. The Capitol is free and open to the public 7 A.M.–10 P.M. weekdays, and 9 A.M.–8 P.M. weekends. Free guided tours are offered 8:30 A.M.–4:30 P.M. Monday–Friday, 9:30 A.M.–3:30 P.M. Saturday, and noon–3:30 P.M. Sunday.

Capitol Visitors Center

If you're itching for more information on the Capitol walk over to the Capitol Visitors Center (112 E. 11th St., 512/305-8400, 9 A.M.–5 P.M. Mon.–Sat., noon–5 P.M. Sun., free), at the southeast corner of the Capitol grounds. Here you'll find exhibits, a video presentation on the secret rooms and spaces in the Capitol, and a salute to O. Henry.

Old State Capitol Building Ruins

Directly across from the Capitol, at Congress and 11th, is the Old State Capitol Building Ruins, the remains of Austin's first state house. There's not much there but the original crumbling foundation and a cistern. It's also the original location where University of Texas classes were held back in the late 1800s.

UNUSUAL THINGS YOU'LL NOTICE

There are many subtle and strange things you may notice while exploring this town that prides itself on being weird. Here's a list in no particular order.

Yard Art and Lawn Statuary: While driving around town you may notice Austin's pervasive veneration for yard art and lawn statuary. Popular yard decorations are pink flamingoes, metal kinetic art, bizarre sculptures, and yard gnomes, some of which have an uncanny resemblance to George W. Bush.

Freak Storms: Austin and the Hill Country is notorious for its freak ministorms that pass through the area in a matter of minutes. One second it's a nice evening at about 70° and all of a sudden the wind will whip up and lightning will fill the skies. Then the next thing you know hail the size of golf balls is plummeting to the earth. In an hour or so the sky clears up as if nothing happened.

Liberal Bumper Stickers: If you had to figure out which city you were in solely by the bumper stickers on cars you would probably guess you were in Berkeley, California. A city in Texas would be your last guess. This is one of the great conundrums of Austin. The capital of the conservative state of Texas is liberal Austin.

Bosom Buddies Theme Song: You have to completely tap into your subconscious to catch this one. When you are about town, shopping for groceries at H.E.B., in the lobby of a motel, or even sitting in a piano bar, you will begin to notice Billy Joel's lyrics, "I don't care what you say anymore, this is my life. Go ahead with your own life, and leave me alone." This melody is a subliminal and curious soundtrack to Austin life.

Governor's Mansion

Not too far from the Capitol is the Governor's Mansion (1010 Colorado St., 512/463-5516, 10 A.M.–noon Mon.–Thurs., free). This Greek Revival–style house has been the home for every governor since it was designed and constructed back in 1856. Built with Austin-made bricks, and timbers from Bastrop, this fine architectural work has survived years of politics, stuffy decor, and a number of renovations. Today the mansion is the oldest standing public building in downtown, and is the fourth-oldest governor's mansion continuously occupied in the United States. Over the years paranormal activity has been reported, and in plain English that means some have seen "dead people." Some think it's the ghost of Sam Houston, while others think it's the ghost of a lovesick 19-year-old that shot himself in the guest room. However, the mansion suffered extensive damage from a fire in 2008 so visiting the mansion is not possible at this time.

◖ BARTON SPRINGS POOL

In the dead of summer, when few stray too far from the air-conditioning, there's one place that's sure to be a cool 68 degrees, and that's Barton Springs Pool (2101 Barton Springs Rd., 512/867-3080). This age-old artesian spring–fed pool in Zilker Park has faithfully provided Austinites with a cool place to swim, relax, and socialize for over 100 years. On any given summer day Barton Springs Pool is packed with families, flirting teenagers, sun seekers, and daredevils at the diving board showing off their tricks.

The 1,000-foot-long swimming hole is fed by several underwater springs. When the springs were damned off to create the pool, the natural rock and gravel bottom was wisely left unaltered, preserving the natural ambience. If you're concerned about pollution or hygiene you'll be glad to hear the pool has a legion of advocates (the Save Our Springs Coalition) that closely guard this precious resource. When it comes to pollution Barton Springs' pure waters have been tirelessly defended from the constant threat of damaging development on the aquifer that feeds the pool. As for hygiene, the pool is closed when the fecal coliform count is high. The pool is open daily (except Thursdays) 5 A.M.–10 P.M. in the summer. Access to the

© JUSTIN MARLER

Barton Springs Pool

pool is $3 for adults, $2 for ages 12–17, and $1 for seniors and kids 11 and under. Swimming before 8 A.M. is free but "swim at your own risk." Lifeguards are on duty only during the fee periods. There are two ways to access the pool; the main entrance is off Barton Springs Road. For the back entrance off Barton Springs Road, turn away from Lady Bird Lake on Robert E. Lee Drive, go up the hill and park at the gravel parking area next to the baseball field. Words of advice: call before you go to make sure the pool is open, check the hours (which change seasonally), and don't bring food (eating on the grounds is prohibited).

☾ SOUTH CONGRESS AVENUE

The bat colony at Congress Avenue Bridge marks the beginning of a strip of curiosity shops, eateries, and clubs on South Congress Avenue. If 6th Street is too touristy for you, you'll love this street. Enjoy strolling around with a cup of coffee from the parking-lot kiosk café at Jo's. Be sure to always look up as you walk up South Congress, because many of

these businesses have great signs and sculptures attached to their roofs and storefronts. For example there's a cowboy made out of a muffler, riding a giant rabbit, and a zebra dressed up like Carmen Miranda. Up here you're sure to be lost for hours in the multifarious shops and boutiques like the folk art gallery Yard Dog, the vintage shop Uncommon Objects, the costume shop Lucy in Disguise with Diamonds, and the Western-wear shop Allen's Boots. South Congress is at its best between 6 and 10 P.M. the first Thursday of each month when the businesses stay open late. The streets are full of vendors and artists selling their wares and bands play on the sidewalks.

☾ 6TH STREET

Besides bats, Austin is probably most known for 6th Street, which is Austin's version of New Orleans's Bourbon Street. 6th Street features bars, pubs, live music venues, and sidewalk pizza kiosks. After dusk live music comes from every crack and crevice. On Thursday, Friday, and Saturday nights around 10 P.M. the Austin police department closes off the street and the

AUSTIN'S JACK THE RIPPER

Early Austin history has many shades, characters, and shady characters. One of Austin's darkest chapters took place in 1885 when the young city was haunted by the shadiest character in all the town's history. Lurking in the shadows was a serial killer who is now known as the Servant Girl Annihilator. For an entire year there was a chill of horror on the streets of Austin. This Texas version of Jack the Ripper was never seen, nor caught, but his trail of blood was everywhere. He brutally murdered seven servant girls of poor origins and one man; all were hacked to death with an ax. The bodies turned up in alleys and behind homes, and one of the bodies was found on what is now West 6th Street. Headlines for that year were horrifying and all the city's residents could do was hope and pray that either the killing spree would stop, or the murderer would get caught. On Christmas Eve the last murder took place, and after that there were no more. Eventually three arrests were made and one suspect went to trial, but he was acquitted. All of the murders have remained unsolved. The uncanny twist to this tale is that three years after the Austin murders, Jack the Ripper began his infamous spree in England.

If this bit of Austin's history interests you, novelist Steven Saylor's historical fiction work **A Twist at the End** (St. Martin's Minotaur, 2001) probes into this dark tale. You can also walk in the footsteps of the Servant Girl Annihilator with **Austin Ghost Tours** (512/853-9826, www.austinghosttours.com).

party begins. The scene on 6th Street is pretty rowdy, with hordes of wasted college kids and scantily clad girls. There's always a contingency of men roaming about, afflicted with an acute case of machismo, looking for a date, a fight, or both in one. The scene can get pretty sketchy later in the night when "gangsta" types start mixing with the college kids. A good time to bail on this scene is around midnight, and especially before the bars close at 2 A.M.

Besides clubs and bars there's also a slew of terrible tourist shops that feature belt buckles, Texas memorabilia with the state flag screen-printed on everything, samurai swords (don't ask why), and ridiculous touristy T-shirts that say things like, "F*** Y'all, I'm from Texas," which doesn't represent Texas or Austin in even the slightest way.

Sure there are some good live music spots here, but you have to put up with lots of nonsense to enjoy it. If you like Spring Break at Daytona Beach, or New Orleans during Mardi Gras, you'll probably like 6th Street.

LADY BIRD JOHNSON WILDFLOWER CENTER

Come spring, Austin and the surrounding Hill Country have some of the most varied and beautiful wildflowers in the state. It's no surprise there's a center devoted to these little guys. In 1982 the Lady Bird Johnson Wildflower Center (4801 La Crosse Ave., 512/232-0100, www.wildflower.org, 9 A.M.–5:30 P.M. Tues.–Sat., noon–5:30 P.M. Sun., $8, $7 for seniors and students, $3 children 5–12) was founded under a different name, and at a different location, by two spry advocates of native plants, former First Lady of the United States Lady Bird Johnson and a friend. In 1995 the center was moved to its current location on 279 acres southwest of Austin, and in 1998 was renamed in honor of Lady Bird Johnson. The main grounds include 16 carefully placed and meticulously maintained gardens, all designed after the region's natural landscape, using native plants. The gardens weave though and around several stone buildings that serve as educational centers and galleries, and lead to even more gardens with wisteria-covered pergolas and flower-lined promenades. The center isn't in Austin proper, but it's well worth the drive. Since it's all hinged on wildflowers and seasonal native plants, don't bother visiting in the fall or winter when everything is dead.

◖ THE BATS OF CONGRESS AVENUE BRIDGE

Austin's main attraction isn't always rock stars. The bats of Congress Avenue Bridge are the star attractions every evening when they fly out from under Congress Avenue Bridge by the thousands in search of bugs. When the bridge was reconstructed in the 1980s they had no idea this spot would become the largest urban bat colony in North America. These Mexican free-tailed bats migrate each spring from central Mexico to various roosting sites throughout the southwestern United States, their favorite being here in Austin. Out of the 1.5 million bats in this colony most are females who produce one offspring each June. Every night they eat somewhere between 10,000 and 30,000 pounds of insects. You can catch their dramatic exit into the night from March to early November, but the best months are July and August. Best spots for viewing the bat flight are the **Bat Observation Area** at the Austin American-Statesman (at the southeast corner of the Congress Ave. Bridge), the patio at **TGIF's** (at the Radisson Hotel, 11 E. 1st St.), on Lady Bird Lake from a **canoe** (rent from Zilker Park Boat Rentals for $10 an hour, www.zilkerboats.com), or on an authentic **double-decker paddle-wheel riverboat** (Lone Star Riverboat, 512/327-1388, $8 per person). Best time for viewing is sunset, and parking is offered at the Austin American-Statesman after 6 P.M. No public restrooms are available. For more information on the bats, such as flight times, call the Bat Hotline at 512/416-5700, ext. 3636.

◖ LBJ LIBRARY AND MUSEUM

Considered the most visited presidential library in the United States, the LBJ Library and Museum (2313 Red River St., on the UT campus, 512/721-0200, www.lbjlibrary.org, 9 A.M.–5 P.M. daily, free) explores the life and politics of Lyndon Baines Johnson. If you know little to nothing about LBJ, the permanent exhibit that unveils his life is sure to capture your interest and foster an appreciation of the 36th president. Midway through the exhibit, expect

LBJ Library and Museum is the most visited presidential library in the U.S.

© JUSTIN MARLER

an emotional sucker punch. The exhibit unveils the assassination of JFK in a moving way. From here on out it explores the period in U.S. history that ushered in a new era in culture and politics—the 1960s. When you surface in the gigantic main room and look up, your breath will be taken away by a towering wall of glass, behind which are floors of red archives containing everything LBJ ever wrote, did, and darn near thought. Be sure to listen to the mechanical LBJ tell jokes.

MUSEUMS, HISTORY, AND ART
◖ Blanton Museum of Art

The only art museum in Austin with a permanent collection to speak of is Blanton Museum of Art (23rd and San Jacinto, on the University of Texas campus, 512/471-7324, 10 A.M.–5 P.M. Tues.–Fri., 11 A.M.–5 P.M. Sat., 1 P.M.–5 P.M. Sun., $9, $7 for seniors, free every Thurs. with extended hours on the third Thurs. of each month). Located at the edge of the university campus in downtown Austin, the Blanton is the largest university museum in the United

who first inhabited the region to the Spanish explorers of the 1500s and the legendary battle at the Alamo, through the oil boom to the present day, Texas's history is chronicled in life-size dioramas and interactive exhibits. The facility also houses two theaters. There's the Texas Spirit Theater, which provides a multimedia, cinematic experience complete with special effects that bring Texas's story to life. The museum also boasts Austin's only IMAX theater, which operates independently of the museum.

So who was Bob Bullock, you might ask? He was a highly regarded state politician who eventually became the lieutenant governor. His vision and passion for all things Texas brought the museum into fruition. Admission prices vary. I suggest getting a combination ticket that includes access to the exhibits and one or both of the theaters. A combination ticket including the Texas Spirit Theater is $10 for an adult.

For those who haven't acquired Texas Pride, or just aren't in the mood for a multimedia Texas experience, "never mind the Bullocks." There are many other museums to saunter through.

© JUSTIN MARLER

Texas history is taken to a sacred level at the Bob Bullock Texas State History Museum.

States. Inside the 180,000-square-foot complex are both temporary and permanent exhibits, and outside is an attractive public plaza with views of the State Capitol. The Blanton's permanent collection includes some 17,000 works of art, including Old Master paintings and contemporary American art, and is proud to be one of the largest public collections of Latin American art in the United States. Works by notable artists include Pablo Picasso, Peter Paul Rubens, and Fernando Botero.

◖ Bob Bullock Texas State History Museum

Texas state pride is bigger than Texas itself. It's fitting that the museum devoted to the big spirit of Texas is gigantic, and adorned with a 35-foot-tall bronze Lone Star. In the grand polished stone halls of the Bob Bullock Texas State History Museum (1800 N. Congress Ave., 866/369-7108, www.thestoryoftexas. com, 9 A.M.–6 P.M. Mon.–Sat., noon–6 P.M. Sun., $9, $8 students, $7 seniors), the "Story of Texas" is told. From the indigenous people

Harry Ransom Center

There's only one place in the world where you can see the Gutenberg Bible, the world's first photograph, an original manuscript by James Joyce, and a painting by Frida Kahlo all in one place, and that's the Harry Ransom Humanities Research Center (21st and Guadalupe St., on the UT campus, 512/471-8944, www.hrc. utexas.edu, 10 A.M.–5 P.M. Tues., Wed., and Fri., 10 A.M.–7 P.M. Thurs., noon–5 P.M. Sat.–Sun., free). Self-billed as "one of the world's finest culture archives," the Harry Ransom Center is a place where scholars conduct research alongside tourists and the curious. The center houses a robust collection of over 36 million literary manuscripts, including ones by Ernest Hemingway, James Joyce, T. S. Eliot, and Tennessee Williams, and over 100,000 works of art that are rotated into view. Along with showcasing its own collections, the center also has temporary exhibits. Parking is at the Dobie Center parking garage on the corner of 21st and Whitis Streets.

ABNER COOK

When exploring Austin you will undoubtedly notice the many elegant old historic homes–or should I say mansions – that summon images of a more genteel lifestyle that has since vanished. The person behind some of these architectural masterpieces is the master builder Abner Cook (1814-1884). In 1837, the young Cook arrived in the small city of Austin where he worked as a carpenter building coffins and furniture and later log cabins. Eventually Cook worked his way to the top and became Austin's foremost master builder, architect, and pioneer of Greek Revival style in Texas architecture.

During his career he was involved in many projects that shaped the overall aesthetic of the city, such as homes, businesses, buildings on the UT campus, a state mental hospital, a state penitentiary, and the State Capitol building. Many of Cook's buildings have been destroyed to make way for more modern development, but some of his elaborate and stately mansions of the late 1800s can still be seen around town. These magnificent homes are exquisite examples of his popular Greek Revival style and bear his unique trademarks, such as the X-and-stick balustrade motif on exterior rails, and Greek Ionic details.

Abner Cook houses that have survived are the **Woodlawn House,** also known as Pease Mansion (6 Niles Rd.); the **Swisher-Scott House** (2408 Sweetbrush); the **West Hill House** (1703 West Ave.); the **Hotchkiss-Graham House** (2605 Salado St.); the **Donnan-Hill House** (2528 Tanglewood); the **Neill-Cochran House** (2310 San Gabriel), which is open to the public; the **Old Depot Hotel** (504 E. 5th St., now Carmelo's Italian Restaurant); and the **Texas Governor's Mansion** (1010 Colorado St.), which is currently closed to the public due to renovations after a fire in 2008.

MEXIC-ARTE Museum

The MEXIC-ARTE Museum (419 Congress Ave., 512/480-9373, www.mexic-artemuseum.org, 10 A.M.–6 P.M. Mon.–Thurs., 10 A.M.–5 P.M. Fri. and Sat., noon–5 P.M. Sun., $5, $4 for seniors, $1 children 12 and under) has emerged as the official Mexican and Mexican-American fine art museum of Texas. Here you can encounter works by contemporary Mexican, Latino, and Latin-American artists in the museum's three gallery spaces. MEXIC-ARTE offers a permanent collection, but the primary focus here is special exhibits and shows that both educate and get people thinking. On any given day the art here is poignant, colorful, and inspiring, offering a glimpse into the inner life of Latino culture through the arts.

O. Henry Museum

The prolific American short-story writer O. Henry (1862–1910) made Austin his home for a brief stint. His little house, now the O. Henry Museum (409 E. 5th St., 512/472-1903, noon–5 P.M. Wed.–Sun., donations encouraged), is a beautiful Queen Anne cottage containing some of O. Henry's personal items. Born William Sydney Porter in Greenboro, North Carolina, he came to Austin when he was 20 years old. Here he started a humorous weekly called *The Rolling Stone* (not to be confused with the pop-culture magazine of today), fell in love, married, and moved into this house, which was owned by his new wife's family. Ten years later he found himself in an Ohio prison where his writing started taking off. Upon leaving the penitentiary he changed his name to O. Henry and moved to New York City. Here his life fizzled out, with a second failed marriage and alcohol problems. The master of surprise endings eventually died of cirrhosis of the liver.

Arthouse at the Jones Center

Arthouse at the Jones Center (700 Congress Ave., 512/453-5312, www.arthousetexas.org, noon–11 P.M. Wed., noon–9 P.M. Thurs.–Sat., noon–5 P.M. Sun., free) is a museum entirely

O. Henry Museum

dedicated to promoting and exhibiting contemporary art by Texas artists. Founded in 1911 to promote the art of locally celebrated artist Elisabet Ney (whose house is now an Austin museum), the gallery space currently has exhibitions and programs to promote art of the Lone Star state. Street parking and garage parking are available.

Austin Children's Museum

Who needs tons of sugar to get kids amped up when there's Austin Children's Museum (201 Colorado St., 512/472-2499, www.austinkids. org, 10 A.M.–5 P.M. Tues.–Sat., noon–5 P.M. Sun.). This is just about the most fun place in central Texas for kids. What started out as a grass-roots organization for children without a facility eventually became a fancy million-dollar institution, thanks to the Dell Corporation. Inside are two stories with several permanent and temporary exhibits, all very cartoonesque, but learning oriented. Kids are bedazzled by colors, sounds, and hands-on exhibits that spin, bounce, roll, swoosh, tumble, and squeak. Caution to parents—a day here will likely end with a climactic post-fun meltdown.

Along with the exhibits the museum also offers events and programs for children and families, all with the goal of inspiring the joy of learning and constructive play. General admission for adults and children 6 years and up is $6.50; 12–23 months are $4.50 and children under 12 months are free. Museum is free for all 4 P.M.–5 P.M. each Sunday. Parking is available for a reduced rate at the AMLI garage, on Lavaca between 2nd and 3rd Streets.

Austin History Center

Austin's rich history has been collected, archived, and made available by the Austin History Center (810 Guadalupe St., next to the Austin Public Library, 512/974-7480, 10 A.M.–6 P.M. Tues.–Sat., noon–6 P.M. Sun., free). Housed in a historic neoclassical building, the collection consists of millions of photos, maps, architectural drawings, documented customs, newspapers, and records, and is the main repository for history in the central Texas region.

Austin Museum of Modern Art

One of Austin's premier venues for modern

art is the Austin Museum of Modern Art–Downtown (823 Congress Ave., 512/495-9224, www.amoa.org, 10 A.M.–5 P.M. Tues., Wed., and Fri. 10 A.M.–8 P.M. Thurs., noon–5 P.M. Sun., $5, children under 12 free). The facility is small but the space is filled with high-profile, national touring exhibits. Although they do have a permanent collection that includes works by artists such as Christiane Kubrick (Stanley Kubrick's wife) and Chuck Close, they aren't out on display very often. In the future AMOA is dedicated to building a larger facility to accommodate both touring exhibits and the permanent collection.

The museum's second location, Austin Museum of Modern Art–Laguna Gloria (3809 West 35th St. west of Mo-Pac/Hwy. 1, 512/458-8191, villa hours noon–4 P.M. Tues.–Wed., 10 A.M.–4 P.M. Thurs.–Sun., $3 suggested donation), is in a spectacular setting—so spectacular that it upstages the art on display. On 12 acres overlooking Lake Austin, on the outskirts of town, this restored 1916 Italianate-style villa was the Austin Museum of Modern Art's original home. Currently the villa has a meager art collection on display that's not necessarily the best reason to visit. Next to the villa is an active art school that offers more than 400 classes annually for adults and children. Weekend public tours of the villa are at 1 P.M.

Austin Nature and Science Center

Ever wanted to pretend you're a scientist? Austin Nature and Science Center (301 Nature Dr., in Zilker Park just off Stratford Dr., 512/974-3888, 9 A.M.–5 P.M. Mon.–Sat., noon–5 P.M. Sun., $2 donation) offers many different ways to discover and explore for a day. Here you can learn about the plants, animals, and geology of central Texas. The Discovery Lab has several mini–science labs that engage and educate through hands-on exhibits. In the Dino Pit you can become a paleontologist and dig up dinosaur bones.

Elisabet Ney Museum

The oldest museum in Texas, and one of the most interesting smaller museums in Austin, is the Elisabet Ney Museum (304 E. 44th St., 512/458-2255, noon–5 P.M. Wed.–Sun., free). In the late 1900s this castlelike home was the only building in the Hyde Park area, and was the home to German-born sculptress Elisabet Ney. Now you can walk through the bright rooms and view over 80 statues and busts of characters from Texas history as well as both known and unknown characters from Europe.

George Washington Carver Museum and Cultural Center

Austin's recently renovated and expanded George Washington Carver Museum and Cultural Center (1165 Angelina St., 512/974-4926, 9:30 A.M.–8 P.M. Mon.–Fri., 1–5 P.M. Sat., free) is celebrated as the first black neighborhood museum in Texas. Permanent exhibits include the country's only permanent exhibit dedicated to the history and development of Juneteenth, the Texas-born day of jubilee celebrating the end of slavery. There's also an in-depth exhibit exploring the lives of 10 African-American families who have contributed to Austin and central Texas history.

Emma S. Barrientos Mexican American Cultural Center

Austin is proud to have a vibrant Latino community comprised of families, business owners, politicians, musicians, and artists. Emma S. Barrientos Mexican American Cultural Center (600 River St., 512/974-3770, www.ci.austin.tx.us/macc, 10 A.M.–9 P.M. Mon.–Thurs., 10 A.M.–5:30 P.M. Fri., 10 A.M.–4 P.M. Sat.) is emerging as the official Mexican-American cultural center in Austin. Here you can encounter works by contemporary Mexican, Latino, and Latin-American artists, participate in educational classes, and screen films from Mexico's Golden Films era with the Cine de Oro "Lunch & a Movie."

Neill-Cochran House Museum

Austin's 19th-century high-society lifestyle has been petrified and is on display at the Neill-Cochran House Museum (2310 San Gabriel, 512/478-2335, www.nchmuseum.

dinosaur footprints. The 1st floor has fossils, gems, and minerals, with a paleontologist on site to answer questions; the 2nd floor displays rare specimens never before seen by the public; the 3rd floor features wildlife exhibits with mounted birds, animals, reptiles, and amphibians; and the 4th floor has an exhibit featuring colorful and unusual insects, microscopic cave fauna, and fish. Parking is available at the UT parking garage located at 2500 San Jacinto Boulevard, just north of the museum.

Texas Memorial Museum

© JUSTIN MARLER

org, 10 A.M.–9 P.M. Mon.–Thurs., 10 A.M.–5:30 P.M. Fri., 10 A.M.–4 P.M. Sat., $5). This old mansion built by famed Austin architect Abner Cook in Greek Revival style offers an interesting glimpse into the past. Here you can see just how stuffy life was "back in the day," with Victorian doilies to hand wash, and collars to starch. The styles of interior decoration represented here are colonial, empire, rococo revival, and Victorian. Over the years this house has functioned as a Civil War hospital and an institute for the blind.

Texas Memorial Museum

For the kids and parents alike there's the Texas Memorial Museum (2400 Trinity St., on the UT campus, 512/471-1604, www.utexas.edu/tmm, 9 A.M.–5 P.M. Mon.–Thurs., 9 A.M.–4:45 P.M. Fri., 10 A.M.–4:45 P.M. Sat., 1–4:45 P.M. Sun., free), which has four floors of exhibits dedicated to the natural sciences. The big draw here is the dinosaur exhibit that features dinosaur models including a 40-foot-long pterosaur, fossils of saber tooth tiger kittens, and

GARDENS AND PARKS

Zilker Park

The heart of Austin's outdoor action is Zilker Park (2100 Barton Springs Rd.). The park's beautiful setting is unparalleled, with 351 acres of green grass at the edge of Lady Bird Lake, groves of old oak trees, and a dramatic view of Austin's city skyline rising from the trees in the distance. Most of the city's outdoor events during the course of the year happen here, such as Austin City Limits Music Festival, Austin Symphony July 4th Concert and Fireworks, Trail of Lights, Zilker Park Christmas Tree, and the Zilker Park Kite Festival that's been held here for almost eighty years. On the grassy knoll next to Barton Springs, classical, rock and everything in between can be heard at the **Zilker Hillside Theater,** which also is home to the **Zilker Summer Musical** and **Shakespeare in the Park.** Down the parking lot from the theater and at the entrance to Barton Springs is the depot for the **Zilker Zephyr,** a miniature open-air train that weaves through the park—a huge hit with kids. Past the Zephyr and down the riverbank you can rent a canoe and paddle around on **Lady Bird Lake** and get a unique view of Austin. **Blues on the Green** happens on alternating summer Wednesdays at the **Rock Garden,** which is in the middle of the large grassy area that is bordered by Barton Springs Road. The park is also home to the **Austin Nature and Science Center,** where everyone can participate in interactive wildlife, nature, and science displays. Zilker Park also has an entrance to the **Green Belt,** which has trails for hiking and biking. At any given day throughout the year, Zilker Park is a safe bet for a day in the outdoors. Parking lots are available, but it's near impossible to find a spot during major festivals.

Zilker Botanical Garden

Austin's unique climate around the south shore of Lady Bird Lake has made a perfect location for the diverse set of gardens at Zilker Botanical Garden (2220 Barton Springs Rd., 512/477-8672, www.zilkergarden.org, 7 A.M.–7 P.M. daily, free). Gardens include the waterfall, ponds and bridges of the Taniguchi Oriental Garden, the Cactus and Succulent Garden, the Rose Garden, the Butterfly Trail and Garden, and the City of Austin's Green Garden. Lastly, there's the garden that interests the whole family, the Hartman Prehistoric Garden, located on the site where dinosaur tracks were found in 1992. Plants in this garden represent those that existed at the time of dinosaurs. To jumpstart the imagination, small-scale bronze statues of dinosaurs that roamed here have been placed throughout the gardens. The Garden Center Complex houses a little gift shop with items for kids and those with a green thumb. Parking is available.

Mount Bonnell

What is considered a hill to some is a mountain to others. Since Texas doesn't have much in the way of mountains, I suppose Mount Bonnell (Mount Bonnell Rd.) has earned its title. Towering 785 feet above Austin, Mount Bonnell offers a spectacular panoramic view of the city, the Colorado River, and surrounding area. This is a wonderful spot to romantically gaze upon the world below, or reflect on life, liberty, and the mindless pursuit of whatever you may be pursuing. The 200-foot limestone escarpment is a strenuous climb but worth the effort. When you are on top of the mount consider how it was once called "Antoinette's Leap" in remembrance of a settler who jumped off the cliff rather than perish during a Native-American attack. Don't expect any snow-capped peaks, and don't try to find Mount Bonnell by driving towards "the mountain," as you can't see it from anywhere. It's accessed from Mo-Pac

Expressway/Highway 1 by exiting at 35th Street and heading west. On your way back down the mountain, stop off at **Dry Creek Saloon** (4812 Mount Bonnell Rd., 512/453-9244) for a beer and to reflect some more.

Umlauf Sculpture Garden and Museum

The Umlauf Sculpture Garden and Museum (605 Robert E. Lee Rd., 512/445-5582, www.umlaufsculpture.org, 10 A.M.–4:30 P.M. Wed.–Fri., 1–4:30 P.M. Sat.–Sun., $3.50) is truly a one-of-a-kind Austin sight. Never heard of Charles Umlauf? Well, you're not alone. The prolific and internationally recognized artist donated his home and many of his works to his own cause, and I'm glad he did. Strolling around the grounds of this quasi museum perks the imagination, and sparks curiosity. The style of Umlauf's sculpture is evocative and emotional, with subject matter ranging from alien-looking angels to pieces that tell a story about the Nazi invasion of Poland.

UNIVERSITY OF TEXAS CAMPUS

The three things that drive this city are politics at the State Capitol, live music, and the University of Texas. UT is both big in size and state importance. Founded in 1883 on 40 acres just north of downtown, the campus now occupies over 350 acres and draws some 50,000 students to the main campus alone. Many of Austin's main attractions and museums are located on campus, including **LBJ Library and Museum, Harry Ransom Center, Texas Memorial Museum, Frank Erwin Center,** the **Battle Oaks,** the **Cactus Cafe** for live music, and the **UT Tower and observation deck.** Along with these, UT sports draw a phenomenal number of people to Austin and the campus.

Visitor parking is available at seven garages. Garages are located on Brazos Street (the only parking garage open 24 hours), Manor Avenue (for Bass Concert Hall and sporting events), San Jacinto Street (for Bass Concert Hall), Speedway, Trinity (for Frank Erwin Center), 27th Street (for football games), and San Antonio Street.

Rates are $3 for 1/2–1 hour, $6 for 1–2 hours, $9 for 2–3 hours, $12 for 3–12 hours, and less than 30 minutes is free. For more information visit the **Texas Union Information Center** (24th and Guadalupe, 512/475-6636, www.utexas.edu, 7 A.M.–3 A.M. Mon.–Fri., 10 A.M.–3 P.M. Sat., noon–3 A.M. Sun.).

The Drag

Every campus needs it's slightly seedy but commercial area where students can get textbooks and booze. The busy section of Guadalupe Street that runs along the western edge of the University of Texas campus, aptly called The Drag, is Austin's version. Although not as wild as earlier years, The Drag is a bustling area similar to Telegraph Avenue near University of California–Berkeley, with students mixing with street folk at late night cafés, record stores, clothing outlets, live music venues, and bars. It may have passed its prime, and is no longer the cultural epicenter it once was, but there's still lots to see and do here. There are several chain clothing shops clinging to any remaining threads of trendiness, great bars such as **Hole in**

© JUSTIN MARLER

The Drag near the UT Campus

the Wall, tattoo shops such as **Diablo Rojo,** restaurants like **Kerby Lane** and **Madam Mam's,** and a couple of notable vintage clothing outlets. As a side note, The Drag is where *Austin City Limits* and Dell computers began. The giant square, dark, ominous, brown building (across from Madam Mam's) was home to the famous *Austin City Limits* studio where all the classic live performances were taped (before the studio moved downtown), and the Dobie Center (UT dorms) is where Dell computer corporation was cooked up. Parking on and near The Drag can be challenging, so plan on driving in circles and eventually parking a couple blocks away.

AUSTIN'S WEIRD SIGHTS
Cathedral of Junk

History will one day refer to our age as the age of waste, and when future archaeologists discover the Cathedral of Junk (4422 Lareina Dr., 512/299-7413) they may think we worshiped the gods of garbage. In the backyard of a small house in South Austin is Artist Vince Hannemann's life work. Here you'll find over 60 tons of post-market-consumer junk weaved, stacked, stuffed, twisted, and screwed together, all amidst overgrown vegetation. The final effect is astonishing. This temple of refuse has been featured in motion pictures such as *Spy Kids 3D,* and has been the backdrop for top-model photo shoots as well. The artist didn't create this masterpiece to express some profound point about our consumer culture of obsolescence, or because he believes in worshiping transcendental refuse. In his own words he did it "because it was kinda cool." Bravo! It should be noted that the cathedral was nearly scrapped when the city tagged it as a blatant code violation. Luckily the city and the artist figured out how to retrofit the structure to make it safer so it could be preserved. The artist opens the cathedral to the public Saturday and Sunday noon–6 P.M., and by appointment during the week.

South Austin Museum of Popular Culture

It should come as no surprise that there's a home spun South Austin Museum of Popular

Culture in Austin (1516 S. Lamar Blvd., 512/440-8318, 1–6 P.M. Thurs.–Sun., free). The best way to explain this place is by completely dismantling its name. First of all, this DIY museum is really more of a shrine than a museum—a shrine to 1960s and '70s music. And it's actually not about pop culture per se, but about the counterculture. The only thing that's correct in the title is that it is, in fact, in South Austin. Here you can marvel at the incredible world of music from the pioneering age of sex, drugs, and rock 'n' roll. The walls are filled with posters, T-shirts, and memorabilia from this era. For those who don't think poster art is fine art, the founder of this museum says, "'Fine' is a four-letter word. It's the F-word of the art world."

Treaty Oak

When you arrive at this sight you may wonder why an old tree with a plaque on it is worth seeing. Well, this venerable 500-year-old Treaty Oak tree is all about legend, history, and drama that includes religion, truces, chainsaws, poison, and endurance. It is the last survivor of the Council Oaks, a grove of trees that was once a place of religious ceremony for the area's Commanches and Tonowas populations. According to legend, it is also the site where Stephen F. Austin signed a boundary treaty with local Native Americans in the 1800s. In the 1920s, when the Council Oaks were being cleared for urban growth, this one ancient tree was saved from a violent death by chainsaw and consecrated a historic U.S. tree by the American Forestry Association. By most folk the Treaty Oak is remembered not for having witnessed Austin's history, but for what happened to it in the 1980s when a lovesick lunatic poured lethal amounts of poison on the tree to get back at a lover. Don't ask why. In the ensuing months Treaty Oak made national headlines as dendrite doctors tried to save the tree. Now about 35 percent of the tree is alive, and Treaty Oak has become a symbol of endurance for Native Americans and Anglos alike.

If you want to see this historic tree there's no need to make a special trip. Just check it out while you're eating at Z'Tejas Southwestern Grill. Treaty Oak is located on Baylor Street in between 5th and 6th Streets, just west of Lamar Boulevard.

Live Music and Nightlife

At night Austin lights up like a pinball machine. Downtown transitions from all business and politics to neon lights, live music, techno-thumping bars, dressed-up folks, honky-tonks, comedy clubs, fine dining, curbside pizza, and drunks young and old doing the bar crawl. All of this happening at one time and place can provide a vibrant backdrop to one's night. Under Austin's city glow you can have an evening that consists of eating at an expensive restaurant, catching a performance of a local singer-songwriter, and having a drink at a swank bar. Or you can eat a slice of pizza on a street corner and catch a metal band, do some dive bar–hopping, and wake up at 11 A.M. the following day on a stranger's kitchen floor.

There are a few areas with the greatest concentration of action. In downtown there's famous (becoming infamous) **6th Street,** which is Austin's version of New Orleans's Bourbon Street. It features bars, live music venues, tattoo parlors, and some tourist shops (traps). This is largely dominated by UT college students, tourists, and crazies looking for craziness. On Thursday, Friday, and Saturday nights around 10 P.M., the Austin police department closes off the street. The scene on 6th Street can get pretty rowdy, especially after midnight.

For a less sketchy scene downtown, where you'll find men who pluck their eyebrows and women who prefer tapas to an entrée, there's the **Warehouse District** on West 4th Street and the bars on West 6th Street. Historically the Warehouse District was the brothel district,

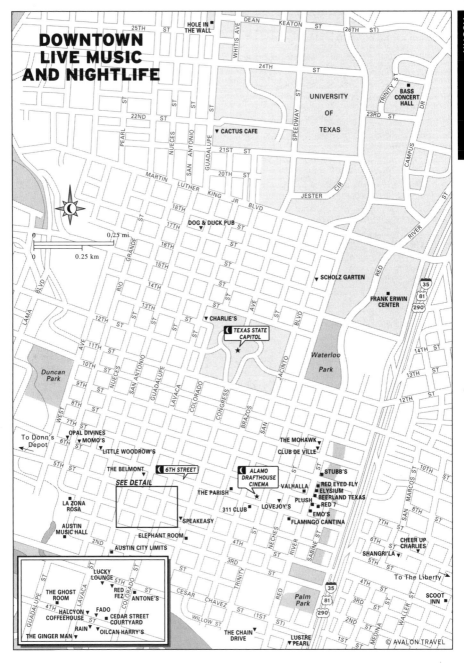

DOWNTOWN LIVE MUSIC AND NIGHTLIFE

25TH ST
HOLE IN THE WALL
DEAN
KEATON ST
26TH ST
WHITIS AVE
24TH ST

UNIVERSITY OF TEXAS

TRINITY ST
BASS CONCERT HALL
23RD ST
CAMPUS DR

22ND ST
PEARL
NUECES
SAN ANTONIO
GUADALUPE
CACTUS CAFE
21ST ST
SPEEDWAY

MARTIN LUTHER KING JR BLVD
20TH ST
JESTER CIR

18TH ST
RIVER ST

GRANDE
17TH
DOG & DUCK PUB
16TH ST
0.25 mi
0.25 km
15TH ST
RIO
14TH ST
SCHOLZ GARTEN
RED
35
81
290
13TH ST
FRANK ERWIN CENTER
LAMA
12TH ST
CHARLIE'S
Duncan Park
11TH ST
TEXAS STATE CAPITOL
JACINTO BLVD
14TH ST
AVE
NUECES
SAN ANTONIO
GUADALUPE
LAVACA
COLORADO
CONGRESS
BRAZOS
SAN
10TH ST
Waterloo Park
13TH ST
9TH
8TH ST
12TH ST
WEST
7TH ST
OPAL DIVINES
To Donn's Depot
6TH
MOMO'S
THE MOHAWK
CLUB DE VILLE
10TH ST
SAN MARCOS ST
LITTLE WOODROW'S
5TH
THE BELMONT
6TH STREET
STUBB'S
RED EYED FLY
ELYSIUM
BEERLAND TEXAS
RED 7
ALAMO DRAFTHOUSE CINEMA
VALHALLA
PLUSH
SEE DETAIL
THE PARISH
EMO'S
8TH
LA ZONA ROSA
311 CLUB
LOVEJOY'S
FLAMINGO CANTINA
7TH
AUSTIN MUSIC HALL
SPEAKEASY
NECHES
RIVER
SABINE ST
6TH
CHEER UP CHARLIES
ELEPHANT ROOM
2ND
SHANGRI'LA
5TH
AUSTIN CITY LIMITS
4TH ST
To The Liberty
3RD ST
4TH
SCOOT INN
LUCKY LOUNGE
5TH ST
RED FEZ
ANTONE'S
CESAR CHAVEZ
TRINITY
RED
35
81
290
3RD
WALLER ST
MEDINA
THE GHOST ROOM
LAVACA
COLORADO
GUADALUPE
HALCYON COFFEEHOUSE
4TH
FADO
CEDAR STREET COURTYARD
RAIN
ST
Palm Park
2ND
THE GINGER MAN
OILCAN HARRY'S
WILLOW ST
(1ST)
THE CHAIN DRIVE
LUSTRE PEARL
1ST

© AVALON TRAVEL

LOCAL MUSICIANS YOU HAVE TO SEE

The city of Austin prides itself in being the Live Music Capital of the World, and for a very good reason: It *is* the live music capital of the world. There are more venues, musicians, and music lovers here than anywhere else outside of heaven. There are over 2,037 recording acts and a total of 8,785 musicians in all genres of music, but I've narrowed the list down to the top artists and bands that live and perform here. If you see any of the following names in the music section of the *Austin Chronicle*, be sure to check them out.

- **Alejandro Escovedo:** Musicians the world 'round are huge fans of Alejandro, but somehow this remarkable singer-songwriter never lands a hit song on the radio. In his case, this is a good thing. As a Hispanic coming out of the late-'70s punk rock movement, Alejandro blends what he knows into a fascinating, moving arrangement of words, melodies, and rhythms that reach all audiences. The best place to see him is at the Cactus Café.

- **And You Will Know Us by the Trail of Dead:** This punk-influenced alternative rock band got their start by playing Emo's as much as possible, but somehow they became more popular in the rest of the country before they really got recognized in Austin. Occasionally they still play in front of a sold-out crowd at Emo's and other smaller venues around town.

- **Asleep at the Wheel:** Austinites, and all of Texas for that matter, have always tapped their toes to the traditional country music pumped out by Asleep at the Wheel. This prolific Grammy award-winning band has survived the terrors of Nashville by sticking to their cause of keeping western swing alive and kicking. If you can catch them at Gruene Hall in the Hill Country you are sure to enter Western nirvana, and the only way to get there is by dancing.

- **Band of Heathens:** This group is a true Austin singer-songwriter collective that draws because of their unique performances that feature all three singer-songwriters up front. These great singers have got soul, blues, rock, country and especially heart. Catch them any time they play at one of the many venues around town.

- **Del Castillo:** Renowned Austin Latin band fronted by Rick del Castillo and Mark del Castillo, Del Castillo is a high energy band that blends many styles including flamenco, rock, Latin, and world music. From their live performance you will never forget the dueling Latin guitar solos. Del Castillo has performed with many legendary acts such as Don Henley and Willie Nelson.

- **Dixie Chicks:** Everyone has heard of the popular but controversial self-made all-girl country band the Dixie Chicks. Although they generally have to stick to stadiums they occasionally surface around town.

- **Joe Ely:** Ely, a country, bluegrass, and rock 'n roll artist, grew up in Lubbock. He later relocated to Austin to pursue his music career. Over his career, Ely has been in numerous bands in a variety of genres. He has performed and toured with Chuck Berry, Carl Perkins, Merle Haggard, Bruce Springsteen, and The Clash.

- **Ghostland Observatory:** After gaining a fast and steady following in Austin, followed by playing a slew of festivals, a taping at the famed **Austin City Limits** set, and an appearance on **Late Night with Conan O'Brien,** Ghostland secured their place in the stripped down electro-rock stratosphere. With programmed beats, minimal guitars and vocals, "no Austin act as achieved so much with so little," as an *Austin Chronicle* writer noted.

- **Grady:** This southern hard rock band consistently puts on powerful shows fraught with hooks and riffs inspired by blues and '70s rock. Grady features seasoned musicians Grady Johnson from the Canadian band Sugar and Whip Layton, who played with Stevie Ray Vaughan and the Arch Angels.

- **Patti Griffin:** This spectacular singer-songwriter has been deep in the background of the music industry and hasn't fully walked onto the mainstream stage for reasons unknown. She has performed with and written songs for some of today's top folk and country acts such as the Dixie Chicks, Lucinda Williams, and Emmylou Harris.

- **Iron & Wine:** Soft-spoken alternative folk master Sam Beam recently relocated to the beautiful Texas Hill Country. This Sub Pop artist doesn't perform live that often, so if his name is listed in the *Chronicle* you best buy your tickets ASAP.

- **James McMurtry:** Blue collar singer-songwriter James McMurtry is a staple around town. He's perpetually performing, and people are perpetually enamored by his unique folk- and blues-based songs that talk about real down-home people in tough real-life situations.

- **Willie Nelson:** Country music legend Willie Nelson is one of the hardest-working artists in Texas. He performs all over Austin and the Hill Country. Seeing him perform here is seeing him perform in his own backyard, and his comfort on local stages really comes through. In fact, despite his age he cuts loose and takes his audience on a ride through his standards, coupled with lots of country classics, all faster and juiced up.

- **Bruce Robison:** The tradition of country ballads of love gone wrong is carried on by Bruce Robison. But don't expect a Stetson and boots on Bruce because he's more of a quiet, contemplative, urban guy that resembles John Cusack. Catch him at the Broken Spoke and other Hill Country venues.

- **Charlie Robison:** Contemporary country that I like to call tractor pop is provided by Charlie Robison. He's a strong country staple for Central Texas, and performs all over the state and the United States. The best place to see him live is at Gruene Hall in the Hill Country.

- **Bob Schneider:** The artist that has the power and charisma to reach fans of many music genres is Bob Schneider. He's a skillful

songwriter who puts on a spectacular show and somehow comes across as honest in his search for mainstream appeal. His folky rock approach sounds like Neil Young meets Beck.

- **Charlie Sexton:** Not many Austinites have graced the cover of *Rolling Stone* in their teens, but Charlie Sexton is one of those few. This prodigy had a hit in the 1980s with "Beat's So Lonely," which was an MTV hit, then he seemed to vanish. For most of the '90s and into the 21st century he was a studio musician and songwriter for some top musicians such as Bob Dylan. Recently Charlie has released a folk/alternative record to much acclaim.

- **Spoon:** Alternative rockers Spoon are Austin's music scene personified. They've been around for years and years performing and recording records that fly beneath the radar. It wasn't until 2005 that they finally broke into the mainstream, and this didn't break their original sound as mainstream often does. They still pop up around town for a low-key show from time to time.

- **The Sword:** Heavy metal and stoner rock has found its way to Austin with the rise of The Sword. These young, semi-nerdy, fully cool kids blast audiences with riff after riff — the kind that made Black Sabbath scary. If you catch them at Emo's be sure to wad up some toilet paper in your ears unless you enjoy tinnitus.

- **Stevie Ray Vaughan:** This American blues guitar legend may have passed away back in 1990, but I'm confident his ghost is cruising all around Austin's music venues. You can pay homage to one of the most influential electric blues musicians in history by visiting his life-size statue on Town Lake.

- **Dale Watson:** Country music has been carefully preserved by local legend Dale Watson. When Nashville gave the boot to country legends such as Johnny Cash and Willie Nelson and started pumping out atrocious pop Western sounds, Dale dug deep into the classics for inspiration. Dale is best enjoyed while sipping on a Lone Star at the Broken Spoke or the Little Longhorn Saloon.

but today the scene is a bit more upscale, with classy bars, dance clubs, live music, gay bars, and pubs. These are all in converted warehouses with entrances that have steps and concrete landings that are uneven and hard to navigate after you've had a few drinks.

The area where new music can be found is **Red River District.** Just a few years ago this area was the dead tooth of downtown—now it's a bustling center for the more alternative and indie forms of live music. Some of the best live music venues in town are all within a two block radius, which makes sampling different bands and drinks easy and fun. The scene here is mostly rockers, punks, and hipsters. Don't let the slew of tattooed folks wearing black and sporting extreme piercings deter you, as the scene here is generally friendly and fun.

Outside of downtown there are a couple areas where you'll find action. First there's **South Congress Avenue.** Here's you'll find a few clubs, some local bars, and some restaurants featuring live music. Far away from the young angst of downtown, this area is a safe bet for a low-key and predictable night on the town.

Austin's newer scene that is being pioneered by hipsters and do-it-yourselfers is **East Austin.** This area, just on the other side of the freeway from 6th Street is where all the artsy musician locals like to hang out. Strewn about on the side of town that has historically been considered the sketchy side of town you'll find a slew of alluring dive bars, food trucks, music venues, and unusual shacks and backyard patios to explore.

Whatever your preference is for a night on the town in Austin, before stepping out the door, grab a free copy of the *Austin Chronicle* (issued every Thursday) and check out what's happening in the events section. With the *Chronicle,* coupled with the listings below, tailor an evening that best suits you, or just wander around and let the night be a "Choose Your Own Adventure" type of experience.

LIVE MUSIC

Austin is compulsive about music. After all it's simply and indisputably the best U.S. city for live music, and has the distinguished honor of being the Live Music Capital of the World. The town is forever inundated with touring national acts, local favorites, and unknowns crawling out of the woodwork seeking their 15 minutes of expression. Venues, clubs, and bars all across town have something going on every night of the week. Live music is so pervasive here that you'll find it in unusual places such as clothing stores, supermarkets (Central Market), the airport, and even the post office. One thing I've noticed in recent years is many venues are offering two stages, one smaller stage inside and a bigger stage outside for larger national acts. This makes sampling music a blast.

Although venues are everywhere, the greatest concentration of music is downtown. No matter where you stand in the downtown area the sounds of live music can be heard, merging in stereophonic cacophony, and the sound is sweet. The concentration gets thick on 6th Street and Red River, where you can stand on any corner and hear blues, pop, and heavy metal all at once. Thanks to Austin's multifarious musical pallet the venues and acts are diverse. There's a thriving scene here for absolutely every kind of musical taste.

It's hard to say how live music got its footing in Austin and how it has become so extraordinary over the years. But, from Willie Nelson to Janis Joplin to *Austin City Limits,* from Stevie Ray Vaughan to Alejandro Escovedo to Spoon, Austin has been greatly blessed in its calling to live music greatness. With this calling comes great responsibility, and Austinites take this seriously by religiously supporting local music. It's not uncommon for someone to catch a live act every night of the week and during the day maintain a "normal" life at the office.

Tickets for most concerts and venues can be purchased at **Waterloo Records** (600 N. Lamar Blvd., 512/474-2500) or online at **Austin 360** (www.austin360.com) or **512 Tickets** (www.512tickets.com). The outlet for theater, music, and dance tickets is **Now Playing Austin** (512/472-8497, www.nowplayingaustin.com). Tickets purchased online are often cheaper than at the venue. For smaller venues tickets are sold only at the door.

Big Venues

The term "big" is relative when it comes to venues. The following listings are venues I consider to be "big" because of their size and seating capacity, and/or "big" because they feature big-name national acts. Tickets can range from $15 to $55 depending on the act or lineup and the night.

Antone's (213 W. 5th St., 512/320-8424, www.antones.net) has been Texas's outlet for the blues for decades. In recent years they've expanded their repertoire to include pop, rock, and indie, bringing in some major national acts. This is the best place to catch Austin's own Jimmie Vaughan. The founder, Cliff Antone, had his highs and lows, operating the venue for the past 30 years until his death in 2006. Highs include receiving an award from the National Blues Foundation for his contribution to the blues, and lows include doing prison time for drugs. The record store on Guadalupe Street with the same name is owned by the venue. Scene: national acts, blues, rock, pop, and country.

***Austin City Limits* Moody Theatre** (310 Willie Nelson Blvd., 877/471-4225 venue, 877/435-9849 tickets, www.acl-live.com) is the new home of the famous *Austin City Limits* stage. Located in the 2nd Street district at the new W Hotel, this new live music venue and studio set has made ACL accessible to the masses. The Moody Theater is a state-of-the-art, 2,700+-person capacity live music venue and studio set. Scene: rock, pop, alternative, country, folk, world.

Newly renovated **Austin Music Hall** (208 Nueces St., 512/263-4146, www.austinmusichall.com) is one of the main venues for artists you hear on the radio, such as 30 Seconds to Mars and Interpol. Located at the edge of downtown near Lady Bird Lake, the venue has a seating capacity of 3,000, a full bar, and folding chairs that you can chose to sit in or stand on. Scene: mainstream rock, pop, alternative rock.

The Backyard (13742 Bee Cave Pkwy., 512/263-4146, www.thebackyard.net) is Austin's premier open-air venue. Here you can catch big-name national acts in a down-home outdoor setting that used to feel like a giant backyard until the town of Bee Cave swallowed it. Artists love playing here and their performances show it. When Willie Nelson plays here he cuts loose. The amphitheatre has seating and standing room that can fit 5,000 people, and beer and merchandise huts line the perimeter. Shows are put on March–October. The Backyard is outside of Austin so you'll need a car to get there; parking can be tricky so show up early for a good spot. Scene: national acts, pop, country, folk, rock.

Frank Erwin Center (1701 Red River St., 512/471-7744, www.uterwincenter.com) is Austin's stadium for mega-entertainment. The coliseum can seat up to 18,000 people, so don't expect an intimate show. The center hosts acts like George Strait, Metallica, and Lady Gaga, and has also hosted the Dalai Lama and the Ringling Bros. and Barnum & Bailey circus. This is also the home of UT sports. Scene: mega-entertainment of all kinds.

La Zona Rosa (612 W. 4th St., 512/472-2293, www.lazonarosa.com) is Austin's favorite Mexican food joint turned music venue. With two stages that can open up into one big room, they can pack in over 1,000 sweaty people. Scene: rock, pop.

Stubb's (801 Red River St., 512/480-8341, www.stubbsaustin.com) is the place to get famous barbecue sauce and famous national acts. Housed in a historic limestone building, Stubb's is the place where the hip parties go down during SXSW. There's a small indoor stage and a big outdoor stage in the backyard. Scene: national acts, local acts, rock, alternative.

Small Venues

There are so many smaller venues in town that it's not practical to give them all a nod here so I've distilled the list down to the very best. Generally doors open for these venues sometime around 8–9 P.M. and there's almost always a cover charge that is somewhere between $5 and $20.

311 Club (311 E. 6th St., 512/477-1630) is the top venue for blues on 6th Street. This

21-and-up venue features local and national acts every night of the week in a bar atmosphere. Scene: blues, R&B, cover bands.

Beerland Texas (711 1/2 Red River St., 512/479-ROCK, www.beerlandtexas.com) is one of the older rock venues in the Red River District. The proprietors best describe their own place by saying, "Rock & roll club seeks bands, fans, and hangers-on for all-out orgy of loud music and cheap beer." Also here are arcade games and pool. Scene: rock.

◖ Broken Spoke (3201 S. Lamar Blvd., 512/442-6189, www.brokenspokeaustintx. com) really should be a sight as well as a venue. This remarkable local institution will blow your Stetson off when you walk through the door. Remember John Travolta in *Urban Cowboy*? Well forget it, because the Broken Spoke is the real deal. First-timers have a hard time blending in because they end up standing there with their jaws hanging. This real honky-tonk is an original Texas dance hall where people still come to dance to live country bands.

Authentic country music and two-stepping happen at the legendary Broken Spoke.

There's a front-room restaurant that serves up home cooking, but the real reason for being here is the humble dance floor, under a low ceiling that I swear is going to cave in in the near future. Finally there's the makeshift museum, containing dusty artifacts from country music legends and photos of the proprietor with famous folks. No one ever seems to go in there, except for newcomers and nerds. Word for the nerd: If the lady bartender asks, "What can I get ya, sugar?" she's not asking you if you want sugar. Scene: country, dancing.

Cactus Cafe (Texas Union on the UT campus, 512/475-6515) is the premier intimate venue for all things unplugged (nowadays everything's actually semi-plugged). Big-name acoustic, singer-songwriter, country, and folk acts have graced the small corner stage for over 70 years. Among them are Janis Joplin, Bob Dylan, Lyle Lovett, Bill Monroe, Ralph Stanley, Ani DiFranco, and Sean Lennon. The space is small, upscale, and outfitted with a full bar in the back. People tend to dress up a bit for shows at the Cactus. It's a safe bet that any show here is worth seeing. Scene: unplugged, singer-songwriter, folk, Americana, bluegrass, and jazz.

Cedar Street Courtyard (208 W. 4th St., 512/495-9669), in the Warehouse District, always has a groove on. The space is like none other in town: It's an open courtyard flanked by basement bars that have a party-in-the-dungeon vibe. Music on the stage is always groovy and upbeat, and dancing is unavoidable. Scene: jazz, funk, tango, groove.

◖ Continental Club (1315 S. Congress Ave., 512/441-2444, www.continentalclub. com) is Austin's legendary retro hook-up that has been around since the 1950s. With a steady lineup of regular local musicians as well as touring acts in a throwback atmosphere, the Continental is another venue where you're sure to catch something good on any given night. Patrons love showing up on their hogs or in their classic cars, looking like a million bucks. Regular acts include Dale Watson and Jon Dee Graham among others. Scene: country, blues, rockabilly, rock, singer-songwriter.

The best way to experience live jazz music is in the basement of the **Elephant Room** (315 Congress Ave., 512/473-2279, www.elephantroom.com). Jazz lovers come from all over to descend into this unique environment and sink back in a chair for a couple hours of toe tapping. The Elephant Room has a full bar with over 20 drafts and wine by the glass. Scene: jazz, big band, swing, smooth.

Elysium (705 Red River St., 512/474-2285, www.elysiumonline.net) is the venue for goth and industrial music. Here the unspoken dress code is black, makeup, and chains, and the attitude is depressed and sullen. For the most part this is a dance club with a beat going on, but there's also live music. Scene: goth/industrial dance club.

◖ **Emo's** (603 Red River St., 512/477-EMOS, www.emosaustin.com) is the town's premier punk, metal, stoner, and indie venue and has been for a long time. You can't use the word "alternative" to describe this scene or the music, as this is sacrilegious, and people will smirk. Spoon and Trail of Dead got their start here, Johnny Cash has played here, and sometimes Emo's offers a surprise by featuring an unusual headliner such as De la Soul or Cheap Trick. Scene: punk, heavy metal, stoner rock, indie.

Flamingo Cantina (515 E. 6th St., 512/494-9336, www.flamingocantina.com) is the premiere reggae venue in town. This 18-and-up roots venue has big-name acts from all over the United States and from "the Islands." Scene: reggae, hip-hop, funk.

The Ghost Room (304 W. 4th St., 512/879-4472, www.theghostroom.com), formerly the location of the Ginger Man, is one of Austin's newer venues. The inside is dark, with an Old West meets gothic feel, and the crowd is friendly and upbeat, which makes for a personal and accessible setting for live indie rock. Scene: indie, pop, singer-songwriter.

Hole in the Wall (2538 Guadalupe St., 512/477-4747, www.holeinthewallaustin.com) is a historic little venue on The Drag that puts on all sorts of music in an average bar atmosphere. As for history, Stevie Ray Vaughan

played here. $1 beer on Monday is crucial for the students. Scene: alternative rock, country, pop, singer-songwriter, bar bands.

Jovita's (1619 S. 1st St., 512/447-7825) serves up great Mexican food and excellent live music. Here you can sit at one of the many small tables, eat tacos, drink beer, and be only a few feet from the band. Scene: Americana, rock, country, folk, singer-song writer.

If Dracula lived in a loft in Manhattan it would probably look a lot like ◖ **The Mohawk** (912 Red River St., 512/482-8404, www.mohawkaustin.com). This space has been through so many incarnations over the years—from club after club, to swank bar, to full-on cocaine den. This time around The Mohawk is a micro-scene unto itself. One of Austin's bustling two-stage venues, this is the place to let your hair down and head bang, shoe gaze, and drink. Catch touring bands such as Bad Brains, Sleep or No Name, or discover popular local indie acts such as The Authors or Stereo is a Lie. Scene: punk, metal, indie, rock.

Momo's (618 W. 6th St., 512/479-8848), on the quieter side of 6th Street, is a versatile, upscale night spot with great live music and atmosphere. The Las Vegas styling, coupled with rooftop deck, and intimate stage with tables have made this place into a popular place to experience local music. The crown is diverse, and friendly on any given night. Scene: indie folk, Americana, pop.

The Parish (214 E. 6th St. upstairs, 512/473-8381, www.theparishroom.com) is one of the newer live venues on the 6th Street scene. The upstairs venue caters primarily to the punk/alternative scene, and often features the type of bands that take themselves too seriously. If you are a band playing here be sure to have roadies, because you have to carry everything up a flight of stairs. Scene: indie, punk, hard rock.

Red 7 (611 E. 7th St., 512/476-8100, www.red7austin.com) is the new punk/rocker/DIY scene that's gaining footing in the Red River District. Like Emo's and Mohawk, Red 7 is the place to be during SXSW or Austin Free Week. Here you'll find a great outdoor stage and a bar that's often so packed you can't see the bartender. There's a loud PA system, and bands push it to the limit. Toilet paper wadded up and stuffed in the ear won't save your hearing because the sound will travel straight through your skull. Scene: punk, metal, indie rock, stoner rock, grunge.

Red Eyed Fly (715 Red River St., 512/474-1084, www.redeyedfly.com) is one of the tried-and-true venues in the Red River District. Red Eyed Fly has two stages and a juke box featuring Jane's Addiction, Son Volt, Tool, Fugazi, Johnny Cash, The Shins, and Queens of the Stone Age. Scene: punk, metal, indie rock.

Saxon Pub (1320 S. Lamar Blvd., 512/448-2552, www.thesaxonpub.com) is a venue down South Lamar that's guarded by a giant knight in shining armor. The best of Austin's local musicians are found here, both enjoying music and playing it. Besides being a great venue it's also a pub complete with darts, pool, and microbrews. Scene: folk, Americana, blues, country, bluegrass, light rock.

Touted as the oldest continuously running beer joint in central Texas, **Scoot Inn** (1308 E. Fourth St., 512/478-6200) is the east side's quintessential dive bar music venue. Supposedly this shack was built in 1871 and was a place where weary pioneers would party. If someone from then visited now they might feel right at home. Patrons are sweaty, unshaven, and look like they rode in on mustangs. A full selection of Hill Country microbrew Real Ale is on tap, which is a treat, and staff are nice. Scene: rock and alternative.

Threadgill's (301 W. Riverside Dr., 512/472-9304, www.threadgills.com) is one of Austin's venues with the most history, as the young Steve Miller, Janis Joplin, and the Doors, among many others, have played here. In fact, Threadgill's claims to have been the first outlet in town for the '60s counterculture movement. Today, you can find all sorts of acts here as well as Austin's new residents, the Neville Brothers and Family, who relocated here after New Orleans was flooded by Hurricane Katrina in 2005. Scene: country, rockabilly, Americana.

Valhalla (710 Red River St., 512/476-0997) is a cigarette loosely hanging from the bottom lip on Red River Street. It's not cool to smile too much here, or to be exuberant. The scene is a mix of denim-overall-wearing tattooed folks, cow-punks, and hipsters. Just stand around with a drink in hand and gently bang your head to the music. The bands can be diverse here but for the most part it's punk, thrash, or metal, all of it loud. The wagon-wheel bar is an interesting feature that divides the bar from the live music. It's not absolutely necessary to pay a cover fee because you can see the band from the bar area. Scene: Hardcore, metal, punk.

BARS AND CLUBS

Texas has many counties that are dry or partially dry, but Austin is definitely not in a dry county. There are thousands of bars here—some local dive bars with Merle Haggard on the jukebox, others ultra-swank clubs that feature DJs. The following are the best watering holes in town.

The high end multilevel lounge experience has been made perfect by **《 The Belmont** (305 W. 6th St., 512/457-0300). This popular joint is plush and custom, outfitted with Vegas overtones and Manhattan undertones. If Dean Martin were alive, and if he was cool enough to live in Austin, he would probably oft be found smoking in one of the private rooms such as the Dakota Lounge, or on the outdoor patio—slightly hammered of course. The signature drink is the Belmontini, which features locally made Tito's vodka and pineapple juice, and live music often helps to set the tone.

One of the more popular watering holes for beautiful people is **Club De Ville** (900 Red River St., 512/457-0900). Style is set with upholstery on the walls and near-darkness. Inside feels a lot like being at a sophisticated party in a darkroom for developing photos. The best feature here is the patio in the backyard, chiseled out of limestone cliffs. This is one of the better spaces in the Red River District for sipping and chatting with friends. Happy hour goes to 8 P.M., which works to bring folks in early.

On the quieter side of downtown towards

NIGHTLIFE TIPS

Before embarking on a night on the town in Austin there are a few things you should take into consideration.

- Be sure to always have your ID with you. Clubs, venues, and bars have very strict ID policies, and you will get carded no matter what. If you don't have a valid ID you will definitely be barred from having a great night out in Austin.

- Drink lots of water in the summer months because you will quickly find yourself dehydrated, especially if you are seeing performances in the hot outdoors and drinking alcohol at the same time. All clubs, venues, and bars are eager to hand out water and often you can find a self-serve water bucket somewhere.

- Have enough cash in your pocket before you start out. ATMs at bars and on the street charge a bundle for cash withdrawal. However, if you are caught in a jam, my favorite

ATM is the one sticking out of an old wood fence at Stubb's on Red River Street. It charges a big fee, but it's entertaining pulling money out of a fence.

- If you are underage, be aware that bartenders, bouncers, and door dudes aren't fools. Consider the experience of one of George W. Bush's daughters, who was caught drinking at Chuy's bar.

- If you're merrily drinking at bars and clubs, don't get bent out of shape if a bartender cuts you off and won't give you another drink. According to Texas state law, bartenders are liable for those who stagger out of bars, and liable for their actions. They are very cautious about this and are looking out for the best interest of everyone.

- Don't drink and drive, and watch out for drunk drivers. It's not uncommon to see someone completely wasted struggling to find the keyhole in a car door.

Mo-Pac/Highway 1 is **Donn's Depot** (1600 W. 5th St., 512/478-0336). This fantastic old-time bar is housed in a former train depot and a real choo-choo. The crowd is very diverse, with old folks looking for a dance as well as spry youngsters seeking a cultural experience. Live and canned music is generally jazz, big band, bluegrass, country, and porch. Donn himself has two bands that perform here.

Amidst all the live music is **Plush** (617 Red River St., 512/478-0099), Austin's premier DJ, mix, hip-hop dance club. Towards the wee hours people can get a little too crazy and loose—think Jersey Shore. Yes, pumping beats, sexy dancing, and throwing up in the bathroom. It's always packed to the gills so if your claustrophobic you may freak out. If so head to the secret chill spot in the back. If it's vacant you will be pleased to kick it in here, near but at a safe distance from the craziness of the main dance floor.

It's hard to pigeonhole **Halcyon Coffeehouse** (218 W. 4th St., 512/472-9637, www.halcyonaustin.com, 7 A.M.–2 A.M. Mon.–Thurs., 7 A.M.–3 A.M. Fri., 8 A.M.–3 A.M. Sat., 8 A.M.–2 A.M. Sun.) as anything specific. This lack of definition is what makes it one of my favorite places to hang out any night of the week. Halcyon (pronounced HAL-see-yon) is a night-owl café, a classy bar, a sophisticated art gallery, and a laid-back smoke shop all rolled into one Zig-Zag. The front half is a great café space with low-lying chairs and couches, the back is the bar with loud music thumping, and on the side is a fish bowl that contains the tobacco shop. Everywhere in this place you will find great artwork hanging on the walls, and people surfing wireless Internet and socializing. If you're craving sweets they will bring fire to your table so you can roast marshmallows and make s'mores.

Most people don't go to bars to be reminded

of death. But if you're one of those people who want to drink a beer on a coffin try **Lovejoy's** (604 Neches St. at 6th St., 512/477-1268). Here you'll find around 20 beers on tap, local and regional brews, wines, and a full bar. The scene is generally a flock of bikers and intellectuals sitting around on garage-sale furniture. If you want to be near, but not on, 6th Street, this is a great place to be. Every night most pints are only $2.

If the downtown 6th Street scene is wearing on you simply walk under the freeway to **The Liberty** (1618 1/2 E. 6th St., 512/600-4791). Here you have a friendly jukebox joint with potent but cheap drinks. The space out back is huge and includes East Side King food truck too. It should be noted that this food truck has a connection to famed local restaurant Uchi. What more would one want for a low pressure evening with friends.

Another great spot on the east side of the freeway is **Shangri'La** (1016 E. 6th St., 512/524-4291). The drinks aren't fancy but they are cheap and strong. This place is fun because it's often packed, has a great juke box, and pool tables. As with most joints east of the freeway, this place is generally free of college folks.

Lucky Lounge (209A W. 5th St., 512/479-7700, www.theluckylounge.com) is a trendy bar with '60s decor and occasionally good live music. If you want to lounge around, have live background music, and sip apple martinis, you're in luck at Lucky's. The crowd is primarily heterosexual singles looking to schmooze and flirt in a sophisticated way.

Just on the west side of Congress Avenue downtown is the ever-popular **Red Fez** (209B W. 5th St., 512/478-5120). Part bar, part nightclub, and all Middle Eastern decor make this an interesting place to find yourself at the wee hours on any given night. It can get loud and intense inside, which can either rev you up or turn you off depending on if you want a wild evening or a mellow one. Although the atmosphere is panache, the drink prices aren't.

Lustre Pearl (97 Rainey St., 512/469-0400) is one of Austin's best bars off the beaten path.

Located in Austin's new downtown area just south of Cesar Chavez near I-35, this stylish bar in an old house that was renovated to look like it was never renovated has a large outdoor area with seating and hula hoops. Yes, you heard right. This is the place where you can drink *and* hula in front of others. In addition, there is table tennis for those who want to look a little less silly. The faux dingy rooms inside the house (which are dangerously close to looking like rooms in a crack house) make for a great place to meet a large party of friends.

One of the best martinis in town is at **Speakeasy** (412D Congress Ave., 512/476-8017). The entrance is in the alley, which harkens back to the Prohibition era. Suave and divine is a way of life here, with live music, relaxed atmosphere, brick-and-wood interior, and walls covered in vintage posters.

The bar for aspiring singers is **Ego's** (510 S. Congress Ave., 512/474-7091). Tucked away in a parking garage off South Congress, Ego's always has a wild cast of vocalists, drinkers, and people-watchers who are willing to let their guard down and be silly. The combination of karaoke and dive bar is genuine here. Karaoke starts at 10 P.M. Sunday–Thursday, and 9 P.M. Friday–Saturday. I'd suggest stopping by when hosted by Diamond Karaoke. Ego's is also home to a competitive karaoke league, Downtown Division of the National Karaoke League, on Thursday nights.

Little Woodrow's (520 W. 6th St., 512/477-2337), on the quieter side of 6th Street, is a great place to hang out with friends for an extended stay. Sports fans will be pleased to find that there are distracting TVs everywhere, and the ladies will enjoy the great outdoor space with picnic tables. Unlike the dive bars and hipster hangouts in town, the beer selection is broad so there's always something here for everyone.

Dive Bars

Have you recently been dragged through the briar patch of love? Have you lost faith in humankind because humans don't seem to be kind? Or are you just lonely and want to sit around with others that are lonely, pretending you don't want to be bothered, when you're really crying out for human contact? Austin's world-class dive bars can help you. Some of these joints have historical significance, although you would never know it from the outside—they look like they've been closed since REO Speedwagon broke up. Many of these drinking institutions are owned and operated by spry, older ladies who've created their own unique cultures in their bars. For obvious reasons these places dredge up images from Nick Cave ("Jangling Jack"), Frank Sinatra ("Strangers in the Night"), and Johnny Cash ("Sunday Morning Coming Down"). Be sure to bring cold hard cash to these places because most of the following joints don't take plastic.

If your inner child likes to drink check out the age-old **Carousel Lounge** (1110 E. 52nd St., 512/452-6790). The circus theme is taken to the limits with a big pink ceramic elephant, circus murals, and a mini-carousel. It summons images of Red Skelton's hobo clown combined with Dean Martin. A special tip of the hat goes to Stella Boes, the 80-year-old hostess who has won awards for her charisma. Only beer and wine are offered here.

Just east of I-35 is one of the more unique home-spun establishments, **Cheer Up Charlie's** (1104 E. 6th St., 512/431-2133). This tiny vegan dive bar is an experience that must be treasured. Here you have food trucks, live music, beer and wine, DJs, and an outdoor movie screen that shows everything from kung fu to cult classics. Or better yet, *The Wizard of Oz* synched up with Pink Floyd's "Dark Side of the Moon."

Jukebox joint **Deep Eddy Cabaret** (2315 Lake Austin Blvd., 512/472-0961) will make you feel at home. Here you can swim in your own head while listening to the eclectic tunes on the jukebox. We've all heard of Elvis (both Costello and Presley), but what kind of dive bar patron has heard of Edith Piaf (often confused with eat a pilaf)? The early 20th century French singer gone heroin addict surprisingly adds a nice depressed touch to this dive bar experience. Pitchers of Lone Star are only $6, and snacks consist of hot nuts and pretzels.

Dry Creek Saloon (4812 Mount Bonnell Rd., 512/453-9244) is one of the oldest bars in town. This rustic shack is nestled among extravagant, million-dollar homes, but I assure you that all the patrons come from elsewhere. Only a couple kinds of beer are available, so don't expect marvelous microbrews on tap. The owner is an unpleasant, cantankerous woman who's known to have kicked sober people out for being drunk. I used to think this added to the charm of Dry Creek Saloon but now I'm way over it. The saloon is high up Mount Bonnell Road, but don't expect some great mountain peak cause this is a Texas mountain, measuring in at a whopping 780 feet above sea level. This doesn't, however, diminish the fact that there's an extraordinary view from the saloon's rooftop deck.

You don't have to be drunk at a Christmas party to see elves dancing over the bar, because it's always Christmas at **Lala's Lounge** (2207-09 Justin Ln., 512/453-2521). Years of cigarette smoke and liquor-stained carpets produce a marvelous smell. Just like the patrons, the Christmas tree is always lit, with presents under her branches—and the skeleton over the pool table is riding a giant beer bottle. There's hidden symbolism in all this I'm sure. Frank Sinatra and Dean Martin provide the soundtrack for this joint.

The legendary mini-honky-tonk (**Ginny's Little Longhorn Saloon** (5434 Burnet Rd., 512/458-1813) is a place steeped in character, booze, and bird poop. Local mother to the bar divers, Ginny Kalmbach is the owner/operator and has achieved mythical status in her own right. Besides being known as a place to get a drink and to hear real country music (as opposed to country pop), Little Longhorn is famous for Chicken Shit Sunday. This is when Ginny puts a specially designed bingo board on the pool table along with a chicken in a cage. People place bets on a number and if the chicken shits on your number you win the pot. The soundtrack is provided by a live performance by Dale Watson and his Lone Stars.

If you thought poodles and heavy metal had no place being together, check out the **Poodle Dog Lounge** (6507 Burnet Rd., 512/465-

POLITICIANS, PROSTITUTES, AND SECRET TUNNELS

During the last quarter of the 19th century Austin had a blossoming red-light district on the west side of Congress Avenue, in the area now referred to as the Warehouse District. Official city documents of the time called this area the First Ward, but everyone really called it Guy Town. With several brothels, slews of hard-working prostitutes, and a client base that consisted of city council members, legislators, and businessmen, Guy Town flourished under the noses of an unsuspecting genteel society. In order to conceal the identities of the "upright citizens" that were patrons of Guy Town, many brothels had tunnels that connected to secret locations. But Guy Town wasn't just for the well-to-do, it was also a place for gamblers and outlaws, and some of Austin's dubious chapters unfolded in the streets, buildings, and tunnels of Guy Town.

Only one remnant of Austin's era of prostitution can be found in town and it's actually not in the historic area of Guy Town, but north of downtown at 1601 Guadalupe Street. This historic stone structure known as the Bertram Building (currently the finest Indian restaurant in Austin) has a basement tunnel that historically led to a conveniently located brothel next door.

© JUSTIN MARLER

Today the Warehouse District is a hip, bustling part of town full of great pubs, bars, and restaurants.

© JUSTIN MARLER

A night of live music at Ginny's Little Longhorn Saloon.

9468). You know you're there when you see a seemingly abandoned building with the faint image of a giant poodle on the outside. The Poodle is a wacky scene. On one hand it seems like it's an old bar in its death throws, and then on Friday nights, when heavy metal bands play, the place springs to life. A poor assortment of beers is all that's available here. Just up the road is Top Notch Hamburgers, which was one of the shooting locations for the movie *Dazed and Confused*.

PUBS

A pub with dark nooks and crannies similar to an English pub is **Dog & Duck Pub** (406 W. 17th St., 512/479-0598). Dog & Duck has 29 beers on tap, including the local Celis line, and dozens of bottled beers to choose from. The Austin Beer Club and the Homebrewing Club both meet here, which says a lot about the pub. Besides being a great place to suck down pints, Dog & Duck is a great place for the whole family. And just like an English pub the food is greasy and is good only because

it goes with beer. On St. Patrick's Day, Dog & Duck is packed. Drink specials are offered throughout the week.

The pub that most successfully replicates English-pub atmosphere is **The Draught House** (4112 Medical Pkwy., 512/452-6258, www.draughthouse.com). Dark spaces, a good selection of microbrews and commercial beers, and a mellow atmosphere make this one of the best pubs in town. They have their own Old World–style brew house where they cook up some excellent beers using a traditional recipe. Ask for a taste before ordering one of their micros. Every day of the week they offer great deals that are sure to draw you in. Free bratwurst on Saturday, free pizza on Wednesday, and pints for $2.75 on Tuesday. The pub lets people take their brews outside, which has spawned a unique lawn-chair-parking-lot social scene. After dark don't drive in with your headlights on, as this will elicit the evil eye from patrons.

Fado (214 W. 4th St., 512/457-0172) in the Warehouse District is hailed as one of the most popular Irish pubs in town. Guinness

CHICKEN S#@T BINGO

The game of bingo, which is the ultimate game of chance and boredom, has become a lively way to spend an afternoon at Ginny's Little Longhorn Saloon. Every Sunday night this tiny honky-tonk features an amusing game of Chicken S#@t Bingo that relies entirely on the unpredictable bowels of a chicken in a cage on a pool table. Contestants throw down hard-earned cash on a number and cheer and jeer for about an hour waiting for that special mo-

ment, while Austin's favorite country singer, Dale Watson and his Lone Stars, perform and provide commentary. Free chili and hot dogs are served, along with cheap Lone Star Beer. The lucky winner can walk away with up to $100. If you want to participate in this spectacle, plan on showing up early and hanging around for a while. The band starts at 4 P.M. and tickets go on sale at 5 P.M. The winner is announced when the chicken takes a dump.

© JUSTIN MARLER

Don't confuse Chick S#@t Bingo with craps.

may flow in rivers here but that doesn't make it Irish, or even a pub for that matter. The interior is faux Irish pub, featuring four different motifs: Victorian Dublin, the Gaelic Pub, the Traditional Pub, and the Irish Country Cottage Pub. You might expect to trip over a faux "Irish" sheep as you walk to the bathroom. However this doesn't diminish Fado's popularity and the fact that it's consistently hopping and always packed after dark.

(The Ginger Man (301 Lavaca St., 512/473-8801) is another one of my favorite pubs in town. Knowledgeable staff serve up bottles and pint glasses of brew produced at local breweries, as well as the ones you're most familiar with. This is the place downtown with the largest selection of beer on tap. Last I heard the number was around 82. No matter where you sit—at the booths inside or on the outside patio—Ginger Man is a comfortable place to hang out with family, friends, or all alone.

A great place to have a beer on a second-story deck overlooking Austin is **Opal Divine's** (700 W. 6th St., 512/477-3308). Opal's is housed in an old building with lots of character, is staffed with knowledgeable and friendly people, offers food one notch above average pub fare, and is so comfortable that it's easy to waste away your whole evening. Take note of the floors and stairs. Much beer has been spilled on these wooden floors, which has created a remarkable protective coating.

Legacy and history make **Scholz Garten** (1607 San Jacinto, 512/474-1958) Austin's one and only *biergarten*. Established in 1866 over an old boarding house by a German immigrant, Scholz became a cultural center with beer as the communal glue. Over 100 years later Scholz is still a cultural center, and the beer still flows. Along with being one of Texas's oldest continuously operated businesses, Scholz also has the distinction of being one of the top 25 best sports bars in the United States according to *Sports Illustrated*. True to the German *biergarten*, Scholz offers schnitzels, along with American fare. Out back is a huge space with a stage for live music and picnic tables, which makes this a grand place for big crowds of family and friends to gather.

GAY AND LESBIAN

You may be thinking, "Austin is in Texas. There can't be a gay scene!" Well, all you have to do is close your eyes, click your heals, and pretend you're not in Texas, and voilà—a thriving gay and lesbian scene is before your eyes. Austin's propensity for open-mindedness has allowed lots of room for a unique gay scene that is completely unrivalled—at least in Texas. Where else in the world can you see a room of cowboys in Stetsons two-step dancing with each other? Nowhere my friends!

The gay neighborhood hole-in-the-wall is **'Bout Time** (9601 N. I-35, 512/832-5339, www.bouttimeaustin.com). Here you can play volleyball, drink cheap drinks, and enjoy the company of friendly, good-humored bartenders.

Austin's gay leather bar is **The Chain Drive** (504 Willow St., 512/480-9017). Not everyone that comes here sports black leather and a 'stache, but it's definitely on tap. Chain Drive is also the headquarters of the Heart of Texas Bears. Thursday is Disco Inferno night.

On the north end of downtown, under the bright lights of the State Capitol, is Austin's most beloved gay hang out, **Charlie's** (1301 Lavaca, 512/474-6481). Charlie's lays claim to being the city's first gay bar. The crowd here is mostly male, all ages and types. For entertainment there's dancing and drag shows.

The gay men's nightclub is **Oilcan Harry's** (211 W. 4th St., 512/320-8823, www.oilcanharrys.com). This Warehouse District gay staple has lots of attitude Thursday–Sunday, from DJs spinning dance hits to the Malebox. The patio area is a great place to meet your mate or hang with your mates. Check out their website for drink specials and a calendar of events.

Also in the Warehouse District is the new guy lounge bar **Rain** (217 W. 4th St., 512/494-1150). It's a classy martini joint with a disco dance and snooty bartenders. Some nights there's dancing and some nights live music. Happy hour is every night of the week.

Entertainment and Events

There's much more besides live music going on in Austin. After all this is a world-class city with opera, symphony, ballet, and roller derby. Tickets for most concerts and events can be purchased at **Waterloo Records** (600 N. Lamar Blvd., 512/474-2500) or online at **Austin 360** (www.austin360.com) or **512 Tickets** (www.512tickets.com). The outlet for theater, music, and dance tickets is **Now Playing Austin** (512/472-8497, www.nowplayingaustin.com). Tickets can also be purchased at the venues depending upon availability, but purchasing online is often cheaper.

THEATERS AND EVENTS CENTERS

The City of Austin's Convention Center Department operates two massive facilities that provide space for some of the area's biggest indoor events. The bigger space is the **Austin Convention Center** (500 E. Cesar Chavez St., 512/404-4000), and the smaller space is **Palmer Events Center** (900 Barton Springs Rd., 512/404-4500). Both host a wide variety of events such as conventions, consumer shows, conferences, roller derby, concerts, public dances, and trade shows. For a comprehensive calendar of events for both venues check out www.austinconventioncenter.com.

Bass Concert Hall (23rd St. at Robert Dedman Dr. on the UT campus, 512/471-2787 or 800/687-6010 for ticket information) is the largest space in UT's Performing Arts Center. This venue has the best acoustics in town, and although it's big, you don't feel far from the stage even in the back seats. Here's where most of the classical and dance performances take place, including touring Broadway acts, and on occasion big stars such as Tony Bennett take the stage. The UT campus parking lots on Manor Avenue and San Jacinto Street are the most convenient places to park.

If you are driving on I-35 and wonder what the gigantic cylinder that resembles the space ship from *Close Encounters of the Third Kind* is,

© JUSTIN MARLER

One World Theatre

it's the **Frank Erwin Center** (1701 Red River St., 512/471-7744). This mega-venue hosts UT sports and big name performers such as Metallica, Lady Gaga, George Strait, and the Harlem Globetrotters. Parking can be downright depressing during a major event; there are a few garages in the area (San Jacinto St.) but don't count on there being a space for you.

Austin's newly renovated **Long Center** (701 W. Riverside Dr., 512/457-5100, www.thelongcenter.org) is the changing city's latest effort to offer a classy venue for cross-cultural classics. Events held here range from opera to modern, making the Long Center the premier venue for the classical arts. Although the performances inside can ennoble, the grand promenades outside, which offer breathtaking views of Lady Bird Lake and the downtown skyline, are just as inspiring.

On the outskirts of town is the beautiful **One World Theatre** (7701 Bee Caves Rd.,

512/330-9500, www.oneworldtheatre.org). This is a favorite for world-class performers in all genres of music. Here you can see the Cowboy Junkies, the Doobie Brothers, Ricky Skaggs, George Winston, and world music and dance. The theater is housed in one of the most famous green/eco-friendly buildings in the area, designed by Marley Porter, and proves that comfort and world-class entertainment can take place without impacting the environment too much. Parking is available.

Paramount Theatre (713 Congress Ave., 512/472-5470, www.austintheatre.org), in the center of downtown near the Capitol, is a beautiful historic theater that hasn't changed much since World War I. It still hosts some of the town's best shows, offering a wide variety of entertainment such as country, folk, jazz, and classical music; comedy shows; dance; spoken word; and theater. This is also the place to see classic movies and random cult classics on the big screen. The art deco interior, ornate ceilings, and original red curtain from the early 1900s make for a great environment in which to be entertained. Downtown garage parking is available.

Wonder where John Tesh performs when in Austin? **Riverbend Centre** (4214 N. Capital of Texas Hwy., 512/327-9416, www.riverbend-centre.com) on the edge of town hosts all sorts of events such as live music, Austin Symphony performances such as the Christmas Sing-A-Long, and world music and entertainment. The center is in a beautiful spot, and the facility is a stunning limestone-and-wood structure that makes performances here a treat.

The State Theatre (719 Congress Ave., 512/472-5143, www.austintheatre.org), next door to the Paramount, primarily offers theater. This is the home of the State Theatre Company, which provides the community with high-quality plays September–June. Wine, beer, and other beverages are sold in the lobby and are allowed in the theater, which makes for a great experience. Downtown garage parking is available.

Zachary Scott Theatre Center (1510 Toomey Rd., 512/476-0541, www.zachscott.

com) is central Texas's oldest and most popular residential theater. Here audiences are captivated by some of the best plays and musicals put on in the state. The season runs September–August, offering about eight performances by an award-winning cast. Parking is available.

PERFORMING ARTS

Austin may not have a world-renowned performing-arts scene, but that is bound to change in the future as the community's various companies, troupes, and organizations keep putting on world-class performances.

Austin's young opera scene is quickly gaining a footing thanks to **Austin Lyric Opera** (512/472-5992, 800/31-OPERA or 800/316-7372, www.austinlyricopera.org). This remarkable troupe is pushing the envelope with avant-garde versions of Mozart's *Don Giovanni*, more traditional expressions of Verdi's *Il Trovatore,* and modern operas such as *Dead Man Walking.* All operas are held at the newly renovated Long Center on Lady Bird Lake. Tickets range $15–$100 depending on the seat and the day of the week. Tickets can be purchased by phone or at the box office (901 Barton Springs Rd.).

Austin Symphony (512/476-6064, www.austinsymphony.org) is keeping classical music alive and well in Austin. Throughout the year the symphony has performances and series with a wide range of interests. They offer the Classical Series, which is strictly classical music performed at Bass Concert Hall on the UT campus, and the Pops Series, which is a fun and eclectic combination of arrangements in conjuncture with contemporary artists at Riverbend Centre and Palmer Events Center. For the whole family there's the Family Series, which includes the Halloween Children's Concert at Paramount Theatre and a Family Concert in June at Symphony Square Amphitheatre. Finally there are the ever-popular Holiday Concerts, including Handel's Messiah in December and the July 4th Concert and Fireworks at Zilker Park, which is probably the most popular symphonic event of the year. Tickets range free–$42 depending on the event and the venue.

Proving its wide range of cultural interests, Austin also has **Ballet Austin** (501 W. 3rd St., 512/476-2163, www.balletaustin.org). The *Washington Post* proclaims Ballet Austin "one of the nation's best kept secrets." Productions include staples such as *The Nutcracker,* but you can also catch more innovative productions as well. Most of the bigger events take place at Bass Concert Hall on the UT campus, and smaller events take place at the Paramount Theatre.

CINEMAS
Alamo Drafthouse Cinema
The only place in town where you can get dinner, drinks, and a movie all at one establishment is the Alamo Drafthouse (320 E. 6th St., 512/476-1320, www.drafthouse.com). This popular independently owned goldmine offers the usual new Hollywood fare complete with explosions and drama, as well as cult classics such as *Repo Man.* The Alamo's schedule also has some off-the-wall stuff such as the Michael Jackson Sing Along, or a special viewing of *Fast Times at Ridgemont High* with a special guest appearance by the pizza delivery boy. Seating begins 45 minutes before screening, which is just enough time to order food and drinks and settle in. The theater has a clever system of writing down requests to keep the food and beer coming during the film with little distraction. Check out their website for schedule and other locations.

Other Cinemas
Austin's only IMAX theater is the **IMAX Theater at Bob Bullock** (1800 N. Congress Ave., 512/936-4649 or 866/369-7108, www.thestoryoftexas.com). Unlike many IMAX theaters, this one is equipped with an IMAX projector that has both 2-D and 3-D capabilities. Tickets cost $7 for general admission, $5 ages 5–18, and $6 for seniors and military. If you plan on visiting the Bob Bullock Museum you might consider buying a package that includes tickets to both the museum and the IMAX theater.

Have a beer with your movie at Alamo Drafthouse.

© JUSTIN MARLER

The **Paramount Theatre** (713 Congress Ave., 512/472-5470, www.austintheatre.org) is the venue in town that screens classic and cult classic movies. In the comfort of the classic art deco theater you can catch *Gone with the Wind, Lawrence of Arabia,* and *2001: A Space Odyssey.* Tickets are on sale at the box office in front of the theater and cost $7 for adults ($6 for showings before 6 P.M.) and $5 for seniors, students, and children.

COMEDY CLUBS
Austin's comedy district consists of two venues on the corner of 6th and Red River Streets. Life offers so much to laugh at and **Esther's Follies** (525 E. 6th St., 512/320-0553, www.esthers-follies.com) mixes it up, boils it all down, and flings it in the face of the audience. Named after Esther Williams, the famed actress and water ballet pioneer whose career sunk like a stone in the 1960s, this comedy troupe is comprised of a wide variety of clever folks from the community. Esther's dishes out dangerously funny satire, spoofs, and monologues bedecked

The Highball is Austin's retro-hip place to have a plush dinner with cocktails — and knock down some pins.

with costumes, clever wit, and cunning 8 P.M.– midnight Thursday–Saturday. Tickets cost $20 for open seating and $25 for special reserved seating. A $2 discount is offered for students and seniors.

Next door to Esther's is Austin's stand-up and open-mic comedy club, **The Velveeta Room** (512 E. 6th St., 512/469-9116, www. thevelveetaroom.com). Local and visiting comics take the stage here and showcase their stuff. This is definitely not for the kiddies. Admission is $5.

OTHER ENTERTAINMENT

Why some people would travel all the way to Austin to spend their time doing mini-golf is beyond me. However, miniature golf enthusiasts will enjoy putting around at **Peter Pan Mini-Golf** (1207 Barton Springs Rd., 512/472-1033, call for hours). Founded in 1948, this small course on a hill overlooking the world's great fast-food chains is a great place to battle pirates, the skull bunny, and a dinosaur, all with the mighty putter. Considering the age of

this institution, the course and holes are in surprisingly decent shape. Before or after golfing here, instead of eating at one of the fast-food joints go up Barton Springs Road to Green Mesquite or Shady Grove restaurants.

A friend once said to me, "If you want to take the pulse of America, put your finger on the artery of any bowling alley in the nation. Bowling alleys are a microcosm of the whole US-of-A." If that's true then the country is in a strange state of affairs. Shoe- and ball-sharing, meals from vending machines, and carpet murals on the walls keep us all coming back to the ancient subculture of knocking down pins. Legendary bowler Ernie McCracken of *Kingpin* fame would endorse the following bowling alleys. **The Highball** (1142 South Lamar Blvd., 512/383-8309, 4:30 P.M.–2 A.M. Mon.–Fri., 1 P.M.–2 A.M. Sat. and Sun.) is Austin's retro-hip place to have a plush dinner with cocktails, sing some karaoke, and knock down pins. This dimly lit place is covered in upholstery and chock-full of all kinds of folks looking for an unusual evening. This retro aspect of the

AUSTIN

AUSTIN CITY LIMITS

With the advent of PBS's most popular and longest-running program, *Austin City Limits* (310 Willie Nelson Blvd., 512/475-9077, www. austincitylimits.org), Austin walked on to the U.S. stage and became a household name. Since the first live taping back in 1976, the program has showcased only the very best artists, musicians, and bands, and has single-handedly chronicled the greatest musicians of our time. It's futile to list all the acts that have performed in front of the famous back-drop of Austin's skyline in the studios of KLRU, but here's a sampling: Ray Charles, B. B. King, Johnny Cash, Leonard Cohen, The Flaming Lips, Beck, Cold Play, Pearl Jam, and Austin's own Willie Nelson and Stevie Ray Vaughan.

In 2011, the *Austin City Limits* stage moved to the 2nd Street District and is now located at the new W Hotel on Willie Nelson Blvd. The move was a massive shift in direction for the legendary show, but they felt that it was time to allow for growth, and to give the public more access. The new studio, called The Moody Theater, is a state-of-the-art, 2,700+ person capacity live music venue and studio set. Live tapings are free – that's right, *free!* Unfortunately you have a better chance at going on a bike ride with the president than you have of getting tickets to a live performance at ACL. There are a very limited number of seats available and these are taken by "insiders" and people "in the know." However if you like playing the lottery, here's how it works. Ticket giveaways are posted on the ACL blog (http://austincitylimits.org/interact/blog). Notices post a few days before a giveaway. You have to check daily for postings and instructions. If you are notified that you have won tickets to a taping, your name will be added to the Space Available list at will call. Two tickets per person are allowed, but a ticket doesn't guarantee admission to a taping.

Since the new location doubles as a live music venue, buying tickets to see a live show is a great way to gain access. For more information about live music visit www.acl-live.com.

bowling experience is pretty authentic because lanes were built out of the legendary Rock and Bowl, which was New Orleans's oldest bowling center until it closed. Since there are only eight, reservations are a must on weekends. If you can't figure out what you want to do on a weekend night, and are burnt out on live music, this is sure to give you some memories.

If you want a bowling experience that is less hip and more gutter visit **Dart Bowl** (5700 Grover Ave., 512/452-2518, 9 A.M.–midnight daily). This 32-lane bowling alley with big TV screens and a popular restaurant that serves an award-winning steak draws a diverse crowd. Also in North Austin, up past all the dive bars, is **Highland Lanes** (8909 Burnet Rd., 512/458-1215, 9:30 A.M.–midnight Sun.–Thurs., 9:30 A.M.–1 A.M. Fri.–Sat.). The culture here is a bit more underbelly, and the food is terrible. Here's where you can find the best carpet mural in Texas, which covers two entire walls. Word of advice: Keep your mind out of the gutter.

The scene where all walks of life merge for the pool, shuffleboard, darts, and foosball is **Buffalo Billiards** (201 E. 6th St., 512/479-7665, 11 A.M.–2 A.M. Mon.–Sat., noon–2 A.M. Sun.). This downtown entertainment joint for the 21-and-older crowd is a great place to either begin or end an evening on the town. Here you can shoot pool, eat dinner, and drink a few beers.

For late-night pool in a dive bar, **Poodle Dog Lounge** (6507 Burnet Rd., 512/465-9468) in Old North Austin always seems to have tables available, and Lone Star beer by the can.

FESTIVALS AND EVENTS

Thanks to the great weather that Austin and the Hill Country enjoy for most of the year, the calendar of events is chock-full of things to do. Texans love their festivals. In fact it seems there's a festival for just about anything you can think of, from kite flying to German festivals that salute the sausage, and from jamborees that honor various fruits such as peaches and apples to festivals that venerate the wide variety of wildflowers in the spring. And one can't forget the many rodeos and local fairs that feature vats of chili, clouds of cotton candy, zany rides, and sunburned families with smiling, nauseous children.

In step with Austin's reputation of being diverse and eclectic one can take in pink tutus, Harley Davidsons, and gay pride all in a single weekend, by walking the Austin Pride Parade during the day, catching Ballet in the Park in the evening, and partying at the ROT Biker Rally the next day. Much of the festivities go down right in Austin.

For a complete guide to absolutely everything going on in Austin throughout the year check out www.austin360.com and click on the calendar link, or www.austintexas.org and click on the events link.

January

The very best way to sample a wide range of Austin bands and musicians is by stumbling through all the Red River/6th Street venues during **Austin Free Week** (http://freeweekaustin.com). It is as it's name implies, a completely free week of live music. There are no cover or door charges at venues such as Emo's, Red Eyed Fly, Beauty Bar and Red 7 during this buffet of music that takes place during the first week of January.

If you thought that yacht racing and Texas were diametrically opposed due to geography and culture, think again. Every year on New Year's Day, Austin Yacht Club puts on a boating spectacle rightly called the **Red-Eye Regatta** (www.austinyachtclub.org), when 50 first-class sailboats race out at Travis Lake.

February

For over two decades, every February **Carnival Brasileiro** (www.carnavalaustin.com) has brought Austin a party straight out of Brazil. Hailed as one of the city's weirdest and wildest

celebrations, Carnival Brasileiro features only Brazilian music played on Brazilian instruments and sung in Portuguese, all for a crowd of drinking gringos.

Although Tinsel Town is far away, Oscar fever can be caught at the Academy-sanctioned **Oscar Night Party** (512/478-4795 or 800/310-3378, www.austinfilmfestival.com). Hosted by the Austin Film Festival, this swank event offers cocktails, hors d'oeuvres, and a silent auction, as well as a live broadcast of the Academy Awards. Tickets are pricey, but all proceeds benefit the Austin Film Festival's nonprofit Young Filmmakers Program. Individual tickets are $90, $75 for AFF members.

March

It's an amazing sight to see thousands of kites in the sky with the Austin skyline as the backdrop. **Zilker Park Kite Fest** (www.zilkerkitefestival.com) has been going on for almost eight decades. Not much can beat a glorious day under the sun in Zilker Park eating hot dogs, people-watching, and trying not to get your kite entangled in the trees or thousands of strings connected to the sky. The day is packed with scheduled events such as kite-building for kids and a kite contest featuring stunt kite-flyers. The festival is free and is the first Sunday in March unless it's rained out. Parking gets close to impossible as the day progresses.

For those with a green thumb, or plant and garden lovers in general, **Zilker Garden Festival,** held at Zilker Botanical Garden Center (2220 Barton Springs Rd., 512/477-8672, www.zilkergarden.org) in Zilker Park, is a great way to learn about the latest trends in gardening. Best described as a garden, plant, and craft fair, this event includes plant vendors and garden-equipment suppliers with booth spaces along with purveyors of other various garden-themed goods such as jewelry, books, and games. Garden Fest is held in either April or May so check the schedule in advance. Admission is $5 and parking is extra.

Every year spring comes unusually early in the Hill Country, and with it springs up a vast array of spectacular wildflowers. Every March

SXSW

Imagine a major U.S. city handing over its streets, Mexican restaurants, barbecue joints, and public areas to hundreds of musicians, celebrities, rock stars, and thousands of fans for two weeks. Picture a backdrop of fireworks and dozens of film premieres. Sounds amazing, but impossible, right? Well, every spring all of this takes place in Austin during the spectacular event called **South by Southwest,** hitherto referred to as SXSW. This music and film festival has grown to mythic proportions in the last decade and is now the premier event in the nation for new music and independent films.

HISTORY

SXSW started back in 1986 when the founders of the local weekly magazine *Austin Chronicle* came up with the brilliant idea of creating a music conference dedicated to independent artists. At the time, the music industry was in dire need of change, as power ballad groups like Cinderella and Bon Jovi dominated the airwaves. The idea was quite simple: bring amazing music from outside the mainstream to one place (Austin), organize a conference with discussions about contemporary music, invite industry folk as well as fans, and have lots and lots of bands perform in venues all over town. The end result: The shape and sound of modern music has been altered forever.

Over the years SXSW has successfully brought attention to quality music that existed below the radar of the music industry. Wisely, the organizers opened the festival and conference to all genres, making the festival a cornucopia for all music lovers. Because of this, bands and musicians that have been featured at the festival over the years vary widely. A small sampling would include Jayhawks, Lucinda Williams, Mudd Puppies, Dixie Chicks, Beck, Wilco, Guided by Voices, The Fugees, Queens of the Stone Age, Trail of Dead, The Hives, The Shins, Black Eyed Peas, White Stripes, and Death Cab for Cutie. All these acts were buzz bands at the festival way back before they became household names. One of the greatest highlights in the history of SXSW was in 1994 when Johnny Cash played an acoustic set at punk rock club Emo's. A rediscovery of Cash ensued that made him a hero and icon for a new generation.

Today, SXSW is the biggest festival for new music in the world. It includes a conference with keynote speakers, private parties for indie record labels, and hundreds of shows featuring the very best new artists. SXSW has been known to have over 1,600 bands performed in over 60 venues – and that's just the official numbers. On the periphery is a whole world of unofficial shows, parties, and showcases

---

Wildflower Days (www.wildflower.org.) begin at Lady Bird Johnson Wildflower Center (4801 La Crosse Ave., 512/292-4100). The gardens and facility are extraordinary—a must-see for those who love the outdoors and who have allergy medication. From mid-March through the end of April the center is open 9 A.M.– 5:30 P.M. every day.

The biggest festival all year long— the mother of all mothers—is **South by Southwest** (www.sxsw.com). For one week (usually mid-March) the city of Austin is completely overrun by hundreds of musicians and celebrities and thousands of music fans. The town is plastered with the festival's acronym,

SXSW, and the restaurants, clubs, music stores, and barbecue joints are teeming with greasy-haired, tattooed, ripped-jean-wearing rock stars and rock star wannabes. What once was a unique underground event tailored for the ambitious DIY musician has now become a beer-sponsored, globally recognized event that includes independent film as well. If the earth opened up and swallowed Austin whole (God forbid) any day in mid-March, nearly all indie rock bands would be erased from the face of the earth, along with a few celebrities.

In Texas the county fair historically was the big event of the year when the whole town gathered to eat barbecue, be mesmerized by

that take place in small juke joints, barbecue restaurants, bars, and vacant parking lots all over town.

In recent years SXSW has expanded its vision to include film. Theaters all over town premiere cutting edge and innovative independent films, accompanied by panels and discussions on the indie film industry.

ACCESS BADGES

To attend the SXSW music or film conference you must buy an access badge. There are several different types of badges for varying levels of access for both the music and film portions of SXSW. Prices range $450-1,250. A badge gets you access to certain SXSW festival events, showcases, and the SXSW Trade Show. You also get a "Big Bag" filled with magazines, CDs, and souvenirs, as well as the program book with registrants directory. Buying your badge in advance is recommended as walk-up prices are higher.

To attend both the film and music conferences it's best to buy a platinum badge. This offers access to all music, film, and interactive events. Platinum badges cost $900-1,050.

The easiest way to register for SXSW is online at www.sxsw.com, but registration forms can also be mailed in. Keep in mind that tickets are cheaper the earlier you buy them and

students can buy film badges at a discount. Badges are picked up at the Austin Convention Center when the festival begins.

TIPS

There are hundreds of free shows and "unofficial" shows all over town. Some are low-key and some are major events. Before the festival begins, a schedule of free shows is circulated among those who have "connections." If you can get your hands on it, you can enjoy SXSW without buying an expensive badge. Mind you, you can't be as selective and won't get to see many of the "official" shows, but the free show circuit is a great way to experience SXSW.

Everyone shows up the first day of the festival to pick up their badges. The wait in long lines can be brutal, so pick up your badge a day early if you can.

For both music and film events that are getting lots of buzz, it's important to show up early and get in line. Admission is subject to venue capacity and when big-name acts and films are being showcased, it can be very disappointing when you can't get in after paying big bucks for the "all access" badge.

Finally, if you are itching to see somebody famous, your best bet is to eat lunch at Güero's Taco Bar or Lambert's barbecue any day during the festival.

snake oil salesmen, and get sick on rides. The vestiges of this era can still be seen at **Star of Texas Fair and Rodeo** (512/919-3000, www.rodeoaustin.com). The fair is held at the Travis County Exposition Center (7311 Decker Ln.). The rodeo is the real deal, and the people that come out of the woodwork are the real deal too. Pressed jeans and Stetsons is what I'm talking about. Parking is available in an adjacent field.

April

The first weekend in April, local artists, as well as artists from across the country, are peddling their wares at the **Art City Austin**

(www.artallianceaustin.org, $8 for adults, children under 12 free). Here you'll find sculpture, metal and woodwork, crafts, and painting in all media. This art festival is a big deal; it's the second-best art festival in Texas according to The Harris List. Downtown streets are blocked to traffic at Republic Square Park for the weekend, and artists set up booths so art lovers and the curious can mull about in a daze looking at all the swirling colors as they eat fair fare and live music sets an upbeat mood.

Eeyore's Birthday Party (512/448-5160, www.eeyores.com) is one of the more popular and interesting city-wide birthday parties held throughout the year. Founded by hippie

© JUSTIN MARLER

Art City, held every April

UT students decades ago, this family festival has grown into an extravaganza of costumes, cake, and live entertainment, all in honor of the depressed donkey friend of Winnie the Pooh. He's getting up there in age so try to catch one of these before he dies. Proceeds go to nonprofit groups in town.

For the wine and food connoisseur willing to throw down some bucks there's the **Texas Wine and Food Festival** (www.texaswineandfood.org). Sponsored by Whole Foods, this four-day taste bud and buzz extravaganza showcases local and national wine and food artisans who converge in Austin to share their culinary creations. The festival takes place in venues all over town. Tickets range $55–$450 depending on how much of the event you want to experience.

A favorite rite-of-spring for Austinites is running the **Capitol 10,000** (www.statesman.com/cap10k), a 10K race on foot that begins in downtown Austin and ends on Auditorium Shores. Some run, some walk, and some just parade about in silly getups. If you have bad knees or just don't like running or walking 10K, it's worth watching the start of the race at Congress Bridge as the thousands of participants clog the arteries of downtown. The event happens the first Sunday of April and early registration costs $20. Every participant is actually placed and timed, so it's possible to cross the finish line in 5,142nd place.

Every April the Clyde Littlefield **Texas Relays** are held on the UT campus. This event is one of the nation's largest and most prestigious track-and-field meets. The four-day event features high school, collegiate, and professional athletes from across the nation. It is one of the earliest outdoor meets of the year and the combination of weather and high-profile athletes draws sellout crowds.

At the end of April, down-home acoustic music enthusiasts make the **Old Settlers Music Festival** (www.oldsettlersmusicfest.org) their home for a four-day weekend where the banjos will be plinkin'. Held at the Salt Lick Pavilion in Driftwood just outside of Austin, the festival features over two dozen of the top performers of bluegrass and Americana music on four stages. Camping at the festival is encouraged, but reserve your tent or RV spot in advance. Admission varies.

Canned food for reggae! The **Austin Reggae Festival** (www.austinreggaefest.com), the city's premier reggae event, celebrates the legacy of peace, world unity, and great reggae music that Bob Marley introduced to the world. Held at Auditorium Shores, this Rasta mecca includes performances by reggae artists along with food vendors offering third-world delicacies. Bring something to sit on, sunscreen, and a Hacky Sack. One-day pass admission is $10 and two cans of nonperishable food.

Get in touch with the more sensitive and expressive side of your soul with the **Austin International Poetry Festival** (www.aipf.org). Held at various venues throughout town, this competition brings in over 200 poets from around the world for a four-day event dedicated to rhyme and time.

Wildflower Days at Lady Bird Johnson Wildflower Center continues though April.

May

If your sense of humor is on the level of Bazooka Joe (I used to work in a blanket factory but it folded . . .), and if you enjoy clever wit, check out the **O. Henry Pun-Off World Championships** (512/472-1903). This duel of puns between a slew of clever word butchers is held in the backyard of the O. Henry Museum (409 East 5th St.) with some 2,000 pun fans watching. Admission is free.

Zilker Garden Festival, held at **Zilker Botanical Garden Center** in Zilker Park, sometimes takes place in May.

Every year during the **Old Pecan Street Arts Festival** (www.oldpecanstreetfestival. com), 6th Street is shut down and the arts become king. Full of some 300 vendors selling arts and crafts, live music stages in the streets, children's carnival games, street performers, and the smell of beef in the air, 6th Street becomes a first-world, Austin-style bazaar. This free event is held every spring in the first weekend of May and every fall in the last weekend of September, between 11 A.M. and 8 P.M.

June

The first weekend in June, women in pink tutus and men in tights are gracefully dancing about under the starry Texas sky. **Ballet under the Stars** (512/502-8634, www.ade-ybt.org) is a free, open-air ballet featuring talented local dancers at the Zilker Park Hillside Theatre. For over a decade Austin Dance Ensemble has put on this nimble affair the first Friday and Saturday of June at 8:30 P.M.

Hailed as the biggest biker parade and street party in Texas, the **Republic of Texas Biker Rally** (www.rotrally.com) fills Austin with acres of hogs, custom choppers, leather, facial hair, and sheer brawn for an entire week. The event stretches over a four-day period at the Travis County Exposition Center (7311 Decker Ln.). Entertainment includes monster-truck rallies, white-knuckle motorcycle stunts, and live music. Headliners in the past have included Charlie Daniels, Hank Williams Jr., and George Thorogood. On Friday night the rally proceeds through downtown with an Austin Police escort, and ends at Congress Avenue. Traffic is shut down for the night for an ensuing all-night biker bash. Tickets for the Expo Center are $45. The party on Congress Avenue is free.

Imagine the symbol of Texas—the Lone Star—on a rainbow backdrop, or a giant Texas-shaped rainbow flag proudly carried as a standard of victory by men dressed up like Cher. At the **Austin Pride Parade** gay pride is as big as Texas. Although it's only been going on for a couple years, this is an important event that is all about tolerance, acceptance, and being proud of who you are. The parade is a family event replete with floats, music, and classic cars, but it can have moments that aren't necessarily rated G.

Starting this month, the local rock station KGSR 107.1 (www.kgsr.com) brings the blues to Zilker Park Rock Island for **Blues on the Green.** Free shows are put on every other Wednesday 7:30–9:30 P.M., mid-June–mid-August. As for all events in the dead of summer, bring sunblock and lawn chairs.

July

Strike up the band and let our independence be commemorated! A grandiose way to celebrate the 4th of July is to attend the **Austin Symphony 4th of July Concert and Fireworks** (www.austinsymphony.org) on Auditorium Shores' outdoor stage. A free, two-hour classical music performance culminates in Tchaikovsky's famous 1812 overture, accompanied by the firing of 75-millimeter Howitzer cannons, and ending with a spectacular fireworks show over Lady Bird Lake.

August

In August it's too darned hot to do anything outside. Nevertheless the *Austin Chronicle* cranks up the heat with the **Austin Chronicle Hot Sauce Festival.** This is an amateur and professional hot sauce competition that includes live music and great food at Waterloo Park. Warning: The combination of the 100-degree heat and hot sauce may make you feel like you're trapped in a structure fire.

During **Bat Fest** (www.roadwayevents. com), Congress Avenue Bridge turns into a fair with more than 100 booths featuring arts, crafts, and food, and more than 20 musicians and bands perform on two stages. All this is in honor of North America's largest urban bat colony, which lives under the bridge during the summer months. The bridge and Congress Avenue, Cesar Chavez Street, and Barton Springs Road near the bridge are all closed from 2 A.M. Saturday to midnight Sunday. Admission is $3 a day. A portion of the proceeds goes to Bat Conservation International.

September

Spun out of the famous public television show, **Austin City Limits Music Festival** (www.aclfestival.com) is the biggest music fest of the year. For three days the festival features top acts, bands, performers, and musical legends in nearly all genres of music. In the past the festival has featured artists such as REM, Ben Harper, Coldplay, and the list goes on. The scene: 200,000 people, portable potties, the smell of sunscreen, parking miles away, dust in every orifice, and heat exhaustion, all in beautiful Zilker Park. Tickets can be purchased for one of the three days (Friday, Saturday, or Sunday), or you can throw down more cash for a three-day pass. In the spring an early-bird ticket special is offered, but these sell out in a matter of hours. After that tickets can be bought at a premium online. There's a long list of things that won't pass security; check the website before you bring all kinds of stuff to survive the weekend.

The fall occurrence of **Old Pecan Street Arts Festival** is held on 6th Street.

October

Founded by former librarian and First Lady Laura Bush, the **Texas Book Festival** (www.texasbookfestival.org) has become one of the biggest literary events in the Southwest. Book signings, awards ceremonies, celebrity-author book readings, and a black-tie Literary Gala including cocktails and dinner provide a great weekend that benefits the Texas Public Libraries. Tickets range $50–75, and the Literary Gala is $350 per person.

Over the past few years Austin has been attracting quite a bit of attention from the film industry. In fact Austin scored the number two spot of Best Cities for Moviemakers (by *MovieMaker* magazine, 2005). The event that highlights Austin and celluloid is the **Austin Film Festival** (www.austinfilmfestival.com). For eight days hundreds of film-industry folk and silver-screen fans converge in downtown Austin's many cinemas and hotels to view some 100 films. The festival also includes a screenwriter's conference.

Local hero, Tour de France champion, cancer survivor, and cyclist extraordinaire Lance Armstrong hosts **Ride for the Roses** (512/236-8820, www.livestrong.org) every October. This hugely popular event brings out crowds of cyclists, fans, celebrities, and spectators for a whole weekend of cycle-related events, all to raise money for cancer research.

Perhaps the most obscure event that goes on in these parts is the **Texas Gourd Society Show and Sale** (www.texasgourdsociety.org). Talk about niche: This society is comprised of artists that enjoy painting and decorating gourds. The show and sale also includes a competition. Whoever has the most gourd-geous gourd wins! Believe me, some of these gourds are pretty spectacular.

When writing up events for Austin's calendar in October one can't omit **Halloween on 6th Street.** Some 60,000 dressed up freaks and ghouls take over downtown's historic 6th Street. Overstimulated by sugar and whatever else, people party all night. The costumes are unbelievable. If you want to trick-or-treat, but don't want to put time into inventing a costume, rent something from **Lucy in Disguise with Diamonds** (1506 S. Congress Ave., 512/444-2002).

November

The funnest festival in Austin throughout the year is **Fun Fun Fun Fest** (www.funfunfunfest. com). Or at least it's pretty fun for all who are interested in indie rock, punk rock, hardcore, metal, and hip-hop/DJ. The festival, which started 2006, is held in Austin's Waterloo

Park close to downtown. The promoters of this show, Transmission Entertainment, have an uncanny knack for getting bands from the bygone era of rock underground to resurface and put on amazing shows. Past lineups have included the Circle Jerks, 7 Seconds, The Hold Steady, Descendents, High on Fire, Spoon, Explosions in the Sky, and Okkervil River. Even Weird Al Yankovic has done his thing, whatever that is. There are multiple stages for music and one for stand-up comedy.

Austin's entertainment district takes on the look of 19th-century London during **Victorian Christmas on 6th Street.** From Thanksgiving to Christmas, weekend shoppers browse the booths filled with holiday crafts and gift items.

A great way to sneak a peek into the lives of Austin artists is by touring artists' studios during **East Austin Studio Tour** (www.east-austinstudiotour.com). Over a hundred artists, galleries, and studios participate in this East Austin event in mid-November each year. All media and styles are represented, from serene landscapes to bizarre abstract art. A map of the tour is available on the East Austin Studio Tour website.

December
Austin's beloved holiday tradition, **Zilker Park Tree Lighting,** draws thousands to Zilker Park to see the park decorated in lights and to watch the lighting of the 165-foot Christmas tree. I'm sad to report that The Trail of Lights, which was a mile-long display of holiday and wintertime scenes has been cancelled. However, spinning under the tree and eating funnel cake is sure to usher in the Christmas spirit. The tree-lighting ceremony takes place on the first Sunday of December.

The **Armadillo Christmas Bazaar** (512/447-1605 after 11 A.M., www.armadillobazaar.com) is a uniquely Austin holiday market where artists and artisans from Texas and the Southwest sell their works. There's great food and live music here too, and it all takes place at Austin Music Hall. Congratulations on 30 years of pumping up local artists.

Recreation

Being in the most beautiful and diverse outdoor setting in Texas, Austin has become a favorite for lovers of the outdoors. There are an unusual amount of lakes, rivers, hills, caves, trails, and parks that have wisely been preserved for people to use and enjoy. There's kayaking, biking, backpacking, boating, scuba diving, spelunking, rock climbing, camping, rafting, skiing, golf, disc golf, tennis, volleyball, and numerous swimming holes—all for the taking.

◖ LADY BIRD LAKE
The greatest attraction Austin has to offer is the stretch of the Colorado River called Lady Bird Lake, formerly known as Town Lake. This wide, slow-moving river that winds through the heart of downtown Austin, is banked with lush vegetation, ancient trees, and wildlife such as turtles, swans, and ducks. What makes Lady Bird Lake so remarkable? By taking just a few steps you can go from bustling, urban downtown to an alternate world that's peaceful, beautiful, and natural.

Lady Bird Lake's hike and bike trails are some of the best urban trails in the country, with several loops over and around the lake that are in three, 10-mile increments. Each loop's bridge provides a different view of Austin, the lake, and surrounding hills. Although the trails are fit for bikes as well as pedestrians, and during peak hours bikers find it pretty hard to navigate all the joggers and speed-walkers, everyone seems to sweat in harmony. The trails are all lakeside and have lots of shade, benches, water fountains, and Stevie Ray Vaughan. That's right! On the south shore of the lake is a life-size bronze statue of the Austin legend proudly standing as a sentinel with guitar in

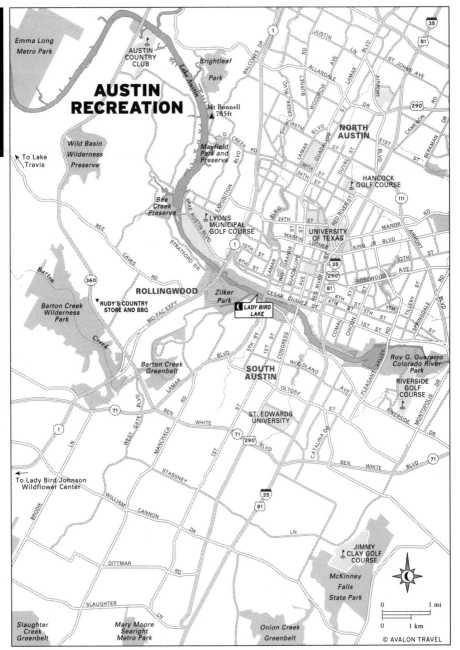

AUSTIN RECREATION

Emma Long Metro Park

Austin Country Club

Brightleaf Park

Mt Bonnell 785ft

To Lake Travis

Wild Basin Wilderness Preserve

Mayfield Park and Preserve

Bee Creek Preserve

Lyons Municipal Golf Course

NORTH AUSTIN

Hancock Golf Course

UNIVERSITY OF TEXAS

Barton Creek Wilderness Park

ROLLINGWOOD

Rudy's Country Store and BBQ

Zilker Park

LADY BIRD LAKE

Barton Creek Greenbelt

SOUTH AUSTIN

Roy G. Guerrero Colorado River Park

RIVERSIDE GOLF COURSE

ST. EDWARDS UNIVERSITY

To Lady Bird Johnson Wildflower Center

JIMMY CLAY GOLF COURSE

McKinney Falls State Park

Slaughter Creek Greenbelt

Mary Moore Searight Metro Park

Onion Creek Greenbelt

0   1 mi

0   1 km

© AVALON TRAVEL

© JUSTIN MARLER

Lady Bird Lake was named after President Lyndon B. Johnson's wife, who saved this natural resource from development.

hand. Free water stations are set up at various locations along the trail. The trail is considered very safe so no need to worry about crazy people doing crazy things. However, the one thing you want to watch out for is poison oak. The trail is laced with this evil plant, and if you are not paying attention, or decide to pet the cute dog running up to you, you may end up with some serious itching. During the peak months nice people will put little flags on branches to help identify the stuff.

Other activities that take place on Lady Bird Lake include crewing, canoeing, and kayaking, which are great ways to get up close to the turtles and other wildlife, not to mention the city looks pretty impressive from the water too. Canoes can be rented by ◀ **Zilker Park Boat Rentals** (www.zilkerboats.com, hours are 9 A.M.–dark Mon.–Fri. summer and early fall, 10 A.M.–dark Sat.–Sun. winter as weather permits, $10 an hour or $40 per day). They have 17-foot Alumacraft, Grumman and Michicraft canoes, and both Frenzy (one

person) and Malibu Two (two person) ocean kayaks. Paddles and life jackets are provided.

Texas Rowing Center (512/467-7799, www.texasrowingcenter.com, 6:30 A.M.–dark daily) on the north side of Lady Bird Lake on the trail near Mo-Pac also has rentals for water sports. Rates start at $10 an hour and go to $45 for all-day rental. There's also a double-decker paddle-wheel riverboat that takes passengers on tours of the lake. **Lone Star Riverboat** (512/327-1388, www.lonestarriverboat.com, $9) operates this Mark Twain–style adventure March–October on weekends at 3 P.M.

Lady Bird Lake's trails can be accessed at any of the downtown bridges and from several of the hotels on the river. The most convenient parking lot is at Auditorium Shores, on the south side of the lake at the foot of the 1st Street Bridge. However, a better place to park is in Zilker Park, on Stratford Drive under the Mo-Pac overpass. Peak recreation hours are before and after the workday, during the weekend, and on holidays. Swimming in

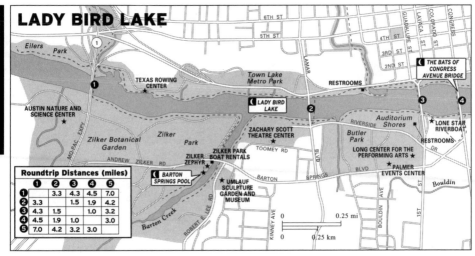

LADY BIRD LAKE

Ellers Park

TEXAS ROWING CENTER

AUSTIN NATURE AND SCIENCE CENTER ★

Zilker Botanical Garden

Zilker Park

ANDREW ZILKER RD

ZILKER ZEPHYR ★

ZILKER PARK BOAT RENTALS ★

BARTON SPRINGS POOL

★ UMLAUF SCULPTURE GARDEN AND MUSEUM

Barton Creek

ROBERT E. LEE RD

KINNEY AVE

ZACHARY SCOTT THEATRE CENTER

TOOMEY RD

BARTON SPRINGS BLVD

Town Lake Metro Park

RESTROOMS

LADY BIRD LAKE

RIVERSIDE *Auditorium Shores*

Butler Park

LONG CENTER FOR THE PERFORMING ARTS ★

★ PALMER EVENTS CENTER

THE BATS OF CONGRESS AVENUE BRIDGE

★ LONE STAR RIVERBOAT

RESTROOMS

Bouldin

BOULDIN AVE

1ST ST

6TH ST
5TH ST
4TH ST
3RD ST
2ND ST

GUADALUPE ST
LAVACA ST
COLORADO ST
CONGRESS

LAMAR

MO-PAC EXPY

Roundtrip Distances (miles)

	➊	➋	➌	➍	➎
➊		3.3	4.3	4.5	7.0
➋	3.3		1.5	1.9	4.2
➌	4.3	1.5		1.0	3.2
➍	4.5	1.9	1.0		3.0
➎	7.0	4.2	3.2	3.0	

0   0.25 mi

0   0.25 km

Lady Bird Lake isn't allowed due to dangerous whirlpools.

LAKE TRAVIS

Just northwest of Austin along the Colorado River is the Highland Lakes area. There are five winding lakes that draw hordes of people from spring to fall: Lake Austin, Inks Lake, Lake LBJ, Lake Marble Falls, and Lake Travis. These lakes are wide spots in the Colorado River that became wider when a series of six dams were built back in the 1930s and '40s. The primary function of these dams was to give water a place to go during flash floods. The lakes that have formed are all about recreation under the sun, the most popular lake being Lake Travis.

People come from all over Texas to lay in the sun on and around Lake Travis and participate in every form of water recreation imaginable. There's swimming, boating, fishing, sailing, scuba diving, parasailing, and all kinds of water sports, as well as the only nude beach in the state. Lake Travis is the second largest of the lakes, and has an average surface area of nearly 19,000 acres to play on.

The best way to gain access to Lake Travis is through Travis County Parks locations. The most popular and largest facility is at **Mansfield Dam Park** (RR 2222, sunrise–9 P.M. daily, $10 for the day, $20 for improved camping). There are four boat-launching ramps, swimming areas, barbeque grills, picnic tables, and restrooms. The other popular access to the lake is at **Pace Bend Park** (RR 2322, 512/264-1482, sunrise–9 P.M. daily, $10 for the day, $15 for primitive camping). With nine miles of Lake Travis shoreline and beautiful vistas, and only 45 minutes from downtown Austin, this park provides an easy way to experience the lake. Here you can camp, swim, hike, and launch boats. To get to Pace Bend take Highway 71 west 11 miles to RR 2322 (Pace Bend Park Rd.). Turn right on RR 2322 and travel 4.6 miles to the park entrance.

If man-made water recreation is more your style there's **Shore Club Volente Beach** (16107 FM 2769, 512/258-5110, www.volentebeach.com, 10 A.M.–8 P.M. daily Apr.–Oct., $15 shorter than 42", $20 42" and taller). This is the closest water-theme park to Austin, and has everything from waterslides to tropical-style swimming pools. To get to Volente Beach go north on Highway 183 then west on Anderson Mill Road, which turns into FM 2769. The park is seven miles up FM 2769.

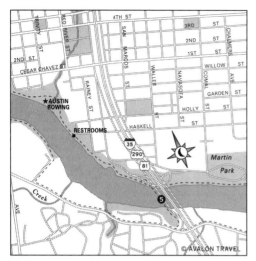

© AVALON TRAVEL

HIKING AND BIKING
Barton Creek Greenbelt

If you want to disappear into nature but don't want to spend any time getting there, Barton Creek Greenbelt (512/472-1267, 5 A.M.– 10 P.M., free) has it all. Second only to Lady Bird Lake, this well-preserved stretch of wilderness along Barton Creek has mountain biking, hiking trails, swimming holes, and rock climbing. The Greenbelt is about 7.9 miles long and consists of 809 acres. The terrain is mostly roughed with sheer cliff walls, lush vegetation, and a creek that is at its peak in the spring. Once you descend into the Greenbelt you feel far away from civilization, provided you don't look up and see the occasional home on the cliff. The trails are rocky and semi-primitive and cut through scenic wildflowers, trees, limestone cliffs, caves, meadows, swimming holes, and waterfalls. The trail varies from narrow ledges to wide walkways. Wildlife is abundant, which can make the park sound and look like the Amazon.

The trail starts above Barton Springs Pool at Zilker Park and extends westward past Loop 360 to Lost Creek. There are several trailheads throughout the park, mostly in adjoining neighborhoods. The three easiest

places to access the Greenbelt are **Spyglass Trail Access** on Spyglass Drive just off Mo-Pac; **Loop 360 Trail Access** at Loop 360 just south from Mo-Pac; and **Gus Fruh Trail Access** at 2642 Barton Hills Drive (wheelchair accessible). Dogs are permitted on leash only. Mountain bikers must yield to hikers, and stay on designated trails. In spring creek crossings may require wading through water. When enjoying the Barton Creek Greenbelt, remember to pack your trash. Call for up-to-date trail conditions.

Mayfield Park and Preserve

One of the more off-the-beaten-path outdoor areas is Mayfield Park and Preserve (3505 W. 35th St., 10 A.M.–10 P.M. daily, free). This often forgotten park, on a small stretch of Lady Bird Lake, is perfect for a casual evening stroll for families and couples. The winding network of paths twists through old groves of oak trees, across several footbridges, over small creeks, and through a lakeside grove of moss-draped oaks. Being next to the historic building of Laguna Gloria Museum just adds to the romance. The park has a paved parking lot, restroom facilities, and drinking fountains. The best way to get to Mayfield is by heading west on the 35th Street exit from Mo-Pac.

Wild Basin Wilderness Preserve

The perfect antidote to a busy schedule is Wild Basin Wilderness Preserve (512/327-7622, www.wildbasin.org, trails hours sunrise–sunset, office hours 9 A.M.–4 P.M. Tues.–Sun., $3). Smaller in scope than Barton Creek Greenbelt and less crowded than Lady Bird Lake, Wild Basin is a favorite secret Austinite retreat. The 2.5 miles of hiking trails on 227 acres are well maintained and generally quiet. The trails take you through a valley, over streams, and to a panoramic view. The trail also includes informative trail markers that give insight into the native plants and animals that live in the region. Interpretive trail brochures are available at the trailhead. Dogs and bikes aren't allowed. The entrance to Wild Basin is right off of Loop 360, which makes it an easy getaway.

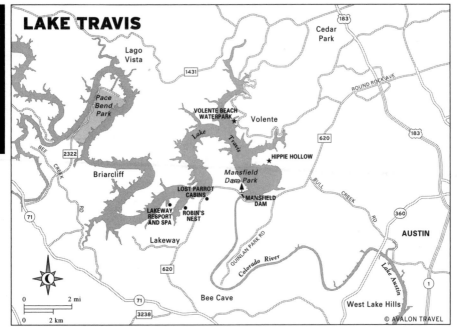

ROCK CLIMBING

Out of the four basic types of rock climbing—sport climbing, traditional climbing (aka Trad), gym climbing, and bouldering—sport climbing is, by far, the most popular and best represented in the Austin area. The **Barton Creek Greenbelt** has a decent number of routes that have their own names like Seismic Wall, Gus Fruh Wall, and New Wall. They are all very short (30–40 ft. max) but really, you can't beat it considering that you don't have to leave the city limits. This sort of "urban cragging" (climber speak for climbing in urban areas) has really put Austin on the map for being a place that you can climb right after work and still make happy hour somewhere.

The Austin Rock Gym (8300 N. Lamar Blvd., Ste. B-102, and 4401 Freidrich Ste., 300, 512/416-9299, www.austinrockgym. com, 3–10 P.M. Mon.–Fri., 10 A.M.–10 P.M. Sat., 10 A.M.–7 P.M. Sun.) is the only gym that is exclusively dedicated to climbing. There are

a couple of great online resources such as www. bloodyflapper.com. Here you'll find lots of good information, a bulletin board for hooking up with other climbers, and great descriptions of all the rock-climbing spots in the Austin area. Another website that has some good info is www.texasclimbers.com, which has a set of rough topographical maps and area descriptions that can be really handy. **Whole Earth Provision Company** (1014 N. Lamar Blvd., 512/476-1414, 10 A.M.–9 P.M. Mon.–Fri., 10 A.M.–8 P.M. Sat., noon–6 P.M. Sun.) offers an extensive line of climbing equipment and shoes. There aren't a whole lot of places where you can rent used gear in town, since climbers' lives depend on the condition of their gear.

SPELUNKING

If you enjoy being in dark places in the belly of the earth, Austin has some good caves waiting to explore. There are two known caves in town. First, there's **Airman's Cave** in the Barton Creek

NAKED IN TEXAS

There's only one place in Texas where you can "be as proud as you can be, of your anatomy" in public, and that's at **Hippie Hollow** on Lake Travis. This little Garden of Eden on the lake is the only clothing-optional public park in the state. The park is in a secluded spot that offers spectacular views of Lake Travis, a paved walking trail, and a hiking trail that hugs the cliffs. Although the shoreline itself is pretty steep and rocky, Hippie Hollow is good for sunbathing, swimming, and fishing. Weather you're a first-timer curious about strutting in the nude, or a dedicated nudist, only the serious are wel-

come here as it's not a place to gawk or giggle at people. Speaking of gawking, a couple years ago a boat passing by Hippie Hollow capsized because everyone rushed to one side of the boat to get a better view.

The park is located 20 minutes from I-35. From Mo-Pac or I-35, take 2222 West to Highway 620. Turn left on 620 and go 1.3 miles. Turn right at the first traffic light onto Comanche Trail. Travel two miles to the park entrance on the left. A paved parking area is available as well as drinking water and restrooms.

Greenbelt. This is the longest known cave in the county. Here you'll see The Keyhole, which is a tight space that can freak out even the most advanced spelunkers, and the Aggie Art Gallery, which is a room full of clay art that has been preserved in this underground environment.

The other cave in town is at **Goat Cave Preserve** (3900 Deer Run) in southwest Austin. For more information on caving in Texas check out www.utgrotto.org.

GOLF

Austin is a golf town—after all it has been home to Harvey Penick, the legendary golf pro and teacher, as well as Ben Crenshaw, Tom Kite, and Hilary Lunke, the U.S. Women's Open champion. There are a slew of excellent world-class courses in the area, both public and private. The following are the best golf courses in Austin.

Hancock Golf Course (811 E. 41st St., on 38th St., 512/453-0276, dawn–dusk daily, $12 for 9 holes) was built in 1899 and is the oldest course in Texas. The 9-hole, par 35 course is in the heart of Austin in the Hyde Park area. No reservations are required. Another course that's been around for a long time is **Lions Golf Course** (2910 Enfield Dr., 512/477-6963, sunrise–sunset daily, $13–20). This 6,001-yard, 18-hole, par 71 course requires reservations.

The Golf Club at Circle C (7401 Hwy. 45, 512/288-4297, www.thegolfclubatcirclec.com, hours vary by season, call ahead) is one of the best public courses in Texas. A picturesque Hill Country setting, covered *biergarten,* and a casual yet elegant clubhouse make this a safe bet for visiting golfers. The Salt Lick barbecue restaurant is nearby and a stop here after golf would finish your day perfectly.

In South Austin there's the tiny but popular **Butler Park Pitch and Putt** (201 Lee Barton Dr., 512/477-4430). This 9-hole, par 27 course is perfect for getting in a quick golfing fix. You only need three clubs carried in hand and a couple golf balls in your pocket. The best golf gear shop is **The Golf Club** (2620 S. Lamar Blvd., 512/916-4653). Well, that's par for the course.

DISC GOLF

When driving past Pease Park on North Lamar Boulevard, you may notice small gatherings of young folks throwing Frisbees into chain hoops with complete concentration, solemnity, and earnestness. This is the fairly young outdoor recreational sport called disc golf, also known as Frisbee golf. Austin has several courses that are very popular to folks that play this niche sport. On the surface this sport seems a bit funny, but people take this very seriously. The most centrally located course is at Pease Park

SPORTING GOODS STORES

- Sports & Outdoor Recreation: **REI** (601 N. Lamar Blvd., 512/482-3357; 9901 N. Capital of Texas Hwy. Ste 200, 512/343-5550)

- Hiking & Outdoor Recreation: **Whole Earth Provision Company** (2410 San Antonio St., 512/478-1577)

- Running & Jogging: **RunTex Lake Austin** (2201 Lake Austin Blvd., 512/477-9464)

- Canoe & Kayak Gear: **Austin Canoe and Kayak** (9705 Burnet Rd., Ste. 102, 512/719-4386)

(Lamar Blvd. at 24th St.). Other courses in town are at Bartholomew Park (51st St. near I-35 in East Austin), and Mary More Searight (Slaughter Lane in South Austin). For more information, check out www.hookshot.com.

SPECTATOR SPORTS

Austin may not have a major league or pro athletic team, but that doesn't stop this sport-loving town from having some of the biggest sporting events in the state. Most of the athletic world in Austin circles around the UT football and baseball teams; both are top in the nation for collegiate sports. UT's sports program also includes tennis, golf, swimming, volleyball, track and field, and women's softball. Beside university games, Austin is also home to the popular minor-league baseball team Round Rock Express, a hockey team called the Ice Bats, and the outlandish return of women's roller derby, which is becoming a wildly popular cult spectator sport.

Football

From the small rural towns where absolutely every citizen can be found in the stands on Friday night to the pro-football mania of the Cowboys, football is Texas's version of the Roman gladiators. Austin happens to be home of **UT Longhorns Football** (www.texassports.com), one of the most popular university football teams in the United States. This excellent team of athletes commands higher ticket prices than pro football, and the networks have hopped on this bandwagon and broadcast Longhorn games with dollar signs in their eyes. The Longhorns fame and athletic superiority hit the national stage when they won the national-championship Rose Bowl game in 2005, considered one of the greatest football games in history. Austin Longhorn season is September–November, and home games take place at Darrell K Royal-Texas Memorial Stadium (1701 Red River St.). Tickets are very hard to get and the ones available are sold as season passes, but it's possible to land tickets for one event for $55–75. Tickets can be purchased at the UT Athletics Ticket Office (Bellmont Hall, first floor lobby, on the UT campus), by phone at 512/471-3333, 800/982-BEVO or 800/982-2386, and online at www.texasboxoffice.com.

Baseball

Baseball may not be as big as football, but it still has an important place in Austin. The **UT Longhorns Baseball** team produces some great ball players, some of whom go on to the majors. In 2005 they were national champions and were ranked number one in collegiate baseball. UT Longhorns baseball season is February–June and games take place at Disch-Falk field (corner of MLK and I-35). Tickets are $8–12 and can be purchased at the UT Athletics Ticket Office (Bellmont Hall, first floor lobby, on the UT campus), by phone at 512/471-3333, 800/982-BEVO or 800/982-2386, or online at www.texasboxoffice.com.

The other baseball team more than worthy of mention is the **The Round Rock Express** (www.roundrockexpress.com). This AAA affiliate of the Houston Astros is owned and operated by Nolan Ryan and tech kingpin Michael Dell. The Express is gaining popularity to such an extent that they often break minor-league attendance records. The team plays about 70 home games April–September at the Dell Diamond (3400 E. Palm Valley Rd.) in Round Rock.

Basketball

The hoop in town is dominated by **UT Longhorns Basketball,** with both men's and women's teams. While both teams are excellent, the women's team is the most popular as it has single-handedly brought women's basketball to public light by drawing the most fans in the sport's history. Both men's and women's basketball games take place at the Frank Erwin Center (1701 Red River St., 512/471-7744). Tickets run $6–15 and can be purchased at the UT Athletics Ticket Office (Bellmont Hall, first floor lobby, on the UT campus), by phone at 512/471-3333, 800/982-BEVO or 800/982-2386, or online at www.texasboxoffice.com.

Roller Derby

One of Austin's hottest and most unique forms of entertainment is the roller derby. Put on by **Texas Rollergirls** (www.txrollergirls.com), this skater-owned and -operated league is comprised of five very competitive teams: Hotrod Honeys, Honky Tonk Heartbreakers, Hell Marys, and the Hustlers. The roller derbies take place every spring and summer at **Playland Skate Center** (8822 McCann Dr. 512/452-1901), **Travis County Exposition Center** (7311 Decker Lane, 512/854-4900), and skating rinks throughout Texas. Every bout at Playland Skate Center usually sells out its 1,100-seat capacity at $15 a ticket so be sure to show up when the doors open at 6:30 P.M.

TOURS
Walking Tours

Austin is best imbibed by strolling around on foot. Most points of interest are within walking distance and the town is easily traversed thanks to good city planning and pedestrian-friendly motorists. Free guided walking tours are put on by **Austin Convention and Visitors Bureau** (512/454-1545, 866/GO-AUSTIN or 866/462-

8784, www.austintexas.org). They offer tours of Congress Avenue, 6th Street, the Capitol grounds, and Bremond Block. Tours are offered March–November at the Capitol's south steps and take about an hour. Call for tour schedules and information.

Austin has enough ghosts in its closet that **Austin Ghost Tours** (512/853-9826, www.austinghosttours.com) came along to give these ghouls their due recognition. Tour organizers have pieced together the past and organized several fascinating tours that include the Haunted 6th Street Tour, Servant Girl Annihilator Tour, and Graveyard Tour, to name a few. Tour guides walk the curious through the streets of Austin and unfold the darker side of town. Tours are about 90 minutes and take place outside for the most part, and all are wheelchair accessible except for the Haunted Pub Crawl Tour. Tickets generally cost $15. Reservations are required for all tours; call in advance.

Sightseeing Cruises

The best view of Austin is from Lady Bird Lake, and the best way to be on the lake is by floating in an authentic double-decker paddle-wheel riverboat. **Lone Star Riverboat** (512/327-1388, www.lonestarriverboat.com) offers narrated sightseeing cruises March–October on Saturday and Sunday at 3 P.M. Boarding begins at 2:30 P.M. and costs $9 for adults, $6 for children under 12, and $7 for seniors over 60. Along with the riverboat, Lone Star also has a pontoon boat that offers a sunset cruise for a buck less. This is the best seat in town for watching the bats fly out of Congress Avenue Bridge. Departure time varies; call in advance.

Also offering aquatic tours on Lady Bird Lake is **Capital Cruises** (512/480-9264, www.capitalcruises.com). Public sightseeing cruises depart Saturday and Sunday at 1:00 P.M. and bat-watching cruises depart before sunset. Rates are $10 for adults, $8 for seniors, and $5 for kids 3–12. Also available is a dinner cruise with cocktails and entertainment. Rates range $26–100 depending on options. The local phone book has a 20 percent

ROLLER DERBY REVIVAL

The golden 1970s' most outrageous form of entertainment, roller derby, is back! The skates are laced up, the short shorts are donned, the roller rink is aflame, and the catfights have begun. But instead of disco, punk and heavy metal is the soundtrack to this over-the-top spectacle. Austin's most unique and dazzling form of underground entertainment is put on by a legion of feisty women from all walks of life. A few years back these ladies started skating for fun and found that people loved the idea of roller derby and would pay to see them beat each other up in the rink. Seeing a grass-roots opportunity to resurrect a spectacle sport that died with disco, they organized and started taking it seriously. A flurry of attention ensued, such as a cover story article in *Rolling Stone* and an A&E TV show.

Today there are two Austin-based, skater-owned and -operated leagues: **Texas Lonestar Rollergirls** and **Texas Rollergirls**. A sampling of team names includes: Hotrod Honeys, Cherry Bombs, Honky Tonk Heartbreakers, Hell Marys, Holy Rollers, and the Texecutioners. With all manner of theatrics, these ladies get dressed up in crazy get-ups comprised of fish-net stockings, plaid skirts, and war paint, and take on various personalities such as Lucille Brawl, Rice Rocket, Kitty Kitty Bang Bang, Cherry Chainsaw, and Dinah-Mite, to name a few.

So what exactly is roller derby? Don't expect this to be a WWF-style choreographed event. This is real women going in circles at high speeds on skates, knocking each other down to win. In brief, here's how it works. There are three positions: pivot sets the pace for the pack and is the last line of defense; blocker tries to stop the jammer and knocks around the opposing team's blockers; jammer sprints through the pack, scoring points by passing members of the opposing team. The pack starts with a pivot from each team in front, three blockers from each team in the middle, and a jammer from each team in the back. When the whistle blows, the pack takes off, and on a second whistle, the jammers start fighting their way through the pack in an attempt to be named lead jammer. The jammers lap the pack and when they re-enter the pack they receive

one point for each member of the opposing team that they pass. A jam lasts a maximum of two minutes, but the lead jammer has the right to call off the jam at her discretion.

If you're feeling brave the best seating is rink side. There are no rails, and very few seats, so plant yourself down on the rink just outside the ring of flashing lights. At rink side you can get up close to the action so much so that you can smell the B.O. as it mixes with the smell of popcorn. Always be on guard and keep your eyes on the women on skates. They often crash, wipeout, or barrel off into the crowd. Spacing out even for one moment can cost you your fingers.

The roller derbies take place every spring and summer at **Palmer Event Center** (900 Barton Springs Rd.) and **Austin Convention Center** (500 E. Cesar Chavez St). Ticket prices are usually $15 a seat and doors usually open at 6:00 P.M. A band always performs at half time. For times and dates and more information check out www.txrollergirls.com and www.txrd.com.

discount coupon. Both Capital Cruises and Lone Star Riverboat offer cruises March–October, and docks for both are located on the south side of Lady Bird Lake between 1st Street Bridge and Congress Avenue Bridge near the Hyatt Regency.

Land Tours

If you don't have sea legs, **Austin Overtures** (512/659-9478, www.austinovertures.com) offers great comprehensive 90-minute tours of town in a brightly colored minibus. Tours include over 30 points of interest and are narrated by a father-son team of Texas history buffs who know their stuff. Tickets are $25 for adults and $17 for children 12 and under, and can be purchased at Austin Convention and Visitors Bureau visitors center at 209 E. 6th Street downtown. The bus departs from this location as well.

Perhaps the most touristy thing to do in Austin is to take the amphibious tour of town with **Austin Duck Adventures** (209 E. 6th St., 512/4-SPLASH or 512/477-5274, www.austinducks.com). Board a domesticated British Alvis Stalwart (amphibious military vehicle from the 1960s) and traverse both land and water, exploring Austin's main sights such as the State Capitol, historic Congress Avenue, and 6th Street before splashing into Lake Austin.

For a nostalgic chug into the past the **Austin Steam Train** (512/477-8468, www.austin-steamtrain.org) is a great way to see parts of Austin and the beautiful countryside north of town. The Austin Steam Train Association operates two classic steam trains on a leg of the original Southern Pacific railroad between Austin and the town of Llano. There are two boarding locations downtown. One is conveniently located at Brush Square on 4th Street in front of the Austin Convention Center, and the other is in Plaza Saltillo in East Austin at E. 4th Street and Comal Street. Although walk-up tickets can be purchased at the boarding locations advance reservations are recommended. Coach fares range $18–28 and lounge fares range $23–43, depending on the route

and the train. Call or go online for schedules and fares.

A horse-drawn carriage is the most romantic way to see downtown, provided you don't feel guilty for making the horses sweat. There are two companies vying for your business, **Austin Carriage Service** (512/243-0044, www.austincarriage.com, $50 for half-hour ride) and **Die Gelbe Rose Carriage** (512/477-8824, $45–100). Both companies have Belgian and Percheron horses and charge $100 per hour and $45 for half-hour tours. Carriages can always be seen around downtown, especially in the evenings. You can schedule a ride, flag one down, or call and have one dispatched to a restaurant, nightclub, or wherever you are. Drivers can include narrative on the tours, but they are pleased to shut up if couples want a more romantic ride.

A new and unusual way of touring the town is on a Segway™ Personal Transporter (PT). **Gliding Revolution** (512/495-9250, www.glidingrevolution.com, $75 for a downtown tour) offers these two-wheel tours complete complete with Segway training, and a standing jaunt through the downtown sights with a tour guide. If a tour of building facades and Lady Bird Lake are too mundane for you, consider going on the Ghost Tour for $85.

Adventure Tours

A brilliant idea has come to fruition with **Cypress Valley Canopy Tours** (1223 Paleface Ranch Rd., 512/264-8880, www.cypressvalleycanopytours.com). Out in the Hill Country, just 30 miles west of Austin, this outfit offers an adventure on wires high up in the trees. The tours include three sky bridges and six zip lines that land on tall platforms amidst the trees. Guides prepare the adventurous by running them through a detailed orientation explaining the gear and the tour. Tours cost $75 per person. Reservations are necessary. Specials rates are available for families, but children under 10 are not permitted. During the summer they are open every day except Monday, and in the fall and spring are open only on weekends.

Accommodations

A fly on the wall in any of Austin's motels, hotels, and bed-and-breakfasts would probably report seeing all kinds of folks coming and going throughout the year, such as families, politicians, sports fans, celebrities and movie industry folk, business professionals attending conferences, and leisure travelers. It's risky putting words in a fly's mouth, but I would venture to say the type of traveler a fly would report seeing the most is musicians. Being the Live Music Capital of the World, Austin generates an unprecedented amount of band traffic. That said, Austin has a place to stay for everyone. Here you can find a room in a quiet Victorian with doilies, down pillows, and blueberry muffins, or a room in a plush four-star luxury hotel with a rooftop pool, whirlpool bathtubs, and impeccable room service.

So what's the best area to lay your head? Downtown is the most desirable area because this is where everything is happening. All the chain hotels know this and their prices reflect it. Rates vary depending on the season and weather there's an event taking over the town. But those desiring comfort and a deal shouldn't lose heart. The upswing of this is that bed-and-breakfasts are plentiful and affordable, and many are within close range of downtown.

The main thing to keep in mind when planning your trip to Austin is to book your reservations way in advance. When there's an event in town it can be difficult, and sometimes nearly impossible, to find a place to stay at the last minute. To be sure you have a good chance at getting a reservation where you prefer to stay, book your lodgings at least 2–3 months in advance if possible.

UNDER $50

The one hostel in the Austin area is **Hostelling International-Austin** (2200 S. Lakeshore Blvd., 512/444-2294 or 800/725-2331, www.hiaustin.org). Set on the banks of Lady Bird Lake near downtown, this comfortable, clean, and spacious hostel is the most affordable place to stay in town. Of course, it has dormitory-style accommodations, and no private rooms are available. Rates are $22 per night for HI members, $25 per night for nonmembers. Bed linens and parking are included in the rate, and towels rent for a buck. Bicycle, canoe, and kayak rentals are available, as is Internet access. Front desk hours are 8 A.M.–10 P.M. Dormitories are open 2 P.M.–11 A.M. No curfew.

$50-100

There's something about staying in a dingy motel in Austin that's very appealing, and even romantic. If you want the motel atmosphere minus some of the various dubious activities we all know go down in motels, there's ❰ **The Austin Motel** (1220 S. Congress Ave., 512/441-1157, www.austinmotel.com, $69–154). This family-owned Austin institution is fraught with unique and quirky style, and is in a great location on South Congress Avenue. The motel's motto is "So close yet so far out." The Austin Motel is a favorite place to crash for musicians because it's safe, cheap, and sorta-kinda clean, but has all the charm and charisma of a total dive.

Now that we're knee deep into the good ol' American roadside mainstays we have to mention **Super 8 Motel** (1201 I-35 at 12th St., 512/472-8331, www.super8.com, $65–139). Rates are very cheap so don't expect anything except a bed, clock radio, coffeemaker (with bad coffee), TV, and a bathroom. For lodgings in the vicinity of the University of Texas campus there's also a Super 8 at 5526 North I-35.

Perhaps the most popular locally owned hotel in town is **Hotel San Jose** (1316 S. Congress Ave., 512/444-7322, www.sanjosehotel.com, $95–105). This place is so hip it's almost an entire pelvis. Hotel San Jose is highly rated due to its chic vibe with minimalist decor that I would describe as post-modern Japanese rustique. Some would say Hotel San Jose is all pretense, while others would say it's

© JUSTIN MARLER

The Austin Motel is a popular, inexpensive place to stay on South Congress Ave.

all romance. You decide. The snooty staff can be unpleasant, but the wisteria-covered arbors and quiet atmosphere are pleasant. The hotel offers a great deal that is often overlooked: If you aren't opposed to sharing a bathroom you can get a posh room for a weekend stay for only $95 Sunday–Thursday and $105 Friday and Saturday. Bands and musicians get a 20 percent discount.

Situated in one of Austin's older neighborhoods north of downtown is **Adam's House** (4300 Avenue G, 512/453-7696, www.the-adamshouse.com, $90–139). This beautiful, historic home was tastefully converted into a bed-and-breakfast that offers five charming rooms decorated with antiques. Located in the historic area of Hyde Park, just north of downtown, not too far from the Elisabet Ney Museum and the excellent restaurants of Duval Street, Adam's House is an excellent place to stay for romance. During the weekdays a light breakfast of granola, cereals, homemade muffins, and juices is offered and on the weekends a full breakfast is served in the dining room. Pets

and children under 12 are not welcome. Texas travelers get the "state traveler discount."

Also north of downtown is **Austin Folk House B&B** (506 W. 22nd St., 512/472-6700, www.austinfolkhouse.com). This cheerful bed-and-breakfast offers clean rooms and great hospitality. Breakfasts are a few notches above most bed-and-breakfasts, as they offer *migas* (Mexican-style scrambled eggs), ginger pancakes, crepes, and a few fruit-based dishes such as banana enchiladas. The weekday rate for one person is $85 and $109 on the weekend, and rates for two range $109–155.

The **Star of Texas Inn** (611 W. 22nd St., 512/472-6700, www.staroftexasinn.com, $85–225) is run by the same people that operate the Austin Folk House B&B, and here you will have the same great hospitality, clean bedrooms, and of course the breakfast, all with a down-home touch.

$100-150

A little more money can go a long way. While in Austin, $100–150 is what you will spend if you want to stay in accommodations that don't feel budget, but still offer value for your buck.

On the West End is ◖ **Austin's Inn at Pearl Street** (809 W. MLK Blvd. at Pearl St., 800/494-2261, www.innpearl.com, weekday rates from $100, weekend rates from $125). With wicker chairs, kitsch in every nook and cranny, floral patterns on the walls, and a calm spiritual feel, this establishment personifies the bed-and-breakfast. Does Shirley MacLaine live here? No—but it sure does seem like she's the decorator. There's a two-night minimum on weekends.

The bed-and-breakfast closest to the action downtown is the **Brava House** (1108 Blanco St., 512/478-5034, www.bravahouse.com, $119–195). This old Victorian decked with art deco flair is classy, clean, and understated. Brava House offers appealing prearranged packages for an additional fee. For example there's the "Enchanted Evening" where champagne, chocolate-covered strawberries, and candles are waiting for you in your room; "Romance in the Air," where an entire romantic evening is arranged that includes dinner for two at a local restaurant followed by a carriage ride through downtown; or the "Spa Getaway."

Extended Stay America Austin-Downtown-Lady Bird Lake (600 Guadalupe St. on 6th St., 512/457-9994, www.extendedstayamerica.com) is a cheap choice for centrally located lodgings downtown. What this place lacks in charm it makes up for in privacy and location. Each unit has a full kitchen, wireless Internet, cable TV, and laundry is available on the premises. Weekly rates are $95 (per day) and daily rates start at $130.

A cheap hotel downtown is **Holiday Inn Austin-Lady Bird Lake** (20 North Interregional at I-35, 512/472-8211, www.holidayinn.com). Located on Lady Bird Lake, this archetypal hotel has it all: outdoor pool, a restaurant, Internet access, on-site fitness center, and views of the city, all for around $150 a night. A kayak rental shop is close by, making kayaking on the lake an easy day excursion. The one drawback with this hotel is it's hovering over I-35. If you stay here ask for a room away from the freeway.

Also in this no-frills hotel genre is **La Quinta Inn-Austin Capitol** (300 E. 11th St., 512/476-1166, www.laquinta.com, $109–149). Here you get just the usual inexpensive hotel amenities you would expect from a budget hotel. It's a cheap place to stay, and centrally located, as it's next to the Capitol. But don't be surprised if the paint is moldy in the bathroom. Also, you may see the flashing lights of Austin PD in the parking lot at night, as it can get slightly shady after dark. Non-smoking rooms are available upon request.

One of Austin's best deals for chain hotel lodgings downtown is at **Embassy Suites Downtown** (300 South Congress Avenue, 512/469-9000, 800-EMBASSY or 800/362-2779, www.embassysuites.com, $139–219). Located at the crossroads of South Congress and Barton Springs Road, this hotel is within walking distance of many of Austin's prime attractions. All the suites here have a separate room for entertaining with a bedroom in the back, and a complimentary cook-to-order breakfast is included. The reason for this good deal is probably because the decor throughout the hotel is stuck in the 1980s.

Austin has always been at the forefront of environmental awareness. **Habitat Suites** (500 East Highland Mall Blvd., 512/467-6000 or 800/535-4663, www.habitatsuites.com, $127–187) is a natural outcome of this local ecofriendly movement. Here you can enjoy all the pleasures of a four-star hotel and feel good about not contributing to the world's environmental problems. The hotel provides nontoxic, phosphate-free, natural shampoos and soaps for guests, and uses natural cleansers. The solar system used here is the largest of its kind used at a U.S. hotel. The facility is a nonsmoking, pet-free environment, and a member of Green Hotels Association (www.greenhotels.com). The one drawback is that it's located up in Old North Austin, which is about five miles north of downtown.

On of the best deals in town is at **Hotel Allandale** (7685 Northcross Dr., 512/452-9391, www.hotelallandale.com, $140). Here you can stay in a nice, clean facility in a quiet neighborhood, in suites that are much larger than the average hotel room, all for a great price. And get this—weekend rates are cheaper than weekday rates. The catch is that it's in Old North Austin. This sounds far away but in reality it's only six miles from downtown. In the vicinity are shopping and restaurants, the Alamo Drafthouse Cinema (North), and some of Austin's best dive bars.

For inexpensive accommodations near Austin-Bergstrom International Airport there's **La Quinta Inn & Suites-Austin Airport** (7625 E. Ben White Blvd., 512/386-6800, www.laquinta.com). If you have a flight leaving early in the morning, stay here and catch a free shuttle to the airport. This La Quinta is all about convenience, not four-star comfort. Rates can be as low as $109 even in the high season.

In Hyde Park Historic District one of the finer bed-and-breakfasts is **Woodburn House Bed & Breakfast** (4401 Avenue D, 888/690-9763, www.woodburnhouse.com, $110–120). Set among old trees and singing birds,

Woodburn House is a calm place for the leisure traveler. Sitting on the wraparound porches and reading a book is the best thing one can do here. Duval Street is within walking distance; there you'll find some of Austin's better restaurants such as Hyde Park Grill and Dolce Vita, which has gelato, espresso, and a rare assortment of scotches and liqueurs.

On the shores of beautiful Lake Travis is **Lakeway Resort and Spa** (101 Lakeway Dr., 512/261-6600 or 800/525-3929, www.lakewayresortandspa.com, $139–199), a premier resort designed to make guests do absolutely nothing except bask in leisure resort delights. Here you can have access to top-notch private golf courses, spas, tennis courts, and even charter a sailboat for a day on the lake. Getaway packages for golf, families, and romance cost more but offer more.

The world got you drained? A weekend getaway to a wellness spa is a great way to recharge your inner battery. **The Crossings** (13500 FM 2769, 512/258-7243, www.thecrossingsaustin.com), just 20 miles northwest of Austin, offers peaceful accommodations along with a busy schedule of workshops and conferences for guests. The breathtaking 205-acre campus has hiking trails, pools, green architecture, and a spectacular view of Lake Travis. Guests are welcome to just shack up here or get involved. A 10 percent discount is offered for those who combine spa and/or workshops with accommodations. Rates range from $100 (shared bath) to $245 for a single room. As for accolades, *Cosmopolitan* magazine rated The Crossings as one of the sexiest places in the world. Arrr!

$150-250

In the downtown area there are several luxury chain hotels. They may lack historic charm but they have boilerplate luxury-hotel service and amenities. They're big, they're fancy, and totally predictable, which is what some travelers prefer. At the crossroads of downtown and South Austin is the **Hyatt Regency Austin** (208 Barton Springs Rd., 512/477-1234, www.hyatt.com, $180–350), one of the city's four-star hotels. Perched on the banks of Lady

You don't have be be a millionaire to stay at The Mansion at Judges' Hill.

Bird Lake, the Hyatt is in close range of the Palmer Auditorium, Austin Convention Center, and the great shops and restaurants of South Congress Avenue as well as 6th Street. A good choice for the health-conscious traveler, the Hyatt has a fitness center and a pool and is close to the trails around Lady Bird Lake. The rooms on the north side have views of bats flying out from under Congress Avenue Bridge in summer months. The open atrium inside and artificial creek running through the restaurant make this a classy place to meet and do business.

Another luxury hotel is **Hilton Austin** (500 E. 4th St., 512/482-8000, www.hilton.com, $150–240). Hilton's downtown location, with a terrace pool on the roof of the 8th floor, a fitness center, in-house steak and seafood restaurant, and extravagant decor, will make you forget all the complications of life. Views are spectacular, service is high caliber, and comfort is unavoidable. Promotional rates can sometimes be as little as $100.

For a rustic and romantic experience outside of town there's **Lost Parrot Cabins** (15116 Storm Dr., 512/266-8916, www.austincabinrentals.com, $190–285), which is situated on eight acres near Mansfield Dam, about 1.5 miles from Lake Travis. This wildly colorful little Mexican-style villa is a perfect place to get away from it all. All cabins are private, complete with hammock and rocker, and to make it even easier you can park next to your cabin. Pets are welcome with an additional fee.

If the Driskill is booked up, (**The Mansion at Judges' Hill** (1900 Rio Grande, 800/311-1619, www.mansionatjudgeshill.com, $169–299) is a safe runner-up for a luxury hotel with historic charm and class. Just west of downtown in a quiet neighborhood, this converted mansion has spacious rooms decked with antique furniture, reproduction canvas paintings by the Impressionists, and luxurious spa bathrobes waiting for guests. Some rooms have an added touch of romance with fireplaces, balconies, and courtyard access. The mansion has a classy restaurant that offers breakfast and dinner. All you could need for a pleasant, romantic, relaxing evening is right here.

The hotel with the best central location is the **Sheraton Austin** (701 E. 11th St., 512/478-1111, www.sheraton.com, $200–299). Although it's not at the heart of downtown, the Sheraton Austin provides easy access to everything, such as the Capitol, 6th Street, Red River District, the business district, many attractions, and the University of Texas main campus. Because of this, the Sheraton is a great place to hunker down for a few days. The views are great and the restaurant isn't bad either.

Omni Austin Hotel Downtown (700 San Jacinto Blvd. at 8th St., 512/476-3700 or 888/444-6664, www.omnihotels.com, $200–300) is a four-diamond hotel in the heart of downtown. A favorite of celebrities, rock stars, and rich folks, the Omni is 20 floors of elegance topped with a rooftop pool and hot tub. Guests are spoiled rotten by the in-house fitness center, on-site massage, sauna, cocktail lounge, and restaurant.

The **InterContinental Stephen F. Austin Hotel** (710 Congress Ave., 512/457-8800, www.austin.intercontinental.com, $209–299) embodies the best of old and new in Austin luxury lodgings. The historic hotel is smack dab in the middle of all the downtown action but retains a calm, upscale vibe, standing serenely above it all. Everything is within a stone's throw, such as the Capitol, music clubs, great restaurants, and museums. The hotel was built in 1924, and although it has gone through major renovations, it still retains the historic class of a bygone era. Besides offering guests over 189 elegant rooms with amenities that pamper, the hotel also has a balcony bar that is very popular, especially with legislators. There's also a health club featuring a lap pool, a Mediterranean themed café called Julienne, and a restaurant called Roaring Fork, which serves up first-class Southwestern cuisine.

Radisson Hotel on Lady Bird Lake (111 E. Cesar Chavez St., 800/395-7046, www.radisson.com, $198–300) is one of the better downtown accommodations in this price range. This centrally located hotel offers great views of the city and quality service. If you stay here you simply must take the time to walk around

Lady Bird Lake, which is just out the back door. Breakfast and rooms with stunning views will cost you a tad more; rooms on the south side have views of Austin's famous bats in summer months. Booking online can get you better rates. The TGI Friday's restaurant in the hotel is one of the best spots in town to watch the bats fly from their roosts on summer evenings.

The best weekend-getaway bed-and-breakfast at Lake Travis is **Robin's Nest** (1007 Stewart Cove, 512/266-3413, www.robinsnest-laketravis.com, $149–250). Beautiful views of the lake, comfortable lodgings, and proximity to water sports, fishing, and swimming holes make this nest an easy choice for an excursion away from town. Lodgings include three homes and nine guest rooms.

The **Bed and Breakfast Spa** (1309 Meriden Ln., 512/499-0081, www.bnbspa.com, $150–200) focuses on couples, relaxation, and privacy. Just west of downtown in an upscale residential area, this unique little oasis doubles as a luxury spa and—you guessed it—a bed-and-breakfast. The three-room suite in the east wing has wood interior, cathedral ceilings, a fireplace, and access to the indoor heated massage pool; the Moon Room has a more modest setup with a luxury shower and access to the spa.

$250 AND UP

Romantic fine dining, horse-drawn carriages, and old western gothic architecture collide right in the heart of downtown at ◖ **The Driskill Hotel** (604 Brazos St., 512/474-5911 or 800/252-9367, www.driskillhotel.com). The Driskill has been Austin's premier luxury hotel for over a century. They've mastered Texas charm, opulence, and drama by providing guests with lavish rooms decked with gigantic curtains, fancy tile bathrooms, and ornate beds. The hotel also has an award-winning restaurant, a piano bar, and a fitness studio. With a great downtown location right on 6th Street there's access to bars, live music, museums, touristy shops, and the Capitol. Out front you can catch a horse-drawn carriage for a romantic tour through downtown. Rates vary

© JUSTIN MARLER

The Driskill Hotel is saturated with history and opulence.

depending on room and season but an average rate can start at around $300 a night and go as high as $1,000.

Austin's classiest four-star hotel is **The Four Seasons** (98 San Jacinto Blvd., 512/478-4500, www.fourseasons.com/austin, $300–900). This is a luxury hotel for the crème de la crème, the beau monde, the privileged class, for celebrities, as well as the average Jack or Jill who wants to spend some hard-earned cash on a fancy bed. O-kay, the Four Seasons is more than a bed, it's a swank hotel set on a quiet piece of Lady Bird Lake, affording a tranquil space, rooms with unforgettable views of the skyline, private balconies, oversized cotton bath towels, down pillows, terry-cloth bathrobes, and bend-over-backwards hospitality. The Queen of England stayed here when she visited Austin. If it's good enough for the Queen . . . .

One of the top 10 best spa resorts in the world is right here in Austin. According to *Travel + Leisure* magazine, **Lake Austin Spa Resort** (1705 South Quinlan Park Rd., 512/372-7300 or 800/847-5637, www.lakeaustin.com) is world class. Located only 25 minutes from downtown

Austin on a quiet spot on the shores of Lake Travis, this spa resort is an extraordinary place to immerse yourself in yourself. In their own words, this is "an exquisite escape into natural beauty and personal discovery." With soothing minimalist architecture, classy modern-Asian flair, beautifully manicured gardens, and exquisite hospitality, you can't help but completely forget about the outside world. Although they offer vacation packages, they also offer day packages. So what goes down here? Water aerobics, water yoga, swimming in indoor and outdoor pools, tai chi classes on the shores of the lake, kayaking, cooking classes, boat cruises, and relaxing in hammocks. Vacation packages can be 3–7 days, and rates vary depending on what you want to experience, ranging anywhere between $1,400–2,300. Guests are free to participate as much or as little as desired.

Austin's new fancy place to stay is the **(W Austin** (200 Lavaca St., 512/542-3600, www.starwoodhotels.com). Besides being the hotel in the middle of Austin's newer downtown 2nd Street District, where shopping and restaurants

© JUSTIN MARLER

the W Austin

are plentiful, the LEED-certified W Austin shares a roof with the new *Austin City Limits* studio where live performance taping happens. Guests can expect the ultimate in service with the hotel's signature Whatever/Whenever service, pampering guests with "whatever you want, whenever you want it." Rates range $300–400 depending on size and amenities. If you are a rock star or want to be treated like one, you can enjoy one of the Marvelous Suites for $1,000 per night.

EXTENDED STAY

If you plan on being in town for an extended period and enjoy the atmosphere of a bed-and-breakfast, the best place to hang your hat is **Austin's Inn at Pearl Street** (809 W. MLK Blvd. at Pearl St., 800/494-2261, www.inn-pearl.com). Their monthly rate is only $49 per day. With the daily breakfast included, this works out to be a great value. The inn is filled with charm and tranquility, with little nooks for reading and relaxing. All rooms have private bathrooms. The inn is located in the West End, which is not in downtown, but close to downtown.

For extended travel accommodations downtown there's **(Extended Stay America Austin-Downtown-Lady Bird Lake** (600 Guadalupe St. on 6th St., 512/457-9994, www.extendedstayamerica.com, $50–89). What this place lacks in charm it makes up for in privacy and a great central location downtown. Each unit has a full kitchen, wireless Internet, cable TV, and laundry is available on the premises.

In north Austin there's **Hotel Allandale Suites** (7685 Northcross Dr., 512/452-9391, www.hotelallandale.com). Here you can stay in a nice, clean facility in a quiet neighborhood, in suites that are much larger than the average hotel room. Nightly rates are around $119, rates for 7–29 nights are $70, and rates for 30-plus nights are as low as $59 and the hotel eats the taxes. In the vicinity are shopping and restaurants, the Alamo Drafthouse Cinema (North), and some of Austin's best dive bars. The hotel is only six miles from downtown.

Food

In Austin, eating out is a pleasure and a pastime. There's an endless amount of breakfast tacos, barbecue brisket, microbrews on tap, organic veggies, and confections waiting to be devoured, and it's "all good." Austin is chock-full of hundreds of eateries, many of which have their own unique story and funky spin on ambience and food, keeping in step with the town's flavor for weirdness. On occasion the gimmick of the restaurant is better than the food. One word of caution is offered: Your money goes a long way in Austin's eateries, making it easy to eat out until you either burn out on restaurants, burn a hole in your wallet, or simply implode. With the exception of fine dining, your average meal will cost somewhere between $5 and $10. Hours of most establishments are typical: Breakfast joints open around 6 A.M., lunch is generally served 10:30 A.M.–4 P.M., and dinner happens 5–10 P.M., with some eateries staying open as late as midnight. So come hungry—all the eateries below are sure to satisfy.

AMERICAN AND DINERS

Austin is inundated with burger joints and diners that offer up hearty plates of American standards. Texas has proven that anything can be chicken fried and that acid reflux is a virtue. Due to Austin's love of health there are some eateries that offer healthier versions of these standard plates. But let the salt pour, the oil flow, and the butter fry cause it's all about good old-fashioned sodium and cholesterol at the some of the following greasy spoons.

For the fickle person that has a hard time deciding what to eat, **Austin Java** (1206 Parkway at 12th and Lamar, 512/476-1829, 301 West 2nd St., 512/481-9400, and 1608 Barton Springs Rd., 512/482-9450, www.austinjava. com, 7 A.M.–11 P.M. Mon.–Fri., 8 A.M.–11 P.M. Sat. and Sun., $8) has an eclectic menu that

© JUSTIN MARLER

Eat 24-hours a day at Magnolia Cafe.

FOOD TRUCK SCENE

Austin has fallen head over wheels for the new food truck craze. Carts, trucks, silver bullets, and even wagons are strategically set up all around town, making a variety of foods readily available. Besides amazing taco trucks, you can also find trucks that serve up Indian food, duck, *pho*, crepes and even cupcakes. There are even a couple farm-to-market trucks that specialize in fresh and organic foods. New carts are popping up everywhere, almost daily it seems. Although they can be found on sidewalks and street corners all over downtown, there are mini food trailer parks on South Congress, South Lamar, South 1st, and on Red River just south of downtown. The best way to sample food truck cuisine is by attending Austin's festival dedicated to these mobile food vendors, **Gypsy Picnic Trailer Food Festival,** which takes place in the fall. It should be noted that most of these trailers don't serve alcohol, and some are BYOB establishments. Also, it's a good idea to show up with cash not plastic. The best resource for food truck info, hours, maps, and reviews can be found online at www.austinfoodcarts.com. Here is a list of some local favorites:

- **G'Raj Mahal** (91 Red River St., 512/480-2255) serves up the best Indian Food.

- **Odd Duck Farm To Trailer** (1219 S. Lamar Blvd., Thurs. dinner only) features locally sourced, whole-animal cooking.

- **Hey Cupcake** (1600 Block of S. Congress Ave., 512/476-CAKE) has, you guessed it! Cupcakes.

- **Holy Cacao** (1311 S. 1st St., 512/851-2253) serves cake balls and other sweet stuff.

- **Mighty Cone** (1600 S. Congress Ave., 512/383-9609) specializes in breaded chicken, beef, or shrimp in a cone.

- **Not Your Mama's Food Truck** (2209 E. Cesar Chavez) features fancy fried comfort food.

- **Kebabalicious** (450 E. 7th St., 468-1065) has chicken, beef, and lamb kebabs, and other Middle-eastern foods.

- **Torchy's Trailer Park** (1311 South 1st St., 512/366-0537) is the best taco truck in town.

- **East Side King** (1618 1/2 E. 6th St. behind Liberty Bar, 512/422-5884) has unusual plates such as fried beets, brussel sprout salad, and pork belly buns.

---

can offer up something for every one for either breakfast, lunch, or dinner. If after looking at the soups and salads you still can't decide what you want you can piece together a lunch combo that suits your taste buds. Thai sesame salad, smoked-gouda bacon burger, and Cajun-blackened crawfish pasta are among the favorites. Then there's the wide variety of organic coffees of various blends, flavors, and colors.

In Old North Austin everybody loves **Billy's** (2105 Hancock Dr. at Burnet Rd., 512/407-9305, 11 A.M.–midnight Mon.–Fri., 11 A.M.–1 A.M. Sat., noon–midnight Sun., $7). Here sports fans, neighborhood locals, and families can eat burgers, drink the best beers on tap, and see Billy sweeping the floor. Happy hour is 2–7 P.M. Monday–Friday. There's also a huge deck outside, beer specials, a jukebox, a pool table, and the game on TV.

For the cheapest meal in town there's **Dirty Martin's** (2808 Guadalupe St., 512/477-3173, 11 A.M.–11 P.M. daily, $6). Dirty's is one of the older continuously owned and operated eateries in Austin. But this doesn't necessarily mean that as with wine, the food at Dirty's is better with age. But the onion rings and fries are homemade, the hamburger meat is fresh, and the shakes and malts are terrific.

If you're in south Austin on South Congress Avenue and you see a giant papier-mâché girl holding a Fender guitar on top of a building, you've made it to **Fran's Hamburgers** (1822

S. Congress Ave., 512/444-5738, 10:30 A.M.–10 P.M. daily, $6). This famous burger spot serves up burgers that come in three juicy sizes: large, larger, and way huge. Fran's also has one of the better hand-dipped milk shakes in town.

If you've ever wanted to rifle through someone's personal photo albums, eat burgers, and throw massive washers at a stake in the ground, try **Freddie's** (1703 S. 1st St., 512/445-9197, 11 A.M.–10:30 P.M. daily, $8). This restaurant embodies Austin's clever character in a fun, weird overdose. The back patio dining area is on a creek, under ancient oaks. There's live music, washers (similar to horseshoes) to throw, and happy hour with free brisket Tuesday–Thursday. How was/is Freddie? Find out for yourself by taking at gander at his photos.

Hoover's Cooking (2002 Manor Rd., 512/479-5006, 11 A.M.–10 P.M. Mon.–Fri. and 8 A.M.–10 P.M. Sat. and Sun., $10) is a classic place to eat barbecue on Sunday after church in East Austin. Hoover describes his cooking influence as "Home cooking—nicely seasoned vegetables, smoked foods, pan-fried dishes and spicy foods with a nod toward Tex-Mex and Cajun." Hoover's has the best meatloaf in Austin and the Jamaican jerk chicken is sent from Jah. This is a popular brunch and breakfast spot so a wait may be necessary, but it's well worth it.

After going through many decades of transformations (from drive-in, to Mexican, to lounge) **Hut's Hamburgers** (807 W. 6th St., 512/472-0693, 11 A.M.–10 P.M. daily, $10) finally settled on the American staple—hamburgers. Hut's is always packed at mealtime and there's a reason. The menu is "outside the bun" with items such as the Ritchie Valens Burger: guacamole, grated cheese, chopped tomatoes, onions, and jalapeños. Their vintage/retro decor of semi-nude photos, pop memorabilia, sports heroes, and music posters only add to this distinctive flavor.

[**Magnolia Cafe** (2304 Lake Austin Blvd., 512/478-8645, and 1920 S. Congress Ave., 512/445-0000, $8) is a good bet for a good dish any time of the day or night. Great breakfasts, hamburgers, sandwiches, soups and salads, as well as some Tex-Mex dishes, can be

ordered any time, as this is Austin's best 24-hour grub facilitator.

One of the top picks of a former U.S. president is **Moonshine Patio Bar and Grill** (303 Red River St., 512/236-9599, 11 A.M.–10 P.M. Mon.–Thurs., 11 A.M.–11 P.M. Fri. and Sat., and 10 A.M.–10 P.M. Sun., $12). Popular for making typical American fare classy and a little pricey, Moonshine is always a hub of important folks. Although this is a great spot for dinner, Austin's best Sunday brunch can be found here. The buffet tables are chock-full of every breakfast food imaginable, all cooked to please those with a refined appetite. Southwestern-style eggs, sausage links, waffles, buckets of fruit, smoked salmon, goodies from the bakery, and jugs of sauces and syrups. Although pricey it's darn worth it.

The best milk shake in town happens to be in an inconspicuous establishment—the pharmacy. Decades ago **Nau Enfield Drug and Old Fashion Soda Fountain** (1115 W. Lynn St., 512/476-1221, 8 A.M.–4 P.M. Mon.–Fri., 8 A.M.–2:30 P.M. Sat., $6) was the place to get a burger, a shake, and your prescriptions, and nothing has changed in the past half a century.

The **Omelettry** (4811 Burnet Rd., 512/453-5062, 7 A.M.–5 P.M. daily, $7) is one of Austin's best-kept secrets. Slackers, students, old-timers, and young families have chosen it as the best place to start a weekend morning. It's a no-frills restaurant that specializes in tasty omelets and pancakes that prove that crepes are just too flat. Don't expect flashy decor or bells and whistles, just great breakfast food. Make sure you bring cash, as they don't accept anything else.

The hamburger is one of the world's most profound culinary creations. It is inexpensive yet rich with flavor, it is globally accepted yet markedly strange in how it is made, how it is eaten, and what it tastes like. I have no fear in going out on a limb by saying that Austin is home to the world's greatest hamburger. It is cooked up at a little burger stand just around the corner from Barton Springs, called [**P. Terry's** (404 S. Lamar, 512/473-2217, 11 A.M.–11 P.M. daily, $5). The owner opened this place up after reading the book *Fast Food Nation*.

The burger is simple and old-fashioned, and made of 100 percent all-natural Black Angus beef and all-natural ingredients. The focus here is quality and taste, so don't expect a flashy menu or quirky decor. Actually the only place to eat is under the trees as there is no indoor seating.

The crossroads of Louisiana and Texas are on North Lamar at **Shoal Creek Saloon** (909 N. Lamar Blvd., 512/474-0805, 11 A.M.–midnight daily, $10). This sports bar was transformed when Chef Bud George moved in from Louisiana, bringing with him authentic Cajun cuisine. Gumbos, fried catfish, crawfish étouffée, oysters, and hush puppies flow like the bayou. Wait—does the bayou flow? Daily specials are a great value, and happy hour is 11 A.M.–7 P.M. Monday–Friday.

A fairly new addition to the South Congress neighborhood is **South Congress Cafe** (1600 S. Congress Ave., 512/447-3905, 10 A.M.–4 P.M. and 5 P.M.–10 P.M. daily, $13). Their approach to things is minimalist. They don't believe in dramatic decor, fancy signs and logos, or anything of a commercial nature. They simply offer quality food and service in a modern, sophisticated atmosphere. Items on the menu vary from crab cakes to pan-seared tuna salad, which sounds expensive, but don't be deceived by the fancy-sounding menu—it's affordable.

South Austin's morning-all day, breakfast-all-day hangout is **Bouldin Creek Coffee House** (1900 South 1st St., 512/416-1601, 7 A.M.–midnight Mon.–Fri., 9 A.M.–midnight Sat.–Sun. $9). The previous location was basically a shack chock-full of Austin's weirdest. Now Bouldin has officially entered the mainstream, and to me this is a good thing. The food is fantastic for egg or tofu scramble eaters, and the vibe is electric with art tips, students, and shoe gazers getting jacked on coffee. Along with scrambled tofu or eggs, the menu include some creative plates that are uniquely hippie Tex-Mex. Example: tofu chorizo tacos, hummus, gluten-free offerings, Slacker's Banquet.

Star Seeds Cafe (3101 N. I-35, 512/478-7107, $7) is one of those places in town that completely personifies Austin. This 24-hour joint, in the truest sense of the word, has no pretense, just past tense, as it seems to be frozen in time. Here you can eat greasy, nothing-fresh diner food, such as sandwiches, burgers, nachos, and breakfast. Effortlessly funky and offbeat, Stars is a great place to eat after waking up at noon, without showering or brushing your teeth.

If you've just finished a tour of the Texas State Capitol and you're fixin' to eat, stroll down the street to the **Texas Chili Parlor** (1409 Lavaca St., 512/472-2828, 11 A.M.–2 A.M. daily, $7). This sports bar is where Texas politicians, UT students, and UT sports fans converge to enjoy a beer and some food. Obviously they are known for their chili, which comes in three variations of spiciness: X for mild, XX for medium, and XXX for habanero hell. They may even make you sign a release form when you order the triple-X. Note for non-Texans: There are no beans in Texas chili, just meat and sauce.

One restaurant that is a historic landmark in its own right is **Threadgill's Home Cooking** (301 West Riverside Dr., 512/472/9304, 11 A.M.–10 P.M. Mon.–Thurs., 11 A.M.–10:30 P.M. Fri.–Sat., 10 A.M.–9:30 P.M. Sun., $10). Founded in 1933 by bootlegger Kenneth Threadgill after obtaining the county's first alcohol license, this down-home kitchen became a local favorite for hootenannies and old-time cookin'. In the '60s, Threadgill's was one of Austin's cultural epicenters for live music. Hippies and rednecks alike would converge here to watch the cultural revolution go down. It's said that Janis Joplin even developed her unique singing style here. As for the down-home cooking, it's just like granny cooks it—lots of butter and oil, meat and potatoes, sodium and white bread. Threadgill's is especially famous for its meatloaf, chicken-fried chicken, and chicken-fried steak.

◖ **Upper Crust Bakery and Cafe** (4508 Burnet Rd., 512/467-0102, 6:30 A.M.–6:30 P.M. Mon.–Fri., 7 A.M.–5 P.M. Sat., 7 A.M.–1 P.M. Sun., $7) serves gorgeous baked goods and sandwiches. You don't have to take my word for it; the *Austin American Statesman* ranked the avocado sandwich one of the top 10 sandwiches in Austin. This is easily the best place in town for any kind of sandwich.

BARBECUE AND STEAK

Eating meat in Austin can be a profoundly gluttonous experience. At many barbecue joints you order brisket by the pound, choose from a selection of sides such as coleslaw, beans, and potato salad, and eat it all off butcher paper. This approach to eating can pose a hazard to those whose eyes are bigger than their stomach. Texans love their beef and you will too at the following restaurants.

Austin Land and Cattle Co. (1205 N. Lamar Blvd., 512/472-1813, 5:30–10 P.M. Sun.–Thurs., 5:30–11 P.M. Fri.–Sat., $30) is Austin's most popular steakhouse. Although the menu offers enough choices for everyone (except the vegetarian), people come here for beef. It can be served up in many different ways, but the best is the 22-ounce bone-in rib eye or sirloin cooked medium rare. The white stucco walls and exposed-beam ceiling make for a comfortable environment. The staff knows the menu and can guide you through your beef-eating experience. As for the sides, they tend to be a notch above your average steakhouse, with baby spinach leaves sautéed in olive oil, and carrots julienne. The portions are so big you might as well ask for a to-go bag when you order.

If you have a car to get there, the **County Line BBQ Restaurant** (5204 FM 2222, 512/346-3664, 11:30 A.M.–2 P.M. and 5–9 P.M. daily, $14) is a terrific spot on the lake that feels rural but is close to town. The waterfront patio looks out onto limestone cliffs and dense tree cover. After chowing down on great barbecue everyone will have a blast feeding the ducks and turtles that come right up to the dock. The food is a little pricey but very tasty.

In South Austin there's **Green Mesquite** (1400 Barton Springs Rd., 512/479-0485, 11 A.M.–10 P.M. Sun.–Thurs., 11 A.M.–11 P.M. Fri.–Sat., $8). Standard, inexpensive barbecue, burgers, and some Cajun food are what's on offer at this staple Austin lunch and dinner joint. It's near Zilker Park, has a friendly staff, relaxed atmosphere, and live music on Friday,

Saturday, and Sunday nights. This is a good place for families with children.

Fancy and barbecue usually are a contradiction in terms. However **ⓒ Lambert's** (401 W. 2nd St., 512/494-1500, lunch 11 A.M.–2:30 P.M., dinner 5:30–10:00 P.M. Mon.–Fri., Sunday brunch 11 A.M.–2 P.M. $12) has concocted a combination that works. Located in the up and coming 2nd Street shopping district makes Lambert's an easy springboard for a night on the town. Besides barbecue, chefs Louis Lambert and Larry McGuire have put together some classic dishes in true to Austin form—casual but classy—such as steak and seafood with family-style sides accompanied by locally made microbrews.

Downtown Austin has been in dire need of a kick-ass good BBQ joint. **Franklin Barbecue** (900 E. 11th street, 512/653-1187, 11 A.M.–1 P.M. Tues.–Sun., $10) has risen out of the ashes of the food truck/trailer trend to deliver the best cracked pepper corn brisket and ribs in Central Austin. The founder started as Texas kid helping out with his dads BBQ joint, did the trailer thing, and now has a wildly successful thing going. The brisket slices are thick and the pork ribs are salty with the right amount of large cracked pepper chunks. The ribs are so tender you don't have to roll up your sleeves and get messy to eat em. Justin pull the meat off with your plastic fork. The vibe in here is unpretentious but with the right amount of retro to be comfortable, the music is old county classics playing loud, and local Live Oak beers are on draft. There's only one drawback. Franklin is only open until they sell out of food. Most days this happens by 1 P.M.

There's also **Iron Works** (100 Red River St., 512/478-4855, 11 A.M.–9 P.M. Mon.–Sat., $9), a local favorite for barbecue. Set in the historic iron shop, this is the one meat joint where you can counterbalance all the beef with all-you-can-eat salad.

Nearly every barbecue spot in the state has the shingle out front that claims, "Best BBQ in Texas." But **Rudy's Country Store and BBQ** (2451 Capital of Texas Hwy., 512/329-5554, and 11570 Research Blvd., 512/418-9898,

7 A.M.–9:30 P.M. daily, $7) gladly proclaims "The Worst Bar-B-Q in Texas." Don't be fooled by this slogan and the fact that Rudy's is a chain, albeit a small Texas franchise. The barbecue is fabulous and the beans are musical. No dishes required, just fingers, a fork, and the need for beef. After fully glutted, wash your hands and face in the industrial-size kitchen sink in the dining room.

The area's best barbecue is provided by the ◖ **Salt Lick** (18300 FM 1826, Driftwood, 512/858-4959, 11 A.M.–10 P.M. daily, $10). It's so far out of town that it's in another town, but that shouldn't stop you from enjoying an Austin tradition. Eating here is one of the great experiences central Texas has to offer. Here's why: It's located in an old limestone ranch house, the recipe is ancient, the barbecue pit is the dining room, you bring your own alcohol, and the barbecue is brutally good. Also on the menu are sausage, turkey, ribs, the usual sides, white bread, and those pickles that every barbecue restaurant seems to have. Warning: There is no air-conditioning. For some this adds to the appeal, but for those who fear perspiration it can ruin their day. Otherwise, sit in front of the fan, relax, and eat beef. Salt Lick only accepts cash, so be sure, if you drive all the way out there, to bring greenbacks.

In the downtown area there's **Stubb's BBQ** (801 Red River St., 512/480-8341, 11 A.M.–10 P.M. Tues.–Wed., 11 A.M.–11 P.M. Thurs.–Sat., 11 A.M.–9 P.M. Sun., $8). Yes, this is the establishment behind the famed Stubb's BBQ Sauce. Christopher Stubblefield founded the first Stubb's restaurant in Lubbock, Texas, where he combined good live music and barbecue. Perfect combo! Artists such as Johnny Cash, John Lee Hooker, and Muddy Waters would "play for their supper." Stubblefield eventually moved to Austin, bringing with him his concept of live music and barbecue. Today Stubb's is one of Austin's premier live music venues and still serves up great barbecue.

MEXICAN

Remember, Austin is only 250 miles from the border, giving the town a great advantage over

Celebrities, presidents, and common folk intermingle at Güero's Taco Bar.

© JUSTIN MARLER

most places for serving up excellent Mexican as well as creative variations on south-of-the-border foods. These variations need some clarification. First, there's good old-fashioned Mexican food, which is rice, beans, tacos, enchiladas, chopped beef, chicken, and salsa. Second, there's Texas's version of Mexican, called Tex-Mex. All you do is add catfish to the enchiladas, corn to the rice, and smoke to the salsa. Finally, there's the new hybrid that has emerged in recent years, which I call gringo-Mex. This is an upscale Mexican and Tex-Mex combination where you "encrust" the enchiladas, "sear" the meats, add citrus to the sauces, and charge more. Think Pancho Villa but replace the bullet straps with a silk scarf.

East Austin's best place for upscale Mexican is ◖ **El Chile** (1809 Manor Rd., 512/457-9900, 11 A.M.–10 P.M. Mon.–Sat., 11 A.M.–9 P.M. Sun., $12). The food is very sophisticated gringo-Mex. Everything on the menu is well crafted, from the smoky salsa that's so tasty I wish they had it on IV drip, to their signature spicy, orange-infused margaritas (the best in town); El Chile is worthy of high accolades. Although it's upscale, the atmosphere is casual. Happy hour is 4–7 P.M. Parking is kitty-corner from the restaurant.

For more casual and affordable Mexican El Chile's opened up a small taco shop **El Cilito** (2219 Manor Rd., 512/382-3797, $6) just down the street that offers street versions of their award-winning food. This place is great for takeout, or relaxing in their outdoor covered patio. No air-conditioning here as there is no indoor seating. Braised pork and carne asada tacos are top menu picks.

On the corner of 6th and Red River is local favorite for Mexican breakfast and brunch **El Sol Y La Luna** (1224 S. Congress Ave., 512/444-7770, 7 A.M.–10 P.M. Wed.–Sat., 7 A.M.–3 P.M. Sun.–Tues., $7). Along with excellent traditional meals such as enchiladas, the menu also has a healthy slant with items such as tofu tacos, which are brilliant. El Sol also caters to those who get up around 2 P.M. and want breakfast, as it's served all day.

While on South Congress, after a day of shopping for retro clothes and antiques, stop off at the best Mexican/Tex-Mex restaurant in Austin: **⟨ Güero's Taco Bar** (1412 South Congress Ave., 512/447-7688, 11 A.M.–11 P.M. Mon.–Fri., 8 A.M.–11 P.M. Sat.–Sun., $12). In 1994 the old Central Feed & Seed building was transformed into this fabulous taqueria. The aged brick walls are adorned with giant photos from the Mexican Revolution. The dining is casual, the handmade corn tortillas are excellent, and the margaritas are a local favorite. The portions are hearty, and the food, such as the shrimp fajitas, is truly mind-blowing. Let's not forget the self-serve salsa bar, which is a crucial part of the experience. Former President Bill Clinton loved this restaurant—hence his favorite dish is called the El Presidente.

The closest you can come to having Mexican food on a beach is at **Takoba** (1411 E. 7th St, 512/628-4466, 11 A.M.–12 A.M. Mon.–Fri., 9 A.M.–12 A.M. Sat.–Sun., $11) in East Austin. Yes, there is a beach in the side yard—or should I say large sandbox. The food is fresh authentic Mexican with homemade chips, creative drinks

(white sangria), and some of the best fish tacos around. The ambiance is a little polished and gringo, but makes for a pleasant environment for a friendly lunch or dinner.

South Austin's **Polvos** (2004 S. 1st St., 512/441-5446, 7 A.M.–10 P.M. daily, $10) is famous for build-your-own enchiladas, the salsa bar, and margarita pitchers. The atmosphere is loud, and the patio is big, which can be fun for some and overwhelming for others. Parking and wait times can be tricky so plan ahead.

The Mexican food restaurant that has something for everyone, **⟨ Torchy's Tacos** (2801 Guadalupe St., 512/494-8226, and 1311 South 1st St., 512/366-0537, $6) started out as a food truck on South 1st Street. They have the predictable tacos and burritos, along with a more creative menu that features mouthwatering creative combinations such as the Jamaican jerk chicken taco. Their most popular plates are the Green Chili Pork tacos and the Trailer Park, which is fried chicken with pico de gallo. They are also famous for amazing breakfast tacos heaping with cheese and bits of bacon, and *migas* tacos. For SXSW folks Torchy's is your morning hangover cure.

Jovita's (1619 S. 1st St., 512/447-7825, 11 A.M.–10 P.M. Tues.–Thurs., 11 P.M.–midnight Fri.–Sat., 11 A.M.–8 P.M. Sun., $9) successfully wears two hats—one is for Mexican food (a sombrero), and the other is for a great live music venue (a cowboy hat). The enchiladas are what you would expect for above-standard Mexican. The political murals on the exterior walls would make any fan of César, Che, or Subcomandante Marcos proud. The music is definitely part of what keeps people coming back.

Everybody's favorite breakfast taco comes from **Maria's Taco Express** (2529 S. Lamar Blvd., 512/444-0261, 7 A.M.–3 P.M. Mon., 7 A.M.–9 P.M. Tues.–Fri., 8 A.M.–9 P.M. Sat., 9 A.M.–2 P.M. Sun., $8). Now run by Maria's son, this taco shack has become legendary for its cheap Mexican fare, fast service, and friendly neighborhood clientele. During SXSW Maria's is overtaken by musicians and fans who come here to start off their day.

AUSTIN

The beautiful hacienda setting at **Matt's El Rancho** (2613 S. Lamar Blvd., 512/462-9333, 11 A.M.–10 P.M. Sun.–Mon. and Wed.–Thurs., 11 A.M.–11 P.M. Fri.–Sat., $12) is a safe bet for Mexican for the family. It's one of the older Mexican restaurants, as it's been in business for more than 50 years. The food gets passionately mixed reviews yet the restaurant has been an Austin tradition for decades. Try the Bob Armstrong dip, steak tampiqueña, and a margarita.

Local favorite Mexican breakfast and lunch joint is **Juan in a Million** (2300 E. Cesar Chavez St., 512/472-3872, 7 A.M.–3 P.M. daily, $8)—the place to get a solid mexican breakfast. The experience at this hole-in-the-wall (said with deep affection) begins with a greeting at the door from Juan himself. Then take a seat and order, but before you do, understand that everything here is huge and heaping. If you're thinking this place is familiar, it landed on the map when Adam Richman of *Man v. Food* was unable to eat eight of the breakfast tacos. Remember I said they were heaping.

© JUSTIN MARLER

Elvis and Tex-Mex at Chuy's is an essential Austin experience.

TEX-MEX AND SOUTHWESTERN

Near the Capitol is popular lunch spot **Arturo's Bakery and Cafe** (314 W. 17th St., 512/469-0380, 7 A.M.–2:30 P.M. Mon.–Tues., 7 A.M.–10 P.M. Wed.–Fri., 9 A.M.–1 P.M. and 5 P.M.–10 P.M. Sat., $8). Don't let bakery or café in the name fool you, as this place is much more than either. The fare is reliable southwestern/Tex-Mex and some American items. This basement restaurant looks like a New York loft, with modern art hanging on brick walls and hip clientele. With low-key but hip decor and a diverse yet affordable menu, Arturo's has become a favorite downtown breakfast and lunch spot.

For Tex-Mex with a thrift-store Elvis flair **Chuy's** (1728 Barton Springs Rd., 512/474-4452, 11 A.M.–10 P.M. Sun.–Thurs., 11 A.M.–11 P.M. Fri.–Sat., $8) will make your hips shake. The first thing one sees when entering Chuy's is a grandiose shrine to Elvis built into the entrance. From this point on it's all an experience. Yes, this establishment is heavy with gimmick, with its ceiling covered in hubcaps and fish and its retro/Salvation Army decor, but the food is great and the service is fast! They're famous for their handmade tortillas, fajitas, margaritas, over-stuffed enchiladas, and Mexi-Cobb Salad. Order their charro beans instead of refried.

Trying to place some food establishments in a particular category can be tricky. **Freebirds World Burrito** (515 S. Congress Ave., 512/462-3512, and 1000 E. 41st St., 512/451-5514, 11 A.M.–10:30 P.M. Sun.–Thurs., 11 A.M.–10 P.M. Fri.–Sat., $7) is free of categorization. It's not Mexican, it's not Tex-Mex, it's not American, and it's definitely not Eritrean, but it is good, filling, and cheap. This place was built with spare parts from a Harley Davidson, your local Mexican joint, Whole Foods, and of course, the remaining members of Lynyrd Skynyrd. If you don't like what you eat, it's your fault, because you build your own burritos, tacos, and wraps here.

◖ **Shady Grove Restaurant** (1624 Barton

Springs Rd., 512/474-9991, 11 A.M.–10 P.M. Sun.–Thurs., 11 A.M.–11 P.M. Fri.–Sat., $12) is one of the best places in town to eat out on the patio. A stylized '50s theme mixes with reliably good Tex-Mex, American, and health-nut fare. This place can get extremely crowded, so go when you have time to wait for a table. Have a beverage, enjoy the outdoors, and watch the beautiful people. Through the summer months Shady Grove is a great spot to see top-notch local musicians perform for the "Unplugged at the Grove" concert series presented by local radio station KGSR.

With a friendly environment that is light on the gimmick and heavy on the taste buds, **(Z'Tejas Southwestern Grill** (1110 West 6th St., 512/478-5355, 11 A.M.–10 P.M. Mon.–Thurs., 11 A.M.–11 P.M. Fri., 10 A.M.–11 P.M. Sat., 10 A.M.–10 P.M. Sun., $10) is the eatery extraordinaire of Austin. A culinary zenith can be reached by sitting outside under the trellises on a sunny afternoon while eating their famous blackened-catfish enchiladas, stuffed pork tenderloin, crab-stuffed chicken, diablo chicken pasta, or virtually anything on the menu. After a big meal at Z'Tejas, walk down the street to the Treaty Oak and ponder the venerable tree's history filled with ceremony, legend, poison, love, and lunacy.

Some of the best fish tacos in the area happen to be served up by surfers. The landlocked folks at **Wahoo's Fish Tacos** (509 Rio Grand St., 512/476-3474, 11 A.M.–10 P.M. Mon.–Sat. and Sun 11 A.M.–9 P.M., $8) seem like fish out of water in Texas. The walls are lined with giant graphics of surfers, giant waves, and skateboarding stickers, and the vibe is straight from Santa Cruz, California. It's hard to wrap your head around the fish taco component, however the food is remarkably well put together and tasty, and the price is in the budget range.

ITALIAN

The genuine Italian food experience must have big tables, Italian songs tableside, big bowls of noodles, olives, cheerful waiters in white, wine, and lots of family. One might think this would be hard to find in Texas, but it's possible at the following Italian eateries.

One of the best places to eat in the Hyde Park area is **Asti** (408C E. 43rd St., 512/451-1218, 11 A.M.–10 P.M. Mon.–Thurs., 11 A.M.–11 P.M. Fri., 5–11 P.M. Sat., $10). This popular lunch and dinner spot looks like it was decorated by a graphic designer, not an Italian grandmother. Here you'll find classy versions of the Italian favorites such as salmon and goat cheese pizza, penne with grilled chicken and spinach, a great wine list, and the best fried calamari this side of the Colorado River. The best part about Asti? This upscale menu at great prices.

The best upscale pizza in town is at the **Brick Oven** (1209 Red River St., 512/477-7006, and 10710 Research Blvd., 512/345-6181, 11 A.M.–9 P.M. Mon.–Thurs., 11 A.M.–9:30 P.M. Fri., 5–9 P.M. Sun., $18). The core of this casual family restaurant is the 100-year-old brick oven and the smoky flavored, thin-crust pizzas it produces. The crust is infused with "special ingredients" that the proprietors will not reveal. This lends to an amazing, soft, flavorful crust that is unparalleled in Austin. Also on the menu are lasagna, chicken formaggi, ravioli, pasta primavera, and calzones. Being close to the Capitol, 6th Street, and the UT campus makes Brick Oven an easy, safe pick for lunch or dinner.

A great place to bring the family is **Frank and Angie's Pizzeria** (598 West Ave., 512/472-3534, 11 A.M.–10 P.M. Mon.–Sat., 5–10 P.M. Sun., $12). This downtown establishment has bizarre murals, Frank Sinatra memorabilia, and a patio overlooking Shoal Creek. Two-for-one specials are offered on Monday and Tuesday. The themed menu includes gourmet pizzas, pasta, calzones, and salads, all prepared well, and at great prices.

If you're on South Congress Avenue and "the moon hits your eye like a big pizza pie," make way to **Home Slice Pizza** (1415 S. Congress Ave., 512/444-PIES, 11:30 A.M.–11 P.M. Mon. and Wed.–Thurs., 11:30 A.M.–midnight Fri.–Sat., noon–10 P.M. Sun., $6). This innovative pizzeria has mastered the art of interior decorating for the trendy crowd. Luckily they've also mastered the world's most popular Italian dish. What makes this place so great is that it's a great place to hang out with friends because they have Italian wines, a couple beers on tap, and an upbeat environment.

The downtown Italian food scene is dominated by **La Traviata** (314 Congress Ave., 512/479-8131, 11:30 A.M.–2 P.M. and 5–10 P.M. Mon.–Fri., 5:30–10:30 P.M. Sat., $15). During the day La Traviata is a popular business lunch spot, and at night it becomes a place for romance. Wine connoisseurs will be pleased to find there's an extensive wine list here, and fans of exquisite Italian dishes will be thrilled by the creative, but traditional menu. It's a bit pricey, but worth it. Note for non-opera people—it's named after one of the best Italian operas of all time.

If Liberace was a goth punk and opened an Italian restaurant it may have been a place like **Romeo's** (1500 Barton Springs Rd., 512/476-1090, 11 A.M.–10 P.M. Sun.–Thurs., 11 A.M.–11 P.M. Fri.–Sat., $10). Decked with red and black walls, a ceiling of plastic grapes, cupids, empty gold frames, and a piano, Romeo's has good Italian food with ambience. The parmesan chicken is my top pick. From 6–9 P.M. every night someone's playing the piano. Expect to hear piano versions of Led Zeppelin, the Beatles, Billy Joel (the *Bosom Buddies* theme song), and Garth Brooks.

Rounder's Pizzeria (1203 W. 6th St., 512/477-0404, 11:30 A.M.–10 P.M. Sun.–Thurs., 11 A.M.–11:30 P.M. Fri.–Sat., $12) has received the award for best pizza every year since its inception. This sounds great—however they've been open only a few years. This Las Vegas–theme pizzeria serves a special pie with unique presentation and a smile. The crust is crunchy, which soft-crust pizza fans won't admire. Besides pizza, Rounder's serves up classic arcade games such as Galaga and Ms. Pacman.

OTHER INTERNATIONAL FOOD

◖ **Clay Pit** (1601 Guadalupe St., 512/322-5131, 11 A.M.–2 P.M. and 5–10 P.M. Mon.–Thurs., 11 A.M.–2 P.M. and 5–11 P.M. Fri.,

noon–3 P.M. and 5 P.M.–11 P.M. Sat., $12) is one of America's best Indian food restaurants, according to *Bon Appétit* magazine, and I am in full agreement! This five-star restaurant serves contemporary Indian cuisine in a sophisticated atmosphere. The orgy of flavors includes several curries, naan, and tandoori dishes. Although this is a great spot for dinner, the $6.99 lunch buffet brings in hordes of folks looking for a bargain for upscale Indian. Clay Pit is affordable yet upscale, which makes it a perfect place for any type of occasion.

Imagine sitting at a table near a lake, drinking mango margaritas and eating pupu, all in the presence of the Polynesian Tiki gods. **Hula Hut** (3825 Lake Austin Blvd., 512/476-4852, 11 A.M.–10 P.M. Sun.–Thurs., 11 A.M.–11 P.M. Fri.–Sat., $10), situated on the banks of Lake Austin, is a world unto itself. The atmosphere is festive, especially on weekends when the weather is nice. The cuisine is a "unique mix of Mexican and Polynesian, otherwise known as Mexonesian." Getting into specifics this means dishes such as Thai barbecue fajitas and mango poblano chile quesadillas. Sitting outside is an absolute must.

Many different cultures have introduced the world to the noodle. **Madam Mam's** (2514 Guadalupe St., 512/472-8306, and 4514 West Gate Blvd., 512/899-8525, 11 A.M.–10 P.M. Mon.–Sun., $8) brings the noodle to Austin in an affordable and reliable way. Although the core of this place is Thai cuisine, with dishes such as pad thai, you can also order up curry dishes with tangy lime and Chinese mushrooms. The versatility of the menu, and the good prices, make Madam Mam's a great place to come with friends before a night on the town.

If you find yourself at the top of Congress Avenue near the Capitol, and you're hankering for something different, **Marakesh** (906 Congress Ave., 512/476-7735, 11 A.M.–10 P.M. Mon.–Sat., $7) will satisfy your curious taste buds. This Mediterranean grill and café offers a healthy menu with variations of hummus, chicken, falafel, and veggies, all surprisingly inexpensive.

Locals with a diverse palate love to eat under the freeway at **Aster's Ethiopian** (2804 N. I-35, 512/469-5966, 11 A.M.–9 P.M. daily, $9). The tender beef and greens mixed with lintels is super filling. With a wide variety of vegetarian and meat dishes, this is a great low-key place to bring a few friends and sample a variety of tasty and healthy dishes. The lunch buffet is all you can eat so be careful.

Thai Kitchen (3009 Guadalupe St., 512/474-2575, 11 A.M.–midnight Mon.–Thurs., 11 A.M.–1 A.M. Fri., noon–2 A.M. Sat., noon–midnight Sun., $9) simply has to be mentioned when expounding on Austin's Asian cuisine options. A popular place for both people and pigeons, Thai Kitchen has consecutively been rated the best Thai restaurant by *Austin Chronicle*. As with many good things, there are pluses and minuses. Here the plus is the Thai food, which is exceptionally good. The minus is that the place is absolutely filthy. The windows and front door are perpetually foggy and smeared with grease, and the walls, floor, and ceiling are disgusting. The trick is you have to just sit down and eat, and try not to think about it too much. The food is surprisingly expensive for a dive Thai joint, but it's worth it. The Thai tea (often mispronounced as tai chi or chai tea) summons contentment and pleasure.

The healthiest and tastiest meal on a shoestring is at **Zen** (3423 Guadalupe St., 512/300-2633, and 1303 S. Congress Ave., 512/444-8081, 11 A.M.–11 P.M. Mon.–Sat., 11:30 A.M.–10 P.M. Sun., $6). Their motto is Japanese Food Fast. It may be fast, but it's healthier than fast food. What can beat four-piece California rolls for $3 or a bowl of spicy chicken with noodles for $5? And what beats sushi prepared by gringos? The restaurants are clean, the decor is modern, and the concept is brilliant!

For an unusual outdoor Indian food dining experience try **G'Raj Mahal** (91 Red River St., 512/480-2255, hours vary so call ahead, $10). Tucked away in Red River Street just south of 6th Street on an empty lot, you'll find a canopy with tables, wait staff, and a shiny food truck that churns out some of the best food in town. Traditional fresh Indian plates are flying out of the tandoor oven in the trailer. No alcohol is served as this is a BYOB establishment, so be sure to bring your favorite wine or beer.

HEALTHY AND VEGETARIAN

Being the Berkeley of Texas, Austin has some great fare for the health nut, vegetarian, and vegan.

In East Austin there's **The Eastside Cafe** (2113 Manor Rd., 512/476-5858, 11:30 A.M.–9:30 P.M. Mon.–Thurs., 11:30 A.M.–10 P.M. Fri., 10 A.M.–10 P.M. Sat., 10 A.M.–9:30 P.M. Sun., $10), which has its own vegetable garden on-site, thus extraordinarily fresh produce graces their plates. Patrons have the choice of eating in the soothing garden room or the classy antique interior of a converted bungalow. Delicious menu options include baked brie with chutney, sesame catfish, and salmon dumplings with coconut curry sauce. On weekends, an extremely popular brunch is offered 10 A.M.–3 P.M. with scrumptious choices like apple almond waffles and smoked salmon Benedict. It's wise to make a reservation, especially on the weekends.

A great choice for healthy food for everyone is **Kerbey Lane** (3704 Kerbey Ln., 512/451-1436; near UT campus at 2606 Guadalupe St., 512/477-5717; and in south Austin at 2700 S. Lamar Blvd., 512/445-4451, $8). Here you can have vegetarian fare and your friends can have meat if they prefer. Expect locally grown, organic, pesticide-free vegetables, and free-range beef and pork, prepared with precision. Kerbey Lane is known for their excellent queso, salads, and unusual entrées. All this is available 24 hours a day.

Mother's Cafe and Garden (4215 Duval St., 512/451-3994, 11:15 A.M.–10 P.M. Mon.–Fri., 10 A.M.–10 P.M. Sat.–Sun., $9) is the oldest and probably the best. All dishes are prepared with the highest quality ingredients and without any meat products. Many items on the menu can be prepared vegan as well. The food is so good here that the skeptic of vegetarian fare is sure to forget that the food is vegetarian.

WHOLE FOODS

Well before eating healthy and organic was trendy, Austin was a center for everything all-natural. People are always surprised to hear that this Texas town was the place where organic supermarket giant Whole Foods got its start back in 1980. At the time there were less than half a dozen natural-food supermarkets in the United States. These stores were pricey and relegated to the hippie fringes of our society. Thanks to the popularity of eating organic, the profile of healthy foods has become accessible to all. Whole Foods may still be pricey, but food tastes so much better when it hasn't been genetically modified, manipulated, and bleached to death.

Whole Foods corporate headquarters is above their flagship store at the corner of Lamar and 6th Street west of downtown Austin (525 North Lamar Blvd.). Folks from out of town are consistently bedazzled, enamored, and overwhelmed by the sheer quantity and quality of the products here. If you're in the neighborhood it's suggested you poke your head in here and look around. Or better yet, stay and have lunch here. If you happen to be buying CDs at Cheapo Discs down the road, take a moment to ponder that the building was the original location of the first Whole Foods.

© JUSTIN MARLER

The owners take great pride in the very eclectic menu choices that range from enchiladas to stir-fry to quiche.

For pauper vegetarians and non-vegetarians broadening their horizons **Veggie Heaven** (1914A Guadalupe St., 512/457-1013, 11 A.M.–9 P.M. Mon.–Fri., noon–9 P.M. Sat.–Sun., $6) offers up a fresh, Asian-based vegetarian menu that's quite overwhelming. Most dishes have textured vegetable protein or tofu, and are so well put together even carnivores can walk away satisfied. This sunken little restaurant is popular, and usually so packed the windows are completely steamed up. Oh wait—maybe that's just grime. Service is curt and to the point, but it's hard to complain because it's so cheap.

If you are vegetarian or vegan, and you're on the verge of backsliding, quickly make haste to **Mr. Natural** (1901 E. Cesar Chavez St., 512/477-5228, 8 A.M.–8 P.M. Mon.–Sat., $6). This humble restaurant in East Austin is nondescript, but don't pass it over. Vegetarian and vegan Mexican has been perfected by Mr. Natural. Each intelligently designed plate is filled to the brim with all-natural ingredients and flavors. Besides great vegan meals, Mr. Natural also has a vegan bakery, with sweets such as tofu cheesecake, and tres leches cake (a brilliant contradiction!). Mr. Natural is sure to seduce any questioning vegan back to the healthy side.

FINE DINING

Of the five senses we humans are equipped with, the one that is the most finicky to please is the sense of taste. Luckily, fine dining in Austin satisfies, with open kitchens, chef hats, long wine lists, Texas-style hospitality, and brilliant tastes whose origins you can't quite pin down.

True to Austin's laissez-faire approach to everything, most fine-dining establishments have no dress expectations. In fact most high-end restaurants don't even want to be classified as "fine dining"; they just want you to be comfortable and enjoy the ride. Plan on bringing plenty of money because the ride can be pricey.

Austin's most enduring high-end restaurant is the **Driskill Bar and Grill** (604 Brazos St., 512/391-7162, 5:30–10 P.M. Tues.–Sat., $40), located inside the Driskill Hotel. The Driskill has been winning awards for years. The interior is dark and Victorian with a rich Texas flair. Popular among the city's elite, such as musicians, politicians, actors, and local celebrities, the Driskill has mastered fine dining. Chef David Bull has developed a three-course menu that includes duck, seared foie gras, baked Alaska halibut, and tenderloin among others. Here you can find nothing but the very best in service and taste. The Driskill is a perfect place to start a romantic evening, followed by a horse-drawn carriage ride.

When you see the giant fork in the sky you know you have arrived at **Hyde Park Bar and Grill** (4206 Duval St., 512/458-3168, 11 A.M.–midnight daily, $15). The interior is swank, the staff are professional, and all meat products are organic. The cows may not be drinking fine wine and getting massages, but they are range-fed and hormone free. Hyde Park is famous for their batter-dipped fries, chicken-fried steak, and peach pudding. The restaurant and bar are open until midnight every day.

Being at the center of the state of Texas you may think good, fresh seafood just isn't a possibility in Austin. **Eddie V's Edgewater Grill** (301 E. 5th St., 512/472-1860, 4:30–11 P.M. Mon.–Thurs., 4:30 P.M.–midnight Fri.–Sat., 4:30–10 P.M. Sun., $30) proves all logic wrong. Every day fresh fish are flown in from Boston, because their motto is "we won't serve it unless it's fresh." When the menu is five pounds and

leather bound, you know it's fine dining. This steak and seafood menu includes Chilean sea bass steamed Hong Kong style, snapper and crab, seared Pacific ahi tuna steak, broiled Georges Bank sea scallops, roasted rack of Colorado lamb, and filet mignon. The menu is à la carte, which adds up pretty quickly, but once you have a nice glass of wine in front to you, you won't even think about it.

If you want to instantly feel like you've come to the right place go to **Jeffrey's** (1204 West Lynn Ave., 512/477-5584, 6–10 P.M. Mon.–Thurs., 5:30–10:30 P.M. Fri.–Sat., 6–9:30 P.M. Sun., $30). A creative and gregarious chef is behind the menu, and this comes through in each dish. Latin and Southwest flavors, coupled with wine and total confidence, make this menu superb. For starters there are crispy oysters on yucca-root chips and ginger beef dumplings. For entrées there are duck and shrimp with a rice pecan cake, beef tenderloin with rosemary potatoes, and Alaskan halibut with linguine, trumpet royale mushrooms, and orange champagne cream. Is your mouth watering yet? It should be!

A mainstay for upscale Mexican food is **Fonda San Miguel** (2330 W. North Loop Blvd., 512/459-4121, 5:30–9:30 P.M. Mon.–Sat., 11 A.M.–2 P.M. Sun., $20). The environment is quite impressive, with its extravagant hacienda interior complete with original Mexican paintings, tall ceilings, lush foliage, and large tin lanterns. Everything on the menu is excellent, but my favorite is the carne asada a la Tampiqueña. The beef is the best-tasting meat in town. All of the above is why Fonda San Miguel has been one of Austin's premier restaurants for 30 years. Be sure to make a reservation for Fonda San Miguel, as the seats fill up quickly.

If you enjoy a gigantic wine list and small entrées **Malaga Tapas & Bar** (440 W. 2nd St., 512/236-8020, 5–10 P.M. Sun.–Thurs., 5 P.M.–12 A.M. Fri.–Sat., $12) is waiting for you in the 2nd Street District. For those who don't know, tapas are a Spanish tradition of serving an appetizer-sized portion of meats, cheeses, or other items to accompany a drink. Along with tasty food, Malaga has one of the most extraordinary wine lists in the world according to *Wine Spectator* magazine. If this is your main meal, be sure to order enough for everyone so you don't walk away hungry at the end of the night. Also, a word of warning for the person new to tapas: Since the food is light and spread out over the course of the evening, the wine tends to go straight to your head.

Also in the Warehouse District is **Truluck's** (400 Colorado St., 512/482-9000, 5–10 P.M. Mon.–Thurs., 5–11 P.M. Fri.–Sat., 5–9 P.M. Sun., $20). Signs of a classy restaurant are waiters in chef coats and art deco employed for decor. With a wide variety of wines, perfectly prepared seafood dishes, and big-band music piped in, Truluck's will convert seafood haters to lovers. The first time I'd ever eaten lobster was here, and it was a profound experience.

Perhaps the most popular dining venue in the city is **◖ Vespaio** (1610 S. Congress Ave., 512/441-6100, 5:30–10:30 P.M. Tues.–Sat., $18). This darling of all the critics, and glamorous star of the people, is housed in a small space on popular South Congress. The kitchen is run by celebrated chef Alan Lazarus, who engineers brilliant Italian food by mixing innovation with tradition. The wine list is excellent, the food is perfectly designed and prepared, the atmosphere is lively—and did I mention the food is perfect? Italian flavor reaches a climax with dishes like veal ravioli, gnocchi with duck, cioppino (Livorno style seafood stew), and spaghetti alla carbonara with handmade noodles. Vespaio is Italian for beehive, and the restaurant lives up to its name by always buzzing with action. There aren't many tables in this small space, and they're guaranteed to be full every night of the week, so the wait may be long, but worth every second.

According to *Texas Monthly* magazine, **◖ Uchi** (801 S. Lamar Blvd., 512/916-4808, 5–10 P.M. Sun.–Thurs., 5–11 P.M. Fri.–Sat., $30) is one of the top five best new restaurants in Texas. It's considered Japanese, but don't expect the usual Japanese fare. It's actually Asian fusion with a dramatic, original flair. I consider Uchi the best white-knuckle eating experience I've ever had. If you have a fat wallet and razor-thin nerves, order anything from the menu and explore the mind of highly decorated chef Tyson Cole. Every item on the menu is extremely flavorful, wildly unique, and highly recommended. Warning to the squeamish—you may end up going away hungry. Praise for the brave—you will walk away an enriched person. The one item on the menu that deserves mention is the sawagani. This is a plate of several miniature freshwater crabs cooked whole to perfection and eaten like popcorn. You'll be surprised how easy the shell crunches and pinchers go down the hatch.

The founders of Lambert's go fishing with the owners of the South Congress fancy seafood joint **Perla's** (1400 S. Congress Ave., 512/291-7300, $20). This is Austin's best place for raw or fried oysters. Sampling the different oyster sauces with wine out on the front deck is the height of decadence. Notable menu items include lobster stock grits, calamari, and escolar. The decor gives one the impression you're eating with the rich in the Hamptons. Perla's is a great choice for seafood far from the sea, for either brunch, lunch, or dinner.

DESSERTS AND CONFECTIONS

There are just a few boutique dessert and confection shops in town, and **◖ Amy's Ice Creams** (1012 W. 6th St., 512/480-0673, 5624 Burnet Rd., 512/538-2697, and 3500 Guadalupe St., 512/458-6895, www.amysicecream.com, 11:30 A.M.–midnight daily, $4) is the queen of them all. Rated as one of the top 12 best ice-cream parlors in the United States by *Saveur* magazine, Amy's uses natural ingredients, a local dairy, and offers 16 flavors daily. One of the tricks to this parlor's popularity is that they manually smash and blend your favorite candy bars into your choice of ice cream using a dramatic process that goes down before your eyes. There are nine locations in Austin.

One of the grand new additions to the South Congress strip is **Big Top Candy Shop** (1706 S. Congress Ave., 512/462-2220, 11 A.M.–7 P.M. Mon.–Fri., 10 A.M.–8 P.M. Sat., 11 A.M.–7 P.M.

Sun., $2–25). These folks have created a bizarre and wonderful atmosphere that can only be described as a 19th-century circus of candy that has an honest to God soda fountain. Everyone under 60, who never had the chance to experience this "back in the day," should rush here without haste. Besides hand-jerked sodas, there are bins of hard candy, rivers of malts, and mountains of chocolate. A visit here is bound to leave you totally hyper and with a sick belly.

For classy and refined fineries there's **Dolce Vita** (4222 Duval St., 512/323-2686, 6:30 A.M.–midnight Mon.–Fri., 8 A.M.–midnight Sat.–Sun., $6). If you have dinner at any of the restaurants in the Hyde Park area such as Hyde Park Grill or Asti, a stop here is essential. Dolce Vita offers espresso along with a selection of ever-changing gelato, ice creams, pastries, and chocolate desserts. They also have an exceptional assortment of scotches and liqueurs that can't be found anywhere else in town.

When walking downtown on a hot summer day in the new 2nd Street District nothing can be more gratifying than making a stop at **Tart** (241 W. 2nd St., 512/803-1156, 11 A.M.– 10 P.M. daily, $4) for a cup of yogurt. With a wide selection of both soy-based frozen yogurt and 100 percent organic yogurt, free Wi-Fi, and a friendly atmosphere one tends to want to put up their feet here for a while.

Austin's original socializing parlor is the **1886 Cafe and Bakery** (116 6th St. at the Driskill Hotel, 512/391-7066, 7 A.M.–midnight daily, $8). With checkered floor, stained glass, dark woodwork, pillars, and arches, the interior looks like it hasn't changed much since 1886. Although this historic café offers breakfast, lunch, and dinner, the reason for coming here is the pastries and desserts. With a great location in the center of downtown in the Driskill Hotel, this is a great place to go if you get a craving for coffee and something sweet.

Imagine eating a small tower of chocolate mousse in a flower shop without flowers with Sandra Bullock. Sounds like heaven right? It's actually **Walton's Fancy & Staple** (609 West 6th St., 512/542-3380, 7 A.M.–8 P.M. Mon.– Fri., 8 A.M.–8 P.M. Sat., 9 A.M.–5 P.M. Sun.,

$6). Although Walton's is actually a deli, I recommend this place for the sweet stuff. Baked goods are absurdly decadent, and sodas are in bottles which means they are sweeter. Everything is sweet about this place including the fact that it was founded by Ms. Bullock.

COFFEE SHOPS

In this day and age, when nearly everyone has a daily caffeine maintenance, cafés are everywhere. Some frequent cafés to sip coffee with friends, some to surf wireless Internet, some to read the paper or a book, but all just want a place to go. Humans, like fish, are social creatures, and humans drink lots of water, only many humans like their water to be filtered through the "bean." Below are some of the top places to hang out and drink coffee.

◖ **Flipnotics** (1603 Barton Springs Rd., 512/480-TOGO or 512/480-8646, 7 A.M.– midnight Mon.–Sat., 8 A.M.–11 P.M. Sun., $2–5) is a perfect place to hang out, read the *Austin Chronicle*, and drink a cup of coffee after waking up at noon. This coffee shop features bitter coffee, various eatables, and live acoustic music in the evenings. With a motif of black and red, a fishbowl TV, and covered outdoor seating, Flipnotics is the best daytime hipster hangout. Downstairs there's an excellent retro clothing and accessories shop worthy of veneration as well.

◖ **Halcyon Coffeehouse** (218 W. 4th St., 512/472-9637, www.halcyonaustin.com, 7 A.M.–2 A.M. Mon.–Thurs., 7 A.M.–3 A.M. Fri., 8 A.M.–3 A.M. Sat., 8 A.M.–2 A.M. Sun., $2–5) is a night-owl café, a bar, an art gallery, and a smoke shop in one, and a great place to hang out. People come here to surf wireless Internet, to socialize, and to meet people. If you happen to have a random craving for s'mores, staff will bring fire to your table, as well as chocolate and marshmallows, so you can satisfy that craving. Seriously!

Jo's Cafe (1300 S. Congress Ave., 512/444-3800, 7 A.M.–9 P.M. Sun.–Fri., 7 A.M.–10 P.M. Sat., $2–5) is the boy who can do no wrong. This outdoor café is strategically positioned in the best area on South Congress Avenue, near all the great curiosity shops and boutiques. Jo's is a shack, albeit a stylish shack, that offers only outdoor seating in a parking lot. They're proud to serve up hot coffee, a few food items, and cold beer to a stream of people all day.

The café with the absolute best location is **Mozart's Coffee Roasters** (3825 Lake Austin Blvd., 512/477-2900, 7 A.M.–midnight Mon.–Thurs., 7 A.M.–1 A.M. Fri., 8 A.M.–1 A.M. Sat., 8 A.M.–midnight Sun.). Set on a quiet part of Lady Bird Lake, with outdoor seating, an in-house bakery, classical music playing, and coffee being roasted in the background, Mozart's is simply marvelous. Baked desserts are $6 and sweet pastries are $3. Wireless Internet is available. The only drawback is that parking can require patience.

Pacha (4618 Burnet Rd., 512/420-8758, 7 A.M.–9 P.M. Mon.–Fri., 8 A.M.–9 P.M. Sat.–Sun., $2–5), north of downtown, is one of those charming little home-spun cafés that everyone prays will survive. Everything in here, from the tables to the hand-forged doorknobs, was made by family and friends of the two owners. Besides great coffee, Pacha sells imported Bolivian handmade arts and crafts from two cooperatives. Buying any of these crafts helps boost families in rural Peru and Bolivia.

Doesn't matter if it's morning or nighttime, one of my favorite places to hang out is **Spider House Cafe** (2908 Fruth St., 512/480-9562, www.spiderhousecafe.com, 7 A.M.–2 A.M. daily, $5). This mostly open-air café features coffee, breakfast, beer, and free Wi-Fi, all in one of Central Austin's best patio settings. Junk is stuffed in every corner of this place, and christmas lights are on year-round, and sometimes there is live music on the tiny stage.

Shopping

Before you defer your shopping fantasies to New York, Los Angeles, or Paris, I recommended you give Austin a full-hearted leap of shopping faith, keeping in mind one thing: Austin is the splendid crossroads of country, kitsch, and pop culture. For shopping this means obscure, secondhand vintage clothing shops, cowboy boots and Western wear, and boutiques featuring the latest in contemporary fashion. Because of all this, Austin is one of those places where the stylists of rock stars and celebrities find some of their clients' greatest fashions.

Along with fashion boutiques Austin also has a wide variety of other shops such as toy stores, galleries, music stores, and an array of curiosity shops, all displaying their wares with personalized weirdness and flair. Concept shops that I would describe as weird gift shops and oddity boutiques are springing up everywhere. They're a hip and zany version of Hallmark stores for the 21st century, peddling weird trinkets, Japanese toys, pop memorabilia, reissued lunchboxes, and risqué cards. These do-it-yourself shops are run by creative folks who parlay their personal fetishes, hobbies, and interests into viable businesses.

Austin also has outlets of many of the big national chains, but in this book we will focus our attention on the one-of-a-kind Austin boutiques, as these are what make Austin so fabulous.

Although there are great shops all over town, there's a concentration of good shops in a few pockets of the city. The most famous shops are on **South Congress Avenue,** which is lined with funky storefronts, vintage boutiques, and trendy clothes and accessory shops. For fashionable new clothes and home decor items the shops in **2nd Street District** downtown, **6th and Lamar,** and **Guadalupe Street** are popular. For vintage and retro stuff there are the shops on **South Lamar** and **North Loop.** And for tacky touristy junk there's a smattering of shops on **6th Street.** Finally, in North Austin there's the shopping mecca of the **Arboretum,** which is a contemporary outdoor strip mall with all the big retail giants such as Gap and

Pottery Barn. Hours for most of these shops are generally 10 A.M.–7 P.M. On the first Thursday of every month merchants on South Congress keep their doors open until 10 P.M. So get on out there and support local business at any of the following choice establishments.

CLOTHES, SHOES, AND ACCESSORIES

South Congress is home to one of the area's finest Western-wear shops, **Allen's Boots** (1522 S. Congress Ave., 512/447-1413, 9 A.M.–8 P.M. Mon.–Sat., noon–6 P.M. Sun.). Once you open that door, be prepared to be knocked down by the smell of cow skin. Inside this wood-paneled, leather-lined cowboy emporium, you'll find everything for your modern cowboy, the closet cowboy, and the wannabe, such as classy belt buckles, bolo ties, Western shirts for men and women, and did I mention boots? Allen's has the most extraordinary cowboy and cowgirl boot collection in the United States. They have everyday boots for the working cowboy, but they specialize in dress boots with ornate patterns, colors, and designs, fetching up to $6,000. Even if you don't want to own a pair of cowboy boots, poke your head in here and marvel.

Finally, there's a clothing shop that sells nothing but black. Gothic meets country at fashionable **Blackmail** (1202 S. Congress Ave., 512/326-7670, 10:30 A.M.–6 P.M. Mon.–Sat., noon–5 P.M. Sun.). What two words personify the style here? Johnny Cash. Here you can buy anything from a black leather jacket to a pair of black jeans to black accessories for both men and women. They even have black lotion. The only color to be found in here is in the back, where they sell vintage cowboy boots.

For fashion-conscious women and men with a fat wallet there's the local institution of fashion known as **By George** (524 N. Lamar Blvd., 512/472-5951, 10 A.M.–7 P.M. Mon.–Sat., noon–6 P.M. Sun.). Owned and operated by the same folks since 1977, By George has had its pulse on the state of fashion for decades. They offer the latest hip rags from contemporary big-name designers as well as some up-and-coming designers. No dusty vintage duds

Allen's Boots on South Congress

© JUSTIN MARLER

and faux vintage here, just the guilty pleasures of passing fads.

Eco-wise (110 W. Elisabeth St., 512/326-4474, 10 A.M.–7 P.M. Mon.–Fri., 10 A.M.–6 P.M. Sat., noon–5 P.M. Sun.) is the place to shop for all things green, and by this I don't mean the color green, I mean made with hemp. As people become increasingly environmentally conscious, shops like Eco-wise are important places to get just about anything. This place carries a small collection of clothes and accessories, as well as natural duds for kids, but don't expect much in the way of flashy design. All products are down to earth in the truest sense of the phrase. Here you'll also find hand creams, building supplies, toys, flooring, and other items for the home, all environmentally friendly.

Emeralds (624 Lamar Blvd., 512/476-4496, 10 A.M.–9 P.M. Mon.–Sat., noon–7 P.M. Sun.) is one of those hard-to-pigeonhole shops. Here you can buy sexy casual dresses, flashy shoes, gifts, cards, and jewelry. This place is best described as Paris Hilton–esque. Styles include designs by BCBG, Volcom, Michael Stars, Killah, French Connection, and many others.

When shopping in Austin, get some brownie points by buying locally made goods in support of local designers from **Parts and Labour** (1117 S. Congress Ave., 512/326/1648, 11 A.M.–9 P.M. daily). The little shop is filled with edgy designs, clever and trendy graphic T-shirts, and unusual accessories. There is no specific "look" that the proprietor is going for fashion-wise, which in turn has created a look that is totally unique. This is achieved by simply stocking the space with all locally made designs and fashions.

Finally, a boutique for the fashion-conscious male. **Service Menswear** (1400 S. Congress St., 512/447-7600, 10:30 A.M.–8 P.M. Mon.–Sat., 11 A.M.–6 P.M. Sun.) is a small space that is easy to overlook. In here men can buy designer, surf, and skate apparel made by Spiewak, Ben Sherman, Tyler Speed, Almost Evil, and age-old Vans and Penguin. Service is known for their great collection of graphic T-shirts and vintage belt buckles.

MUSIC

Being the music lovin' town that it is, Austin has some great music caches around town that have it all—vinyl, CDs, cassettes, and even eight-tracks, in any and every genre of music. For the vinyl fiend there are some excellent record stores.

Remember when record stores carried records? Remember that distinct smell of cardboard and plastic? At **Antone's Record Store** (2928 Guadalupe Ave., 512/322-0660, 10 A.M.–10 P.M. Mon.–Sat., 11 A.M.–8 P.M. Sun.), vinyl junkies are sure to find some old records they've been looking for. Besides having the biggest collection of vinyl in town Antone's also has a great selection of Texas music. So dig in that junk drawer and find your yellow 45 adapters.

Cheapo Discs (914 N. Lamar Blvd., 512/477-4499, 9 A.M.–midnight daily) is the best music store in Austin. Here the music fan can flip through bins of millions of CDs all day long and into the wee hours. Cheapo

is housed in the original location of the first Whole Foods. What used to be the location for overpriced organic foods now serves up gourmet new and used music at great prices. From the outside the store looks like it's been closed since Whole Foods moved out. Don't be deceived by the inconspicuous exterior. Weekend nights there's often a live band playing in the corner while you shop.

Vinyl enthusiasts will be pleased when they visit Austin's true indie record store **End of an Ear** (2209 S. 1st St., 512/462-6008, www.endofanear.com, 11 A.M.–9 P.M. Mon.–Sat., noon–8 P.M. Sun.). Although the space seems small, the collection of vinyl is full of surprises. Dig a little and you will uncover more "must-haves" than you can afford. Beside LPs and 7 inches, they also carry record players, and used and new CDs of your favorite punk and metal bands, along with a meager selection of country, metal, and jazz. The folks here are experts in vinyl and can help troubleshoot or answer questions.

Austin's most popular source for both new and used music is **Waterloo Records** (600A N. Lamar Blvd., 512/474-2500, 10 A.M.–11 P.M. Mon.–Sat., 11 A.M.–11 P.M. Sun.). They specialize in the most current releases in pop, country, and indie, and offer a great selection of Texas artists. Besides peddling CDs, Waterloo is the place to get tickets for local concerts, and they even put on their own live shows in-house.

BOOKSTORES

The largest bookstore in Texas is **BookPeople** (603 N. Lamar Blvd. at 6th St., 512/472-5050, 9 A.M.–11 P.M. daily). They have everything that a major chain has, and then some. Here you'll find new books in every category, by nearly every author, as well as gifts, journals, children's books, magazines, and a café. BookPeople is also the area's top venue for author book signings, lectures, and literary information. As the name implies, it's a community bookstore and resource.

For the ladies, and the ladies that like ladies, there's **Book Woman** (5501 N. Lamar,

512/472-2785, 10 A.M.–8 P.M. Mon.–Sat., noon–6 P.M. Sun.). This female-oriented bookstore and community information center stocks feminist, gay and lesbian, and women's studies books, as well as T-shirts and gifts.

The area's biggest used-book resource is **Half Price Books** (5555 N. Lamar Blvd. at Koenig, 512/451-4463, www.halfpricebooks. com, 9 A.M.–10 P.M. Mon.–Sat., 10 A.M.–9 P.M. Sun.). Along with racks and shelves of used books you will also find new overstock coffee table books, color folio books, and bestsellers at a discount. In the back is a rare book room for the collector in search of that first edition *Wizard of Oz*. For other locations visit their website.

Want to bring down "the man"? Need a copy of *The Anarchist Cookbook?* **Monkey Wrench Books** (110 North Loop Blvd., 512/407-6925, 11 A.M.–8 P.M. Mon.–Fri., noon–8 P.M. Sat.–Sun.) carries literature for the counterculture and the cultural revolution. Monkey has a wide variety of zines, punk and pop culture journals, as well as socialist and anarchist books.

ART GALLERIES

Every outlet for creativity abounds in Austin. Although music takes center stage, the fine arts also deserve a nod. There are a slew of galleries around town that represent all types of artists in all mediums and styles. However, the most prevalent style is contemporary folk art best described as John Wayne meets Andy Warhol.

Wally Workman Gallery (1202 W. 6th St., 512/472-7428, 10 A.M.–5 P.M. Tues.–Sat.) is the gallery in town where you can always find something beautiful and captivating to look at no matter what your tastes may be. Every month this small gallery in an old retrofitted victorian house has a new exhibition that features new and innovative artists which never disappoint.

One of Austin's most intriguing art spaces is **d berman gallery** (1701 Guadalupe St., 512/481-1088, 11 A.M.–6 P.M. Tues.–Sat.). This gallery specializes in contemporary American painting, sculpture, and photography, with an emphasis on regional artists. The gallery is in a contemporary, alluring urban exhibition space—an historic commercial art deco building.

Local artist Todd Sanders has created a little world for himself at **Roadhouse Relics** (1720 S. 1st St., 512/442-NEON or 512/442-6366). A while back he bought the corner storefront location, plunked a trailer in the back, and hunkered down. Now he flings paint and neon where he wants without worrying about a thing. He opens his world to the public by appointment or by chance. If you drop by and he's not there, peek into the backyard at the giant chicken, the huge AUSTIN neon sign, and all the other bizarre things Todd has collected. His stuff is best described as vintage neon and decor.

Austin's only outlet for master artists of Europe is the **Russell Collection** (1137 W. 6th St., 512/478-4440, www.russell-collection. com, 10 A.M.–6 P.M. Tues.–Sat.). This gallery is perfect for the art collector who wants to own a Chagall, Renoir, Manet, Pissarro, or Picasso, but has a budget of around $1,000–5,000. You may shudder at this and ask how this is possible. Well, the collection consists, for the most part, of signed lithographs and works on paper that were cranked out either during the artist's lifetime or were produced by the original plates in recent years. How about the original oils? Well, look closely at the name and you will see these are painted by relatives of the masters, not the masters themselves.

Yard Dog (1510 S. Congress Ave., 512/912-1613, www.yarddog.com, 11 A.M.–5 P.M. Mon.–Fri., 11 A.M.–6 P.M. Sat., noon–5 P.M. Sun.) is an art gallery that represents artists from around the country that create abstract folk art with a bite. The artwork in here is always amusing, quirky, and both colorful and off-color. Paintings, sculpture, and a unique array of things in between seem to take a tongue-in-cheek approach to Americana without becoming irreverent.

WEIRD GIFTS AND ODDITIES

One place I find hard to classify is **Atomic City** (1700 San Antonio St., 512/477-0293,

AUSTIN'S FUNKY SIGNAGE

Driving around Austin one can't help but take notice of the numerous funky, creepy, bizarre, and clever signs that many Austin businesses are adorned with. When it comes to zoning laws for signage Austin is pretty laissez-faire, which has opened the door for some creative approaches to attract the passerby. These businesses and their signs have become landmarks for locals and tourists, and collectively give Austin an amusing and fascinating image.

For example, what would normally be a very mundane light-bulb shop is completely transformed when topped with a three-dimensional bust of a giant, creepy, grinning man with a light bulb suspended over his head. Like a moth drawn to a light bulb one can't help but stroll into **The Light Bulb Shop** (6318 Burnet Rd.), even if there's no need for a light bulb. Just down the road is another peculiar sign worth noting. In front of **Atomic Tattoo** (5533 Burnet Rd.) is a pole topped with a skull, wearing a cap, (not to be confused with a skullcap) mounted on an octopus. Eye-catching? Yes! But whether this makes one crave a tattoo or not is another story.

Other signage worth mentioning would be the grotesque massive red bulging arm in full flex protruding from **Hyde Park Gym** (4125 Guadalupe St.). Or there's the much more soothing retro/hippie sign of **Groovy Lube** (3511 Guadalupe St.) or the lesser-known, daffy-looking boxer standing proud and tall above **Richard Lord's Boxing Gym** (5400 N. Lamar). One can't leave out the string of shops on South Congress Avenue. The sign and sculpture above **Uncommon Objects** (1512 S. Congress Ave.) begs the question, "What the heck were they thinking?" A cowboy made out of a muffler, riding a giant rabbit? Wow!

© JUSTIN MARLER

Among all of Austin's landmark signs there are two vying for the position of sign diva. One is a little waitress girl with a big Fender guitar on top of **Fran's Hamburgers** (1822 S. Congress Ave.); the other is the mother of all mothers, the colossal woman's bust with open arms beckoning all the world to enter **Maria's Taco Express** (2529 S. Lamar Blvd.). This sign features the actual likeness of the proprietress. Once you see Maria's open arms from the road it is highly suggested you pull over and let her embrace you with her delicious tacos.

noon–6 P.M. Mon.–Sat., 2–6 P.M. Sun.), as it's a unique store filled will pop culture memorabilia, Japanese toys, tin toys, punk rock T-shirts, and risqué postcards, all crammed into the bottom floor of an old two-story house. In the back room is a great collection of fashionable leather boots and shoes that lean towards the rocker/goth/punk crowd (this was the first place in Austin to sell Doc Martens). All the above products are passions of the owner, who's an Austin attraction in his own right.

Electric Ladyland, aka **Lucy in Disguise with Diamonds** (1506 S. Congress Ave., 512/444-2002, 11 A.M.–7 P.M. Mon.–Sat., noon–6 P.M. Sun.), is the biggest costume and prop outlet around. Here you can rent or buy costumes for anything, and this is not hyperbole. There's a wall of costume jewelry that can make any woman—or man for that matter—into Cleopatra, Carmen Miranda, or the Jolly Green Giant. Inside the showroom there's an amazing collection of theme park–quality get-ups such as Tweety Bird, which includes a big, fuzzy, unwieldy mask. There's also an entire room of scary rubber masks and prosthetics that range from a Freddie Kruger mask to a triple "breast"-plate.

Monkeys are known for "aping" what others do, but **Monkey See, Monkey Do** (1712 S. Congress Ave., 512/443-4999, 11 A.M.–8 P.M. daily) isn't copying anyone. This new boutique filled with new junk such as Japanese toys, silly kitsch, retro clocks, pop culture books, and the largest refrigerator-magnet collection in Texas, fits in perfectly on South Congress Avenue.

Oat Willie's (617 W. 29th St., 512/482-0630, 10 A.M.–10 P.M. Mon.–Sat., 11 A.M.–9 P.M. Sun.) is the oldest continuously operating smoke shop in town. Oat's straddles the fine line between selling tobacco and being a head shop. I tip my hat to all who smoke tobacco in a bong.

The shop with the most color is **Tesoros** (1500 S. Congress Ave., 512/447-7500, 11 A.M.–6 P.M. daily), Austin's Latin-American import extravaganza. Here tourists can be bedazzled by an enormous space filled with treasures, religious and superstitious items,

and folk art, all imported from south of the border. This emporium of colorful kitsch is a great place to get unique gift ideas. The endless litany of items includes hand-made jewelry, unusual trinkets, colorful wall-hangings and tapestries, carved figures and figurines, Mexican wrestling masks, pottery, toys made from soda cans, *ex-votos/milagros,* religious paintings and art, woodblock prints, and much, much more.

South Congress's Latin import connection is the **Turquoise Door** (1208 S. Congress Ave., 512/480-0618, 10 A.M.–7 P.M. Mon.–Sat., 10 A.M.–6 P.M. Sun.). This small retail space is chock-full of Latin-American folk art including hand-woven ceremonial Peruvian wall-hangings, larger-than-life Oaxacan Día de los Muertos (Day of the Dead) figures, folk dolls, Mexican punched-tin art, religious items, wooden masks, and colorful and exotic jewelry. Chances are you aren't going in this place looking for something specific, but you'll like what you find.

FOR KIDS

Austin is an all-around fun place with a persistent lightheartedness and an unspoken maxim: "Don't take things too seriously." That said, everything in town for children isn't exclusively for children. Frank Sinatra's famous song explains what I'm trying to say with the lyric: "For it's hard, you will find, to be narrow of mind, if you're young at heart," and especially if you are in **Toy Joy** (2900 Guadalupe Ave., 512/320-0090, 10 A.M.–11 P.M. Mon.–Thurs., 10 A.M.–midnight Fri.–Sat.). Rated one of the top 10 toy stores in the nation by *Child* magazine, Toy Joy is lined floor to ceiling and beyond with toys, gags, flying things, shooting things, noisemakers, squishy things, giant things, and tiny things, all in primary colors. One very important word of advice to grown-ups: Before you enter, leave your inner adult at the door. Open late at night, this is a great place to visit in the "wee" hours. Inside Toy Joy you'll find things that cheer up every girl and boy, such as: things that go swish, things that go squish, flying birds, and swimming fish.

Things that tumble, things that roll, and music by Raffi, not Dave Grohl.

If the commercial plastic side of the toy industry has you turned off consider visiting Austin's minihaven of homemade wooden toys, **Rootin' Ridge Toymakers** (1206 W. 38th, Suite 1105, 512/453-2604, 10 A.M.–5 P.M. Mon.–Sat.). This little shop, founded by husband and wife team Georgean and Paul in 1976, has all kinds of toys and games that seem like they were made for the set of *Little House on the Prairie*. The fun part about visiting this little shop is you can watch the toys being made on the spot.

Another great locally owned toy store is **Terra Toys** (2438 W. Anderson Ln., 512/445-4489, 9 A.M.–8 P.M. Mon.–Sat., noon–6 P.M. Sun.). If you're a kid, it's as good as a candy store, and if you're a depressed and jaded adult, Terra Toys will cut a smile into your face. This collection of toys steers clear of the consumer garbage that has captivated kids for so long such as action figures and Barbie. Instead, here parents can find educational toys, handmade toys, learning games, wooden toys, musical instruments for tots, and a small selection of expensive clothes.

RETRO, VINTAGE, AND ANTIQUES

Austin's love affair with kitsch is best experienced by strolling through the many shops and boutiques that specialize in the wacky and rare retro furnishings, vintage clothing, and country and folk antiques. In any number of these shops you can throw down some hard-earned dollars for a musty old Western shirt that looks like something worn by a member of the Carter Family on the stage of the Grand Ole Opry, an amoeba-shaped chair that looks like it came from Frank Sinatra's Las Vegas home, a hand-carved shrine to the Virgin de Guadalupe, or an antique stuffed rabbit perched on a lacquered piece of burl. By stuffed I mean taxidermy—you can tell by the creepy smell.

For the most part these shops are clustered together on a few of the main drags in town, which makes it easy to just step out on a street and follow your curious nose where it leads you. South of town there are some fantastic shops on South Lamar and South Congress, and just north of downtown there are a couple shops on Guadalupe Street. Farther north there are some shops on Old Burnet Road and North Loop. Generally these places are close to great coffee shops and excellent places to break for lunch. For a complete list of vintage outlets in Austin check out: www.vintagearoundtownguide.com.

South Congress

First of all, I highly suggest kicking off your shopping on South Congress by fixing your caffeine maintenance at Jo's Cafe. Only then will you be able to focus properly for the transactions of the day. Then walk up to **New Bohemia Retro Resale** (1606 S. Congress Ave., 512/326-1238, noon–10 P.M. daily), a thrift store cool enough for teenagers and retro enough for the parents. This upbeat environment seems to draw them in and keep them coming back. In here you will find old clothes one notch above Goodwill, art that appears to be inspired by the great Bob Ross (the public television guy with the afro), some furniture, and of course that classic junk-store smell that is similar to granny's living room. Hats off to whoever made the catchy sign out front.

For upscale trinkets **Off the Wall** (1704 S. Congress Ave., 512/445-4701, 10 A.M.–6:30 P.M. Mon.–Sat., noon–6 P.M. Sun.) has lots of oddities you can buy at collectors' prices. The proprietors have made a living out of treasure hunting. With 25 years of experience they've developed an excellent sense for what attracts the antique moths to the virtual flame. Here you'll find furniture along with an intriguing array of collectibles ranging from swords to early versions of Mickey Mouse in porcelain, from weird inventions from foregone times to expensive antique ashtrays.

The best curiosity shop in town is **Uncommon Objects** (1512 S. Congress Ave., 512/442-4000, 11 A.M.–7 P.M. Fri.–Wed., 11 A.M.–9 P.M. Thurs.). Here 18 purveyors of random items, knickknacks, oddities,

© JUSTIN MARLER

Uncommon Objects

trinkets, and collectibles peddle their weird stuff. Everything in this dark, 4,000-square-foot space is a conversation piece, such as vintage priest vestments, Victorian and cowboy clothes, human bones, bronze busts of whoever, and taxidermy animals corpses. Take your time browsing because there's stuff in every corner and junk hanging from the ceiling. You won't want to miss a thing.

Cream Vintage (1714 S Congress Ave., 512/474-8787, and 2532 Guadalupe St., 512/474-8787, 11 A.M.–9 P.M. Mon.–Sat., noon–8 P.M. Sun.) has flawlessly merged vintage and modern fashion, without being too dusty or too slick. This small retail shop specializes in '70s period duds, used T-shirts, shoes, retro sweaters, and accessories. For instance you can get Izod shirts, polyester pants, Daisy Duke cutoffs, and corduroy. Think *Repo Man*. The prices are a little steep, but when you find that '80s Euro trash pleather jacket you've always wanted you'll throw down the cash. If you're on The Drag at the UT campus area, be sure to visit their other location, just across the street from the site of the original *Austin City Limits* studio.

South Lamar

One of the long-living staples in Austin's vintage/retro scene is **Amelia's Retro-Vogue & Relics** (2213 S. 1st, 512/442-4446, noon–7 P.M. Tues.–Sat., noon–5 P.M. Sun.). This is a favorite place for designers and stylists to the celebrities, musicians, as well as drag entertainers to get ideas. Inside you'll find dramatic glamour outfits from the '50s show-business era, children's vintage clothes, and a massive hat collection. You know you have arrived at Amelia's when you see a giant wire globe in the front yard of an old house.

Up South Lamar is **Bitchin Threads** (1030D S. Lamar Blvd., 512/441-9955, 11 A.M.–7 P.M. Mon.–Sat., noon–5 P.M. Sun.). I think the name may be a play on words. Bitch in threads—get it? Where's the crook and gong? Anyway, in here ladies who dress vintage with a witch flair can find all sorts of long dresses, formalwear, handbags, sparkly glam outfits, and trays of accessories. This is the place in town—and for that matter in Texas—to buy rare, antique silk kimonos. As a side note, the lady who runs the shop is a hoot to chat with.

For vintage and retro shopping for men and women, there's **Flashback** (1805 S. 1st St., 512/445-6906, 11 A.M.–7 P.M. Thur.–Sat., noon–5 P.M. Sun.). Here you'll find an excellent collection of early-20th-century women's evening wear, men's shirts, and thrift-store art. The amount of vintage duds in here is phenomenal. The most interesting vest in the world is in here—a snake vest outfitted with pockets made from cobra heads, no joke.

North Loop

If you're out and about in Old North Austin and want to hunt for nothing in particular, make your way to the burgeoning North Loop DIY business district. This small bend in the road of a residential area is well worth your time. Here you'll find **Hog Wild Texas Vintage** (100 E. North Loop Blvd #A, 512/467-9453, 11 A.M.–7 P.M. daily), one of Austin's oldest and largest vintage stockpiles featuring a vast collection of toys, clothes, and furniture, and stuff from the '70s TV show *All in the Family*.

Just across the street is **Room Service Vintage** (107 E. North Loop Blvd., 512/451-1057, 11 A.M.–7 P.M. daily). Upon entering through the double doors one can't help but be overwhelmed by the lights, colors, and shapes in here. With over 3,500 square feet of "modern" amoeba-shaped furniture, '50s light fixtures, costume clothes and jewelry, vinyl records, vintage *Playboy* magazines, and paint-by-numbers artwork, everyone is bound to find something that tickles their fancy.

Wrap up your North Loop retro shopping

day at **Blue Velvet** (217 W. North Loop, 512/452-2583, 11 A.M.–8 P.M. Mon.–Sat., noon–8 P.M. Sun.). Blue Velvet, six-time winner of *Austin Chronicle*'s Reader's Poll for Best Vintage Store, is a one-stop shop for all your trendy clothing wants. In addition to the large collection of both new and vintage duds, this retro shop also sells costumes and unique handmade items from local DIY craftsters.

Old Burnet Road

One man's junk is another man's treasure, especially at **Out of the Past** (5341 Burnet Rd., 512/371-3550, 10 A.M.–6 P.M. Mon.–Sat., noon–6 P.M. Sun.). This place wins the award for most stuff crammed into a small room. Browsing here is like digging through your uncle's garage and uncovering movie, music, and sports posters; collectible toys such as Star Wars, Barbie, and Hot Wheels; miniature furniture made from clothespins; and religious kitsch. They have the whole kit and caboodle—whatever that means.

Antique Marketplace (5806 Burnet Rd., 512/452-1000, 11 A.M.–6 P.M. Mon.–Sat., noon–6 P.M. Sun.) offers shelter to 50 dealers in over 19,000 square feet of stuffy antique bliss. It's all old, and it's all good. One of the dealers inside the market is **Aqua 20th Century Modern.** They have a great website, www.aquamodern.com, that's worth checking out if you're into '50s modern furniture and furnishings.

Top Drawer Thrift Shop (4902 Burnet Rd., 512/454-5161, 10 A.M.–7 P.M. Mon.–Sat.) is a secondhand store with a fashion sensibility. Sixties paint-by-numbers art, old clothes and graphic tees, old appliances, and shelves of weird stuff are sitting around begging to find a home.

Information and Services

TOURIST INFORMATION

The **Austin Convention and Visitors Bureau** (800/926-2282, www.austintexas.org) is a great resource for travel and tourism information before you land in Austin. Their easy to navigate website offers lots of concise information, and the person at the other end of their toll-free number can offer advice and information on anything Austin-related as well. For a brick-and-mortar information center, there's the **Austin Visitor Information Center** (209 E. 6th St., 866/GO-AUSTIN or 866/462-8784, 9 A.M.–5 P.M. Mon.–Fri., 9:30 A.M.–5:30 P.M. Sat.–Sun.). Their knowledgeable staff can help you find the right accommodation at short notice, maps of the town, and anything else necessary for survival in Austin.

EMERGENCY INFORMATION

In the event of an emergency involving injury or danger dial **911.** Other non-emergency numbers are as follows: **Austin Police Department** (311 or 512/974-5000), **Brackenridge Hospital** (601 E. 15th St., 512/324-7000) located downtown, **St. David's Hospital** (919 E. 32nd St., 512/476-7111) located north of downtown, **Seton Medical Center** (1201 W. 38th St., 512/324-1000) located near the UT campus, **Dell Children's Medical Center of Central Texas** (4900 Mueller Blvd., 512/324-0000), **People's Community Clinic** (2909 N. IH 35, 512/478-4939 or 512/478-8924) for uninsured patients who pay on a sliding scale.

If you're on vacation and have a shoe emergency there's **Austin Shoe Hospital** (720 Congress Ave., 512/477-5078). In addition to the downtown location they have several others in the Austin area where they can fix your sole.

PUBLICATIONS

The local newspaper, the *Austin American Statesman* is an average medium-size-city newspaper—nothing to write home about. The *Statesman* covers all the basics including local, national, and international news; sports; business; classifieds; and entertainment. Every Thursday the paper has an entertainment section called "Xlent." The *Statesman* can be found anywhere in town.

The city's alternative weekly rag, the **Austin Chronicle,** on the other hand, is excellent. What it lacks in design and layout it makes up for in colorful, opinionated content. Look to the *Chronicle* for information on music, events, films, the arts, food, kids' activities and local politics. The *Chronicle* comes out every Thursday and is free for the taking at almost every restaurant, café, and shopping center in town.

Many U.S. cities take a stab at having a classy, sophisticated, hip magazine and most totally fail. But *Austin Monthly* is a high-caliber city magazine that works. In here you'll find articles that cover everything current including culture, politics, entertainment, and tasteful celebrity cover stories.

The full-color, glossy magazine *Texas Monthly* is the best state magazine in the country. It can be purchased at most supermarkets and corner stores and is a great resource for state news, politics, and celebrity gossip, and offers a great listings section in the back with restaurant reviews.

INTERNET AND WI-FI

Internet access is so readily available in Austin it's literally in the air. If you have a laptop with a wireless card you will be pleased to know that Austin has more free Wi-Fi hot spots than anywhere else on the planet. Walk into almost any café in town and chances are you can surf for free on your own computer. Businesses in the downtown area sure to have wireless Internet are: **Flipnotics** (1603 Barton Springs Rd., 512/480-TOGO or 512/480-8646), **Halcyon Coffeehouse** (218 W. 4th St., 512/472-9637), **Jo's Cafe** (1300 S. Congress Ave. and 242 W. 2nd St., 512/444-3800), **Little City Cafe** (916 Congress Ave., 512/476-2489), **Mozart's Coffee Roasters** (3852 Lake Austin Blvd., 512/477-2900), **Progress Coffee** (500 San Marcos St.,

ORANGE, STEERS, AND THAT HAND SIGN

There are a few things the newcomer to Austin will notice around town that may cause some confusion, or at least raise some questions. Now is as good a time as any to clarify a few points. First of all let me explain the color orange. It's technically called burnt orange and is more of a rusty color. This sacred hue is seen everywhere in Austin. People even paint their houses and cars with it. It's so pervasive that it's darn near the official color of the city. However it's actually the official team color of the UT Longhorns.

Secondly, the outsider may notice the simple iconic image of steer horns plastered all over town. This image is just as pervasive as burnt orange, popping up on city street signs, on most cars on the roads, in advertisements, and on flags that are simultaneously flown with the Texas state flag. Again, the image of the steer – or more correctly the longhorn steer – isn't the city's official logo; it belongs to the celebrated college football team the UT Longhorns.

Finally, the most confusing thing for the outsider is the popular hand sign that Austinites display. This gesture, with pinky and index fingers raised, resembles the sinister hand sign of devil horns attributed to heavy metal and Satanism. But in Austin, and Texas in general, this is called the "Hook'em Horns" and has nothing to do with old Beelzebub. In fact, in other cultures it has less evil meanings: In Buddhism it's a prayerful symbol that wards off evil, in parts of Africa it's a curse, and in sign language it means "bullsh–." In Austin this symbol is the hand sign of UT fans, devised back in the 1950s, which definitely predates heavy metal.

512/493-0963), **Dominican Joe** (515 S. Congress Ave, 512/448-3919), **Thunderbird Coffee** (2200 Manor Rd., 512/472-9900), **Austin Java** (1608 Barton Springs Rd., 512/482-9450 and 1206 Parkway, 512/476-1829), **Opal Divine's** (700 W. 6th St., 512/477-3308), **La Tazza Fresca** (519 W. 37th St., 512/453-0403), **Spider House** (2908 Fruth St,. 512/480-9562). Most hotels have Internet service as well.

For those without a laptop there are many outlets to get connected. All Austin public libraries offer free Internet access provided you have a valid ID such as a driver's license and one other form of ID. For locations call 512/974-7400. For everyone else there's a **FedEx Office** (327 Congress Ave., 512/472-4448) downtown and elsewhere around Austin. Rates are $0.20 or $0.40 per minute depending on the computer.

MUSICIAN'S RESOURCES

Since thousands of bands and musicians make their way through Austin on tour every year, it seems fitting to offer some tips on where to get your guitar set up, where to rent gear, and where to sneak in a rehearsal. The largest selection of equipment and gear rental is offered by **Rock N Roll Rentals** (1420 Oltorf St., www.rocknrollrentals.com, 512/447-5305). Here you'll find the largest selection of guitars, basses, amps, drums, and keyboards. When festivals are happening gear can be hard to find so reserve equipment in advance.

If you are on tour and want to work on new material or brush up on your chops **Music Lab** (1306 Oltorf St. and 500 E Saint Elmo Rd., www.musiclab.net, 512/326-3816) offers affordable rehearsal rooms by the hour. Prices range $12–15 per hour and rooms include PA and mic stands. Any gear beyond this can be rented for reasonable hourly rates.

There are several shops in town that offer guitar and amp repair but most are generally booked out a few days. The best shops in town for guitar repair are **Austin Vintage Guitars** (1112 South Lamar Blvd., 512/428-9100), **Strait Music** (2428 West Ben White Blvd., 512/476-6927) and **South Austin Music** (1402 S. Lamar Blvd., 512/448-4992). The best shops in town for amp repair are **Austin Vintage Guitars** (1112 South Lamar Blvd.,512/428-9100) and **Audiotech Austin** (2213-B S. 1st St., 512/673-7141).

With many vintage guitar boutiques and new music shops in austin, buying new and used gear can be a blast. Amazing selections of vintage guitars and basses can be found at **Austin Vintage Guitars** (1112 South Lamar Blvd.,512/428-9100), **South Austin Music** (1402 S. Lamar Blvd., 512/448-4992) and **Bass Emporium** (1720 W Anderson Ln., 512/691-7445). The place to buy drums and accessories is **Tommy's Drum Shop** (1100 South 8th St., 512/444-3786). Lastly, the music store that offers just about everything is **Strait Music** (2428 West Ben White Blvd., 512/476-6927).

LAUNDRY

For coin-operated laundry machines and dry cleaning all-in-one there's **EcoClean** (2915 Guadalupe St., 512/236-8645). In the South Congress area there's **Spincycle** (2424 S. Congress Ave., 512/447-2700), and near UT campus there's **Spincycle Washateria** (3501 Guadalupe St, 512/380-0218) for coin-op laundry.

POST OFFICE

The centrally located post offices are as follows: **Downtown** (510 Guadalupe St., 512/494-2206); **Capitol Station** (111 E. 17th St., 512/477-7082) downtown near the Capitol; **Central Park Station** (3507 N. Lamar Blvd., 512/420-0310) in Central Austin; and **University** (2201 Guadalupe, West Mail Building, 512/232-5488) on the UT campus. For information on other locations call 800/275-8777. UPS Stores are all over town; refer to a local phone book, call 800/PICK-UPS (800/742-5877), or visit www.ups.com for locations.

MONEY

It takes money to get money. ATM kiosks are everywhere, but beware: The ATMs you find on the street, such as on 6th Street, Red River, and Congress Avenue, all charge extraordinarily high fees. It's always best to get money from your own banking institution, but if your bank isn't to be found, at least use a national bank. You may still incur a fee, but it will be much less than at kiosk ATMs. My favorite ATM in town, and possibly in the world, is the one planted in the old rickety wooden fence on Red River Street at Stubb's BBQ. I would never get money from it—it's just an interesting sight to behold. Also, Austin doesn't seem to have a problem with pick-pocketing so you don't need to be looking over your shoulder like you do in other cities.

USEFUL PHONE NUMBERS

Here are a smattering of useful phone numbers in no particular order. You can call for up to the minute **weather** (512/451-2424), current **time** (512/973-3555), and **Lost and Found** (512/974-5000). The *Statesman* has an **Information Hotline** (512/416-5700 or 800/862-8784) that provides pre-recorded information at each of the following extensions: **News** 2236, **Sports** 2083, **Fishing** 3474, **Today in History** 7177. For up-to-date information on the Bats of Congress Avenue Bridge, such as flight times, call the **Bat Hotline** (512/416-5700, ext. 3636).

Getting There

BY AIR

The main airport that services the Austin metropolitan area is **Austin-Bergstrom International Airport** (300 Presidential Blvd., 512/530-2242), located eight miles southeast of downtown. This converted Air Force base offers international connections that can get you to anywhere in the world.

Major passenger airlines include America West (800/235-9292), American Airlines (800/433-7300), Continental Airlines (800/525-0280), Delta (800/221-1212), Frontier Airlines (800/432-1359), Northwest (800/225-2525), Southwest (800/435-9792), and United (800/241-6522).

The airport terminal has a couple restaurants

including the famous barbecue of the Salt Lick, coffee shops, and, of course, the usual airport gift shops filled with irritating flying toys, paperbacks, coffee mugs, tourist T-shirts, and key chains. There's one shop that is worth making an attempt to check out if you aren't running to catch a plane, and that's the **Austin City Limits** store. And, true to Austin's love of live music, the airport also has live music. Because of this Austin's airport has landed on *USA Today*'s list of "10 great places to hang out during a layover."

The one big drawback to Austin-Bergstrom International Airport is that passengers often have a connecting flight, and this can eat up most of a travel day. There are only 52 destinations with nonstop service to and from Austin, and nearly all are domestic cities that are "lesser traveled." However, what ABIA is lacking in connections is made up for by convenient parking, which is close to the terminal and easily accessed, with no wait and no hassle. Airport parking is free under 30 minutes, $2 for 31–60 minutes, and each additional hour is $2. Day rate for the covered parking garage is $19 and long-term parking nearby runs $7 a day. Travelers heading to Austin-Bergstrom can call the airport for parking availability and other airport information 24 hours a day.

There are several ways to get from the airport to town. The most economical way is **SuperShuttle** (512/258-3826 or 800/258-3826), which costs about $13 to take one person to the downtown area. Taking a cab to downtown costs about $22–25, but this may go up with the high cost of gas.

BY BUS AND TRAIN

If you have a fear of flying, a low budget, or a fascination with the underbelly of America, there's always ground transportation to get you to and from Austin. The bus station is inconveniently located far north of downtown at 916 East Koenig Lane. The two bus lines available are **Greyhound** (512/458-4463 or 800/231-2222), which services just about anywhere in the contiguous United States, and **Kerrville Bus Company** (800/474-3352), which serves many of the smaller Texas towns, including many in the Hill Country. Capital Metro buses numbers 15 (Red River) or 7 (Duval) going south can get you from the bus station in North Austin to downtown. As for train access to Austin, **Amtrak** (512/476-5684 or 800/872-7245) has a station conveniently located right in the heart of downtown, near Lady Bird Lake at 250 North Lamar Bouvelard.

Getting Around

It's fairly easy to get around Austin, which makes for less time traveling and more time enjoying the city. Most everything is conveniently accessible either by foot, bus, cab, or bike. However if you plan on hiking some of the trails in and around Austin, visiting the Lady Bird Johnson Wildflower Center, or if you want to explore the Hill Country, you'll want to rent a car.

BY CAR

Getting around Austin by car is not necessary, but a car can provide the most freedom, and the best way to make the most of your time.

There are only a few major freeways in the metropolitan area, and only a few major streets that connect everything to downtown, which makes it easy to figure out your way around. One minor drawback to using a car is downtown parking, which can require patience and a good eye. Fee parking garages are available to eliminate parking woes.

All the usual rental car companies are represented on the ground floor at Austin-Bergstrom International Airport as well as around town. Car rental agencies include **Advantage Rent-A-Car** (800/777-5500), **Alamo Rent-A-Car** (800/462-5266), **Avis Car Rental** (800/331-

1212), **Budget** (800/527-0700), **Dollar Rent-A-Car** (800/800-3665), **Enterprise** (800/261-7331), **Hertz Rent-A-Car** (800/654-3131), **National Car Rental** (800/222-9058), and **Thrifty** (800/847-4389).

BY BUS

Austin's public transportation system, **Capital Metro** (512/474-1200, www.capmetro.org) is intuitive, easy to get the hang of, and inexpensive. Most individual rides are 50 cents (exact change only), but you can get the most for your money if you buy a $5 card that's good for 20 rides or a $10 pass that offers unlimited rides within a calendar month. Passes are available at any H.E.B. Grocery store and at the **Capital Metro Transit Store** (323 Congress Ave.). Capital Metro's very informative website is a great place to get schedule and route information. This information can also be found at most supermarkets in town and at the Capital Metro Transit Store.

TAXI

Taxi service is available 24 hours a day, seven days a week. Smoking and nonsmoking cabs are available thanks to city regulations. Hailing a cab downtown can take some time so I recommend calling one of the following cab companies to get faster service: **Yellow Cab Austin** (512/452-9999), **Austin Cab** (512/478-2222), and **Lone Star Cab** (512/836-4900).

BICYCLE

Austin is an ultra bicycle-friendly town, but it hasn't always been that way. Before Lance Armstrong became a celebrity athlete, cyclists were considered an inconvenience out on the motorways. Now Austin has miles of designated bicycle lanes and very respectful motorists. The City of Austin's Bicycle and Pedestrian Program (www.ci.austin.tx.us/bicycle) has a helpful map of suggested routes. It's also good to note that all Capital Metro buses are equipped with bike racks. However, if you plan to use a bicycle to get around be forewarned that Austin has a dreadful problem with bike thievery.

The premier place to rent a bicycle for the day is **Bicycle Sport Shop** (517 S. Lamar Blvd., 512/477-3472). They rent just about anything, including mountain bikes, road bikes, tandems, kids' bikes, and trailers. Prices range $28–35 for four hours and $18–50 for 24-hour rentals. Rates vary depending on the type and make of bike.

For quick and easy transportation around downtown, **Heart of Texas Pedicab** (512/930-8791), **Austin Bicycle Cabs** (512/930-8791), **Capital Pedicab** (512/448-2227, www.capital-pedicab.com) and **Metrocycle** (512/825-1276) can sweat it out for you. Service is available primarily around 6th Street, Congress Avenue, and the Warehouse District.

THE HILL COUNTRY

The central region of Texas, known as the Hill Country, is perhaps the most lush, beautiful, and culturally interesting area in the state. It's characterized by rolling hills, oak trees, dance halls, wildflowers, wineries, abandoned cars in fields, honky-tonks, dude ranches, state parks, and frontier towns scattered throughout the hills. Every square mile and every corner of the Hill Country is spilling over with history and legend. From clashes between the native Apache Indians and Spanish settlers, to the founding of towns by German settlers, to old ranches as large as 50 square miles, the history here is rich and compelling. Over the past 150 years the Hill Country has been home to many wildly interesting characters such as outlaws, pioneers, presidents, rodeo cowboys, and musicians.

Today the Hill Country is a place where people come to get away and have a unique Texas experience. In the Hill Country you can be a cowboy for a weekend at one of Bandera's many dude ranches; hike to the top of an enormous pink granite rock at Enchanted Rock State Natural Area; see an original Rembrandt hanging on a wall in a bank in Uvalde; go horseback riding in the Hill Country State Natural Area; catch a live performance at Gruene Hall, Texas's oldest dance hall; tube down the Guadalupe River in New Braunfels; and encounter the German heritage of Central Texas by visiting Fredericksburg. Although it's expected that visitors will romanticize the Hill Country as being a living Wild West, it's still 21st-century America. Some areas in the Hill Country look like scenes from the movie *Deliverance,* while some are reminiscent of

HIGHLIGHTS

◖ **Hamilton Pool Preserve:** This extraordinary place is the most beautiful spot in all of the Hill Country. The grotto-like pool is a great swimming hole as well as a gorgeous place to hike (page 128).

◖ **The Salt Lick:** This famed barbecue mecca offers a Civil War-era brisket recipe, unmatched hospitality, and a remote setting that is worth the drive (page 129).

◖ **Becker Vineyards:** Sipping a glass of wine on the porch at sunset at Becker Vineyards is one of the top Hill Country experiences. Be sure to walk away with at least one bottle of Texas's best wine (page 132).

◖ **Fredericksburg:** This historic town settled by German immigrants in the 1800s is a favorite Hill Country getaway. Bed-and-breakfasts, quaint shops, schnitzel, and polka music make this a Texas version of Bavaria that bewitches and bedazzles visitors (page 133).

◖ **Enchanted Rock State Natural Area:** Legend and mystery surround the natural wonder that is Enchanted Rock. The giant pink granite dome is the highlight of this park, affording spectacular panoramic views of the Hill Country (page 140).

◖ **Natural Bridge Caverns and Wildlife Ranch:** The Hill Country is beautiful on the outside and dark and mysterious on the inside—that is, in the many caves that have been discovered in the hills. See a great example at Natural Bridge Caverns (page 145).

◖ **Stonehenge II:** In a field in the middle of nowhere is a smaller version of the mysterious monument in Salisbury, England. This version wasn't created by aliens or Druids, but by a local attorney with a crazy idea (page 148).

◖ **Lost Maples State Natural Area:** This remote state park explodes with color in the fall when the bigtooth maple trees turn from green to bright red (page 153).

◖ **Tubing the Guadalupe:** In the summer you'll find thousands of folks sunning, relaxing, and drinking as they bob down the Guadalupe River through groves of bald cypress and over mild white-water rapids (page 161).

◖ **Gruene:** Although small and off the beaten path, the old town of Gruene is a place visitors to the Hill Country have to visit. Eat in the ruins of an old cotton gin at the Gristmill, hunt for antiques, and catch some of the Lone Star State's best live country music at famous Gruene Hall, Texas's oldest dance hall (page 162).

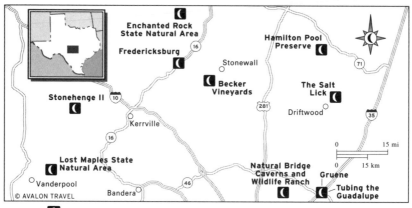

LOOK FOR ◖ TO FIND RECOMMENDED SIGHTS, ACTIVITIES, DINING, AND LODGING.

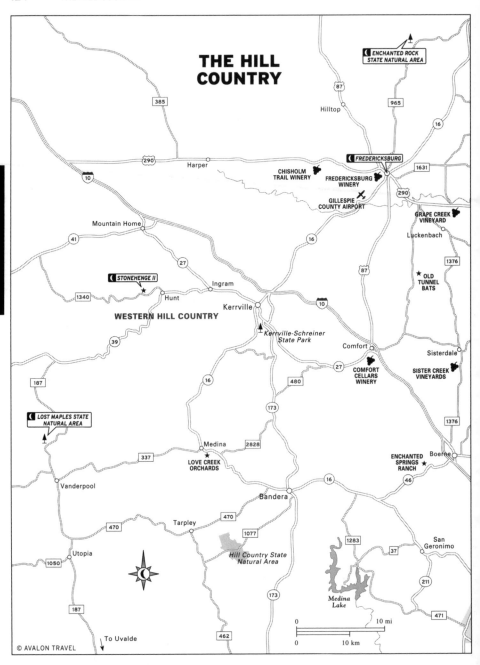

THE HILL COUNTRY

ENCHANTED ROCK STATE NATURAL AREA

87

965

Hilltop

385

16

290

Harper

CHISHOLM TRAIL WINERY

FREDERICKSBURG WINERY

FREDERICKSBURG

1631

10

GILLESPIE COUNTY AIRPORT

290

GRAPE CREEK VINEYARD

Mountain Home

Luckenbach

16

1376

41

27

16

OLD TUNNEL BATS

STONEHENGE II

87

Ingram

10

1340

Hunt

Kerrville

WESTERN HILL COUNTRY

Comfort

Sisterdale

39

Kerrville-Schreiner State Park

27

COMFORT CELLARS WINERY

SISTER CREEK VINEYARDS

187

16

480

1376

173

LOST MAPLES STATE NATURAL AREA

Medina

2828

337

LOVE CREEK ORCHARDS

ENCHANTED SPRINGS RANCH

Boerne

Vanderpool

16

46

Bandera

470

Tarpley

470

1077

San Geronimo

Utopia

1050

1283

37

Hill Country State Natural Area

211

187

Medina Lake

471

0   10 mi

0   10 km

173

462

To Uvalde

© AVALON TRAVEL

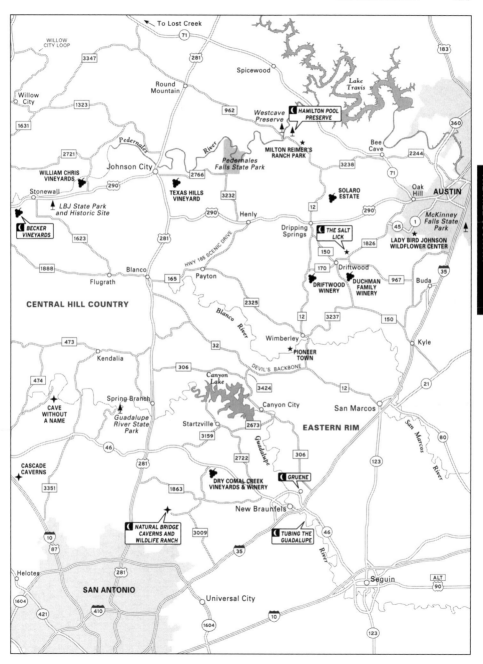

HILL COUNTRY FESTIVALS AND EVENTS

Thanks to the great weather that the Hill Country enjoys for most of the year, the calendar of events is chock-full of things to do. Here are the main events that you shouldn't miss.

APRIL

Folks in Wimberley love butterflies so much they have a day dedicated to these little larva that turn beautiful. On a weekend in April the **Emily Ann Theatre Butterfly Day** (1101 FM 2325, 512/847-6969, www.emilyann.org) becomes the focus of town. There's live music, plays and skits, and fun for kids and the whole family.

MAY

The biggest and longest-running festival that goes down in the Hill Country is the **Kerrville Folk Festival** (830/257-3600 or 800/435-8429, www.kerrvillefolkfestival.com). Starting the Thursday before Memorial Day, this 18-day folk implosion draws the biggest names in Americana, folk, bluegrass, acoustic rock, blues, and country. In addition to the live music, arts and crafts, fun for the kids, camping, and food and beverages are all within arms' reach. The festival takes place at Quiet Valley Ranch, nine miles south of Kerrville on Highway 16. Tickets vary by day, but generally run $30 in advance and $40 at the gate.

The small art town of Wimberley offers a peek into the studios of some of its artists during **Arts Fest** (Wimberley Visitors Center, 512/847-2201, www.wimberleyartleague.com). Wimberley Square is lined with booths and arts spaces visited by over 3,000 art lovers. Artists represent a number of media including oil painting, watercolor, mixed media, and sculpture. Most artists are locally, nationally and even internationally renowned.

JUNE

For a peach of a time the town of Stonewall has its annual **Peach JAMboree and Rodeo** (830/644-2735, www.stonewalltexas.com). At the height of peach season, locals get together for live music and dancing in honor of the fuzzy fruit.

SEPTEMBER

Celebrate Bandera (www.celebratebandera.com) is where to be on Labor Day weekend in the Hill Country. Every year the town of Bandera becomes a giant celebration that includes a real cattle drive, intertribal Native American Pow Wow, bull-riding competitions, concerts, parades, rodeos, and a Bloody Mary street party. Some events charge a fee and some are free. Check out their website for specific information.

Also on Labor Day weekend is the **Kerrville Wine and Music Festival** (830/257-3600 or 800/435-8429, www.kerrville-music.com). Songwriters and entertainers from all around the United States make their way to Kerrville for this three-day festival that includes wine-tasting, crafts, and camping. All this goes down at Quiet Valley Ranch, nine miles south of Kerrville on Highway 16. Tickets are $25 in advance and $30 at the gate.

Every year Fredericksburg hosts the **Renewable Energy Round-up** (512/326-3391, 877/3ROUNDUP or 877/376-8638,

Napa Valley. This intense combination is what makes this region so interesting.

PLANNING YOUR TIME

Because all the points of interest in the Hill Country are spread out, it's wise to plan your time before setting out on your journey. There are two ways people experience this region; the most common is by choosing a town and settling in for the weekend. This approach is great for a weekend getaway as it is low stress, low travel, and totally relaxing. The other approach, which is less common but becoming more and more popular, is road-tripping through the Hill Country. It can take up to seven days to fully explore the whole region as outlined in this chapter. However, a 3–4 day weekend can be sufficient for a road trip that includes major attractions.

www.theroundup.org). This green building fair features exhibits, demonstrations, and workshops all espousing the new products and technologies related to the field of renewable energy and green building. It's hard to determine whether this environmental awareness spills out from Austin's liberal hippie-ness, or whether it comes from Texas's long history of DIY independence from everything. Nevertheless, this event is essential for the green do-it-yourselfer. The roundup is held downtown at Market Square; tickets cost $10 for Friday and Sunday and $12 for Saturday.

OCTOBER

Festivals abound in the historic German settlement town of Fredericksburg, but the one that gets everyone's lederhosen in a bunch is **Oktoberfest** (830/997-4810, www.oktoberfestinfbg.com). Held every year during the first weekend in October, this three-day bratwurst, schnitzel, and German beer extravaganza draws big crowds. Two stages, two tents, great food, polka and waltz contests, smiles, and music with an oompah make this a great family weekend getaway. Oktoberfest takes place at Marktplatz in the center of downtown. Hours are 6 P.M.–midnight Friday, 10 A.M.–midnight Saturday, 10 A.M.–6 P.M. Sunday. Tickets cost $6 for single-day passes, $10 for two-day passes, and $15 for three-day passes.

At the end of the month there's the **Fredericksburg Food and Wine Fest** (830/997-8515, www.fbgfoodandwinefest.com), a celebration of Texas food and wine that includes live music, specialty booths, and lots of clinking of glasses. The festival is held at Marktplatz in downtown Fredericksburg and admission is $20.

NOVEMBER

For over 40 years Bandera has hosted the annual **Hunters BBQ and Outdoor Expo** (830/796-3280, www.banderahuntersbbq.com). Everyone gets all gussied up in camo and heads out to Mansfield Park Showbarn for barbecue and beer and hunter-gatherer fellowship. The expo includes interactive exhibits, demonstrations of the latest hunting equipment, wildlife exhibits, and a live auction.

The best fest in New Braunfels is **Wurstfest** (800/221-4369, www.wurstfest.com). This 10-day salute to sausage features accordion music, dancing, and, of course, bratwurst. The fest takes place at Landa Park and admission is $8.

The Saturday after Thanksgiving the historic downtown of Comfort is taken over by **Christmas in Comfort** (830/995-3131, 10 A.M.–9 P.M., free). Over 150 vendors sell arts, crafts, and homemade foods, all to the soundtrack of live music. A trolley brings shoppers to the various shops around the downtown area.

DECEMBER

For the whole month of December it's **Lights Spectacular** in Johnson City. The Blanco Country Courthouse at the center of Johnson City's downtown is bedecked with 100,000 Christmas lights. It's a remarkable show of BTUs and candlepower worthy of checking out. Local homes and businesses also get into the spirit.

All towns in the Hill Country are a 1–2 hour drive from Austin and/or San Antonio. The distance between towns is generally under 50 miles, some being as close as 30 miles, which is great because drive time doesn't eat up too much of the day. Out of the dozens of towns in the Hill Country there are only a few that will lure you in for a night or two; these are Fredericksburg, Bandera, Kerrville, Boerne, Gruene, New Braunfels, and Wimberly. For these towns plan on setting aside a full day for exploring, eating, and just meandering. All the little towns in between are good for some barbecue, roadside peaches, antiques, and maybe an hour or two of poking around.

ORIENTATION

Although there is no agreed-upon boundary that circumscribes the Hill Country, it can generally be defined as the incredibly vast area smack dab in the center of the state of Texas. The area of the Hill Country with towns and attractions that merit mention as travel destinations is best broken into the following regions: the **Central Hill Country,** which includes some of the more touristy spots, the **Western Hill Country,** which stretches as far as Vanderpool, and the **Eastern Rim,** also known as the Austin–San Antonio corridor, which travels along I-35 south of Austin en route to San Antonio.

Central Hill Country

The gateway to the Hill Country is the small town of Dripping Springs on Highway 290 heading west from Austin. This little backgammon-loving, slow-moving wide spot in the road is known to locals simply as Drippin'. Dripping Springs once was a country-bumpkin ranch town but it's quickly being swallowed by Austin. People are buying acreage, building mansions, and driving SUVs to and from the "big city." Once you pass through Dripping Springs into the Hill Country, all its grandeur rolls out like a red carpet before your very eyes.

HAMILTON POOL ROAD

Just north of Dripping Springs, and about 30 miles west of Austin, there's FM 3238, better known as Hamilton Pool Road. Out on this rural country thoroughfare there are three main attractions that are increasingly drawing outdoor lovers, with caves, waterfalls, rivers, swimming holes, and trails all within a matter of a few miles of each other. This off-the-beaten-path region of outdoor activities has been discovered and developed only in recent years. As this area's popularity grows I hope and pray it doesn't get overrun.

From Dripping Springs go north of Highway 12 and turn left on FM 3238 (Hamilton Pool Rd.). From Austin take Highway 290 west, then go north on Highway 71. When you come to FM 3238 (Hamilton Pool Rd.), turn left. Everything is about 10 miles up the road near the Pedernales River.

◖ Hamilton Pool Preserve

This preserve may be over 230 acres but the main attraction here is a swimming hole.

Whether you want to take a dip or not, Hamilton Pool (Hamilton Pool Rd., FM 3238, Dripping Springs, 512/264-2740, 9 A.M.–5:30 P.M. daily, $10 per vehicle, cash only) is a sight worth seeing. It's considered the most beautiful natural swimming hole in Texas because a majestic 45-foot waterfall spills into a deep, grotto-like pool that was formed when the dome of an underground river collapsed hundreds of years ago. In the hot summer months the preserve is usually filled to capacity. The parking lot can fit about 75 cars, and when all spaces are taken, cars are held up at the gate until a space opens. Drinking water or concessions are not available at the preserve, but there are toilets.

Thanks to a diligent parks and recreation department, the pool is carefully protected, and visitors are asked to be respectful of the environment. Swimming is allowed only when the water quality meets safe standards, so it's best to call for swimming information before trekking out to the preserve. The preserve also offers limited day use for picnicking, hiking, swimming, and nature study. Pets are not allowed, even on leashes. Hamilton Pool Preserve is located about 30 miles west of Austin.

Westcave Preserve

Just down the road from Hamilton Pool Preserve is Westcave Preserve (FM 3238, Hamilton Pool Rd., at RR 962, 830/825-3442), another natural spot that demonstrates the dramatic topography and geographical history of the Hill Country. At this well-preserved, often overlooked park, there's a cave, spectacular waterfalls, and an award-winning environmental

© JUSTIN MARLER

THE HILL COUNTRY

Hamilton Pool Preserve, God's temple in the Hill Country

learning center. The trail in the park can only be accessed with a guide. Canyon trail tours are offered Saturday and Sunday at 10 A.M., noon, 2 P.M., and 4 P.M. and cost $5 for adults, $2 for children under 12, and $15 for families. No pets are allowed on the grounds, even in cars. Toilets are available but there is no drinking water.

Milton Reimer's Ranch Park
In recent years Milton Reimer's Ranch Park (Hamilton Pool Rd., 512/264-1923, 7 A.M.–sunset, $10 per vehicle) has exploded on to the scene as a popular spot for outdoor recreation in the Hill Country. Reimer's was originally a privately owned ranch where people could pay a few bucks to do some fishing, camping, and rock climbing. Recently mountain bike trails have increased the list of activities. The ranch is on the banks of the beautiful Pedernales River, which makes for a great place to cool off on hot days. Getting to the ranch can be tricky. On Hamilton Pool Road there's a sign that says Milton Reimer's Fishing Ranch. Turn here and follow the rugged dirt road until you come to a gate. Go through the gate and stop at the house, where someone will come out to take your money. Then park and play.

◖ THE SALT LICK
Animals on the ranch congregate around what's called a salt lick, which is a big block of sodium sitting in a field. Humans in Central Texas have a place to congregate too, and it's called The Salt Lick (18300 FM 1826, Driftwood, 512/858-4959, www.saltlickbbq. com). If barbecue was a religion, its devout followers would make this age-old landmark their hallowed pilgrimage sight. This mecca for the golden calf of brisket is nearly 45 minutes outside of Austin in a wide spot in the road called Driftwood. The Salt Lick's award-winning barbecue is truly legendary, as their recipes have supposedly been handed down since the Civil War. With time-tested and time-honored beef brisket, sausage, smoked pork tenderloin, moist smoked turkey, potato salad, and beans on the menu, it's hard to find something even

Legendary barbecue is cooked up at the Salt Lick.

remotely close to this Texas tradition else-where. Besides having the best barbecue in the Austin vicinity, the Salt Lick is also known for its remarkably beautiful location. Situated on an old ranch in rolling hills of oak trees, the restaurant is housed in old buildings made of stone quarried from the ranch. The setting is almost European in feel.

One important thing to know before driving all the way out to the Salt Lick is that you need to bring cash—they don't have debit or credit card machines. Also, if you like beer with your beef, you must bring your own beverages, as the Salt Lick doesn't sell alcohol (however they do have non-alcoholic drinks available). It may seem weird to some to show up with your own beer, but that's the way it's done here.

From Austin take MoPac (Hwy. 1) south. MoPac will turn into Highway 45 and dead-ends at FM 1826. Turn left on FM 1826 and the Salt Lick is about seven miles down the road on the right. If for whatever inexcusable rea-son you can't make it out to the Salt Lick dur-ing your visit, you can have a mini–Salt Lick

experience at Austin-Bergstrom International Airport. However, nothing is as good as driv-ing out to the original great barbecue mecca in the Texas Hill Country.

PEDERNALES FALLS STATE PARK

Along a dramatic and twisting part of the Pedernales River is Pedernales Falls State Park (830/868-7304 or 800/792-1112, 8 A.M.– 10 P.M. daily, $5 per person). This rugged 5,000-acre park, featuring cypress-lined riv-erfront, waterfalls, and Hill Country nature trails and located just east of Johnson City, was acquired from private owners in 1970. The main attraction here is the falls, viewed from a scenic overlook at the north end of the park. Crashing down over a distance of about 3,000 feet onto limestone, the falls are most dramatic after a heavy downpour. Besides the waterfall, the park also offers hiking, mountain biking, fishing, bird-watching, horseback riding, and picnicking, and there are some wide spots in the river that are great swimming holes.

The park is located between Dripping Springs and Johnson City. From Austin take Highway 290 past Dripping Springs and go north on RR 3232. From Johnson City take RR 2766 east until you come to the entrance. Leisure camping with restrooms, showers, water, and electric is available as well as primi-tive camping, and both are available on a first-come, first-serve basis when the park isn't full. Reservations are suggested. If camping isn't your thing there's a great bed-and-breakfast just outside the park called **Room with a View** (103 Ridgeview Dr. just off RR 3232, 830/868-7668, $80–180). Here you can have a room with a view of rolling hills with the comforts of a bed-and-breakfast.

JOHNSON CITY

The podunk town of Johnson City (pop. 1,200) is far from being a city. Things haven't changed a whole lot in the past 50 years in these parts. A testament to this resistance to change is that the old limestone jail built back in 1894 is still in use. The town center, where

THE STORY OF LBJ

Most people agree that in the 20th century, the 1960s was the tipping point in American history for social and political change. The one man at the center of this tipping point was Lyndon Baines Johnson, a native son of the Hill Country. His story is one that both exemplifies and defines the character of this heartland of Texas. LBJ was born in 1908 in the small town of Stonewall, between Johnson City and Fredericksburg. When he was five years old his family moved to Johnson City where he graduated from high school. He received a college education in San Marcos at Southwest Texas State Teachers College, where he supported himself by working as a janitor.

A few years later he ended up in Washington, D.C., where he landed a job as the secretary to a U.S. Congressman. Here he learned the trade of politics and acquired a taste for public office. In 1934, while visiting his hometown of Johnson City, he met Claudia Alta Taylor (the future Lady Bird Johnson) and shortly thereafter they got married in San Antonio. The following year his political career exploded on the Washington scene when President Roosevelt appointed LBJ as the Texas Director of the National Youth Administration (NYA). In the subsequent years LBJ was elected to the 10th Congressional District, reelected to a full term in the 76th Congress, as well as succeeding Congresses. After the bombing of Pearl Harbor, Johnson became the first member of Congress to volunteer for active duty in the armed forces, and ended up receiving the Silver Star from General Douglas MacArthur for heroic efforts during an aerial combat mission over New Guinea. After World War II, LBJ was elected to the U.S. Senate.

In 1958 John F. Kennedy and LBJ ran for the presidency and in 1960 the candidates were elected president and vice president. The accomplishment LBJ is most noted for during his stint as vice president is jumpstarting the space program's goals of getting a man on the moon. Toward the end of his first vice presidential term, on a street in Dallas, Texas, President JFK was assassinated. Beneath a shroud of turmoil, tragedy, and mourning, high up on Air Force One, LBJ was sworn in to the office of the presi-

Historic buildings have been both preserved and replicated at LBJ's Ranch outside of Johnson City.

© JUSTIN MARLER

dency. LBJ's career in politics culminated in the highest office, in the lowest of circumstances. His presidency has been characterized as one of the most complex in history. He achieved many great things, such as furthering the U.S. space program, signing the Civil Rights Act of 1964, signing the Voting Rights Act, creating the Great Society program, and ushering in landmark legislation such as Medicare. It's also important to note that he was the first president to host a barbecue on the White House lawn. The more complex side to his term in office relates to his ushering in the Vietnam War, and the cultural upheaval that ensued. In 1969, LBJ's presidency ended. He chose not to run for another term, but instead he retired to his ranch outside Johnson City. He died only three years later.

LBJ is most characterized by his love of his Texas roots. The Hill Country, or as he called it, "a special corner of God's real estate," was where he hung his hat and left his heart. Today you can hear a virtual LBJ tell stories and jokes at the LBJ Library and Museum in Austin. You can also visit his ranch in the Hill Country, and his boyhood home in Johnson City.

© JUSTIN MARLER

the courthouse in Johnson City

the jail is located, is a relic from the past. It's laid out in the typical town square fashion with the historic limestone county courthouse at the center surrounded by old businesses, most of which are windswept and vacant.

So what's the reason for mentioning this little town? Johnson City was the boyhood home of President Lyndon B. Johnson (LBJ), which is a big deal to small-town Texas. Although Johnson City was originally named after an ancestor of his, LBJ has become its patron saint. Everything around these parts revolves around him and his memory in one way or another.

Sights and Activities

The main attraction in Johnson City is the **Lyndon B. Johnson Boyhood Home** (two blocks south of Hwy. 290, 9 A.M.–noon and 1 P.M.–5 P.M. daily, free) in the heart of downtown. LBJ lived in this old house from age 5 to 26, when he married. Today the house is furnished with items from LBJ's childhood such as photos and quilts made by relatives. Unfortunately it's hard to get into the house

due to funding and staff cuts. Nevertheless, the history buff may find the home interesting.

Between Johnson City and Fredericksburg is the land of LBJ known as **LBJ State Park and Historic Site** (Hwy. 290 near Stonewall, 830/644-2252, 8 A.M.–5 P.M. daily, free). This beautiful sprawling ranch belonged to LBJ and his wife, Ladybird, and was their special retreat from the world. Highlights of the park include the old house where LBJ was born, the house the president had built called the Texas White House where he met with heads of state, and the cemetery where he is buried. LBJ referred to his Hill Country ranch as a "special corner of God's real estate," and this hasn't changed. The visitors center has lots of great information about the life of LBJ and his ranch. You can also watch a 25-minute movie presentation that shows LBJ driving around the ranch explaining the history and telling stories about the area. Tours of the ranch are available by bus with a tour guide. The ranch is still owned by the family, and former First Lady Johnson still lives at the Texas White House.

During the winter holidays the beautiful old county courthouse downtown is draped with thousands of Christmas lights. People all around the Hill Country come to gaze at the dramatic display of holiday cheer that's called **Lights Spectacular.** The lights are on sunset to sunrise from the end of November to January.

The most popular local business in town is **Whittington's Jerky** (604 Hwy. 281/Hwy. 290, 877/868-5501). Founded in 1963, this favorite country jerky maker has a little store on the highway where you can find all sorts of Texas-style canned goods, country knickknacks, gifts, and of course, the jerky. It comes in several flavors, including original beef jerky, garlic beef jerky, teriyaki jerky, and turkey jerky, all smoke-dried the traditional way. The result is sticks of meat that are dry and tough to chew—perfect for gnawing during a road trip in the Hill Country.

◖ BECKER VINEYARDS

It should come as no surprise that one of the most beautiful settings in the Hill Country is

© JUSTIN MARLER

wine tasting at Becker Vineyards

at a winery. Visiting Becker Vineyards (464 Becker Farms Rd., 830/644-2681, www.becker-vineyards.com, 10 A.M.–5 P.M. Mon.–Thurs., 10 A.M.–6 P.M. Fri.–Sat., noon–6 P.M. Sun.) is like being transported to Napa Valley in Northern California. Honestly, you would never know you were in the heart of Texas. At Becker Vineyards the hills are golden and the fields are rife with grapes on the vine. The wine-tasting room and attached wine production area are housed in buildings made of limestone with expansive porches affording spectacular views. A quintessential Hill Country moment is had sitting on this porch with a glass of wine at sunset. The winery is located four miles west of Stonewall, off Highway 290 on Jenschke Lane.

◖ FREDERICKSBURG

The most popular getaway destination in Central Texas is Fredericksburg (pop. 9,700). This big town, one of the largest in the Hill Country, is spilling over with German charm, Wild West allure, and Texas hospitality. Main Street, which runs straight through town, is lined with old historic limestone buildings with wrought-iron balconies, historic storefronts, and German *biergartens,* all in a Wild West setting. In a few words, Fredericksburg is Roy Rogers in Bavaria. This German frontierism isn't just made up for tourism—it's the real deal. In the mid 1800s after Annexation, Europeans, most of whom were German, were the first white folks to settle this frontier region. These Euro-pioneers brought with them all their traditions, including schnitzel, oompah music, and beer. The vestiges of this German heritage haven't eroded over time, but on the contrary, have become what defines Fredericksburg.

In recent years Fredericksburg has become a major tourist attraction for Central Texas. The town is a small grid of old streets lined with old trees, creating neighborhoods with historic houses and bungalows. These neighborhoods are small-town America at its height, and remind one of the sentimental paintings of Thomas Kinkade. Main Street is lined with

TEXAS HILL COUNTRY WINE TRAIL

For thousands of years grapes have grown on the banks of rivers and streams all over Texas. The climate is so conducive to the vine that there are more grape species here than anywhere else on the planet. Of the 36 species of vines in the world, 15 are native to Texas. For some strange reason, when the Spanish arrived in the 1500s they never took advantage of these local varieties. They made the first wine on American soil in El Paso with a variety brought over from Europe. It wasn't until the 1800s that the grape potential of Texas was recognized. It all began when German immigrants in the Hill Country started fermenting the local grapes, as well as producing wine from grapes brought from the Old World.

By the late 1800s wine research and production in Texas was fully underway. At the same time in Europe the phylloxera epidemic was wreaking havoc on French grape crops, threatening the future of French wine production. A grape researcher by the name of Thomas V. Munson of Denison, Texas, discovered that American species were resistant to the insect and brought vines from Texas to France, essentially saving the French wine industry. Ironically, 40 years later the U.S. Congress was successful in killing the Texas wine industry when they created Prohibition.

In recent years the Texas Hill Country has rediscovered its viticulture roots. Recently Orbitz ranked the Texas Hill Country as the second fastest growing wine destination in the country. Wineries have been cropping up all throughout the state, 27 of which happen to be west of Austin in the beautiful Texas Hill Country. These wineries have joined forces to create what is called the **Texas Hill Country Wineries Trail** (866/621-9463, www.texas-winetrail.com). Here are a few of the best wineries in the Hill Country.

- **Becker Vineyards** (464 Becker Farms Rd., Stonewall, 830/644-2681, www.beckervineyards.com) Location: 4 miles west of Stonewall, off Highway 290 on Jenschke Lane

- **Chisholm Trail Winery** (2367 Usener Rd., Fredericksburg, 830/990-2675, www.chisholmtrailwinery.com) Location: 9 miles west of Fredericksburg on Highway 290 west, 2.4 miles south on Usener Road

- **Comfort Cellars Winery** (723 Front St., Comfort, 830/995-3274, www.comfortcellars.com) Location: I-10 exit 524, Highway 87 one mile then left on Highway 27

- **Driftwood Vineyards** (4001 Elder Hill Rd./CR 170, Driftwood, 512/692-6229, www.driftwoodvineyards.com) Location: Six miles south of Highway 290 on RR 12 between Dripping Springs and Wimberley

- **Duchman Family Winery** (13308 FM 150 W, Driftwood, 512/858-1470, www.duchmanfamilywinery.com) Location: Two miles south of Driftwood on FM 150

- **Dry Comal Creek Vineyards & Winery** (1741 Herbelin Rd., New Braunfels, 830/885-4121, www.drycomalcreek.com) Location: Six miles west of New Braunfels off Highway 46 west

- **Fredericksburg Winery** (247 West Main St., Fredericksburg, 830/990-8747, www.fbgwinery.com) Location: Downtown Fredericksburg

© JUSTIN MARLER

- **Grape Creek Vineyard** (97 Vineyard Ln., Stonewall, 830/644-2710, www.grapecreek. com) Location: Nine miles east of Fredericksburg on Highway 290, three miles west of Stonewall

- **Sister Creek Vineyards** (1142 Sisterdale Rd., Sisterdale, 830/324-6704, www.sister creekvineyards.com) Location: Twelve miles north of Boerne on FM 1376

- **Solaro Estate** (13111 Silver Creek Rd, Dripping Springs, 832/660-8642, www.solar estate.com) Location: North of Dripping Springs off Highway 12

- **Texas Hills Vineyard** (878 RR 2766, Johnson City, 830/868-2321, www.texas hillsvineyard.com) Location: One mile east of Johnson City on RR 2766

- **William Chris Vineyards** (10352 Highway 290, Hye, 830/998-7654, www.william chriswines.com) Location: Off FM 1320 between Johnson City and Fredericksburg

LUCKENBACH, TEXAS

Between Johnson City and Fredericksburg, just a few miles south of Highway 290, is the sleepy town of Luckenbach. Not much is happening here, but this dusty old town deserves some sort of a nod. After all, it was the subject matter for a hit song by Waylon Jennings and Willie Nelson called "Luckenbach, Texas." Ironically, the chaps who wrote the song were a couple songwriters from Nashville who had never been to the remote, out-of-the-way, three-building town. In fact Waylon had never been there either. So how did it merit mention in a country song? Maybe the songwriters threw a dart at a map of Texas?

shops and boutiques that peddle all sorts of stuff for the middle class, such as home furnishings and decor, Western wear, country kitsch, and frontier-themed souvenirs. There are also a few interesting museums and historic sights to meander through, antique stores in which to find treasures, and wine-tasting shops, as well as hundreds of bed-and-breakfasts to pamper you during your stay. Just north is Enchanted Rock State Natural Area, which adds to the town's draw. With a rich history, a lot to see and do, and quaint places to spend money, it's no surprise people keep coming back to Fredericksburg. The **Fredericksburg Convention and Visitors Bureau** (302 E. Austin St., 830/997-6523, www.fredericksburg-texas.com, 8:30 A.M.–5 P.M. Mon.–Fri., 9 A.M.–5 P.M. Sat., noon–4 P.M. Sun.) is your local source for information.

Sights and Activities

One of the first U.S. Army outposts in Texas was **Fort Martin Scott** (1606 E. Main St., 10 A.M.–5 P.M. Tues.–Sun., free), at the eastern end of Fredericksburg. There's not much here except for a few buildings in a field, but it does offer an interesting look at what a frontier Texas fort looked like before the Civil War.

Only one original building remains; the rest are re-creations. The fort was active 1848–1853; once it closed as a military outpost it was used by Texas Rangers and homesteaders and was the site of the county fair for a few years. The fort grounds are open to the public all the time.

The most off-the-beaten-path attraction in town—which happens to be my favorite—is **Gish's Old West Museum** (502 Milam St., 830/997-2794, by appointment only, free). Joe Gish, collector of Wild West memorabilia and artifacts, has opened his collection to the public. The museum is in an old cabin on his private property. The place is covered from floor to ceiling in sheriff's badges, old rifles, saddles, cowboy hats, chaps, and spurs. Gish also has memorabilia from the silent-movie cowboys, as well as a fascinating collection of old photos of weathered faces from the frontier days.

WWII buffs from all over come to Fredericksburg to visit the **The National Museum of the Pacific War** (340 E. Main St., 830/997-4379, www.nimitz-museum.org, 9 A.M.–5 P.M. daily, $12 general admission, $10 seniors and military, $6 students, under 6 free). The museum, dedicated exclusively to telling the story of the Pacific Theater battles of World War II, has over 1,000 artifacts from the Pacific War including Allied Japanese aircraft, tanks, and guns. The nine-acre complex also includes a shrine to WWII heroes in the **Admiral Nimitz Museum,** which is housed in the historic Nimitz Hotel. Also on the grounds is the recent installation of the **George Bush Gallery;** the **Japanese Garden of Peace;** the **Pacific Combat Zone,** complete with artillery and PT Boat; **Veterans Walk of Honor;** the **Plaza of the Presidents;** and the **Center for Pacific War Studies.**

The **Pioneer Museum** (325 W. Main St., 830/990-8441, 10 A.M.–5 P.M. Mon.–Sat., 1–5 P.M. Sun., $5), is a must-see when in Fredericksburg. This well put together complex of historic buildings furnished with artifacts offers a rare glimpse into the day-to-day life of the first pioneers of the Hill Country. The focal point of the complex is the historic home and store of the Kammlah family. All the other buildings were brought in for preservation. The museum and complex are run by a few elderly women in period clothes. They and their outfits add to the museum's charm by being stuffy and old-fashioned.

Accommodations

There are literally hundreds of bed-and-breakfasts, ranches, and guest cottages in and around Fredericksburg. A few clever people have created companies that help connect travelers to accommodations with an easy one-stop-shop approach. These reservation services have been so successful that it's hard to find lodgings without going through them. The thing that's good about these services is you can easily find just the right accommodation for your liking because the research is all done for you. The drawback is that the personal touch that bed-and-breakfasts are famous for can be lost in the process.

If you like the one-stop-shop approach try **Gastehaus Schmidt** (231 W. Main St., 830/997-5612 or 866/427-8374, www.fbglodging.com), **First Class Bed and Breakfast Reservation Service** (888/991-6749, www.fredericksburg-lodging.com), **Main Street B&B Service** (830/997-0153 or 888/559-8555, www.travelmainstreet.com) or **Absolute Charm,** (866/244-7897, www.absolutecharm.com). All these reservation services have access to hundreds of accommodations ranging from old farmhouses to historic limestone buildings and old Victorian homes. Perusing these websites is a great way to find the bed-and-breakfast that is right for you as they have photos, maps, reviews, and amenity information. Reservation-service accommodations generally start at $129 a night and can go as high as $300. Whether you plan to use a reservation service or find a bed-and-breakfast to your liking on your own, it's important to book far in advance.

One of the cheapest rooms in town is at the **Frederick Motel** (1308 E. Main St., 830/997-6050 or 800/996-6050, $40–129). The proprietors like to call themselves an "unconventional B&B" because they offer quality hospitality and a continental breakfast in the mornings. For a motel, the rooms are clean and well maintained, however they are small and just off Highway 290. Smoking and nonsmoking rooms are available.

A few blocks behind Main Street, in a quiet neighborhood, is **Magnolia House** (101 E. Hackberry, 830/997-0306 or 800/880-4374, www.magnolia-house.com, $115–165). This bed-and-breakfast is housed in a historic landmark that's a perfect example of a craftsman bungalow. The decor of the common rooms and the suites are country Victorian, and the breakfasts include American staples such as bacon, eggs, waffles, and coffee, all served on crystal. The backyard has a pleasant seating area under the trees and a small pond. There

THE HILL COUNTRY

SCENIC DRIVE: WILLOW CITY LOOP

All roads in the Hill Country are beautiful and scenic, but there are a few that are truly unbelievable. Willow City Loop is one of these. This 13-mile celestial drive takes the road-tripper through heavenly landscapes of wildflowers, wildlife, and terrain that seems too beautiful to be real. The road travels along a ridge for many miles, then drops down into what's called the Devil's Kitchen. This is a valley that has a large crater in the ground that was formed by a meteor. Although it's a rural country road, in the spring Willow City Loop can have a surprising number of bicycles, motorcycles, and cars, so don't think this is some unsung Shangri-la.

To get to Willow Loop from Fredericksburg, go north on Highway 16 for about 12 miles, then turn east on FR 1323. About three miles up the road at the small town of Willow City, look for the sign that marks the beginning of the Willow City Loop.

are five guest rooms in all, with the proprietors living in a cottage in the back.

One of Fredericksburg's earliest pioneer homes is now a place to stay. The **Loeffler-Weber Haus** (508 W. Main St., 866/427-8374, www.fbglodging.com, $100–120) may be shockingly rustic and pastoral, but it can be alluring. This Ma and Pa Kettle–style log cabin has been altered just enough to be comfortable for today's traveler. The kerosene lamps are mostly for looks but can be fired up if you want an 1800s experience.

Another place that specializes in rustic lodgings is **Barons Creekside** (316 Goehmann Ln., 830/990-4048, www.baronscreekside.com, $150–200). Just minutes from downtown Fredericksburg, this pastoral location features rolling hills with an assortment of little one-room cabins, and an old Victorian house. The cabins are built out of logs from an old tobacco-drying barn from Kentucky and windows and doors from a 250-year-old house from Switzerland. The accommodations are a perfect combination of rustic and luxury. Think log walls and whirlpool tub to the sounds of crickets while drinking a bottle of exceptional wine. Also, there is a trail that leads down to a creek and a natural pool, and the cantilevered lookout can't be left out.

The romantic place to stay in Fredericksburg is **Austin Street Retreat** (408 W. Austin St., 830/997-5612, www.austinstreetretreat.com, $135–175). This exotic and spectacular setting was originally a 19th-century family home made of Texas limestone. The home was meticulously converted into a lovely guesthouse with five private rooms, all under old pecan trees. Once you step off the street you feel like you're in a small village in Europe. Amenities can include fine linens, custom-designed bedding, whirlpool tubs, and private terraces.

For a private cottage just off Main Street, there's **Camp David** (708 W. Main St., 830/997-7797, www.campdavidbb.com, $99–149). The cottages are under old pecan trees; all are clean, well maintained, and have a great balance of charm and simplicity. For breakfast

© JUSTIN MARLER

Tuscany meets Bavaria at the Keidel Inn.

you don't have to get dressed and mingle with other guests; breakfast is served at your door.

One of the best privately owned and operated bed-and-breakfasts in downtown is **Keidel Inn** (403 E. Main St., 866/244-7897, www.absolutecharm.com, $140–240). This charming villa-style home has rooms with great views, creature comforts such as big fluffy beds, and an outdoor area with brick patio and a fountain. The historic home wasn't renovated to be a bed-and-breakfast, so most rooms share a bathroom with other guests. The best part about this inn is its location. Das Keidel is on Main Street, a block away from everything that's great about Fredericksburg.

Picture the last scene in Casablanca—the airstrip, the old plane, and the romance of it all. The **Hangar Hotel** (155 Airport Rd., 830/997-9990, www.hangarhotel.com, weekday $119, weekend $169) at the Gillespie County Airport brings this scene to life in a unique way. Although this hotel looks like it's in an old WWII airplane hangar, it's actually completely new, with modern amenities worthy

© JUSTIN MARLER

the Hangar Hotel

of a four-star hotel. All 50 rooms have a king-size bed, classy brass New York Library–style lamps, honeycomb-tile bathrooms, Egyptian cotton sheets, and army blankets, all in a South Pacific WWII motif. There's also a diner and a bar on the premises. All this, and you don't have to be a pilot, or even arrive by plane— you can drive up in a car. Rooms are quiet, which is surprising for being on an airstrip. For the quintessential Hangar Hotel experience, pilot John Barnett (210/844-4463) offers plane rides for $100 for 30 minutes. Gillespie County Airport is two miles south of Main Street off Highway 16.

For predictable, chain-style amenities, there's **La Quinta** (1465 E. Main St. on Hwy. 290, 830/990-2899, $105–179) and **Fredericksburg Inn and Suites** (201 S. Washington St., 830/997-0202 or 800/446-0202, www.fredericksburg-inn.com, $99–179).

Food

Fredericksburg is, for the most part, an affluent community, and because of this the dining scene is of a high quality. Thanks to city zoning and planning there isn't a slew of fast food restaurants on Main Street. With the German influence, many of the eateries have a Texas-meets-schnitzel menu, which makes eating here fun and unique. The place that personifies this combination is ◖ **Auslander Biergarten** (323 E. Main St., 830/997-7714, 11 A.M.–9 P.M. daily except Wed., $13). Although this eatery is leaning heavily towards the touristy crowd, locals also claim Auslander for themselves. The menu offers the best of the "wursts," such as knackwurst, pepperwurst, and the popular bratwurst. You can also get local favorite chicken-fried steak and other chicken and fish dishes. Outdoor and semioutdoor seating is nice on a spring evening. Although the restaurant closes after the dinner crowd leaves, the bar is open until midnight.

For a gourmet take on Tex-Mex and southwestern there's **Bejas Grill and Cantina** (209 E. Main St., 830/997-5226, 11 A.M.–8 P.M. Mon.–Thurs., 11 A.M.–9 P.M. Fri.–Sat., 10 A.M.–3 P.M. Sun., $15). There's nothing German and touristy on the menu, just upscale versions of Texas staples such as pan-fried trout, chipotle barbecue quail, enchiladas, and margaritas.

The place on Main Street for authentic German cuisine and atmosphere is **Der Lindenbaum** (312 E. Main St., 830/997-9126, 11 A.M.–10 P.M. daily, $13). Owned and operated by a feisty German woman who is a globally trained chef, Der Lindenbaum produces high-quality soups, salads, schnitzels, and upscale meat dishes. No reservations needed as seating is on a first-come, first-serve basis.

Considered by many to be the best brewpub in Texas, **Fredericksburg Brewing Company** (245 E. Main St., 830/997-1646, 11:30 A.M.–9 P.M. Mon.–Thurs., 11:30 A.M.–10 P.M. Fri.–Sat., 11:30 A.M.–7 P.M. Sun., $11) proudly serves fine microbrews and German and American foods. The founder researched breweries in Europe and eventually decided to pattern this establishment after the Bavarian *gasthhausbrauerei,* which incidentally means bed and brew. The end result? Fredericksburg

THE HILL COUNTRY

Brewing Company has beer vats in the restaurant and guestrooms upstairs.

Many fine dining establishments come and go in Fredericksburg, but one that endures is **Navajo Grill** (803 E. Main St., 830/990-8289, 5:30–9 P.M. daily, $15). This local favorite is a safe bet for a fine dining experience free of the German theme. The seasonal menu includes steak, pork chops, and crab cakes. Since it's casual-elegant you may want to primp or dapper up.

The old █ **Fredericksburg Bakery** (141 E. Main St., 830/997-3254, 8 A.M.–5:30 P.M. Mon.–Fri., 8 A.M.–7 P.M. Sat.–Sun.) has been the place to get baked goods and a cup of coffee for over a century. Housed in a historic building, this little pastry shop is the oldest continuously operated business in town. Along with the usual croissants, you can also get ice cream, locally made fudge, a sandwich, and cooking-related gifts.

Java Ranch (114 E. Main St., 830/990-4517, 7 A.M.–5 P.M. Mon.–Sat., 8 A.M.–5 P.M. Sun.) is the local disseminator of Starbucks coffee. Besides having great coffee, this is the cheapest breakfast in town. Weather you're thirsty or not you have to poke your head in the door and check out the massive mural. Local folks modeled for this excellent work of art, including the local donkey.

If you don't want to make a big deal about lunch and just want a burger, there's **Wheeler's Restaurant** (204 E. Main St., 830/990-8180, 11 A.M.–3 P.M. daily, $8).

Shopping

Although Fredericksburg has museums and historic sights, the reason most people come here is to stroll up and down Main Street and to meander through the many shops and boutiques. Guys who don't like shopping, don't panic! Don't think you'll be dragged through this street all day with nothing to do, because many of the shops have such a thick Wild West theme that your attention will surely be caught. And if you don't want to do the shopping thing at all, go hang out at a *biergarten.*

The best place to get an eatable souvenir is **Rustlin' Rob's** (121 E. Main St.,

830/990-4750, 10 A.M.–5:30 P.M. Mon.–Fri., 10 A.M.–6 P.M. Sat.). This little old-style general store is chock-full of homemade, regionally made, and locally produced canned and dried goods.

The most interesting clothing store for both men and women is **Parts Unknown** (146 E. Main St., 830/997-2055, 10 A.M.–6 P.M. Mon.–Thurs., 10 A.M.–7 P.M. Fri.–Sat., noon–6 P.M. Sun.). Here you'll find fashions fit for upscale Texans such as country western, rockabilly, Patsy Cline–style cowgirl boots, men's bowling shirts, and sequins for the ladies and the men.

The local art gallery that represents many Fredericksburg artists is **Fredericksburg Art Gallery** (314 E. Main St., 830/990-2707, 10 A.M.–5:30 P.M. Mon.–Sat.). Original paintings and works of art are sold for reasonable prices. Although these artists probably won't become world renowned, the pieces here definitely capture the spirit of the Hill Country.

Amish Market (410 W. Main St., 830/990-2977, 10 A.M.–5 P.M. Sun.–Fri.) is an interesting place to pop your head in. This is the local outlet for handmade items from folks in the Amish and Mennonite communities. Things you'll find for sale here are Amish furniture, chests, curios, and arts and crafts. Everything here is made with care and craftsmanship.

If you didn't take the time to visit any of the local wineries, you can taste products from them all at **Texas Vineyards and Beyond** (329 1/2 E. Main St., 830/990-9199, 11 A.M.–7 P.M. Mon.–Fri., 11 A.M.–8 P.M. Sat., noon–6 P.M. Sun., closed Wed.).

█ ENCHANTED ROCK STATE NATURAL AREA

Just north of Fredericksburg is an amazing park called Enchanted Rock State Natural Area (16710 RM 965, 830/685-3636, 8 A.M.–10 P.M. daily, $6). Once you drive around the bend and get your first glimpse of the massive outcropping of pink granite, I guarantee you will be amazed. A popular weekend expedition for locals is to walk up the face of the enormous dome to the top, which offers incredible panoramic views of the Hill Country. The rock is the size of a city

ATTACK AT ENCHANTED ROCK

The granite dome of Enchanted Rock has been witness to some of the earliest Wild West showdowns in Texas. In 1841, Texas Ranger Captain Jack Hays was exploring the region with a company of Rangers. They were looking for members of the Comanche tribe who had recently raided San Antonio. Hays decided to climb Enchanted Rock in order to get a better view of the surrounding countryside. He became separated from his men and while high up on the mountain was attacked by a large band of the Comanche. In ordinary circumstances, this would have been a fatal error on the part of Captain Hays. On this day, however, he was armed with a brand new weapon invented by Samuel Colt. Jack Hays carried a pair of five-shot Patterson Colt revolvers. These pistols were the most modern and innovative handguns yet created.

The tactics of the Comanche were simple. They would rush a lone defender, causing that person to fire his single-shot weapon. Following this, the individual was at the mercy of the Indians. The Comanche charged Jack Hays, he fired his single-shot rifle, and they came at him with a vengeance. However, he used his Patterson Colts to great effect, and the stunned attackers fled in terror. They had never faced multishot weapons before. Ever after Hays was known as "Devil Jack." Having proven themselves in battle, Samuel Colt's revolvers became increasingly popular, and Colt subse-

Enchanted Rock

© JUSTIN MARLER

quently became one of the most successful gun manufacturers in the country. To this day, the scenic beauty and vivid history of Enchanted Rock inspires all those who visit the location.

block, and looks more like it should be set in Australia, or Utah—anywhere but Texas.

Legend has it that the area was considered "enchanted" by the Tonkawa who believed a ghost lived in the rock. The Tonkawa heard weird creaking and groaning at the site, which they attributed to spirits. Today's geologists say these sounds come from the rock contracting and expanding due to hot and cold climate changes. Another story is that a conquistador captured by the Tonkawa escaped by getting lost in the rock area. This gave rise to an Indian legend of a pale man who was swallowed by the rock and reborn as one of their own.

Activities at the park include hiking, camping, picnicking, bird-watching, and rock climbing. Climbers love this spot because it's great for traditional climbing as well as crack climbing. The parking lot fills up early on weekends, and the park often reaches capacity and can be closed because of this.

COMFORT

Like most Hill Country towns, Comfort (pop. 1,500) was founded in the 1850s by German immigrants who left New Braunfels to settle more remote parts of the Hill Country. The name came about just as you might imagine—the location was a comfortable place to settle. The German word for comfort is Gemütlichkeit. They found this to be a little bewildering to non-Germans so they settled on the English translation. This group of settlers was different from other German pioneers in that they were anti-slavery, and they weren't particularly religious. It took them over 40 years to build their first church, unlike other Hill Country towns that erected lots of churches quickly.

Over the years Comfort hasn't changed much. It's a small town with almost no tourism infrastructure and no attractions—just a collection of historic buildings and a few shops, one of which is the oldest general store in Texas. In a sense the town is the attraction. For more information contact the **Comfort Chamber of Commerce and Visitors Center** (630 Hwy. 27, 830/995-3131, www.comfort-texas.com).

Sights and Activities

Comfort's downtown **business district** is considered to be the most intact and original business district in Texas. Taking a stroll around town is one of the top activities here. All the old buildings are appealing to the eye and perk the imagination. Some have historical information inscribed in a cornerstone, or have a name and date in relief somewhere on the exterior. Current business owners often know the history of the buildings they occupy, while other buildings speak for themselves, such as the old post office.

The only monument to Union soldiers south of the Mason–Dixon line is in Comfort. The **Truer der Union Monument,** a simple obelisk erected in 1865, honors a group of German men slain by Confederate soldiers. The daring freethinkers refused to sign a Confederate oath of allegiance, and fled to Mexico to escape. On their way south, they were discovered by Confederate soldiers. Most were executed, while a few escaped and later returned to tell the tale. But all were "true to the Union."

The oldest bowling alley in Texas is at **Phil's Firehouse** (601 Water St., 830/995-2654, www.philsfirehouse.com). There are only four lanes and the bowling pins are all set by hand just like the old days. Besides bowling, Phil's also has food and live music. Bowling is 4–8 P.M. Friday and Saturday, $3.50 per person per hour.

Accommodations

An easy way to find bed-and-breakfast accommodations in Comfort is by going through **Meyer Bed and Breakfast** (845 High St., 888/995-6100, www.meyerbedandbreakfast. com, $99–160). Meyer has several suites in unique historic buildings on beautiful Cypress Creek.

The historic building known as the Ingenhuett-Faust Hotel is home to an excellent bed-and-breakfast, **The Comfort Common** (717 High St., 830/995-3030, www.comfort-common.com, $80–125). Buildings in the complex include log cabins, Victorian cottages, and old farm buildings, as well as some antique shops.

Food

World-class restaurants aren't to be found in Comfort, but the following spots will satisfy hunger. A popular lunch spot is **Hen House Cafe** (5B Hwy. 87 N., 830/995-5793, 11 A.M.–2:30 P.M. Mon.–Sat., 5 P.M.–9 P.M. Fri.–Sat., $7). Here you can get sandwiches, hamburgers, and enchiladas. A diverse menu that includes German and Cajun is to be found at **Guenther's Creekside Grill** (220 Hwy. 473 at 6th St., 830/995-5370, 11 A.M.–2 P.M. and 5 P.M.–9 P.M. Tues.–Sat., $8).

OLD TUNNEL BATS

Just east of Comfort, inside an abandoned railroad tunnel called Old Tunnel is a massive colony of Mexican free-tailed bats. The site has been preserved and is now called the Old Tunnel Wildlife Management Area (866/978-2287). Every evening in the summer months the bat colony flutters off in search of bugs to eat. A few viewing areas have been designated by the park service and on peak days someone will step out and give a presentation on the phenomenon. Another spot to view the bats is **Alamo Spring Café** (107 Alamo Rd.,

830/990-8004, 10 A.M.–10 P.M. daily, $8). Bat viewing is nightly May–October, but the Old Tunnel is open year-round from sunrise to sunset. It's located eight miles east of Comfort off FM 473 on Old No. 9 Highway.

BOERNE

The little bucolic town of Boerne (pop. 6,100), just 30 miles north of San Antonio, is one of the Hill Country's bastions of German heritage. Boerne (correctly pronounced BUR-nee) was originally a village called Tusculum, which was overrun in the mid 1800s by German pioneers who settled here, built a town, and named it after a German writer named Ludwig Börne. Today the attractive downtown features many old limestone buildings built in the 1800s, narrow streets, bridges, and old towering trees. On Main Street, which is also known by its German name of Hauptstrasse, there are hundreds of little shops, boutiques, art galleries, and antique stores that draw tourists year-round.

Although Hauptstrasse is a delight to take in, the most beautiful feature of town is Cibolo Creek, which flows right through the heart of town. This creek—known to locals as the river—is home to ducks, geese, and other wildlife, making the setting almost too charming. For more information stop by the **Boerne Convention and Visitors Bureau** (1407 S. Main St., 888/842-8080, www.visitboerne.org, 9 A.M.–5 P.M. Mon.–Fri., 10 A.M.–2 P.M. Sat.).

Sights and Activities

No one comes to Boerne for major attractions, grand museums, and big entertainment. People come here to stay in a bed-and-breakfast, walk through the shops, and visit the most beautiful attraction in Central Texas—nature.

History and majesty are to be found in the caves at **Cascade Caverns** (226 Cascade Caverns Rd., 830/755-8080, www.cascadecaverns.com, 10 A.M.–5 P.M. daily, $11 for adults, $7 for children 11 and under). These living caves have lots of stories to tell visitors. For example, the first cave was the secret hideout for a German recluse running from the law at the turn of the 20th century. Going back further in time, this same cave was a place for Native American ceremonies. Finally, going back to prehistoric times, the remains of a mastodon were found in the cave; its bones are still in the cave. The cave tour lasts about an hour and ends with a 100-foot inner-cave waterfall. Cascade Caverns is located south of Boerne just off Highway 10.

Another cave in the area is the **Cave Without a Name** (325 Kreutzberg Rd., 830/537-4212, www.cavewithoutaname.com, summer 9 A.M.–6 P.M. daily, winter 10 A.M.–5 P.M. daily, $12 for adults, $6 for children 12 and under). This spectacular underworld was originally discovered in the 1930s. Before it was opened to the public a contest was held to name the cave. Legend has it that a little boy said the cave is too beautiful to name. Thus the cave got its name, or didn't, depending on how you want to look at it. Inside these immense vaulted rooms are intriguing rock formations, stalagmites, stalactites, and delicate soda straws. The cave is located northeast of Boerne on Kreutzberg Road, just off RR 474.

The most intriguing thing in Boerne is the **Boerne Village Band.** This outfit is the oldest continuously active German band in the country, and the second oldest in the world. Established in 1860, this is one of the best obscure, historic traditions in the country. You can see the band perform for what's called **Abendkonzerte** every other Tuesday night in June and July at the Boerne Main Plaza. If you're in town, you have to see this. But don't expect 150-year-old folks on the tuba—the members have changed over the years.

Have you ever dreamed of being Roy Rogers or Dale Evans for a day? **Enchanted Springs Ranch** (242 Hwy. 46 W., 800/640-5917, www.enchantedspringsranch.com, 10 A.M.–5 P.M. Wed.–Sun. June–Aug. and 10 A.M.–5 P.M. Sat.–Sun Sep–May, $12 adults, $6 for children 12 and under) has put together an incredible world devoted entirely to everything everyone loves about the Wild West. In a breathtaking setting in the Hill Country, an entire mock pioneer town was built where guests can see gunfights, ropers, roaming animals, and go on hayrides. All staff are in costume and playing the part, and as you walk around you'll find yourself playing the part too.

Accommodations

The most celebrated historic place to stay in the area is **(Ye Kendall Inn** (128 W. Blanco, 800/364-2138, www.yekendallinn.com, $119–249). In 1859 this grand limestone building rented rooms out to stagecoach travelers seeking upscale comfort in the rustic Hill Country. Today the tradition is carried on by offering 30 rooms filled with antiques and decor that harkens back to the pioneer days. There's also a bar and a restaurant on the premises.

A cheap but charming place to stay is the **Boerne Vistro Inn** (911 S. Main St., 830/249-9563, www.boernevistro.com, $70). Housed in one of Boerne's historic landmark buildings that was originally an old English Sunday House, this is a few notches above a roadside motel. There's a shaded outdoor courtyard area with old live oak trees, and porches outside rooms. All rooms are decorated with authentic Texana furniture. There's also a restaurant on-site.

The best way to find a bed-and-breakfast in Boerne is by going through **Boerne Reservations** (132 S. Main St., 866/336-3809, www.boernereservations.com, 9 A.M.–10 P.M. daily). This reservation service books rooms and cottages in and around town, and can easily match a lodging with a guest. Their website has accommodation information, photos, rates, and amenities all in one place, which makes it easy to find the lodging that best suits your needs. The service is at no extra charge to guests.

For chain hotel accommodations there's **Best Western Texas Country Inn** (35150 Hwy. 10 W., 830/249-9791, $93–127).

Food

The local favorite spot to take visitors is **Po Po Restaurant** (829 FM 289, 830/537-4194, 11 A.M.–9 P.M. daily, $10). The world's largest plate collection in a restaurant covers the walls. American standards are served on the plates.

A popular lunch spot at the center of Boerne, near antique shops and boutiques, is **Peach Tree Kountry Kitchen** (448 S. Main St., 830/249-8583, 11 A.M.–2 P.M. daily, $8). Cajun shrimp gumbo, Texas chili, an assortment of salads, and sandwiches are what's served here. People come here to meet up, socialize, get a late start to a day downtown, and to eat home cooking.

Across from Cibolo Creek is the **(Dodging Duck Brew Haus** (402 River Rd., 830/248-3825, 11 A.M.–9 P.M. Sun.–Thurs., 11 A.M.–10 P.M. Fri.–Sat., $11). Standard American fare such as burgers, beef tenderloin, and salmon are on offer here. They also brew their own beers, which are quite good. Outdoor seating across from the creek makes this a great place to relax any time of day.

The local favorite breakfast joint is **Bear Moon Bakery** (401 S. Main St., 830/816-2327, 6 A.M.–5 P.M. Tues.–Sat., 8 A.M.–4 P.M. Sun., $7). Besides cooking up eggs, pancakes, and waffles, Bear Moon also has the best baked goods in town.

Boerne fine dining happens at **The Creek Restaurant** (119 Staffel, 830/816-2005, 11 A.M.–3 P.M. Tues.–Sun., 5–9 P.M. Tues.–Sat., $12 lunch, $28 dinner). The restaurant is housed in an old bungalow just up the banks from the Cibolo Creek. Taking charm to the extreme, they've also added a water mill, pond, and outdoor decks, all smothered with southern charm that resembles Georgia more than Texas. The food is upscale but affordable, with a menu that has items such as mushroom fondue, crab cakes, and schnitzel.

Shopping

Boerne is a main-street town lined with wine-tasting rooms, trendy boutiques, antique shops, and art galleries, all housed in old historic buildings made of limestone or wood. Walking up and down these sidewalks is an excellent way to not spend your time wisely, which is what this experience is all about. Most shops are open between 10 A.M. and 6 P.M. daily. A shop that all must visit is **Carousel Antiques and Pickles** (118 S. Main St., 877/249-9306, 10 A.M.–5 P.M. Mon.–Sat., noon–4 P.M. Sun.).

The great and unique combination of pickles and antiques is surprisingly brilliant. Other shops worth checking out are **Landmark Antiques** (404 S. Main St., 830/816-8100, 10 A.M.–5 P.M. daily), the Texana crafts and stuff store called **Calamity Jane's Trading Co.** (322 S. Main St., 830/249-0081, 10 A.M.–5 P.M. Tues.–Sat., noon–5 P.M. Sun.), **The Green Bull Jewelry Store** (325 S. Main St., 830/249-7393, 10 A.M.–5 P.M. Tues.–Sat.), and the **Pewter Store** (463 S. Main St., 830/249-2765. 10 A.M.–5 P.M. Tues.–Thurs., 10 A.M.–5:30 P.M. Fri.–Sat., 11 A.M.–5 P.M. Sun.).

GUADALUPE RIVER STATE PARK

A magical place for outdoor recreation of all kind is Guadalupe River State Park (3350 Park Road 31, near Spring Branch, 830/438-2656, 8 A.M.–10 P.M. daily, $7 pp). This 2,000-acre park has miles of river frontage property in a spectacular setting, not too far from civilization (San Antonio). The thing that makes this place so magical is the Guadalupe River, which is lined with bald cypress trees and filled with wildlife. Visitors to the park enjoy a wide variety of outdoor activities including canoeing, swimming, fishing, tubing, hiking, and camping. The park recently opened a five-mile trail for horseback riding and mountain biking. Admission includes a two-hour guided tour through Honey Creek State Natural Area, where visitors learn about local plant life, geology, and wildlife. The tour is usually given Saturday at 9 A.M.; call to confirm. The park is located off Park Road 31 just off Highway 46, eight miles from Highway 281.

◖ NATURAL BRIDGE CAVERNS AND WILDLIFE RANCH

If you've ever wanted to explore the belly of the earth in a safe and easy way Natural Bridge Caverns (26495 Natural Bridge Caverns Rd., 210/651-6101, www.naturalbridgecaverns.com, 9 A.M.–7 P.M. in summer, closes at 4 P.M. the rest of the year, $15–25) has the experience all figured out. They offer three tours that vary

inside the caves at Natural Bridge Caverns and Wildlife Ranch

depending on your interest and lack of claustrophobia. The most popular is the North Cavern Tour, which is a 75-minute excursion that takes you underground for a half-mile exploration of massive caverns. The second is the Jaremy Room Tour, which is a short-and-sweet trip to a 120-foot deep chamber—perfect for the whole family. Finally there's the Adventure Tour, where the brave are outfitted with caving gear, lowered into the entry room by rope, then proceed on a mile-long journey. All the caves are awe inspiring, from the stalagmites, to the stalactites, to the constant temperature of 70°.

Next door to Natural Bridge Caverns is Natural Bridge Wildlife Ranch (26515 Natural Bridge Caverns Rd., 830/438-7400, www.wildliferanchtexas.com, 9 A.M.–5 P.M. daily, $17 for adults, $7 for children 11 and under). Kids love to take the drive through this Texas-style African safari and see giraffes, rhinos, zebras, and many other exotic animals.

Western Hill Country

Although all of the Hill Country shares the age-old brand of the Wild West, the western Hill Country is particularly wild and western. The farther west you travel, the more rural the scenery gets, and the more down-home the folks get. When exploring this region, expect to see things out of the ordinary, such as a replica of Stonehenge, folk music jamborees, and dude ranches with real cowboys.

KERRVILLE

All the hard work and the dreams of the western pioneers are fulfilled in the small main-street town of Kerrville (pop. 20,400), on the banks of the Guadalupe River. Although Kerrville wasn't founded by French settler Captain Charles Schreiner, he has become the iconic figure that everyone remembers. In the 1850s, after serving as a Texas Ranger at fifteen, Charles ended up in Kerrville and quickly became a successful businessman. At the peak of his career he found himself in banking, ranching, and promoting the value of mohair, the product of angora goats, and his empire stretched over 600,000 acres. Through his wealth many of the town's historic buildings were erected, and eventually Kerrville established itself as a viable mark on the map of Texas.

Today Kerrville is considered by many to be the capital of the Hill Country. The town of Kerrville is a must-visit hamlet that promotes leisure, great music, and lots of outdoor activities. The recently revitalized downtown retains old-world charm, but offers modern comfort and style. It's easy to get sucked in to the boutiques, galleries, shops, and cafés, which makes Kerrville a tourist trap in the truest sense of the word. But getting trapped here is exactly what you want. The town is sleepy and quiet until one of the many festivals held here injects hustle and bustle into the streets.

Kerrville is situated on the banks of the Guadalupe River, at the quiet edge of the Hill

SCENIC DRIVE: ROUTE 16 BETWEEN KERRVILLE AND MEDINA

The windy stretch of road between Kerrville and Medina is especially fantastic. At the start you may think, "what's the big deal." But keep on driving because at a certain point you will feel like you drove straight out of small town Texas and right into a Dr. Seuss book. This magical country road takes you through hill and dale, and through mini-gorges that are absolutely gorgeous. The hills are unusually bumpy and pointy, and the road is squirrelly to the point of nausea.

Country just 104 miles from Austin and 65 miles from San Antonio. Because of the town's location, it's considered one of the healthiest places to live in the United States with its clean air, unpolluted environment, and a great climate. Kerrville is located just off Highway 10, south on Highway 16. From Austin you would travel west on Highway 290 and at Fredericksburg take Highway 16 South. Once there, the **Kerrville Convention and Visitors Bureau** (2108 Sidney Baker St., 830/792-3535 or 800/221-7958, www.kerrvilletexascvb.com, 8:30 A.M.–5 P.M. Mon.–Fri., 9 A.M.–3 P.M. Sat., 10 A.M.–3 P.M. Sun.) is a great place to start, as they offer copious amounts of information about the town and surrounding area, including easy-to-use maps, a great brochure on historic buildings of Kerrville, and a guide (with checklist) about local birds.

Sights and Activities

What better place to house the **Hill Country Museum** (226 Earl Garrett St., 830/896-8633, 10 A.M.–4:30 P.M. Mon.–Sat., $5) than the historic mansion of one of the region's earliest pioneers, Captain Charles Schreiner? The mansion—a museum piece itself—offers a glimpse into the life of the wealthier early settlers. Marvel at the elegance of the fiesta gowns worn by the ladies of Hill Country high society, the bronze fountain imported from France, the Texas primitive art, Civil War memorabilia, and bullet molds used to make bullets by hand. People with money were able to pull off a highbrow way of life even though they were in a rugged frontier, thanks to arduous chores performed by laborers. The piano in the formal parlor was brought to Kerrville by covered wagon in the late 1800s.

The talent of local artists is showcased at **Kerr Arts and Culture Center** (228 Earl Garrett St., 830/895-2911, 10 A.M.–4 P.M. Tues.–Sat., 1–4 P.M. Sun., free). Housed in the recently renovated historic post office building, the slick gallery space displays high-quality works including pottery, paintings, quilting, woodwork, and jewelry.

The headquarters of famed jeweler **James**

Avery (145 Avery Road N., on the north side of Hwy. 10 off Harper Rd., 830/895-1122, 9 A.M.–6 P.M. Mon.–Sat., free) is in Kerrville. Whether you're a jewelry buff or not, Mr. Avery's designs are sure to impress. Started in a two-car garage in 1954, this little homespun shop has grown into a national mail order business. Designs include everything from bracelets, to earrings, to crosses, all bearing the unique style of the artist. Here you can visit his shop and purchase jewelry, but the most interesting thing here is the visitors center where guests can watch artisans at work.

This riverside town's best natural feature lays just to the south at **Kerrville-Schreiner State Park** (830/257-5392). At the upper edge of the park the Guadalupe River winds its way through, creating a lush and rugged park filled with rolling hills of live oaks. Camping, fishing, hiking, swimming, canoeing, picnicking, tubing, and wildlife-watching are what people come here for. The hiking is easy, as most of the trails don't have much of an incline and are clearly marked. Wildlife you are bound to encounter here are white-tailed deer, wild turkeys, rabbits, armadillos, and rare birds. Ornithologists should note that the Texas Hill Country is one of a few places to see rare birds such as the golden-cheeked warbler and the black-capped vireo. There are 58 designated tent sites with access to restrooms, 62 RV sites, and 1 park cabin. Entrance fee is $4, tent camping is $15, water and electric sites are $18, and full-hookup sites are $21. Reservations are recommended. The park is located off Highway 173 and access to the park is free.

Museum of Western Art (1550 Bandera Hwy., aka Hwy. 173, 830/896-2553, www.museumofwesternart.com, 10 A.M.–4 P.M. Tues.–Sat., 1–5 P.M. Sun., $7) is a one-of-a-kind gallery that features contemporary art about cowboys and created by cowboys. Dramatic sculptures and paintings romanticize cowboys on the range in a way that captures the imagination and fosters a desire to want to eat rattlesnakes and drink coffee boiled over an open fire, without filters. The artistry and craftsmanship in all pieces on exhibit is spectacular and truly world-class. For the kids there's the permanent exhibit featuring things used in the everyday life of a cowboy. The building is constructed of heavy timbers and limestone, and the grounds are dotted with life-size bronze statues, making this a long lasting monument to the Wild West and the artistic tradition that captures it. The museum is located on the southern side of the Guadalupe River.

Cultural and natural history merge at **Riverside Nature Center** (150 Francisco Lemos St., 830/257-4837, www.riverside-naturecenter.org, 9 A.M.–4 P.M. Mon.–Fri., 10 A.M.–3 P.M. Sat.–Sun., free). This former farm is now a sanctuary for wildlife and native plants. Inside the main building are feature exhibits, educational programs, a gift shop, and a natural sciences library. Outside, on the grounds of the center, there's an arboretum of Texas trees, a wildflower meadow, butterfly gardens, and millions of insects. The gardens and trails are open daily from dawn to dusk.

Accommodations

For an inexpensive bed with no fanfare there are a couple options: **Flagstaff Inn Motel** (906 Junction Hwy., 830/792-4449, $40–70) and **America's Best Value Inn** (1804 Sydney Baker St., 830/896-8200, $45–70).

One of the Hill Country's most famous and historic ranches is **◖ Y. O. Ranch** (1736 Y. O. Ranch Rd., west of Kerrville, 830/640-3222 or 800/967-2624, www.yoranch.net). Picture longhorn cattle drives, a classy lodge-style resort, cowboys, and zebras, and you've envisioned Y. O. Ranch. This exotic game and hunting ranch spans 50 square miles, which is equivalent to 40,000 acres. Zebras, antelope, giraffes, and good ol' fashioned longhorns are among the 56 species of exotic and native animals that roam these parts. Established back in 1880 by Captain Charles Schreiner (of Kerrville fame), the ranch now offers exotic wildlife tours, horseback riding, rustic accommodations, and cowboy suppers featuring—you guessed it—meat and potatoes. Reservations are necessary. Guided hunts cost $250 a day for up to three people. Accommodations are

around $150 per night, per person, and include three meals. Tours for wildlife viewing are $33 for adults, but if you are staying on the ranch tours cost only $18.

The classiest place to stay in the Kerrville area is **Inn of the Hills Resort** (1001 Junction Hwy., 830/895-5000, www.innofthehills.com, $90–250). Amenities include room service, Olympic-size pool and kiddie pool, tennis courts, and fitness club. There's also an upscale restaurant on the premises, which offers breakfast, lunch buffets, and dinner daily.

Food

Every Hill Country town has great barbecue. In Kerrville it's served up at **Bill's Bar-B-Que** (1909 Junction Hwy., 830/895-5733 or 830/367-4624, 11 A.M.–7 P.M. Tues.–Sat., $8). Bill's is *the* local favorite for all meats barbecued to perfection.

Kathy's on the River (417 Water St., 830/257-7811, 8 A.M.–9 P.M. Wed.–Sun., $8) is known for seafood and steaks at reasonable prices. Folks love eating on the outdoor patio overlooking the river.

Hill Country Café (806 Main St., 830/257-6665, 6 A.M.–2 P.M. Mon.–Fri., 6–11 A.M. Sat., $7). This local institution serves American standards for breakfast and lunch only. Being smack dab in downtown, it's popular and often packed.

WEST OF KERRVILLE
◖ Stonehenge II

The area's most peculiar attraction is what's known as Stonehenge II. Situated on a flat spot in a field a couple miles west of the small town of Hunt is a 60 percent scale version of Stonehenge, the iconic rock structure near Salisbury, England. Unknowing folks traveling down this small Hill Country road who happen to see this amazing monument to God-knows-what are completely baffled, and unsure of what they're seeing. Just as mysterious as the original, this smaller version begs the question: "What were they thinking?" Was it created by aliens trying to contact their motherland? No! How about druids? Nope! Stonehenge II was

© JUSTIN MARLER

Marvel at a weird replica of Stonehenge that is out in the far reaches of the Hill Country.

conceived and constructed by two locals, Al Shepperd and Doug Hill. Material: concrete. Reason: none needed. Location: past the town of Hunt on FM 1340. Stonehenge II is on private property but visitors are welcome during daylight hours.

LOVE CREEK ORCHARDS

If you plan on leaving the Kerrville area on Highway 16 going south you will probably want to stop off at **Love Creek Orchards Cider Mill and Country Store** (Hwy. 16 south of Medina, 830/589-2588, $7). This is a place where the apple is worshipped and glorified in its many forms. Although the orchards are lovely the real reason why everybody comes here is the country store. To find it follow the distinct smell of baking apples that wafts down the highway. Once the unsuspecting visitor walks onto the grounds they are transported into a Thomas Kinkade painting where America seems to be perfect and free of sin, until the apple is served up. Here you'll find apple pies, apple cider, applesauce, apple turnovers, apple muffins, apple rings, apple butter, and apple jellies and jams. In all, the folks at Love Creek produce over 33 different products from apples. Yes, the temptation is great, but you can't blame Eve—this place is owned an operated by the Adams family.

BANDERA

The authentic, honest-to-goodness Western town of Bandera (pop. 1,000) considers itself the Cowboy Capital of the World. When you show up you may wonder if this is true because it can come across as a bleak little town at first. Sure, it's not a set from a spaghetti western, and yes it doesn't have a sexy hunk galloping down main street looking for the sheriff. But if you scratch the surface just a little, you will see there's much to discover and experience here that is truly western.

According to legend, many bloody battles between Apache and Comanche and the Spanish conquistadors took place in Bandera Pass (now 12 miles north on Hwy. 173). Supposedly a red flag (*bandera* is Spanish for flag) marked

Bandera was once the boundary between Spanish and Native American territory.

the boundary between Spanish and Native American territory. In 1852 the town was officially founded, and Bandera became a staging area for western cattle drives, a Mormon colony, and the largest Polish settlement in the United States.

Today Bandera is still an emblem of the American frontier as home to world-champion rodeo cowboys, western craftsmen who produce fine furniture and leather products, and old-style Texas dance halls. So what draws people here? The living spirit of the old West, camping under the stars, rodeos, kayaking and canoeing, catfish and bass fishing, honky-tonks and country music, horseback riding, and Texas-style R&R.

Bandera's population hovers around 1,000. The downtown is small and the centerpiece is the Old Bandera County Courthouse, which is now the library. Its distinct Renaissance Revival architecture evokes the Spanish era, while the rest of the town harkens to the old West, demonstrating the richness of Bandera's history.

For more information about Bandera there's **Bandera County Convention and Visitors Bureau** (126 Hwy. 16 S., 830/796-3045 or 800/364-3833, www.banderacowboycapital.com, 9 A.M.–5 P.M. Mon.–Fri., 10 A.M.–3 P.M. Sat.). The helpful staff can assist in finding just the right lodgings for you as well as offer information about anything, from rodeo schedules to the historic walking tour of downtown.

Sights and Activities

The best small-town museum in Texas happens to be in Bandera, the **Frontier Times Museum** (510 13th St., 830/796-3864, 10 A.M.–4:30 P.M. Mon.–Sat., $5). This homespun museum is more like an antique store where you can't buy anything—you can only look. Here you can imbibe the luster of the old days, and breath in the scent of old wood and dusty artifacts from the Wild West's cowboy lore and Bandera's history.

The 5,400 acres that make up the **Hill Country State Natural Area** (830/796-4413) were originally the site of the Merrick Ranch. Located 10 miles west of Bandera on

BACK IN THE SADDLE AGAIN

Bandera is a popular place for saddling up and heading out into the country. Many of the dude ranches in and around Bandera offer horseback riding packages with accommodations or day-trip horseback riding at an hourly rate. Experienced riders can head out on trails alone, and the inexperienced can ride with a guide. Most ranches don't have addresses as they are out in the country, so it's good to look them up on the Internet or call to get directions before heading out. Children under six usually can't ride, and reservations are required.

For a guided stroll through the countryside for a few hours, there's **Bar M Ranch** (RR 1077 West, 2.5 miles southwest of Bandera, 830/796-9096, www.bar-mranch.com, $40 for two hours, $75 for three hours). Trails will take riders over brook and dale, through pastures, and in the shadows of cliffs. Wildlife abounds here so bring a camera, or just take mental pictures. Rates go by trail, and trails are generally 2–3 hours. Trails three hours and longer require experienced riders.

Another ranch that offers hourly horseback riding is **Rancho Cortez** (RR 1077, 830/796-9339, www.ranchocortez.com, $35 per hour). Hourly rates are higher for State Park rides.

For the most experienced ride on trails that go through the beautiful Hill Country State Natural Area, call **Desert Hearts Cowgirls Club** (830/796-7001, $65 for the first two hours, $30 for each additional hour), founded by Jeanne Beauxbeannes (pronounced BOH-bee-nee). She's been riding the park longer than any of the rangers. Her idea of hiking in this park is simply hiking your leg over a saddle. Jeanne offers interpretive guided trail rides for a minimum of two hours. Half-day and all-day rides are offered only in fall and spring.

THE HILL COUNTRY

© JUSTIN MARLER

A dude ranch retreat isn't complete without spending some time in the saddle.

FM 1077, this park has virtually nothing to offer in the way of amenities—just good ol' fashioned nature. Camping is permitted in a 20-acre designated area, but don't expect restrooms and showers here, as primitive camping is what this park is all about. Make sure you bring water, food, and toilet paper, bury all waste matter, and take all your trash with you when you leave. This largely undeveloped, nearly pristine park, offers a rugged place for hiking, walk-in camping, backpacking, mountain biking, and horseback riding among canyons, springs, and rocky hills. There are also over 20 caves and 10 springs that add to the majesty of the park.

Six miles southeast of town on Highway 16 is **Polly's Chapel,** built in 1882 by José Policarpo Rodriguez. José came from Mexico to Texas and became famous as a scout for the U.S. Army and a mercenary. He later joined the Methodist church and became a licensed preacher and built this tiny chapel. José, known by locals as Polly, is buried in the graveyard. The chapel is often open to the public.

Living up to the prestigious working title of Cowboy Capital, Bandera hosts a wide array of **rodeos** from spring to fall. Every Tuesday and Friday night from Memorial Day weekend in May through Labor Day weekend in September, the **Twin Elm Guest Ranch** (Hwy. 470, 830/796-3628, www.twinelmranch. com) hosts open rodeos. Professional rodeos are put on by the **Cowboy Capital Rodeo Association** (www.banderarodeo.com) every year on Memorial Day weekend. For schedules and information on all rodeos in Bandera check out www.banderacowboycapital.com or contact the Bandera County Convention and Visitors Bureau.

Music and Dancing

Bandera is known for keeping honky-tonk alive with live country music, line dancing, and sawdust floors. Live dances are held Wednesday–Sunday nights throughout the year at the various honky-tonks and dance halls in and around town. Bandera is also known for jam sessions that grow into full-on hootenannies.

Expect to see accordions, Stetsons, guitars, and beer bellies at the following bars: **Arkey Blue's Silver Dollar** (308 Main St., 830/796-8826), **Bandera Saloon** (402 Main St., 830/796-3699), newly reopened **The Cabaret Dance Hall** (801 Main St., 830/796-8889), and the **11th Street Cowboy Bar** (307 11th St., 830/796-4849).

Accommodations

Although Bandera has a couple of typical motels, the popular way to lodge is in a dude ranch or a guest ranch. For most people, staying in a dude ranch is a once-in-a-lifetime opportunity. Most ranches offer rustic accommodations and a wide range of activities such as campfire storytelling, marshmallow roasting, horseback riding, swimming, and nature walks. Rates for dude and guest ranches are more than your average motel/hotel, but often include up to three meals a day.

For predictably clean and affordable accommodations within walking distance to shops and restaurants there's **Bandera Lodge** (700 St. ,Hwy. 16 S., 830/796-3093, $63–90). Nothing fancy here, just a TV, a bed, Internet access, and a bathroom.

A comfortable ranch that offers hotel-style amenities is the **Flying L Guest Ranch** (800/292-5134, www.flyingl.com, $180–300). On over 700 acres, this ranch offers 41 cottages and suites, many with fireplaces. Here you can spend the day horseback riding along the San Julian Creek, swimming, fishing, and playing sports. The Flying L also has an 18-hole championship golf course and packages for golfers that make for a resort getaway with a ranch feel. All cottages and suites require a two-night minimum stay.

Fun for the whole family is to be had at **Mayan Dude Ranch** (Pecan St., 830/796-3312, www.mayanranch.com, $130–150 for adults, $70–95 for children under 18). This ranch has been hosting people for decades, providing couples and families with rustic rooms and cottages, horseback riding, hay-bale rides, tubing, fishing, hiking, golf, and tennis. The facility is huge and it takes a lot of concentration to

THE HILL COUNTRY

be bored here. Included in the price are three cowboy-style meals and a horseback ride.

A popular place to hunker down for a weekend in style is the **Old Texas Square** (703 Main St., 830/896-1711, www.texassquare. com, $60–179). This historic building makes for a great hotel, complete with a restaurant and upscale lobby bar. Old Texas Square was and still is the hub of town, which makes this hotel the very best place to stay for those desiring foot-access to everything. The fancy rooms are tempered with a folksy, ranch-style decor, all one notch above the rest.

Across from the Medina River are the cozy cottages of **River Front Motel** (1103 Maple St., 830/460-3690, $74–125). These semirustic, clean rooms are furnished by local craftsmen and offer convenience, location, and quiet.

For rustic ranch lodgings, the **Twin Elm Guest Ranch** (Hwy. 470, 830/796-3628, www.twinelmranch.com, $105–115 for adults, $80 for teens, $65 for children under 12.) can draw the inner cowpoke right out of you. Twin Elm has 21 units, all clean and with air-conditioning; some have bunk beds and porches. Rates vary for high and low seasons. Rates include three big cowboy-style meals a day, access to the rodeos held every Tuesday and Friday night during the summer, marshmallow roasting, swimming, and relaxing in hammocks. For a few more bucks, guided horseback riding is offered by Twin Elm.

Food

In Bandera eating out is cheap and amusing. Sometimes the cuisine can be a bit too cowboy though. By this I mean too greasy, meaty, and salty. You can expect to spend under $10 for a meal and a drink.

For barbecue, there's **Busbee's Bar-B-Que** (319 Main St., 830/796-3153, 10:30 A.M.–8 P.M. Mon.–Thurs., 10:30 A.M.–9 P.M. Fri.–Sat., closed Tuesdays., $7). They unabashedly declare themselves the cowboy's choice for barbecue, and if this is true, how can one go wrong eating here? Beef is served up by the pound with the usual sides.

The landmark eatery in town is **O. S. T.**

Restaurant (305 Main St., 830/796-3836, 6 A.M.–9 P.M. Mon.–Sat., 7 A.M.–9 P.M. Sun., $8), also known as Old Spanish Trail. Downhome cooking here includes chicken-fried steak, roast, meatloaf, and other American fare. One room in the restaurant is entirely devoted to the memory of Marion Morrison. Who's this you might ask? The Duke—better known as John Wayne.

VANDERPOOL

The small town of Vanderpool (pop. 20) is primarily a center for sheep, goat, and cattle ranching. Back in 1885, when a post office was established out here for settlers and ranchers, they decided to give this place a name. Not much has changed since then—the main feature here is still the post office. So what's out here? This quiet area at the western edge of Bandera County is exceptionally beautiful, with some of the most scenic country roads in the Hill Country. The town, if it can even be called a town, is situated on the lazy Sabinal River near a state park, which is a popular getaway for city folk.

The only sight out here is **Lone Star Motorcycle Museum** (Hwy. 187 N., four miles north of Vanderpool, 830/966-6103, www.lonestarmotorcyclemuseum.com, 10 A.M.–5 P.M. Fri.–Sun., $5). This labor of love was pieced together by a motorcycle connoisseur who had extra money to spend on a hobby. The collection spans the entire history and evolution of the motorcycle, from the first motorized bicycles to the hogs of our time. The popular trend that has resurrected the chopper and custom motorcycle has brought more traffic than usual to this small museum. The scenic roads leading up to the museum make this a great destination for a weekend motorcycle ride.

◖ LOST MAPLES STATE NATURAL AREA

The main reason for going as far west as Vanderpool is Lost Maples State Natural Area (37221 FM 187, 830/966-3413, 8 A.M.–10 P.M. daily, $5 Dec.–Sept., $6 Oct.–Nov.). The beautiful bigtooth maples are the big attraction here, and they aren't "lost" or even hard to find. In the fall these delicate but enormous trees explode with color. Fall foliage is most dramatic in November, and that's when the crowds come. Hikers are encouraged to stay on trails as the trees can be damaged by soil compaction. Bigtooth maples require very specific conditions and have shallow roots, making them rare and vulnerable. The park is home to three State Champion Big Trees: escarpment chokecherry, a Texas ash, and a bigtooth maple, nominated by the American Forestry Association. Park facilities include campsites with water and electricity, picnic areas, and restrooms with showers. Primitive camp areas are also available but you have to hike in about 11 miles to get to them. The park is located four miles north of Vanderpool on FM 187.

UVALDE

At the far reaches of the western Hill Country is the slow-paced town of Uvalde (pop. 15,000). This Wild West frontier town was first settled by the Spanish back in 1674 as a missionary effort to convert the Apache population. Spanish bailed on this effort after repeated attacks by local Lipan-Apache, and returned in 1709 under the military leadership of Spanish Governor Juan del Ugalde (Uvalde), who defeated the Apaches. According to legend, Uvalde Canyon is the spot of this final battle.

Although there are traces of the Spanish era, Uvalde is most remembered as a Wild West town, and as the stomping grounds of the notorious gunslinger, outlaw, and sheriff J. King Fisher. Although Fisher died in a gunfight in the Vaudeville Theater in San Antonio he's buried here in Pioneer Cemetery. The other historical character that called Uvalde home was John "Cactus Jack" Garner, vice president under Franklin D. Roosevelt, whose home is now a museum.

Uvalde is the most remote town covered in this guidebook. Although it's out in the middle of nowhere, Uvalde is the most noteworthy town at the farthest southwestern rim of the Hill Country, and can make for an interesting day trip from both San Antonio and

Austin. From San Antonio, go west 80 miles on Highway 90, and from Austin, it's probably best to go through Bandera, and take Highway 173 south to Highway 90, then go west. Upon arrival the **Uvalde Convention and Visitors Bureau** (300 E. Main St., 830/278-4115 or 800/588-2533, www.visituvalde.com, 9 A.M.–5 P.M. Mon.–Fri.) is the best place to get information.

Sights and Activities

Housed in a WWII hangar at the Uvalde municipal airport is the **Aviation Museum of Texas** (201 Sul Ross Blvd., hangar number 1 at Garner Field, 830/278-2552). See WWII aircraft and memorabilia, such as a disassembled Martin B-26, Stearman, PT-17, Liason-4, 1946 Ercoupe, and a Fairchild. Due to a lack of volunteers the museum is only open 9 A.M.–4 P.M. Tues. and Fri., 1 P.M.–4 P.M. Sat. or by request; a donation of $2 will get you in.

If you make it all the way out to Uvalde you have to check out **Briscoe Art and Antique Collection** (200 E. Nopal St., in the First State Bank, 830/278-6231, www.fsbuvalde.com, 9 A.M.–3 P.M. Mon.–Fri., free). People are always completely surprised to find that out in this remote Texas town, inside a bank, there's an extensive, multimillion-dollar art collection that includes original masterpieces by Rembrandt and Gainsborough, and works by American Western artists Salinas and Warren. The collection was developed by rancher, oilman, banker, and former Texas Governor Dolph Briscoe and his wife, and can be seen by simply strolling into the bank and looking around. For a guided tour, call in advance.

Built in 1891, the **Janey Slaughter-Briscoe Grand Opera House** (100 W. North St., 830/278-4184, 9 A.M.–3 P.M. Mon.–Fri., free) was once the center for cultural activity in southwestern Texas. Recently refurbished, the opera house is now an active performing-arts center. Whether there's something happening here or not, it's worth poking your head into this historic building. The stage and most of the interior has the original turn-of-the-20th-century decor.

John Nance Garner Museum (333 North Park, 830/278-5018, 9 A.M.–5 P.M. Tues.–Sat., free) is located in the home of John "Cactus Jack" Garner, vice president under Franklin D. Roosevelt. On display are items associated with Mr. Garner's life, including items from his political career as well as area history. The museum is run by one of four divisions of the University of Texas Center for American History.

Accommodations

Amber Sky Motel (2005 E. Main St., 830/278-5602, $52–62) is your roadside mainstay, with 39 units. A restaurant is on the premises for convenience.

For slightly fancy accommodations there's **Quality Inn** (920 E. Main St., 830/278-4511, $88). This recently remodeled hotel has a pool, a restaurant on-site, banquet rooms, and a cocktail lounge.

For luxury in a bed-and-breakfast atmosphere let **Live Oaks Bed & Breakfast** (6 Tanglewood, 830/591-2340, www.liveoaksbnb.com, $100–130) take care of you. Live Oaks is nestled in a secluded meadow of tall mesquite and live oak trees on a six-acre plot on the outskirts town. When you think of bed-and-breakfast you may think of an old converted Victorian house, but that's not what you'll find here. Think new construction, contemporary design, clean and simple rooms, and great service.

Food

At the Amber Sky Motel is the **Amber Sky Coffee Shop** (2001 E. Main St., 830/278-3923, 6 A.M.–3 P.M. Mon.–Sat., $7), where locals have been getting their coffee and conversation for years. Here you can get a delicious home-cooked meal, a pie and a paper, and start the day slowly.

Long-time Uvalde tradition is offered at **Evett's Barbecue** (301 E. Main St., 830/278-6204, 10:30 A.M.–6 P.M. Tues.–Sat., 10:30 A.M.–4 P.M. Sat., $7). Choose smoked-to-perfection barbecue and sides, or a sandwich, all dirt cheap.

For a plate of the best country cooking "in the country," there's **Golden Corral** (2221 E. Main St., 830/278-3465, 11 A.M.–9 P.M. Mon.–Thurs., 11 A.M.–10 P.M. Fri.–Sun., $9). Satisfy your appetite with over 120 buffet items to choose from, including a dessert bar that's second to none.

Eastern Rim

The Eastern Rim of the Hill Country is defined by I-35, which connects San Antonio to Austin, Dallas, and everything in between. The towns along the freeway were the original settlements of the first German immigrants back in the 1800s. Today these towns are getaway hotspots for city folk who want to tube the beautiful rivers, shop for antiques, and enjoy leisurely meals on outdoor patios.

MCKINNEY FALLS STATE PARK

A bucolic spot on the eastern side of I-35 between San Antonio and Austin is home to McKinney Falls State Park (5808 McKinney Falls Pkwy., 512/243-1643, 8 A.M.–10 P.M. daily, $4). This beautiful area on Onion Creek was settled by one of Steven F. Austin's original 300 colonists, Thomas F. McKinney, back in the 1850s. Ruins of his original homestead have been preserved. Park facilities include 84 campsites with water and electricity, screened shelters with bunk beds, and picnic sites. There's also an interpretive hiking trail that's just under a mile long, as well as over three miles of paved trails. Mountain biking is available on designated trails. Camping costs $16 per site.

SAN MARCOS

Between Austin and San Antonio, on I-35, is the small river town of San Marcos (pop.

SCENIC DRIVE: DEVIL'S BACKBONE

One of many scenic drives in the Hill Country is Devil's Backbone, which is out in the country near Wimberley. This is a winding country road that cuts its way along a dramatic ridge and through a valley of rolling hills. This drive is at its visual climax in the spring. To get to Devil's Backbone from San Marcos, follow RR 12 west to RR 32, where the scenic drive travels west for about 14 miles.

35,000). Over 12,000 years ago Native Americans lived in this area, making it the oldest continuously inhabited place on the continent. It's not hard to figure out why people have always lived here. This lush spot on the San Marcos River is where springs from an underground reservoir burst forth, creating the riverhead. The result: beauty and life.

Today San Marcos is a town that wears many hats. It's home to Texas State University, the state's largest shopping outlet center, and a place for ranchers and country folk to get supplies. But first and foremost San Marcos's most important aspect is the ancient river. For more information contact the **San Marcos Tourist Information Center** (617 I-35 N., 512/393-5930, www.sanmarcostexas.com, 8:30 A.M.–5 P.M. Mon.–Fri.).

Sights and Activities

The fourth most visited attraction in the state of Texas is the shopping mecca of the **Premium Outlets** (3939 I-35 S., exit 200, Centerpoint Rd., 512/396-2200, www.premiumoutlets. com, 10 A.M.–9 P.M. Mon.–Sat., 10 A.M.–7 P.M. Sun.). Every year more than six million shoppers visit the sea of concrete and buildings that make up the shopping center in search of deals, steals, the new thing, the old thing at a discount, and an endless array of bargains. The 110-plus factory outlet stores offer everything from apparel and accessories to health and beauty items to home furnishings and housewares. The outlets have been developed with a Disneyland aesthetic, such as castle-like towers and gondola rides, that only adds to the draw. If you plan to join the hordes shopping here be sure to pick up a map of the complex as soon as you arrive, and plan on making a day of it.

Texas State University's **Aquarena Center** (921 Aquarena Springs Dr., 512/245-7570, www.aquarena.txstate.edu, 10 A.M.–5 P.M. daily, free) is Central Texas's contribution to the science of water. At the center there's an aquarium, an endangered-species exhibit, a wetlands boardwalk, and scientific diving, all to educate visitors about the fundamental element of all life—water. The highlight of the Aquarena is taking a tour in a glass-bottom boat ($9) to explore the watery underworld without getting wet.

San Marcos's version of a theme park is **Wonder World Caverns** (1000 Prospect St., exit 202 off I-35, 877/492-4657, www.wonderworldpark.com). Along with dramatic caverns to explore, Wonder World also has an anti-gravity house, animals on the prowl, an observation tower, and a mini-train to ride. Summer hours are 8 A.M.–8 P.M. daily June–August; winter hours are 9 A.M.–5 P.M. Mon.–Fri., 9 A.M.–6 P.M. Sat.–Sun. September–May. Ticket prices range $7–19 depending on what attractions you want to experience.

The best feature in town is the river, and the best activity is **Tubing the San Marcos River.** Floating the short circuit takes about an hour, and floating the long one can take about six hours. On the float tubers encounter ancient cypress trees, a mini-waterfall, and serene settings around every bend. **Lions Club Tube Rental** (in City Park across from the university, 512/396-LION or 512/396-5466, www. tubesanmarcos.com) makes the experience easy. Just show up at their site, pick out a tube, and jump in the river. The Lions Club folks will pick you up at the Rio Vista Dam (one-hour trip), or Martindale Dam (six-hour trip), and drive you back to the start point at the Lions Club. Rental rates range $7–14 depending on the type of tube. Deposits are required.

Summer hours are 10 A.M.–7 P.M. daily June–August; winter hours are 10 A.M.–7 P.M. on weekends only September–May. Last tube rental is always at 5:30 P.M.

Food

The **☾ Café on the Square** (126 N. LBJ, 512/396-9999, 6:30 A.M.–11 P.M. Mon.–Sat., 8 A.M.–10 P.M. Sun., $8) is where all the town's gossip goes down. Locals converge here all throughout the day and night, and sip iced tea and eat breakfast well past noon. This is the type of place where it's OK to occupy a table for hours. The food is standard American, delivered with above-standard hospitality.

Palmers (218 W. Moore, 512/353-3500, www.palmerstexas.com, 11 A.M.–10 P.M. Sun.–Thurs., 11 A.M.–11 P.M. Fri.–Sat., $10) offers the classiest environment in San Marcos for lunch and dinner. The menu offers a diverse selection of entrées, from pastas to steaks, all served at tables situated among plants and trees.

WIMBERLEY

The wacky little valley town of Wimberley (pop. 5,000) is in an incredible setting on the Blanco River and Cypress Creek. Many residents of Wimberley don't think the outside world knows about their quirky little town, and they want to keep it that way. I hate to disappoint, but people are on to them and their town, and visit by the thousands. Some visit and love the place so much that they move there. In recent decades Wimberley has become home to artists, authors, musicians, and people seeking a simple life away from the city. This has given rise to an organic community of artists, which has made Wimberley into a bona fide art town. This strong art identity has been grafted to an old tradition of ranching, which gives Wimberley a funky, charming, and offbeat identity crisis.

Wimberley has been struggling with its identity ever since its founding back in the 1850s. The town was first settled by a veteran of the

THE HILL COUNTRY

© JUSTIN MARLER

Wimberley Square

Texas Revolution named Williams Winters, who built a mill on the location. The town was called Winters until a man named John Cade bought the mill and renamed the town Cade's Mill. A few years later a wealthy man from Llano named Pleasant Wimberley bought the mill and changed the name to Wimberley. For over a hundred years nothing changed much in the small town. Then in the 1970s and '80s hippies started showing up, giving way to the art scene. Today, what you'll find here is a charming town; a fascinating little shopping area at **Wimberley Square,** where some artists peddle their wares; and over a hundred bed-and-breakfasts in the surrounding countryside. Although Wimberley's status as an art town draws people here, the real reason people come here is to simply do nothing.

For more information stop by **Wimberley Visitor Center** (14100 RR 12, 512/847-2201, 9 A.M.–4 P.M. Mon.–Sat., 1–4 P.M. Sun.).

Sights and Activities

Wimberley's lifeline is the scenic **Blanco River,** which cuts its way through town leaving extraordinarily beautiful surroundings in its wake. The best way to take in Blanco River is to drive up River Road. It only offers about a mile of river frontage views, but it's well worth the trip.

The other feature of town is also a natural one: Cypress Creek. The best spot to see this creek at its best is at **Blue Hole** (RR 3237, north of town). This majestic piece of the river has been a popular swimming hole ever since this area was settled. It's called Blue Hole for a reason—the water is a deep cobalt blue.

People from all over the area converge in Wimberley once a month for **Market Day at Lions Field** (RR 2325, in Lions Field, 6 A.M.–6 P.M., free). Over 450 vendors set up booths under tree-covered paths on the first Saturday of every month from April to December. The scene is third-world bazaar meets country kitsch, with vendors peddling antiques, canned goods, furniture, art, and live music.

To get a good view of the area hike to the top of **Mount Baldy.** It got its name because the trees stopped growing and the top is as bald as Kojak. There are 212 steps to the top. To get to the trailhead from RR 12, go west on Woodcreek Drive, then take your first right. You should see the stairs and a place to park.

One of the weirdest things in Wimberley is **Pioneer Town** (333 Wayside Dr., off River Rd.). This is a small Wild West town created out of old buildings that were going to meet their fate in and around Wimberley. It all started when the founder of 7A Resort, old-timer Raymond Czichos, visited Knott's Berry Farm in California. He came back to Wimberley inspired, and over the course of several years built this bizarre mock town. Initially it had real businesses, run by folks in western getups, but today it's more of a ghost town. 1960s-style mannequins from department stores, dressed up in Western attire, are the only remaining survivors of this dream. Rumor has it that someone bought Pioneer Town and has plans to revitalize it. Until then it's pretty dead and creepy, but makes for an interesting place to take a stroll.

One of the top attractions in town is one of the local artist's studios at **Wimberley Glass Works** (6469 Ranch Road 12, 800/929-6686, www.wgw.com, 10 A.M.–5 P.M. daily). Founded by Tim de Jong in the 1990s, this incredible space has become one of the premier art glass galleries in the Southwest. Handblown glass demonstrations take place daily, where master artists create lighting and art glass. Wimberley Glass Works is located south on RR 12.

Accommodations

There are over 100 different lodgings in and around Wimberley, including bed-and-breakfasts, guest rooms, cottages, and cabins. The following reservation services can help match you with a lodging that suits your budget and needs: **All Wimberley Lodgings** (400 River Rd., 800/460-3909) and **Hill Country Accommodations** (14015 RR 12, 800/926-5028). If you prefer not to use a service, the following accommodations come recommended.

◖ Blair House (100 Spoke Hill Rd.,

512/847-1111 or 877/549-5450, www.blairhou-seinn.com, $125–275) is easily one of the top places to get away in the Hill Country. After all, *Condé Nast Traveler* considers Blair's one of the top 25 inns in the country for a very good reason—or should I say several reasons. Here guests are seduced with all the pleasures one could wish for in a vacation getaway, with fine dining and fine linens in a fine location. In the evening, turndown service includes a beverage and a confection, and in the morning guests wake up to a gourmet breakfast.

For budget travelers, **Mountain View Lodge** (RR 12, south of Wimberley, 512/847-2992, $85–95) has excellent rooms with balconies, and views of the Wimberley Valley. Continental breakfast is included in the rates.

Comfortable cottages and a serene setting are to be found at **Wimberley Inn** (200 FM 3237, 512/847-3750, www.wimberleyinn.com, $85–175). A night's stay here includes an upscale continental breakfast, along with great service. High-speed Internet access is available.

Food
Blair House (100 Spoke Hill Rd., 512/847-1111 or 877/549-5450, www.blairhouseinn.com, $65) offers the best fine-dining experience in the area. A five-star fixed menu is offered at 7:30 P.M. each Saturday evening. Any restaurant that's only open one night a week and still gets the highest of accolades deserves the title of fine dining. Entrées have included coffee-braised short ribs with baked yams and pork tenderloin with orange sauce.

Cypress Creek Café (7:30 A.M.–8:30 P.M. Tues.–Sat., 7:30 A.M.–3 P.M. Sun., $9) serves up American fare that keeps the locals coming back. Coconut shrimp, scampi, marlin, pork— all make this menu diverse and yummy.

On beautiful Cypress Creek is **Ino'z** (14004 RR 12 on Wimberley Square, 512/847-6060, 11 A.M.–9 P.M. daily, $8). The setting is the best in town as restaurants go, however the food is nothing special. The reason to come here is to sit on the outside deck and have chicken-fried steak and a beer under the bald cypress trees next to the creek.

Miss Mae's BBQ (419 FM 2325, 512/847-9808, 10:30 A.M.–7 P.M. Mon.–Sat., $6) has the barbecue connection in Wimberley. The tradition started in 1957 in the founder's grandmother's kitchen. Using her recipe Miss Mae's cooks up barbecue chicken, beef, ham, and turkey.

Shopping
All the shopping in town takes place at Wimberley Square. Here you'll find hundreds of little boutiques filled with Texana crafts, home furnishings, vintage clothes and antiques, along with a couple art galleries. Your shopping strategy should be to park anywhere and spend a couple hours walking around. Shops often come and go within a matter of months in this area.

Boutiques worth checking out are **Brocante** (14015 RR 12, 512/847-8577, 10:30 A.M.–5 P.M. Mon.–Sat., 11:30 A.M.–5 P.M. Sun.) and **Wall Street Western** (13904 RR 12, 512/847-1818, 10 A.M.–6 P.M. daily). An interesting art gallery featuring folk art and wildlife sculptures is **Old Mill Store** (Wimberley Square RR 12, 512/847-3068, 10 A.M.–6 P.M. Mon.–Thurs., 10 A.M.–7 P.M. Fri.–Sun.).

NEW BRAUNFELS
The German heritage of Central Texas all began in the town of New Braunfels (pop. 36,400), located in the Austin–San Antonio corridor off I-35. Back in the 1840s, German entrepreneurs bought a vast amount of acreage here with the intention of bringing in German colonists. The first settlers, led by Prince Carl of Solms-Braunfels in Germany, arrived to find the area far from the coast, and populated by Native Americans, but decided to settle the area anyway. These first German settlers brought their culture and traditions and integrated them into the story of the Texas Hill Country. These traditions have survived to the present day, and define New Braunfels, making it the unique place that it is.

Today people come to New Braunfels for many reasons. City folks in both Austin and San Antonio come here to relax, spend hot

CHEATING DEATH AT THE GUADALUPE RIVER

Driving north from San Antonio toward Austin on I-35, you will cross the Guadalupe River at the scenic town of New Braunfels. As you pass the bridge over the Guadalupe, imagine the winter of 1838. At that time, Noah Smithwick, a Texas Ranger, was making his way from San Antonio to his base in the community of Bastrop on the Colorado River. There were no bridges across the Guadalupe and Smithwick was riding a mule. He thought he could get across, but unfortunately the river was deeper and swifter than he anticipated. He and his mule struggled but were unable to get across. After almost drowning, they both eventually emerged on the same side of the river where they had started. Unfortunately for Smithwick, he had lost his rifle, his gunpowder was wet, and he was soaked to the skin. The temperature was hovering at 30°F and a north wind was blowing at about 30 mph. The sun was going down and Smithwick was in danger of freezing to death.

He could not get a fire started since he had no dry gunpowder and no flintlock to create a spark. It was at this time he remembered a story told to him by David Crockett. Crockett had been in a similar situation and survived by gathering enough armloads of tall grass to create a hay pile. Smithwick did the same and took off his wet clothes and dove into the middle of his fresh pile of grass. Amazingly, he soon became warm as toast and survived the cold night. In the morning he mounted his mule and headed back to San Antonio where he discovered that he had escaped death three times within 24 hours.

A large band of Comanches had struck San Antonio the previous day and his friends in town thought that Smithwick had been caught alone on the prairie and killed by the Native Americans. This would probably have been his fate but for his mishap in the Guadalupe River. If he hadn't lost his rifle, he would have been able to make a fire and the Comanches would have spotted him. If he had successfully crossed the Guadalupe River, he would have run smack into their war party. Thus he almost died of drowning, freezing, and a Comanche attack all in the same day. Smithwick was a living example of that pioneer philosophy that what seems to be bad luck at first is sometimes the best thing that could happen to you.

summer days at the enormous water-theme park, and to imbibe the vestiges of German-meets-Texas culture. People also come here to do some serious antique shopping. There are so many junk and antique shops here that New Braunfels has been dubbed the Antique Capital of Texas. For more information on New Braunfels contact **New Braunfels Visitors Center** (237 I-35 N. at FM 725, 830/625-7973, 9 A.M.–5 P.M. daily).

Sights and Activities

Most people come to New Braunfels for recreation that centers around water. Water fun comes in many forms and sizes here, such as tubing down the Guadalupe River, rafting, or fishing. For those who want water without the mud and in a totally artificial environment, there's **Schlitterbahn** (400 N.

Liberty, 830/625-2351, www.schlitterbahn.com, 10 A.M.–8 P.M. daily in peak summer months, 10 A.M.–6 P.M. weekends at the beginning and end of season, $38 for adults, $30 for children 3–11). This mega-size waterpark with a German theme, open late April–September, draws people by the thousands all spring, summer, and fall. Featuring over 30 water slides, pools, thrill rides, and all sorts of wet fun for the whole family, Schlitterbahn has become Texas's largest waterpark.

New Braunfels has a strange assortment of grassroots museums and historical sights that aren't necessarily worth driving for miles to check out. However, if you have an itch for curious historical things there are a couple places you may want to check out. The **Sophienburg Museum and Archives** (401 W. Coll St., 830/629-1572, 10 A.M.–4 P.M. Tues.–Sat., $5)

© JUSTIN MARLER

Snake Farm houses over 300 reptile species.

has an interesting collection of local artifacts, mostly relating to German pioneers and early folks in the history of New Braunfels. The museum is located on the hilltop site where Prince Carl of Solms-Braunfels built a log fortress. There's also the **Heritage Village-Museum of Texas Handmade Furniture** (1370 Church Hill Dr., 830/629-6504, 1–4 P.M. Tues.–Sun. Feb.–Nov., $5), which features over 75 furniture items that were handmade in Texas during the 1800s. Finally, there's the **Lindheimer Home Museum** (491 Comal, 830/629-2943, 2–5 P.M. weekends, $3) where visitors can tour the home of the father of Texas botany, Ferdinand Jakob Lindheimer (1801–1879).

Just south of New Braunfels is **Snake Farm** (I-35 exit 182 at Engle, 830/608-9270, 10 A.M.–6 P.M. daily Memorial Day–Labor Day, $10). Since 1967 this roadside shrine devoted to reptiles has been drawing in the curious from the highway. Inside the main facility there are over 300 reptile species. Some are endangered, some are poisonous, many you probably have never seen up close before, and all

are intriguing and beautiful. All these curious creatures are stuck in small, dank aquariums, tanks, and cages that seem a bit precariously stacked and neglected. The smell in here is phenomenal. Snake Farm also has what I consider to be one of the weirdest gift shops in the state. As expected there's all kinds of snake-related memorabilia as well as display cases that exhibit dusty souvenirs so old they've become relics in their own right. There's also a rattlesnake pit with live rattlesnakes.

Tubing the Guadalupe

The main attraction in New Braunfels is the Guadalupe River that runs through town. The main activity is swimming, tubing, and rafting down the Guadalupe. This spectacular river is the air conditioner for locals and visitors as it's always cool and always running. In the summer you'll find thousands of folks from all walks of life sunning, relaxing, and drinking as they bob down the river through groves of bald cypress and over mild white-water rapids. The riverhead is at Canyon Lake and

Gruene is the end of the line. The whole length is approximately 20 miles. On any given day May–October you'll find a mob of sunburned, exhausted, tipsy folks staggering out of the exit points along the river carrying inner tubes, ice chests, and empty beverage containers. It's a sight to behold.

There are a number of businesses that offer tube and raft rentals along with shuttle service to various starting and exiting points along the river. There's **Rockin' R River Rides** (1405 Gruene Rd., 830/629-9999, 800/55-FLOAT or 800/553-5628, www.rockinr.com) and **Gruene River Company** (1404 Gruene Rd., 830/625-2800 or 888/705-2800, www.toobing.com). Tube rentals are $14, coolers are $15, and cooler tubes are $18. Inflatable canoes run $30–55 and rafts for 3–6 people are $25.

To reach the main locations for either of these companies from I-35, exit at Loop 337 and go north towards the town of Gruene. After you cross the Guadalupe River, turn right on Gruene Road. Drive up to the river and park.

Accommodations

The best bed in town is at **Prince Solms Inn** (295 E. San Antonio St., 830/625-9169 or 800/625-9169, www.princesolmsinn.com, $125–150). This historic inn was built back in 1898 and was known as the most romantic and most luxurious hotel in this area. It still deserves this distinction with a great central location, fluffy pillows, wines, confections, and breakfast in the morning. If you stay here ask about the ghost tale, if you dare. Speaking of creepy stuff, the inn offers a very unique experience called the murder mystery weekend, when folks rent out the inn and the staff host a clever who-done-it evening.

An excellent bed-and-breakfast is **Das Anwesen Bed and Breakfast** (360 Millie's Ln., 830/625-5992 or 866/526-1236, www.dasanwesen.com, $100–175). This prairie-style home is on historic Karbach Ranch, which was established when the German immigrants first settled New Braunfels in 1844. The interior of the home is filled with fine antiques, tasteful decorations, and country charm. Breakfast is served on antique china, crystal, and silver at 8:30 A.M.

For standard roadside accommodations in New Braunfels there's **Days Inn New Braunfels** (963 I-35 N. at exit 189, 830/608-0004, $54–150). One notch above Days Inn is **La Quinta Inn and Suites** (365 Hwy. 36 S., 830/627-3333, $80) and **Hawthorn Inn and Suites** (1533 I-35 N., 830/643-9300, $80).

Food

In step with New Braunfels' German heritage there's touristy **Oma's Haus Restaurant** (541 S. Hwy. 46, 830/625-3280, 11 A.M.–9 P.M. daily, $12). If you're expecting a super-authentic German food experience you may be disappointed—however If you want a fun experience and pseudo-German fare you will love this place. Oma's offers quite a selection of imported German beers and schnitzels along with some American plates for the less adventurous.

Want to eat beef at any time of day? **New Braunfels Smokehouse** (140 Hwy. 46 S., 830/625-2416, 7:30 A.M.–8 P.M. Sun.–Thurs., 7:30 A.M.–9 P.M. Fri.–Sat., $12) has beef for breakfast, lunch, and dinner, and even for snack time. They specialize in German and American smoked meats. Here you can find any kind of meat you could ever crave—beef brisket, pork, chicken, ribs, turkey, and jerky—all hickory smoked.

Housed in the old Palace Movie Theatre in historic downtown New Braunfels is **Myron's Prime Steakhouse** (136 Castell St., 830/624-1024, 4–10 P.M. daily, $30). People come here for great wine, Chicago prime beef, and a classy fine-dining experience. Myron's has a full bar as well as an extensive wine list. The atmosphere is casual but elegant. Reservations are recommended.

◖ GRUENE

One of the Hill Country's best-kept secrets is historic Gruene (pop. 20). Pronounced like the color green, this small bend in the river is technically a part of New Braunfels called the Gruene Historic District. The slogan on Gruene's promotional material speaks volumes about the town's forward-looking vision: "Gently resisting change since 1872." This happens to be the year the town was born, when German immigrant Henry D. Gruene bought the land to establish a cotton farm. The town's gentle resistance becomes very apparent once you take that last turn and drive into Gruene. Suddenly you find yourself smack dab in the middle of an old-world downtown that's straight out of a bygone era.

Sights and Activities

The town itself is the main attraction. It's nothing more than a few Wild West–style buildings with tin roofs, a large water tower, a historic mansion, and a few restaurants and specialty shops, all with laid-back country charm. This charm is due to the town's perfect combination of strict zoning laws that keep out big business, and laissez-faire fire codes that allow nearly dilapidated buildings to continue to exist. Several of the businesses simply don't have air-conditioning. This may be a deliberate attempt at creating an old-world ambience, or maybe it's simply a way to save money. Either way it adds to the experience.

A nice way to spend half a day is to simply meander through town, going in and out of the old buildings that house new businesses. If you're so inclined, buy some horseshoe art, some locally made wine, or some antiques.

You never would guess it, but Gruene has one of the best venues for music in Texas, and one of the most unique venues in the whole United States. **Gruene Hall** (1281 Gruene Rd., 830/606-1281, www.gruenehall.com) is billed as the oldest standing dance hall in the state. I say "standing" with trepidation as the building is so old and rickety it doesn't look like it's long for this world. The windows are chicken wire, the roof is tin, and the walls are those originally erected back in the 1880s. With chicken-wire windows there's no chance for air-conditioning, so the best way to cool down is with a cold beverage. Adorning the walls are hundreds of signed photos of the performers

that have graced this old hall. Be sure to look for the two photos of Lyle Lovett, one when he was a young upstart without the big hair 'do, and the other when he found his shtick. Many country legends and rock stars have performed here over the years such as Willie Nelson, George Strait, Jerry Jeff Walker, Merle Haggard, George Thorogood, and the alt-country band the Old 97's. There's live music seven days a week in summer and 3–4 days a week the rest of the year, including Saturday and Sunday afternoons.

Accommodations

When visiting Gruene, if you aren't hurried and can stay the night in town, there are a few great options for lodgings. The most famous and certainly the place with the most mystique is **Gruene Mansion Inn** (1275 Gruene Rd., 830/629-2641, www.gruenemansioninn.com), the original house that Henry D. Gruene built. This old mansion offers 30 different rooms, units, and nooks to stay in, ranging $159–209. Rooms are brightly colored, some outfitted with claw foot tubs, hardwood floors, canopy beds, fireplaces, and views of the Guadalupe River.

If an old mansion freaks you out, or if you prefer modern accommodations, **Gruene Apple B&B** (1235 Gruene Rd., 830/643-1234, www.grueneapple.com) has clean rooms with views of the river as well. Amenities in the rooms can include a whirlpool tub, fireplace, a private balcony, and amenities available to all guests include a full-size swimming pool, a media room with theater, and an entertainment room including a pool table and library. Rates range $160–210 and include a hearty gourmet breakfast. Imagine cinnamon pecan-stuffed French toast and you understand the use of the word gourmet.

Other accommodations include **Gruene Homestead Inn** (832 Gruene Rd., 800/238-5534, www.gruenehomesteadinn.com), a collection of historic farm houses on eight acres. Prices range $125–250 depending on the room and time of the year. There's also **Gruene River Inn** (1111 Gruene Rd., 830/627-1600, www.grueneriverinn.com, $125–195), located 100 feet above the Guadalupe River. Every room takes advantage of the great view of the river. And finally, for a great bed-and-breakfast, there's **Antoinette's Cottage** (1258 Gruene Rd., 830/606-6929, www.antoinettescottage. com, $150).

Food

There are a few great eateries in town, a couple hovering above the Guadalupe River. These riverfront restaurants have seating outside on decks and porches under the groves of trees that line the river. One of the best restaurants in all of Texas, the **Gristmill River Restaurant & Bar** (1287 Gruene Rd., 830/625-0684, 11 A.M.–9 P.M. Sun.–Thurs., 11 A.M.–10 P.M. Fri.–Sat., $15), is right here in Gruene at the base of the water tower. With a maze of terraced decks, porches, and covered areas that weave in and out of the ruins of an old historic cotton gin, this top-notch restaurant is a must for dinner. Although there is no air-conditioning in most of the restaurant, once you sit down with a cold iced tea and relax, you can forget about the heat . . . sort of. The fare is standard, such as sirloin, trout, shrimp, and chicken-fried chicken, but all is above standard once it hits the palate.

Gruene's Tex-Mex food establishment, **Adobe Verde** (1724 Hunter Rd., 830/629-0777, www.adobeverde.com, $8), is a great place to bring the family or fill up before a show at Gruene Hall. I recommend relaxing on the covered patio while eating fajitas, chips and queso, or tortilla soup.

Shopping

In a historic town like Gruene it's only natural that there be a number of antique shops to add to the old flavor. If you enter town by way of Gruene Road, coming from New Braunfels, the first antique shop you come to will be the **Gruene Antique Company** (1607 Hunter Rd., 830/629-7781, 10 A.M.–9 P.M. daily). Housed in the original mercantile building is 8,000 square feet of antiques, collectibles, furniture, and gifts. Ask to see the original bank vault from the Henry D. Gruene days.

Just up the road is a string of antique shops, all in historic old houses, starting with **Hampe House** (1640 Hunter Rd., 830/620-1325, 10 A.M.–5:30 P.M. Mon. and Wed.–Thurs., 10 A.M.–6 P.M. Fri.). The proprietors are proud to offer antique furniture and decorative items for the country home, all at great prices. Next door is **Cactus Jacks** (1706 Hunter Rd., 830/620-9602, 10 A.M.–5:30 P.M. Wed.–Mon.), which offers more furniture but with a European flair, along with some handmade gifts and things for the garden.

Getting Around

The best way to get around in the Hill Country is by car. Having the freedom to go where and when you please is the only way you can truly sink your teeth into this big pie. For car rental companies refer to the Austin or San Antonio chapters. If you would like to take a bus from either Austin or San Antonio there's **Kerrville Bus Company** (in Austin 512/389-0319, in San Antonio 210/226-7371, or 800/256-2757, www.iridekbc.com).

Finding your way around the small roads in the Hill Country can be tricky if you're not from the area. Streets in town often have a name, but as they leave town they turn into numbered roads. On maps you may see unusual abbreviations. FM means Farm-to-Market, RM means Ranch-to-Market, and RR means Rural Road. Many dude ranches, state parks, and attractions out of town simply don't have street addresses. Instead they use old-fashioned ranch signs to mark their entrance.

SAN ANTONIO

San Antonio is one of the oldest continuously inhabited places in Texas. Historically, this stretch of lush and scenic land along the San Antonio River was both beautiful and rich in resources, which made it a crossroads of many peoples and cultures including Native Americans, Spanish settlers and missionaries, Latin Americans, and even German immigrants. Throughout the centuries, all this cultural exchange and diversity provided the stage for some of the more dramatic chapters in Texas's history.

Today San Antonio has settled into its role as a laid-back, friendly, gritty, hard-working, family town, and is proud to still be a crossroads of cultures. It is a place where Mexico, the old Wild West, and the New World genuinely and successfully collaborate to create a unique culture and relaxed lifestyle that can't be found anywhere else. It's a place where Spanish colonial architecture and modern skyscrapers emerge out of the ancient San Antonio River's beautiful River Walk, where mariachi mass is still offered at one of the old Spanish missions, where masterfully executed murals on city walls tell the story of Mexico and Texas.

People are always pleasantly surprised by the remarkably unique charm this city has. Most people know of San Antonio as the home of the mother of all American pilgrimage sights—the Alamo. Sure there's the Alamo, Davy Crockett, General Santa Anna, and the fight for independence—but there's also much more. There's the beautiful River Walk, the crumbling Spanish missions, world-class museums, and even overblown theme parks. Because of all this history, natural beauty, and fun, San Antonio has grown

© JUSTIN MARLER

SAN ANTONIO

HIGHLIGHTS

◖ **The Alamo:** The most sacred sight on Texas soil is this old mission that became the location of one of the bloodiest and most infamous showdowns in U.S. history. Although small in appearance, the Alamo is huge in stature and importance (page 169).

◖ **River Walk:** Walk down the old stone steps to the River Walk to find another world filled with little shops, boats, and restaurants with umbrella tables, all lining the twisting San Antonio River. Most visitors stay near the river and spend most of their time here because it's so beautiful and inviting (page 171).

◖ **San Antonio Zoo and Aquarium:** Nationally renowned, this zoo carved into the side of a cliff is a blast for kids and the whole family. See lions, gorillas, alligators, and a flock of other exotic birds and animals (page 172).

◖ **La Villita:** The historic site of the first established village in San Antonio has largely been preserved. Housed in original old buildings are art galleries, cafés, and funky shops (page 174).

◖ **King William Historic District:** An excellent place for a lazy afternoon or evening stroll, this old part of town was built by and for the rich of San Antonio. The mansions are still occupied, and a couple are even open to the public, such as the Guenther House and the Edward Steves Homestead Museum (page 175).

◖ **San Antonio Museum of Art:** Four floors of exhibits containing perfectly displayed prehistoric art, Egyptian mummies, Roman statuary, antiquities, and American and European paintings by the masters are housed in the original Lone Star Brewery (page 176).

◖ **The Missions:** Stroll the ancient grounds of San Antonio's sacred and mysterious missions and learn how the indigenous peoples lived before the arrival of the Spanish, and how the native culture and people changed as a result of the missionaries (page 177).

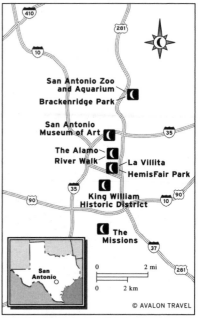

© AVALON TRAVEL

LOOK FOR ◖ TO FIND RECOMMENDED SIGHTS, ACTIVITIES, DINING, AND LODGING.

◖ **Brackenridge Park:** This beautiful park is home to many of the city's main attractions, such as the San Antonio Zoo and Aquarium, the Witte Museum, the Texas Pioneer and Ranger Museum, the Japanese Tea Gardens, and a miniature train called the Brackenridge Eagle (page 180).

◖ **HemisFair Park:** Once the World's Fair of 1968 was over, San Antonio was left with some amazing features that were wisely preserved, such as the Institute of Texan Cultures, the Tower of the Americas, the water gardens, and the Schultz House Cottage Garden (page 181).

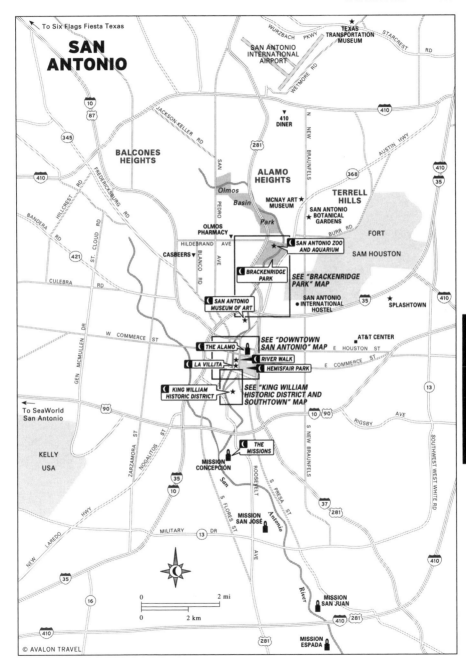

SAN ANTONIO

© JUSTIN MARLER

A good downtown reference point is the strange orange sculpture at the center of Alamo Square, above the River Walk.

SAN ANTONIO QUICK FACTS

- Founded in 1731

- Population: 1,236,249

- Land area: approximately 400 square miles

- Time zone: GMT/UTC -6 (Central Time)

- Second-largest city in Texas

- Eighth-largest city in the United States

- County: Bexar

- Ethnicity: 32 percent white, 58 percent Hispanic, 7 percent African American, 2 percent other

- Sales tax: 7.75 percent

---

into the eighth-largest city in the United States and is Texas's most beloved town.

PLANNING YOUR TIME

San Antonio covers a massive area, but fortunately most of what people come here for is in or around downtown, which makes planning your time fairly easy. Most people prefer to stay at one of the many hotels along the River Walk to make it just that much easier. If you plan on seeing the sights downtown, your trip is a cinch to plan. In fact you can figure it out as you go. However, if you want to take in sights outside of the downtown area such as the San Antonio Zoo, the missions, the Witte Museum, or one of the two theme parks, you will want to plan your time more carefully. Going to any of the above can easily turn into a full-day excursion, once you factor in transportation time and meal breaks.

ORIENTATION

San Antonio is only 80 miles south of Austin, just outside the Hill Country. The border of

Mexico is 270 miles to the south, and the Gulf of Mexico is 140 miles to the southeast. The city itself is a massive sprawling place that can be intimidating for the first-time visitor. For the most part, sights, activities, and points of interest are located in three main areas: downtown, Southtown, and the Brackenridge Park area. The downtown area is where you will most likely spend most of your time. It's stunningly beautiful here and most everything is within walking distance. Because of this, most visitors pitch their tent in one of the many hotels downtown on the River Walk. This is where you'll find sights pertaining to the original Spanish settlement such as the Alamo, the River Walk on the San Antonio River, La Villita, several museums, and Market Square. In Southtown you'll explore the mansions of the King William Historic District, modern art studios and galleries, and some of the best restaurants San Antonio has to offer. Southtown is also the starting point for the missions along the Mission Trail. The Brackenridge Park area is where you'll spend a good chunk of time if you have kids. This beautiful city park is home to the famous San Antonio Zoo as well as museums and botanical gardens geared towards families.

Outside of these three areas is an endless urban and suburban sprawl with neighborhoods, strip malls, industrial complexes, and military bases. There are three attractions worth mentioning out here, and they are Six Flags Fiesta Texas, Sea World San Antonio, and Splashtown.

Sights

San Antonio is Texas's most beloved city for all things touristy. Its rich history combined with a contemporary appeal keeps folks coming here year-round. Besides being home to the top two most visited attractions in Texas, The Alamo and the River Walk, San Antonio also has world-class museums, mega–theme parks, and quirky attractions that are sure to amuse even the most jaded traveler.

◖ THE ALAMO

The most revered historical sight and most venerated landmark in Texas is The Alamo (300 Alamo Plaza, 210/225-1391, www.thealamo. org, 9 A.M.–5:30 P.M. Mon.–Sat., 10 A.M.–5:30 P.M. Sun.; open until 7 P.M. Fri.–Sat. June–Aug., free). Here legends and heroes of Texas history were born, died, and live on in our imaginations. Most visitors are surprised to see that the Alamo is small in size, but the history here is huge. On this hallowed ground in 1836, 188 brave Texans made their stand against 3,000 (give or take a few) of General Santa Anna's finest. For 13 days a bloody battle slowly carried out and finally culminated in the final assault on the morning of March 6. Famous Texans like Col. William Travis, James Bowie, Juan Seguin, and of course, the Tennessean Davy Crockett (Congressman and outdoorsman who was famous in his day for his exploits) made history by defying the dictator Santa Anna and staking their lives for freedom's sake. They lost the battle but through their sacrifice a nation (the Republic of Texas) was born. There is some controversy regarding what became of Davy Crockett, but whatever you do, don't let a revisionist historian tell you that Davy Crockett surrendered (the

© JUSTIN MARLER

Although the Alamo is small in size, it's huge in history.

Pena "diaries" were a forgery . . . Davy died swinging his rifle, Ol' Betsy—that's my story and I'm sticking with it!). Their famous stand bought precious time for the fledgling republic's first president, Sam Houston, who eventually was able to defeat Santa Anna at the Battle of San Jacinto, near Houston. Texas is the only state of the United States that was a sovereign nation before being annexed in 1845.

At the turn of the 20th century, the Alamo was almost converted into a hotel but was saved by the Daughters of the Texas Republic, who to this day impeccably maintain the historic

SAN ANTONIO

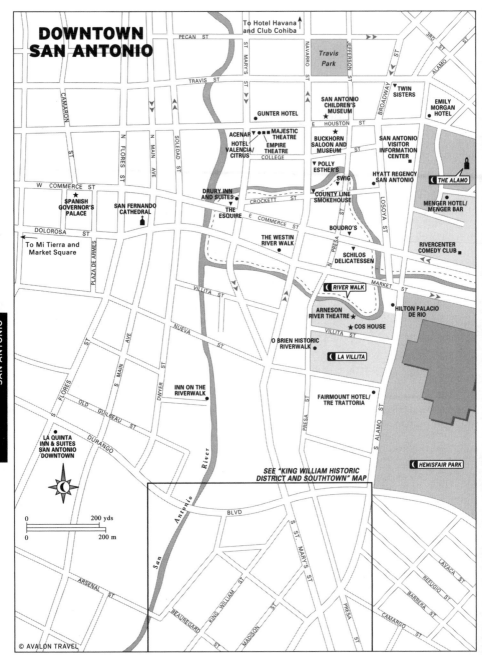

DOWNTOWN SAN ANTONIO

PECAN ST

To Hotel Havana
and Club Cohiba

Travis Park

TRAVIS ST

CAMARON ST

ST MARY'S ST

FLORES ST

N MAIN AVE

SOLEDAD ST

NAVARRO

JEFFERSON ST

ALAMO ST

3RD ST

BROADWAY

TWIN SISTERS

GUNTER HOTEL

E HOUSTON ST

SAN ANTONIO CHILDREN'S MUSEUM ★

EMILY MORGAN HOTEL

ACENAR ▼ ■ ■ MAJESTIC THEATRE
HOTEL VALENCIA/ CITRUS
EMPIRE THEATRE
COLLEGE

BUCKHORN SALOON AND MUSEUM ★

SAN ANTONIO VISITOR INFORMATION CENTER ■

▼ POLLY ESTHER'S

SWIG ★

HYATT REGENCY SAN ANTONIO ●

🕯 THE ALAMO

W COMMERCE ST

SPANISH GOVERNOR'S PALACE ★

SAN FERNANDO CATHEDRAL ♠

DRURY INN AND SUITES ●

CROCKETT ST

COUNTY LINE SMOKEHOUSE

MENGER HOTEL/ MENGER BAR ●

THE ESQUIRE ▼

E COMMERCE ST

BOUDRO'S ▼

DOLOROSA ST

To Mi Tierra and
Market Square

THE WESTIN RIVER WALK ●

SCHILOS DELICATESSEN ▼

LOSOYA ST

RIVERCENTER COMEDY CLUB ■

PLAZA DE ARMES

VILLITA ST

PRESA ST

MARKET ST

🕯 RIVER WALK

ARNESON RIVER THEATRE ★

COS HOUSE ★

HILTON PALACIO DE RIO ●

NUEVA ST

DWYER ST

VILLITA ST

O BRIEN HISTORIC RIVERWALK ●

🕯 LA VILLITA

FLORES ST

S MAIN AVE

OLD GUILBEAU ST

INN ON THE RIVERWALK ●

DURANGO ST

LA QUINTA INN & SUITES SAN ANTONIO DOWNTOWN ●

San Antonio River

FAIRMOUNT HOTEL/ TRE TRATTORIA ●

S ALAMO ST

🕯 HEMISFAIR PARK

SEE "KING WILLIAM HISTORIC DISTRICT AND SOUTHTOWN" MAP

BLVD

S ST MARY'S ST

PRESA ST

0   200 yds
0   200 m

BEAUREGARD ST

KING WILLIAM ST

MADISON ST

LAVACA ST

REFUGIO ST

BARRERA ST

CAMARGO ST

ARSENAL ST

© AVALON TRAVEL

SAN ANTONIO

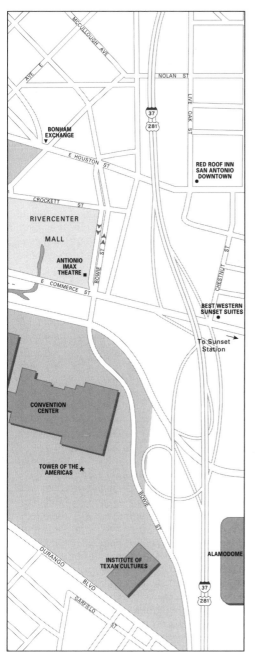

site. Toward the end of the 20th century people knew the Alamo as the place where Ozzy Osbourne relieved himself. He did his time in jail, so let's move on from this moment in rock history and remember the Alamo for the sacrifice, the glory, the honor!

◖ RIVER WALK

The greatest and most pleasant surprise San Antonio has to offer is the age-old Paseo del Río, commonly referred to as the River Walk. This stretch of the San Antonio River winds and twists its way through the downtown area, in the shadows of the city's historic buildings and skyscrapers. With stone bridges, stone stairways, and winding pathways at the edge of calm, teal-colored water, the River Walk is reminiscent of the smaller canals of Venice. Once you descend one of the many stairways and set foot on the River Walk you find yourself in a quiet, romantic, captivating subterranean world with shops, riverside cafés, bars, restaurants, hotels, and historic sites.

The River Walk almost never was. Back in the 1920s, after a disastrous flood, the city nearly filled this part of the San Antonio River in. Thanks to city officials with vision, and the brilliant design of Robert H. Hugman, what began as a catastrophe ended in 1941 as the Paseo del Río (River Walk). In 1968, just before the opening of San Antonio's World Exposition (HemisFair), a second extension and upgrade was completed, which helped put San Antonio on the map as a world-class city. Then in the '70s, the River Walk superseded the Alamo in popularity due to a clever campaign by the city with the slogan "Forget the Alamo. Remember the River Walk."

Today the River Walk is a historic, well-established centerpiece of downtown. The city's locals and frequenters can all too easily overlook this as something for the tourist. Sure it has its touristy side, but it's also a unique and genuinely integral part of San Antonio. Although the River Walk is always active, it reaches a fevered pitch during Fiesta and the winter holiday season. So many people are down on the stone walks that it's not

© JUSTIN MARLER

One of the most beautiful touristy spots in Texas is San Antonio's famous River Walk.

uncommon to see someone fall in to the river. To truly appreciate the River Walk all you have to do is take a seat at one of the riverside cafés, sip a mojito, and watch the boats and people pass by.

◖ SAN ANTONIO ZOO AND AQUARIUM

In beautiful Brackenridge Park is the glorious San Antonio Zoo and Aquarium (3903 N. St. Mary's St., 210/734-7184, www.sazoo-aq.org, 9 A.M.–5 P.M. daily, until 6 P.M. in the summer, $11 for adults, $8 for seniors and children 3–11). This world-renowned zoo is home to over 3,500 animals, with 750 species represented including some endangered species. Virtually every animal that spurs the imagination the world over can be found here, laying around in small cages and faux environments. Of the more popular residents are the lions, zebras, tigers, and gorillas. Along with gawking at those critters in captivity, one can also learn much here, as the zoo is set up to educate and foster a love of animals.

TOWER OF THE AMERICAS

The main focal point in the San Antonio skyline is the Tower of the Americas (600 HemisFair Park, 210/223-3101, www.toweroftheamericas.com, 10 A.M.–10 P.M. Sun.–Thurs., 10 A.M.–11 P.M. Fri.–Sat., $11). The tower is one of the many remnants of the HemisFair (World's Fair) that was held in **HemisFair Park** back in 1968 and is still one of the tallest freestanding structures in the Western Hemisphere. No matter where you are in San Antonio you can see the 750-foot tower, which dwarfs the Space Needle by 87 feet and snubs the Washington Monument by 67 feet. In Texas everything is bigger—get used to it. The observation deck is some 59 stories high and offers the very best view in town. Buying a Tower Ticket for $11 gives you all-day access to the observation deck and a 15-minute ride called **Skies Over Texas,** which is a stadium seating 4-D adventure that offers a short Texas history lesson through a simulated helicopter ride over the state. The tower is also home to the **Chart House** (210/223-3101, $18), a slowly revolving

WHAT HAPPENED TO DAVY CROCKETT?

Some of the details of the battle at the Alamo are enshrouded in mystery. The legend of Davy Crockett and the Alamo is perhaps the most controversial of these mysteries. History has offered us several conflicting accounts of what happened to Crockett. Did he die or was he taken as a slave? And if he died there, where did he die? A slave of William Travis's by the name of Joe and one of the several female survivors, Susanna Dickinson, reported seeing his body at the Alamo surrounded by several dead Mexican soldiers when they departed the chapel after the battle. In 1975, a diary of a Mexican officer by the name of Lt. Jose Enrique de la Pena surfaced. In the diary, Pena reported that Crockett was one of several men taken prisoner after the battle and put to death before Santa Anna "without complaining and without humiliating themselves before their torturers." The authenticity of the diary is subject to much dispute. The diary's account of Crockett's death conflicts not only with the observations of Travis's slave and Dickinson but also with that of the Mexican *alcalde* (mayor) of San Antonio, Francisco Antonio Ruiz. Santa Anna put Ruiz in charge of collecting all the dead and burning their bodies. Santa Anna had him identify the bodies of Travis, Bowie, and Crockett, a task he would not have had to perform if Crockett had been killed in Santa Anna's presence.

restaurant with mediocre pseudo-fancy food, and a low-key cocktail lounge called **Bar 601** (210/223-3101). Heavy drinkers will be pleased to know that, unlike the restaurant, the lounge doesn't revolve. Late hours make this a must for romantics. Parking is $8 at 701 Bowie Street.

AMUSEMENT PARKS
SeaWorld San Antonio

The home of San Antonio's biggest celebrity is SeaWorld San Antonio (10500 SeaWorld Dr., 800/700-7786, www.seaworld.com), the biggest marine theme park in the world. And who might this celebrity be? Shamu, the gentle killer whale. The Shamu Adventure is the top-billing act at SeaWorld and is hosted by world-renowned animal expert Jack Hanna. With a two-story video screen, seven-million-gallon tank, and 3,800 seats, the show inundates viewers with thrills. Warning to all who like to drink water and not wear it—don't sit in the first 14 rows, where you will get seriously drenched. Shows take place throughout the day. Also at SeaWorld is a sea-lion and beluga show with tricked-out dolphins and acrobats, Lost Lagoon water park with wave pool and water chutes, shark aquariums with large viewing windows, bird exhibits, and 100 resident penguins. There is also a large dolphin pool where little ones can feed dolphins. As if this isn't enough, the park also has several roller coasters. I'm not much of a fan of overblown, mega–theme parks, especially ones founded by Anheuser-Busch, but the kids *love* it! There's so much going on here that I highly suggest going online before your visit to help determine what you want to see. Also, plan on bringing swimsuits and a change of clothes cause you will probably get wet. Hours fluctuate, but generally are 10 A.M.–6 P.M. Ticket prices for day passes are $50 ages 3–9 and $60 ages 10 and up. Deals can sometimes be had by buying tickets online.

Six Flags Fiesta Texas

Another mega–theme park is Six Flags Fiesta Texas (17000 I-10 W., 210/697-5050, www.sixflags.com). With over 200 acres of fun for the whole family, Six Flags is a major draw for thrill-seekers all over the state. The park features rides for visitors of all ages, as well as campy shows and theme areas à la Disneyland. The whole park has a Texas spin, flavor, and look, with cartoon-style themed areas like a Hispanic village and a German town. The real reason people come here is to get sick and scared on the roller coasters or get wet on the water slides and chutes. Families will like how the rides are laid out, intermixing the adult rides with the children's rides. This makes for a fun day for everyone, all at the same time. I pity the folks who are walking around dressed up like cartoon characters in the middle of summer. Park hours and days of operation fluctuate so call in advance. Tickets prices are $555 for general admission and $40 for children 48 inches and under. A deal can be had by purchasing tickets online.

Splashtown
A great place for the whole family to cool down in the hot summer months is Splashtown (3600 N. I-35, 210/227-1400, www.splashtownsa. com, hours vary, roughly 11 A.M.–8 P.M. daily Apr.–Sept., $30 for general admission, $22 for children under 48 in., $19 after 5 P.M.). This 20-acre water theme park has hydro-related activities for every age, from Kid's Kove to the Wave Pool, from the seven-story Lone Star Luge to Starflight, a double-tube slide into total darkness. After the sun sets Splashtown offers a teen-oriented program that includes movies every Friday night and live Christian bands most Sunday afternoons. Lockers are available for a fee and parking is free.

MUSEUMS, HISTORY, AND ART
◖ La Villita
Walking on San Antonio's famous River Walk you'll stumble on a little historic yet touristy spot called La Villita (418 Villita St., 210/207-8610, www.lavillita.com, 10 A.M.–6 P.M. daily, free). This is the original site of San Antonio's first neighborhood. It's believed it was first founded as a settlement for Spanish soldiers under Santa Anna who were stationed at the Mission San Antonio (the Alamo). The buildings at La Villita are mostly historic; some have survived the floods and some have been transported to this location. Inside these relics there are galleries, shops, and cafés, all oozing charm. Also at La Villita is the historic outdoor **Arneson River Theatre** that was cleverly constructed of stone with grass patches for

Historic La Villita is the site where General Cos surrendered to the Texans. Today it's a charming shopping district.

comfortable seating, as was seen in the movie *Miss Congeniality*. Also in La Villita is the Cos House, which is believed to be the spot where General Perfecto de Cos signed the articles of capitulation for the Mexican Army after being defeated by the Texan Army.

Institute of Texan Cultures
Texas, and more specifically the San Antonio area, has some of the continent's most ancient history. Many various peoples have inhabited, settled, and in some way contributed to the history and prehistory of the state. The Institute of Texas Cultures (801 S. Bowie St., 210/458-2300, www.texancultures.utsa.edu, 10 A.M.–5 P.M. Tues.–Sat., noon–5 P.M. Sun., $7) has pulled all this history into one place and presented it in a dynamic and moving way. The populations of 26 cultural and ethnic groups are represented and explored through the items they left behind, such as tools, religious artifacts, and household items from daily life. In the 50,000-square-foot space the

institute has developed fascinating permanent and rotating exhibits, educational programs, and even a multiscreen video presentation that unveils these cultures. The institute originally opened at the HemisFair back in 1968, but was so well received it has remained open since. Limited free parking is at the front of the building, and paid parking is available at 701 Bowie Street for $8.

King William Historic District

The amazing little neighborhood just south of downtown called the King William Historic District is the one place in town where you can marvel at historic mansions, visit some of San Antonio's best art galleries, and get a bite to eat at one of a few fantastic restaurants. At the end of the 19th century, this little bastion of opulence initially settled by German immigrants was where the rich and notable of San Antonio lived. Today this historic district is still lined with breathtakingly beautiful historic mansions, some of which are beautifully set on the banks of the San Antonio River. Most of the mansions are Victorian and colonial revival in style and have well-manicured gardens. If you are curious about what the interior of these mansions looks like, you're in luck. Two of the mansions, **The Guenther House** (205 E. Guenther St., 210/227-1061) and the **Edward Steves Homestead Museum** (509 King William St., 210/225-5924) are open to the public. The King William Historic District is circumscribed by Durango Street, St. Mary's Street, Alamo Street, and the San Antonio River.

McNay Art Museum

San Antonio's best repository for paintings by the masters is the lovely McNay Art Museum (600 N. New Braunfels St., 210/824-5368, www.mcnayart.org, 10 A.M.–4 P.M. Tues.–Fri., 10 A.M.–9 P.M. Thurs., 10 A.M.–5 P.M. Sat., noon–5 P.M. Sun., $8 adults, free for children 12 and under). Safely hanging on the walls of a stunning old Spanish colonial revival–style mansion is a spectacular collection of art. The collection focuses on 19th- and

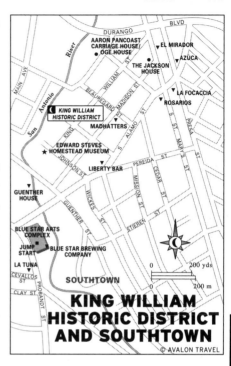

20th-century European and American art, including notable works by Picasso, Cézanne, O'Keeffe, Gauguin, and Van Gogh, and also features a variety of sculpture. The mansion is surrounded in well-tended gardens, making this one of the most scenic and breathtaking museums in Texas. The house and much of the collection belonged to a wealthy woman by the name of Marion Koogler McNay, who donated everything to the cause of the "advancement of art" upon her passing in 1950. Subsequently the McNay Museum was the first modern art museum in the state. Free parking is available.

San Antonio Children's Museum

The stodgy museums of adults can get pretty boring for kids. If you make a pit stop at the San Antonio Children's Museum (305 E. Houston St., 210/212-4453, www.sakids.org, 9 A.M.–5 P.M. Mon.–Fri., 9 A.M.–6 P.M. Sat.,

THE LEGEND OF THE HAUNTING CHILDREN

On the south side of San Antonio, in the vicinity of Blue Star Arts Complex, there's a set of railroad tracks that are believed to be haunted. The story is that a bus full of children stalled on the railroad tracks and was hit by a train. All the children supposedly died. Although there is no record of this incident, people believe children haunt the tracks, especially at one crossing. Supposedly, if you go at night (especially Halloween), put baby powder on the trunk of your car, and put your car in neutral on the tracks, your car will be pushed by the ghosts of the kids. Their fingerprints are often seen in the baby powder. Local residents are tired of people stopping on the tracks and doing the baby powder test, so I won't disclose the location of this crossing. Just know that there may be the ghosts of children in the area.

noon–5 P.M. Sun., $7) you're sure to put a smile on their faces, and get their approval for one more trip to the old missions. With over 80 hands-on exhibits, children can pretend to be a plumber, an H.E.B employee, an airplane pilot, or a construction worker, and learn at the same time. Although the museum is designed for children ages 2–12, adults can also get into this if you let go of your inhibitions and adultness and scream, run, and play.

◖ San Antonio Museum of Art

Housed in the former Lone Star Brewery building, which dates back to 1884, is the San Antonio Museum of Art (200 W. Jones Ave., 210/978-8100, www.sa-museum.org, 10 A.M.–5 P.M. Tues.–Sat., until 9 P.M. Tues., noon–6 P.M. Sun., $8). This truly world-class museum is one of the most comprehensive in the United States, with four floors of exhibits that contain perfectly displayed prehistoric art,

Egyptian mummies, Roman statuary, antiquities, and American and European paintings by the masters. Along with all this, the museum is also home to the Nelson A. Rockefeller Center for Latin American Art, which is the most extensive collection of Latin American art in the nation. To give you an example of the caliber of the San Antonio Museum of Art, this museum is on the same touring-exhibit circuit as the New York Metropolitan Museum of Art and the Louvre in Paris.

San Fernando Cathedral

The oldest cathedral sanctuary in the United States is at San Fernando Cathedral (115 Main Plaza, 210/227-1297, www.sfcathedral. org). Founded in 1731 by a group of families who came from Spain at the invitation of King Philip V of Spain, this picturesque, historic, gothic revival–style cathedral has seen much of San Antonio's history. Probably the most dramatic event was during the siege of the Alamo when General Santa Anna raised the flag of "no quarter" from the rooftop. The cathedral has always been at the center of San Antonio's life and to this day is a main focal point as well as cultural centerpiece. It is the seat of the Roman Catholic Archdiocese of San Antonio and offers mass in Spanish, English, and Latin. The popular mariachi mass is offered at 5:30 P.M. every Saturday, and every Sunday several masses are offered. For the mass schedule visit the cathedral's website.

Spanish Governor's Palace

The Spanish Governor's Palace (105 Plaza de Armas, 210/224-0601, 9 A.M.–5 P.M. Mon.–Sat., 10 A.M.–5 P.M. Sun., $2) is considered "the most beautiful building in San Antonio" according to the National Geographic Society. The "palace" is better described as a mansion. It's a beautiful Spanish colonial home with thick adobe walls and beautiful gardens. It was built as a result of an early-17th-century rivalry between Spain and France for dominance over the territory. No Spanish governor has ever actually lived here but, as the pseudo-home of the local authority, the palace played host to all-important Spanish officials of the Province of Texas. In short, the palace was the crash pad for big shots. The interior is simply but elegantly decorated with period furnishings and unique objects from everyday 19th-century life. For some reason ghosts inhabit the fountain in the garden. According to my research, the gurgling that comes from the fountain isn't the ghosts. The strangely low admission fee makes this the cheapest thrill in town.

Texas Pioneer and Ranger Museum

San Antonio wouldn't be complete without a special museum dedicated to the folks who founded and protected Texas in the beginning. The Texas Pioneer and Ranger Museum (3805 Broadway, 210/822-9011, 11 A.M.–4 P.M. Mon.–Sat., noon–4 P.M. Sun. Sept.–Apr., $5) is a commendable tribute that offers a rare glimpse into the early pioneer days, with exhibits that display items that kept the pioneers alive. The collection includes Texas Ranger artifacts and items from the old trail drivers.

Texas Transportation Museum

The quirkiest attraction in town has got to be the Texas Transportation Museum (11731 Wetmore Rd., 210/490-3554, www.txtransportationmuseum.org, 9 A.M.–3 P.M. Thurs.–Fri., 10 A.M.–5 P.M. Sat.–Sun., $8 adults, $5 children 12 and under, $22 family special). Really this is more a shrine and a personal passion dedicated to the great era of the locomotive. Here you can marvel at miniature-scale model train sets, both indoors and outdoors. The scale models and their detailed environments are a must-see for the train geek and a try-to-see for the curious. It's located to the north of San Antonio Airport. If you can, give a donation on top of your admission to keep this independently owned operation alive.

Witte Museum

The museum that boasts the most is the Witte Museum (3801 Broadway St., 210/357-1900, www.wittemuseum.org, 10 A.M.–5 P.M. Mon.–Sat., until 8 P.M. Tues., noon–5 P.M. Sun.) north

of downtown in beautiful Brackenridge Park. The correct pronunciation is like "witty," and coincidently the museum is pretty clever. The Witte is a spectacular institution that features all sorts of fun and interesting exhibits that are sure to perk the interests of everyone. With real triceratops and tyrannosaurus rex bones, mummies, dioramas, history and natural science exhibits, national touring exhibits, family events, and overnight camp-ins for children, there's almost—dare I say—too much happening here. In fact, the Witte deserves nearly a day of your time, especially if you are bringing children. The biggest draw for kids is the H.E.B Science Tree House, which consists of four floors for the miniscientist and junior anthropologist in the family to explore. General admission is $8 for adults, $7 for seniors, and $6 for children 4–11 years of age.

Buckhorn Saloon and Museum

The Buckhorn Saloon and Museum (318 E. Houston St., 210/247-4000, 10 A.M.–6 P.M. daily Memorial Day–Labor Day, 10 A.M.–5 P.M. daily the rest of the year, $18 for adults, $14 for children) is more an amusing sight than it is a museum. This weird institution has been in continuous operation since 1881. It was founded by Albert Friedrich on Dolorosa Street as a saloon where a man could get a shot of whiskey in exchange for deer antlers. During Prohibition the saloon became a "museum" and resurfaced after Prohibition as a watering hole. Over the years the saloon's collection of horns and antlers grew to include trophy mounts, memorabilia and "artifacts" from the Wild West, furniture made of cattle horns, art made from the rattles of rattlesnakes, antique powder horns, and firearms. In all, there are over 1,200 dead animals, making this a temple to the art of taxidermy. If you don't know whether to take this seriously or not, err on the side of tongue-in-cheek, and you'll have a laugh.

◖ THE MISSIONS

Although San Antonio's history stretches back for hundreds of centuries and beyond, the most visible and best-preserved relics from the past

© JUSTIN MARLER

The San Antonio Missions are remarkably well-preserved.

are the 18th-century Spanish missions established along the San Antonio River. There are five missions in all: Mission San Antonio de Valero (the Alamo), Mission Concepción, Mission San José, Mission San Juan, and Mission Espada. What's known as the Mission Trail historically connected the missions, from the northernmost mission, the Alamo, to the southernmost mission, Espada, a distance of just over eight miles. Collectively these missions form the largest concentration of Catholic missions in North America.

Established by Franciscan friars to convert the local native population, these missions were first built of stone, wood, and adobe and didn't have walls. Because of tensions between tribes and missionary occupants, stone walls were erected as a form of defense. Native Americans built these beautifully ornate buildings under the direction of craftsmen from Spain, using Spanish Colonial architectural style.

Today, the missions are surprisingly intact, although walls are crumbling and ornamental details have eroded. Mission San Antonio de

Valero (the Alamo) is maintained and operated by the Daughters of the Republic of Texas, while the other four missions are active Roman Catholic parishes run in collaboration with the Archdiocese of San Antonio and the National Parks Department.

Recently the Mission Trail has become an amazing outdoor attraction in itself. In the past the Mission Trail wasn't really an actual trail in the traditional sense of the word. However, in 2011 the San Antonio River Authority (SARA) held a soft opening of the first segment of the Mission Reach Hike and Bike Trail which connects the Main Plaza near San Fernando Cathedral to Mission Espada, the farthest mission to the south. Large portions of the trail are along the beautiful San Antonio River, which make exploring the missions via bike or by foot very enjoyable. Although signage on roads helps cars and bikes navigate the trails and roads that make up the trail, it is a good idea to download a copy of the map at www.visitsanantonio.com. Be sure to bring snacks and water as there aren't any stores to speak of along the trail.

If you don't have the time or energy for the hike and bike trail, you can easily explore all the missions in a long afternoon via auto. Here's what I recommend. Do the Alamo separately, and then tackle the other four missions. There's a distance of about three miles between all the missions (excluding the Alamo) so travel time is quick, unless you get lost. From downtown, drive south on South St. Mary's Street to Mission Road where you will land at Mission Concepción. Then take Mission Road south to Mission San José. Just outside the mission is a comprehensive visitors center with video presentations, exhibits, maps (the confusing one I mentioned), and artifacts from all the missions. Then exit the mission on Napier Avenue and head south on Mission Parkway, which will connect you to Mission San Juan, and the farthest of the missions, Mission Espada.

Visiting the missions is free of charge and all are open 9 A.M.–5 P.M. daily except Thanksgiving Day, Christmas Day, and New Year's Day. For more information contact the parks department's mission headquarters

(210/534-8833, www.nps.gov/saan) or the visitors center (6701 San José Dr., 210/932-1001).

Mission Concepción

Transferred to its present location in 1731, Mission Concepción is the largest of the missions. This mission served as the headquarters for all the San Antonio missions. At one time the facade of the mission church was adorned with elaborate, colorful frescoes and detailed artistry that has faded over time. Inside the sanctuary, remnants of this colorful past are still to be found. Some of the religious paintings on the walls contain a blend of Christian, Spanish, and native influences, and reveal how the missionaries used traditional native and religious imagery in their Christian context, in order to convey Christian teachings.

Mission San José

Founded by Franciscan missionary Father Antonio Margila de Jesús in 1720, Mission

San José became the best known of the Texas missions. The colonial baroque architecture of the limestone mission church exceeded the other missions, as did its capacity as a social center. These combined to help the mission earn the name Queen of the Missions. Once the founding ceremonies for the mission took place, leaders of three Native American tribes were appointed governor, judge, and sheriff of the mission community, and mission inhabitants learned to use firearms to defend themselves against the Apache and Comanche. At its height, the mission housed over 350 neophyte Native Americans, had an efficient aqueduct system for irrigation, a Spanish colonial flour mill, granary, and maintained fields and herds of livestock. In 1824 it ceased to be a mission.

Mission San Juan

Originally founded in 1716 in eastern Texas, Mission San Juan was transferred to its present location in 1731. San Juan eventually became

BATTLE OF CONCEPCIÓN

Approximately two miles south of downtown San Antonio is the historic Mission Concepción. Originally founded in 1716, the mission remains one of the oldest and best preserved of all the missions along the San Antonio River. In December 1835, it was the site of an important battle between the Texas colonists and the Mexican Army. The Texas revolution had just begun and 600 colonists, led by Stephen F. Austin, marched on San Antonio to force the removal of General Cos and his 900 Mexican troops. As the Texans approached San Antonio from the south, Austin sent Jim Bowie ahead with 60 men to scout out the enemy. Bowie camped in the bend along the San Antonio River, a few hundred yards in front of Mission Concepción. The following day, Cos marched out with over 300 infantry and cavalry to surround and crush the Texas force.

While lesser men might have considered surrendering, Bowie's inspired leadership led to a Texas victory. He had his men shelter behind

the riverbank and prepare for the Mexican onslaught. The cannon fire of the Mexicans went over the Texans' heads and showered them with pecans from the trees along the bank. At each charge, the Texas long rifles fired and caused heavy casualties among the Mexican Army. After four unsuccessful assaults, the Mexicans retreated back to San Antonio, leaving their cannon behind. It was the first significant victory the Texas forces won over the Mexican Army in the revolution and inspired the troops to subsequently attack the city of San Antonio and force the surrender of General Cos.

It is remarkable that after all of these years the battlefield (so close to downtown San Antonio) remains virtually unchanged. With just a little imagination a visitor can easily envision the positions of the Mexican army and the defending Texans and relive the historic battle. Look for the monument marking the place where the Texans suffered their first fatality of the revolution.

a major regional supplier of produce, once its agricultural potential was reached. Outside the mission walls orchards and gardens produced melons, grapes, sweet potatoes, beans, and even sugar cane. Within the mission walls Native American artisans produced cloth, iron tools, and other items for daily life. These products supported all the San Antonio missions as well as nearby settlements, and trade was established with surrounding states and throughout Mexico.

Mission Espada

Originally founded in 1690 near present-day Weches, Texas, Mission Espada was the first mission in Texas. The mission was transferred to its present location in 1731 and is now the most remote and southernmost mission of the four. Here mission Natives were taught vocational skills such as carpentry, masonry, blacksmithing, and stone cutting. Mission Espada was the only mission to produce bricks, which were used throughout the region. Some claim these bricks are seen throughout many historical sights in the San Antonio area. The church has a unique entrance topped with a three-bell tower known as an *espadana*. According to legend, the wooden cross to the left of the main doorway of the church was carried by parishioners in a procession around the compound as they prayed for rain during a time of drought.

GARDENS AND PARKS
C Brackenridge Park

North of downtown is San Antonio's own Shangri-la, Brackenridge Park (3910 N. St. Mary's St., 210/207-7275, 5 A.M.–11 P.M. daily, free). This beautiful city park has many features and attractions that make it a special place for kids, adults, and adults that act like kids. There's the nationally renowned **San Antonio Zoo and Aquarium,** a miniature train called the **Brackenridge Eagle** (210/735-7455) that travels over two miles around the park, the **Japanese Tea Gardens** (210/821-3120) also known as the **Sunken Gardens,** and the **Sunken Garden Theatre** (210/735-

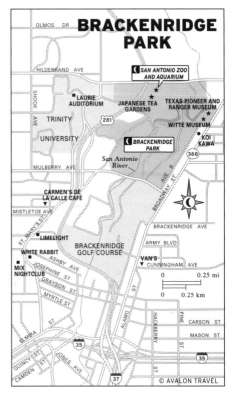

0663). Brackenridge Park is also home to the **Brackenridge Golf Course** (210/226-5612), the oldest 18-hole public golf course in Texas. At the northeastern edge of the park are two excellent museums, the **Witte Museum** (210/357-1900) and the **Texas Pioneer and Ranger Museum.**

Besides these attractions Brackenridge Park is the location of many springs that make up the headwaters for the San Antonio River, which brings the beauty of flowing, twisting lanes of water to the park. The old stone building over the river is the pump house that operated as San Antonio's first public water supply system.

With a mini-amusement park, a mini-train to ride, boats to bob in, museums, and a zoo, who needs *Lost Horizon*? The park is

© JUSTIN MARLER

Brackenridge Park

approximately two miles north of downtown, and the main entrance is in the 2800 block of North Broadway. Although admission to the park is free, fees may apply to some of the attractions within the park.

◖ HemisFair Park

One landmark event that put San Antonio on the map was the city's hosting of the World's Fair in 1968. The fair coincided with the city's 250th anniversary, and people saw this as an opportunity to boost San Antonio's profile as a world-class destination by pulling off a dramatic fair. Thus, HemisFair Park was created. Once the fair was over the city was left with some amazing features that were wisely preserved, such as the **Institute of Texan Cultures,** the **Tower of the Americas,** the **water gardens,** and the **Schultz House Cottage Garden.** In 1990 a children's playground was added that includes a wood-and-sand playground. HemisFair Park is located downtown, adjacent to the Convention Center. Parking is $8 at 701 Bowie Street.

Japanese Tea Gardens

The most serene spot in town is the Japanese Tea Gardens (3875 N. St. Mary's St., 210/207-3121). Also known as the Sunken Garden, this beautiful spot inside Brackenridge Park was the former site of a rock quarry that produced the limestone used to construct the Texas State Capitol in Austin. Someone with vision got the idea of making this beautiful and brought in a Japanese designer, Mr. Jingo, who designed and built the magnificent gardens. In recent years the gardens have been restored to their prime. Highlights of the Japanese Tea Gardens included winding walkways, a waterfall, and serene lily ponds with koi, turtles and ducks. Walking the traditional stone Japanese bridges and exploring these tranquil, lush, overgrown gardens is a relaxing way to spend an afternoon.

San Antonio Botanical Gardens

San Antonio Botanical Gardens (555 Funston Pl., 210/207-3250, www.sabot.org, 9 A.M.–5 P.M. daily, $7), located northeast of downtown, is a whopping 33 acres of well-tended plants, all waiting to be admired, understood, and appreciated. Most of the plants are displayed outdoors in the vast landscape. A slew of well-planned theme gardens are carefully orchestrated, such as the Texas regional gardens, the Old-Fashioned Garden, the Rose Garden, the Sacred Garden filled with Biblical plants, the Japanese Garden, and the brilliant Garden for the Blind. The uniquely shaped glass building that's the focal point of the grounds is the conservatory, which houses plants that have "special needs." Within a fully controlled climate the staff are able to create mini-ecosystems for plants that otherwise would perish in the San Antonio climate. Displays in the conservatory include exotic plants, ferns, desert plants, tropical plants, and palms and cycads. Outside, the conservatory is surrounded by a sunken courtyard and tropical lagoon filled with even more plants. The overlook happens to the highest point in San Antonio, 798 feet above sea level.

Entertainment and Events

San Antonio isn't known for having a crazy nightlife scene filled with live music and all-night dancing. This came about probably because at some point the family-oriented city let Austin take the lead for nightlife and entertainment. However, if you're "in the know," you can find some pretty spectacular places to spend a memorable night on the town.

For complete listings of what's happening in San Antonio, pick up a free copy of the weekly alternative newspaper, the *San Antonio Current,* or check out the Weekender section of the local newspaper, the *San Antonio Express-News.*

San Antonio is one of the largest cities in the United States, so touring national acts often play here. There are two mega-entertainment venues that host everything from hugely popular rock and country bands, to monster-truck extravaganzas, to Disney on Ice, to all spectator sports. The biggest is the ginormous **Alamodome** (100 Montana St., 210/207-3663, www.alamodome.com), located on the east side of Highway 35 near HemisFair Park. Next up is the **AT&T Center** (1 AT&T Center Pkwy., 210/444-5000, www.attcenter.com), which is home to the San Antonio Spurs and has a maximum capacity of 18,500. Finally, the popular big music venue downtown is **Sunset Station** (1174 E. Commerce, 210/222-9481, www.sunset-station.com). This entertainment complex is in the original San Antonio train station at HemisFair Park and can host 3,500 people. Tickets for large events can be purchased through **Ticketmaster** (210/224-9600, www.ticketmaster.com).

LIVE MUSIC

There's no real entertainment district to speak of in town. All venues for live music are scattered throughout the big city, and many venues double as restaurants and bars. For the most part bands strike up on weekend nights between 9 P.M. and 2 A.M. and cover charges vary.

In recent years a popular music and food district has sprouted up on North St. Mary's

Street near Brackenridge Park. This popular hipster area is home to the great music and DJ club **Limelight** (2718 N. St. Mary's St., 210/735-7775). Upon entry you may be a tad intimidated by the tattoos and stares at the door, but hang in there as this place is one of the hottest venues in town for indie rock. Shoe gazers, loud amps, and nerd rebellions rattle this place with sometimes mediocre, but often intriguing, talent. Cover usually starts at $5.

The other popular venue on North St. Mary's is **Mix Nightclub** (2423 N. Sait. Mary's St., 210/735-1313). This dive bar has a built-in scene that is alive most weekend nights starting on Thursday night. The beer is pretty cheap and the place is often packed.

Also in the North St. Mary's area is the local favorite **Carmen's de la Calle Café** (720 E. Mistletoe Ave., 210/737-8272). Thursday–Saturday nights Carmen's comes alive with jazz, Latin, and acoustic acts that always get patrons on their feet. Tapas and live flamenco music are popular on Friday nights.

In midtown, **Casbeers** (1719 Blanco Rd., 210/732-3511) is where locals go to eat burgers and listen to country, blues, rock, and folk. With a rich history that began in the 1930s, Casbeers is singing with character, with portions that are big—both in music and food.

Every town has its legendary music venue. San Antonio's is **Floore's Country Store** (14492 Bandera Rd., north of San Antonio in Helotes, 210/695-8827, www.liveatfloores.com). This "country store" sells nothing but barbecue, beer, and foot-stomping country and rockabilly music. Artists such as Lyle Lovett and Willie Nelson have graced the outdoor stage time and again. Don't expect anything fancy here, just picnic tables in the dirt.

A sure-fire way to have a great time on the town is by listening to jazz on the River Walk at **The Landing** (123 Losoya St., 210/223-7266, www.landing.com). The in-house seven-piece band, headed by Jim Cullum, faithfully performs early big-band jazz pieces, covering

MEXICANS, GERMANS, AND THE ACCORDION

The accordion is a 19th-century European instrument. So how did it become an integral part of Mexican music? It happened right here in Central Texas. The unusual instrument was first patented in 1829 in Vienna. Only a few years later German pioneers headed out to the New World, ended up in Texas, and quickly established many of the Hill Country towns such New Braunfels, Gruene, Boerne, and Comfort. They brought with them sauerkraut, schnitzel, and a strange new musical invention: the squeezebox. As the German and Mexican cultures mingled, a new style of music was pioneered. The final product was an accordion-based, Tex-Mex music that blended traditional Mexican forms such as the *corrido* and western/European waltz and polka. San Antonio was the biggest city in the region and quickly became the experimental grounds for this new music style called Tejano and conjunto. In recent years it has adopted strong influences from rock, blues, and *cumbia*, and is now not just regional ethnic music, but its own genre with wide appeal.

greats such as Benny Goodman, Glen Miller, and Louis Armstrong. The Jim Cullum Jazz Band plays Monday–Saturday starting at 8 P.M. Ask for a Bathtub Gin Martini once the band starts playing.

Leon Springs Dancehall (24135 I-10 W., 210/698-7070, www.leonspringsdancehall. com) is where you can two-step to a live country band along with hundreds of other folks. This family-friendly dance hall has a massive, 18,000 square feet of wooden floor that's packed Friday and Saturday nights. Cover charge is only $5, making this a great place to take a date for a cheap but memorable night out. Minors are welcome, but must be accompanied by an adult.

Teen angst is best experienced at the famous **White Rabbit** (2410 N. St. Mary's St., 210/737-2221, www.sawhiterabbit.com). Here a younger crowd sweats to indie rock, punk, and hard-core music. The venue is all ages and often there's no cover charge. Buy tickets by phone for a discount.

BARS AND CLUBS

Located in the hip Blue Star Arts Complex is the **Blue Star Brewing Company** (1414 S. Alamo, 210/212-5506). This inviting brewpub in the artsy area, Southtown, is a welcome oasis from the hubbub of downtown. The brews cooked up here are best enjoyed on the large outdoor patio or second-story balcony where you can watch the artists and businessmen.

Just around the corner from the Alamo is three stories of par-tay at **Bonham Exchange** (411 Bonham St., 210/271-3811). With five bars, some named after heroes of the Alamo, and three dance floors, the Bonham has oodles of space to mingle. Wednesday is college night, also known as straight night. The rest of the week it's a popular gay hangout.

Yes the Missions are old but **The Esquire** (155 E. Commerce St., 210/222-2521) is old too. This bar is a San Antonio institution that has been around since it opened in 1933, the year Prohibition ended. Okay, so it closed for four years and was recently renovated, but the ancient long bar is the main attraction. This historic saloon which houses the second-longest wooden bar in Texas, is the oldest continuously running watering hole in the state (except for those four years I mentioned). There's a whopping 91 feet of stools, bar, and locals leaning up against it checking out the folks that walk through the door. It can be intimidating drinking a beer in this joint for the first time because no matter who you are, "you're new in these parts," and you'll get the stare-down. The crowd in here is primarily locals and rough characters who practically live here. The ceiling is stamped copper, the walls are bordello-style, and the wait staff sport black shirt and tie.

Blue Star Brewing Company

The highest bar stool in town is at the **Tower of the Americas Lounge.** Located at the top of the Tower of the Americas, this classy bar with a view isn't for those who pinch pennies or have vertigo.

A great spot to stop off after an evening walk in the King William Historic District is **La Tuna** (100 Probandt St., 210/212-5727). This ice house has an inviting atmosphere that is for the whole family. Drinking a beer at one of the outside tables in late spring is a popular way to be in denial about the ensuing heat.

Next door to the Alamo is a bar rich in history called the **Menger Bar** (204 Alamo Plaza, 210/223-4361). A replica of the House of Lords Pub in London, this dimly lit, small room covered in rich cherry wood attached to the famous, ghost-haunted Menger Hotel is the perfect place to sit in a dark corner and have a drink. As you sit and sip, ponder how this pub was the location where Teddy Roosevelt recruited some of his Rough Riders. Who knows—maybe you'll see his ghost if you have enough drinks.

For a modern spin on the Brat Pack approach to booze there's **Swig** (111 W. Crockett St., No.

2205, 210/476-0005). This martini bar is all about cocktails, cigars, and live music. Guys, you gotta have a collar on your shirt to not stand out here, and gals, you gotta be in pumps. With a patio overlooking the River Walk, the best selection of martinis in town, and live jazz bands to set the tone, this place is a class act.

PERFORMING ARTS AND THEATERS

San Antonio has a slew of small performing-arts groups, as well as some more-established companies that keep the local performing-arts scene eclectic, entertaining, and cutting edge. The main performing-arts company in the arena of music is the nationally recognized **San Antonio Symphony** (210/554-1000, www.sasymphony. org). Most performances are held at newly renovated Majestic Theatre. Classical music filling the extraordinarily ornate halls of the Majestic can be a breathtaking experience.

When it comes to theater, San Antonio takes pride in having a handful of performing-arts companies. Most theatrical performances take place at one of several venues. The **Majestic**

JUSTIN MARLER

Jump-Start performances take place in an old warehouse.

Theatre (224 E. Houston St., 210/226-3333, www.majesticempire.com) is the beloved of the city. It's considered one of the most ornate theaters in the country and its history alone seems to add to any drama. Built in the 1920s this grand stage has been the center of the performing arts in San Antonio for decades. Today you can catch major Broadway productions as well as the San Antonio Symphony. The Majestic's sister theater is the **Empire Theatre** (226 N. St. Mary's St., 210/226-5700, www.majesticempire.com). This old opera house built in 1914 now puts on shows and performances of all kinds.

Trinity University Campus is home to **Laurie Auditorium** (715 Stadium Dr., 210/999-8117). It's not possible to pin down all that happens in this performing-arts auditorium. People come here to see comics like Jay Leno, jazz concerts, and world-renowned lecturers speak to packed audiences on all topics imaginable.

San Antonio's cutting-edge shows are put on at **Jump-Start** (108 Blue Star Complex, 210/227-5867, www.jump-start.org). This unique company focuses entirely on new creations that are dreamed up by local artists and writers. Most of what you'll see here is very avant-garde—all appropriately take place on a stage in an old warehouse.

Located downtown on the River Walk at historic La Villita is **Arneson River Theatre** (210/207-8610, www.lavillita.com). This well-designed outdoor amphitheatre is in a spectacular setting. The San Antonio River separates the stage from the audience, who sit on cleverly designed stone seats that are filled with patches of grass for comfort.

CINEMAS

For the magic and clarity of IMAX, there's **San Antonio IMAX Theatre** (849 E. Commerce St., 210/247-4629). Along with the usual movies Hollywood pumps out, this theater also screens those dramatic movies that make IMAX so famous. The one everyone has to see here is *Alamo, The Price of Freedom*. The theater is located on the first level of Rivercenter Mall. Three hours of parking is free at the Rivercenter Mall with the purchase of an IMAX ticket.

COMEDY CLUBS

The one outlet for live laughs is **Rivercenter Comedy Club** (849 E. Commerce St., Suite 893, at the Rivercenter Mall, 210/229-1420). Big-name acts come through here, such as Dennis Miller and comedians from Comedy Central and HBO. Local talent is also appreciated, especially during Comedy Potpourri on Monday. A night here can be complemented by dinner and drinks, as the club has a full kitchen and bar. Doors open at 4 P.M. and shows begin at 8 P.M. Headliner shows are Wednesday–Sunday. Tickets can cost anywhere from $8 to $12 depending on the night of the week and the comedian or act.

FESTIVALS AND EVENTS
January

The yearly maintenance of the San Antonio River has turned into a filthy festival, the **River Walk Mud Festival** (210/227-4262). When the river is drained, a king and queen of mud

SAN ANTONIO

are elected to preside over events that include music, games, and festivities related to mud.

February

Every February the SBC Center is taken over for the 16-day **San Antonio Stock Show and Rodeo** (210/255-5851, www.sarodeo.com). See live music, livestock, and daring cowboys riding raging bulls.

The week before Ash Wednesday, just before Lent, the River Walk features **Mardi Gras** (210/227-4262). Buy or browse arts and crafts made by local artists and artisans for an entire week. The end of the week is marked by the **Mardi Gras River Parade.** Watch a procession of decorated river barges transform the San Antonio River. Costumed revelers and live entertainment celebrate Mardi Gras San Antonio–style.

March

St. Patrick's Day in San Antonio is celebrated with barrels of green dye and even more barrels of beer. As floats pour environmentally friendly green dye into the San Antonio River, the river is renamed "The River Shannon." This is followed by the St. Patrick's Day Parade, which in turn is followed by mass consumption of beer. An estimated 15,000 people flood the River Walk for the event.

April

The most spectacular festival of all is **Fiesta San Antonio** (www.fiesta-sa.org). For 10 days in April San Antonio has a party similar to New Orleans's Mardi Gras. The citywide celebration includes carnivals, sports, fireworks, entertainment, feasts, art exhibits, and parades that float down the San Antonio River. In the past Fiesta has attracted some three million participants and spectators from around the nation. The first Fiesta event was back in 1891 in celebration of the Battle of Flowers, which honored the memory of heroes of Texas history.

May

Tejano Conjunto Festival (210/271-3151, www.guadalupeculturalarts.org) is San Antonio's way of celebrating the unique form

of music that developed in South Texas with both German and Mexican roots. The three-day festival features live performances from top conjunto and Tejano artists, all in Rosedale Park and on the Guadalupe Campus.

June

Texas Folklife Festival (210/458-2224, www.texasfolklifefestival.org) is an annual four-day celebration of the diverse group of folks that settled Texas. Some 45 groups bring their cultures to the Institute of Texan Cultures. Everyone celebrates unity through diversity with crafts, music, dances, and foods.

The most important celebration for African Americans of Texas is **Juneteenth** (www.juneteenthsanantonio.com). June 19, 1865 marked the day that Texas slaves received word of the Emancipation Proclamation. Observances include a picnic, jazz concerts, a parade, and other cultural festivities honoring the first step toward freedom for blacks.

July

Contemporary Art Month (210/222-2787, www.contemporaryartmonth.com) is a month-long contemporary arts festival—the only one in the nation. With more than 400 exhibitions taking place in more than 50 venues, such as galleries, museums, and studios, this month of art offers an amazing look at what's happening in the art world of San Antonio.

September

Marking Mexico's independence from Spain is **Diez y Seis** (800/447-3372, www.sanantoniovisit.com). Every September 16 San Antonio celebrates with a street parade with floats, marching bands, celebrations at Market Square and La Villita, and other activities.

Jazz lovers all over converge in San Antonio for **Jazz'SAlive** (210/212-8423). For two days the nation's top jazz entertainers, along with regional talent, perform in Travis Park.

October

It seems people either love the accordion or they hate it. Either way, every year San Antonio hosts the **International Accordion Festival** (www. internationalaccordionfestival.org), a two-day festival of music, dancing, and food, all for the glory and versatility of the accordion.

November
Connect with your loved ones who have passed on by celebrating **El Día de los Muertos** (210/222-2787, www.sanantonio.gov/art).

Translated as The Day of the Dead, this important and ancient celebration in Mexican culture is a celebration in which the family welcomes back departed loved ones.

Who doesn't want to sip great wine with excellent food? The **San Antonio New World Wine & Food Festival** (210/822-9555, www. nwwff.org) offers a spectacular event for wine and food aficionados.

Recreation

For those looking for fun, the most popular activities are golf, spectator sports, and, of course, visits to the city's massive theme parks. There's not much in the way of outdoor recreation in San Antonio. For hiking, biking, rock climbing, and swimming most people head out into the Hill Country.

HIKING AND BIKING
Most people head out into the Hill Country for the great outdoors. Bluntly put, San Antonio simply doesn't have much to offer in the way of outdoor activities. Perhaps the most convenient place to hike and bike is the **Mission Trail** (6701 San José Dr., 210/932-1001, www.nps. gov/saan). The trails that link some of the missions are, for the most part, scenic. However, some lengths of the trail cut through rundown urban areas that aren't too scenic. The only other place for outdoor activities in the San Antonio metropolitan area is **Brackenridge Park** (3910 N. St. Mary's St., 210/207-7275, 5 A.M.–11 P.M. daily, free). Don't expect any dirt trails for hiking or mountain biking, though, as this park is primarily for families who want to picnic and walk a paved trail near the river.

On the outskirts of town is beautiful **McAllister Park** (13102 Jones Maltsberger Rd., 210/207-7275, 5 A.M.–11 P.M. daily, free). This wooded area 12 miles north of downtown is the best place to get away from the city and hike or bike in semi-seclusion. Lastly there's **Friedrich Wilderness Park** (210/207-7275,

5 A.M.–11 P.M. daily, free), which offers 5.5 miles of trails for hiking.

GOLF
What San Antonio lacks in hiking and biking activities is made up by several world-class golf courses. In fact, some of these courses are recognized by golfers as top spots to swing a club. The favorite resort-golf mecca is **La Cantera Golf Club and Resort** (16401 La Cantera Pkwy., 800/446-5387). The two top-notch courses on the resort grounds are both classic Hill Country layouts. One overlooks Six Flags Fiesta Texas.

One of Texas's best municipal golf courses is **Cedar Creek Municipal Golf Course** (8250 Vista Colina, 210/695-5050). Considered by some to be the poor man's La Cantera, Cedar Creek can get very crowded, so patience and a tee time are absolutely necessary.

Lastly there's beautiful **Canyon Springs Golf Course** (24400 Canyon Golf Rd., 210/497-1770). No setting in golf is better than the approach to the signature 17th green and its waterfall backdrop.

SPECTATOR SPORTS
San Antonio's only major-league franchise is the ever-popular **San Antonio Spurs** (www.nba. com/spurs). This team has fought its way up the NBA food chain and has been the National Basketball Association Champions four times (in 1999, 2003, 2005, and 2007). The season is October–May, and home games are played

in the **AT&T Center.** Tickets can cost anywhere from $25 to $70, and can be purchased at the AT&T Ticket Office (1 AT&T Center Pkwy., 210/444-5819) or through Ticketmaster (210/224-9600, www.ticketmaster.com).

Another popular spectator sport is **drag racing.** The venue for this rubber-smoking speed sport is the **San Antonio Raceway** (3641 S. Santa Clara Rd., 210/698-2310, www.sanantonioraceway.com). There's also the minor-league baseball team, the **San Antonio Missions** (210/675-7275, www.samissions.com), whose season is April–September. Games are played at **Nelson Wolff Stadium** (5757 Hwy. 90 W.).

San Antonio's mega venue is the **Alamodome** (100 Montana St., 800/884-3663, www.alamodome.com), which showcases anything from bull riding to football to the Texas Hunters Extravaganza.

One of the most unique experiences one can have while in San Antonio is spending the day at the **Mexican Rodeo (Charreada)** (6126 Padre Dr., 210/532-0693, Mar.–Oct., $10, 12 and under free). *Charreada* is similar in many ways to American rodeo, but with a distinct Latin flair and showmanship. Among many *suertes* (events) are Colas en Lienzo (Bull Tailing), where a rider grabs the tail of a running bull, wraps it around his leg, and pulls the bull to the ground, and Paso de Muerte (Pass of Death), where a rider jumps from his galloping horse onto the back of a galloping wild horse and rides it until it stops bucking.

For more than 50 years the San Antonio Charro Association has been keeping this old-world sport alive, dazzling audiences with high-stakes horsemanship, daring bull roping, and live mariachi bands. Events are held at the Association's ranch, which overlooks the San Antonio River.

TOURS

Touring the downtown stretch of the San Antonio River by boat is a hoot. Tours are offered by **Rio San Antonio Cruises** (210/244-5700, www.riosanantonio.com) There are three ticket and boarding locations along the River Walk: Holiday Inn River Walk, Rivercenter Mall, and Market Street Bridge. The tour takes passengers on a 2.6-mile excursion along the river in an open, flat-bottom barge. Tours last about 40 minutes and cost $8.25. If you get an experienced tour guide who incessantly shoots out facts and anecdotes about history, famous people, and infamous events, the touristy ride can be quite entertaining. If you prefer to take a ride without the monologue, Rio offers a river taxi service that has 39 stops along the river. Taxi stops are marked by Rio Trans signs along the River Walk. One-way rate is $5, a day pass is $10, and a three-day pass is $25.

Accommodations

San Antonio is a huge, sprawling city with accommodations everywhere. The most convenient area to stay for a visitor who plans on seeing sights is obviously downtown. All downtown hotels are within walking distance to most sights, and many are luxury hotels situated right on the banks of the famous River Walk. Rates for all hotels downtown generally start around $139. During the off-season and slow times many of these hotels offer discounts that can dip as low as $100, and deals can often be found online. Although it's almost impossible to find a room in the downtown area that is under $99, deals can be found at chain hotels and motels along the highways, just outside of downtown.

UNDER $50

The **San Antonio International Hostel** (621 Pierce St. at Grayson, 210/223-9426, $25) is by far the cheapest place to stay in town, but don't expect much in the way of accommodations other than a bunk bed. If you expect to shower here, plan to share with everyone else, as there's one shower and tub used by all guests. And remember, there's a total of 38 bunks (30 male dorm bunks and 8 female dorm bunks). A $10 cash key deposit is required.

$50-100

It's almost a joke having a category for $50–100 in San Antonio. Therefore I must give a disclaimer for the following cheap lodgings. Most of them aren't in the classiest and safest areas of town, and their rooms aren't particularly nice. As for amenities, expect nothing but some sheets, a small bar of soap, and maybe some lousy coffee.

If you desire nothing but a bed, a TV, and an exceptionally low rate, the **Ramada Limited Downtown** (1122 S. Laredo St. at I-35, 210/229-1133, $59–189) offers the most basic accommodations in town. Historic Market Square is just a couple blocks away and the River Walk is just a couple miles north. It may not be centrally located but you'll have more than enough money to get around town with the money you'll save here.

The cleanest affordable bed in town is at the **Red Roof Inn San Antonio Downtown** (1011 E. Houston St., 210/229-9973 or 800/733-7663, $55–119). It's right off I-35 so expect some highway noise.

There are a few exceptions in this price range. A place that has yet to be discovered by the masses of budget travelers is **La Quinta Inn & Suites San Antonio Downtown** (100 W. Durango Blvd. 210/212-5400, $89–139). Your money can go a long way here. The rooms are spacious and clean, there's a pool for splashing around in, and the complimentary breakfast is a real breakfast with eggs and waffles. The location may not be in the River Walk, but it's still centrally located.

Another affordable place to stay near all the Riverwalk action is the **O Brien Historic Riverwalk** (116 Navarro St., 210/527-1111, $93–130). The O Brien has the charm of being in an old building and is a step above the cheaper hotels in the price range. However, keep in mind, you get what you pay for. Nothing super fancy here because it's more about the location and price.

$100-150

C Best Western Sunset Suites (1103 E. Commerce St., 210/223-4400 or 866/560-6000, $99–169) may not be at the center of all the River Walk action, but it's a safe bet for inexpensive accommodations with clean and comfortable rooms. Amenities include nice furnishings, TVs, and minifridges. Also included in your stay is free breakfast and free local calls.

Bonner Garden Bed and Breakfast (145 E. Agarita Ave., 800/396-4222, www.bonnergarden.com, $95–140), a palatial bed-and-breakfast not far from Brackenridge Park, is a romantic place to stay away from the hum of downtown but central to all that San Antonio has to offer. Imagine a spectacular two-story Italian-style villa with lush gardens, a 45-foot swimming pool, and full rooftop patio that overlooks downtown San Antonio, along with all the pampering amenities of a top-class bed-and-breakfast, and you have envisioned Bonner Gardens. Rooms are furnished with antiques, knockoff paintings, TVs, and high-speed Internet. There's a two-night minimum for weekends and a 10 percent discount is offered for three nights or more.

A great deal on the River Walk is often found at **Drury Inn and Suites** (201 N. St. Mary's St., 210/212-5200, $90–189). Amenities include free hot breakfast (the kind with eggs and sausage), free beverages, free long distance for up to 60 minutes, and high-speed Internet access. It may not be classy, but the location and value are great for budget travelers.

Early 20th century San Antonio comes alive at the **Hotel Havana** (1015 Navarro, 210/222-2008, www.havanasanantonio.com, $129–199). This historic landmark building on the River Walk was tastefully renovated and designed to evoke a combination of 1920s Texas meets Cuba. Rooms are decorated with vintage photographs, furnishings from around the world, plantation shutters, ceiling fans, and brick walls. On the premises is one of San Antonio's most intimate bars, **Club Cohiba**. This Latin bar and tapas grill is a favorite hangout for locals and travelers on the town, in the mood, and on the lam. It's best enjoyed with a stogie in hand and a flower in the lapel.

Another good value on the River Walk can be found at **Hilton Palacio del Rio** (200 S. Alamo St., 210/222-1400, $139–189). Hilton Palacio is the longest consecutive recipient of the AAA Four Diamond Award. All rooms feature Spanish decor and have access to private balconies with spectacular views of the city. Much of the main lobby and common area are a bit out-dated looking, but the fitness center has been renovated. There's also a rooftop pool and hot tub with stunning views, a full-service business center, a restaurant, and a river-level bar featuring live music and booze.

The **Gunter Hotel** (205 E. Houston St., 210/227-3241, www.gunterhotel.com, $99–189) is one of many hotels in the Sheraton chain. Housed in a historic landmark building in downtown, the Gunter looks like it might have back in 1909 when it was first built. Old San Antonio upscale charm makes this an enjoyable place to hang your hat for the weekend. Amenities aren't four-star, but who cares—when it comes to downtown hotels, this is the best deal.

One of three classy bed-and-breakfasts operated by Noble Inns is the **Aaron Pancoast Carriage House** (209 Washington, 210/223-2353 or 800/242-2770, www.nobleinns.com, $130–200). Located in the King William Historic District, this carriage house has only three suites, making for personalized service and quietude. Wake up late and take breakfast at your leisure, then relax and read in the garden, followed by a swim in the full-size pool. The large suites feature queen-size beds, separate living/dining areas, and full kitchens, all with privacy. Be sure to ask about the 1960 Rolls Royce, which can be hired for transportation to and from the airport or dinner.

As you walk around downtown you will probably notice a neo-gothic, wedge-shaped building that perks the curiosity. This is the historic **Emily Morgan Hotel** (705 E. Houston St., 210/225-5100, www.emilymorganhotel.com, $139–359), named after the Yellow Rose, the heroine of the Texas Revolution.

Some rooms at the Emily Morgan Hotel have views of the Alamo.

This recently renovated classy hotel is distinguished by neo–art deco decor, spacious rooms with views, and classic jazz be-bopping in the background. Amenities include Aveda skincare products, cotton bathrobes, full-service restaurant and bar, and whirlpool tubs. In the shadows of the hotel is the famous Alamo. Rooms on the Alamo side of the hotel offer the best views.

Affordable yet classy bed-and-breakfast accommodations are found can be found at **Inn on the Riverwalk Bed & Breakfast** (129 Woodward Pl., 210/225-6333, www.innontheriverwalksa.com, $79–199). These three properties at the end of a cul-de-sac overlooking the riverwalk are tucked away at the end of a quiet street south of downtown right on the San Antonio river, which makes it feel as though it's a hideaway right in the heart of the city.

$150-250

A swank place to stay that has a turn-of-the-20th-century aesthetic is the **Fairmount Hotel** (401 S. Alamo St., 210/224-8800, $159–229).

Conveniently located on the River Walk and across the street from HemisFair Park, just down the street from the Alamo, this old San Antonio hotel is housed in a historic brick building that has been renovated for convenience and comfort. There are three floors of charming Victorian-style rooms and suites, each uniquely designed with antiques, European silk fabrics, tiling, and flat-screen TVs. Be sure to request one of the rooms with a view.

The best place to stay in town is the innovative **Hotel Valencia** (150 E. Houston St., 210/227-9700, $159–300). This young upstart hotel is like none other in the state. In an age when all luxury hotels feel and look like they were cut from the same template, the Valencia appears on the scene and completely inverts the model. The interior is dark, dramatic, luxurious, modern, vanguard, and somehow resembles a classy nightclub. The service and integrity here is the best in town, and the rooms are perfectly comfortable and unique. Faux mink throws, balconies, and bathrooms that look more like they're out of a design magazine than a hotel are all trademarks of the Valencia. On site is an upscale bar, and an uptown restaurant called Citrus. Imagine all this style and class situated on a quiet bend on the River Walk and you've envisioned the Valencia. All of the above is why celebrities stay here, and why *Condé Nast Traveler* magazine rated the Valencia as one of the world's top 100 new hotels.

One of the ritziest ways to experience San Antonio is by staying in the King William Historic District at **The Jackson House** (107 Madison, 800/242-2770, www.nobleinns.com, $160–250). Feel wealthy for a day as you are pampered to the point of no return. Spend quiet time in the conservatory surrounded by Victorian stained-glass windows; relax in the large, heated swim-spa; and return to your room and find a chocolate on your pillow. Be sure to arrange to have their 1960 Rolls Royce take you and your date to dinner.

Literally next door to the Alamo is the historic five-story **Menger Hotel** (204 Alamo Plaza, 210/223-4361, www.mengerhotel.com, $195–215). Whether you stay here or not the

Menger deserves a visit, as the history here is worthy of an entire History Channel special. From the famous guests who have stayed here throughout the years, such as Teddy Roosevelt, Babe Ruth, and Oscar Wilde, to the legends that were born here such as Robert E. Lee riding his horse into the main lobby, there's lots of history to encounter. The Menger also boasts having over 40 often-seen apparitions. The hotel features a romantic courtyard, large heated pool, and a full day spa. Rooms are somewhat tiny, but charming. There's also the Menger Bar, which is where Teddy Roosevelt recruited some of his Rough Riders for the Spanish-American War. The "giant" Western painting in the old lobby, by F. L. Van Ness, was featured in the Western classic *Giant,* starring Rock Hudson and Elizabeth Taylor.

One of Texas's most historic bed-and-breakfasts is the **Oge House** (209 Washington St., 210/223-2353, www.ogeinn.com, $155–255). This boutique bed-and-breakfast mansion is located in the King William Historic District and is set on the banks of the San Antonio River. The location is unparalleled. With grand verandas with views, dramatic halls lined with period antiques, and scarlet drapes, one is transported to the era of wealthy, high society, 19th-century Texas money. Most rooms have a fireplace and old-world charm with modern comfort and convenience. Prepare to be dazzled by a gourmet breakfast served on china and white linens.

The four-star hotel on the San Antonio River is **The Westin River Walk** (420 Market St., 210/224-6500, $179–359). For high-end accommodations this is a good bet as the service is impeccable and the comforts abound. From the valet parking service to the rooms with downtown views and the goose-down pillows, everything here is perfectly orchestrated. The entire hotel is decorated with art from local artists and marble and stone is everywhere. Wireless Internet is available throughout, there's a fitness center on-site, shampoos and soaps are above average, and some showers feature spa-style double showerheads. Among the more unusual amenities there's La Merienda, which is a Latin version of afternoon tea available to guests

Tuesday–Saturday. Because of these comforts, this is one of two places where the rich and famous stay when in town.

$250 AND UP

Have you ever wanted to stay overnight at Pottery Barn or Crate and Barrel? The **Hyatt Regency San Antonio** (123 Losoya St., 210/222-1234, $249–329) has recently renovated its rooms to reflect the most current trends in decor. The bustling grand lobby is an open-air atrium with waterfall, chichi bar, and mediocre service. The location is what this Hyatt is all about. It's both on the River Walk and at the center of downtown, just a stone's throw away from the Alamo.

La Mansión del Rio (112 College St., 800/292-7300, www.lamansion.com, $239–379). This Spanish hacienda–style hotel has everything you could ever want in a San Antonio stay. Of course it comes with a hefty price. It's located on one of the most beautiful stretches of the River Walk, within walking distance of all that downtown San Antonio has to offer. With arches, antiques, verandas, wrought-iron balconies, scarlet drapes, rough-hewn-beam ceilings, and amenities fit for General Santa Anna himself, guests are encouraged to feel like world rulers. Rooms on the River Walk are very expensive, and are often occupied by the rich and famous. By expensive I mean they can run upwards of $2,000.

Food

San Antonio's proximity to the Mexican border and its rich Latino history make this one of the best places for Tex-Mex and Mexican food. Even restaurants that aren't billed as Mexican offer enchiladas at the very least. When it comes to Mexican food, expect guacamole prepared tableside, margaritas, breakfast tacos, live mariachi music, handmade tortillas, and some gringo-Mex variations of all the above, all at great prices.

If you are one of those few people in the world that doesn't like Mexican, or just want to try something different, there are lots of other eateries to choose from. Fabulous restaurants are scattered all throughout town, but many are in the downtown area. The River Walk is a popular place to eat for both locals and tourists, as the atmosphere is remarkably serene and alluring. The narrow winding paths along the river are lined with umbrella tables and charming eateries that are packed from spring to fall. There's also a slew of very popular restaurants that have popped up in burgeoning Southtown, along South Alamo Street. These special eateries, rich with character and bubbling with action, are favorite spots for hip locals and tourists in the know.

AMERICAN

A local favorite for brunch is **Madhatters** (320 Beauregard St. at S. Alamo St., 210/212-4832, 7 A.M.–9 P.M. Mon.–Fri., 8 A.M.–9 P.M. Sat., 9 A.M.–3 P.M. Sun., $9). With a creative selection of sandwiches and salads, all made with breads baked in-house, as well as French toast and other breakfast items, Madhatters is the perfect place to relax in the King William Historic District. In spirit with *Alice in Wonderland,* they also offer a large selection of fabulous teas under the trees.

Although it's a chain, albeit a small Texas chain, **County Line Smokehouse** (111 W. Crockett St., 210/229-1941, $14) has some of the best barbecue in the downtown area. Beef brisket is moist and smoldering with flavor, and comes with the boilerplate smokehouse sides such as potato salad, beans, and cole slaw.

American, '50s-style *Leave It to Beaver* home cooking is served up at **410 Diner** (8315 Broadway St., 210/822-6246, 11 A.M.–9 P.M. Sun.–Thurs., 11 A.M.–10 P.M. Fri., $8). This true diner is where you'll find meat loaf and vegetables, along with a few attempts at upscale menu items such as snapper with artichoke hearts. Its proximity to the airport makes it a great stop before an evening flight out of town.

The historic **Guenther House** (205 E. Guenther St., 210/227-1061, 7 A.M.–3 P.M. daily, $7) offers great high-society class at a great value. For under $10 one can have a fabulous meal in a mansion overlooking the San Antonio River, in the King William Historic District. The smell of breakfast with freshly baked goods wafting through the mansion's Victorian-style parlors is what keeps a steady fan base coming back. And it tastes as good as it smells. Patrons are generally older folks, but youngsters shouldn't be scared to claim this for their own too. While there, be sure to take a tour of the gift shop and the historic Guenther House.

The best place for lunch and a cocktail is **◖ Liberty Bar** (1111 South Alamo St., 210/227-1187, 11 A.M.–10:30 P.M. Sun.–Thurs., 10:30 A.M.–midnight Fri.–Sat., $12). With interesting food, in-house baked breads, and one-of-a-kind ambience, Liberty is a bona fide San Antonio legend. Although they have moved from their previous location, which was a building that was near collapsing, the style and eating experience has not changed. If you want to impress someone, or yourself for that matter, have a classy lunch or dinner in this former convent. Crab cakes, New York strip, or portobello sandwich all go excellent with your choice of wine. Afterwards a stroll through the historic King William District seems like a given.

North of town in Alamo Heights is **Olmos Pharmacy** (3902 McCollough, 210/822-1188, 4 P.M.–12 A.M. Mon.–Fri., 4 P.M.–1 A.M. Sat., 10 A.M.–12 A.M. Sun., $7), an old-style pharmacy serving up medicine in the form of milk shakes and burgers. Founded in 1938, this neighborhood fountain makes a mean root beer float at a price that hasn't changed in 30 years.

Nothing beats a deli sandwich for lunch, and nobody beats the classic yet upscale fixin's at **Schilos Delicatessen** (424 E. Commerce St., 210/223-6692, 10 A.M.–2:30 P.M. Mon.–Fri., $12). The interior of Schilos (pronounced shee-lows) is best described as caravan meets an Italian meat wagon. The food is remarkably

tasty and summons authentic visions of German pioneers who settled in South Texas and transplanted their food heritage. Here you build your own sandwich, or order a meat-filled egg breakfast, and between the slices of bread expect only the very best in sandwich craftsmanship. Be sure to try their homemade root beer.

MEXICAN, TEX-MEX, AND SOUTHWESTERN

Walk into **◖ Acenar** (146 E. Houston St., 210/222-2362, 11 A.M.–10 P.M. Sun.–Thurs., 11 A.M.–11 P.M. Fri.–Sat., 5–9 P.M. Sun., $12) and let yourself be overwhelmed by the bright colors and delectable foods. The sophisticated menu is upscale and creative, and not traditional Mexican, which is refreshing. Be sure

THE INVENTION OF FRITOS CHIPS

Legend has it that the tasty snack food known as Fritos Corn Chips was invented in San Antonio in the early 1900s. At the time, the city's Mexican restaurants were in the custom of frying up the day-old tortillas and selling them. One establishment that was peddling these recycled corn snacks was the Santa Rosa Macaroni Factory, which was owned by a distinguished Italian immigrant named Carmelo Ruffo. Some say it was a Mexican immigrant who created and sold the original recipe, but others say it was Ruffo, whose tantalizing day-old fried "Fritos" were made with his macaroni press. One day Carmelo was approached by an entrepreneur named Elmer Doolin, who offered Carmelo $100 for his fried chip recipe and the macaroni machine. Carmelo walked away with the $100 thinking to himself, "Who would buy those chips when everyone in town is making them already?" Well, the rest of the country bought into the idea and to this day are suckered into paying for the unique taste of Fritos chips.

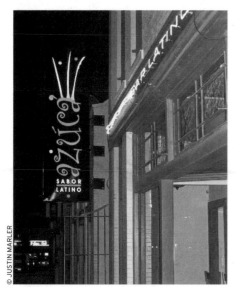

Azúca is the place for great Latin food and music.

to ask for their famous guacamole made table-side. It's the best I've ever had in my life. If it's not too hot, eat outside on the porch above the River Walk, and you're guaranteed to have one of those "life is good" moments.

Caribbean and Latin-American cuisine has been skillfully brought to the King William Historic District by **Azúca** (713 S. Alamo, 210/225-5550, 11 a.m.–9:30 p.m. Mon.–Thurs., 11 a.m.–10:30 p.m. Fri.–Sat., 5 p.m.–9:30 p.m. Sun., $18). This hip bar and restaurant is known for making potent mojitos and well-crafted meat dishes. On weekend nights Azúca is the place in town for live tango, salsa, and flamenco music and dancing.

On the River Walk is upscale **Boudro's** (421 E. Commerce St., 210/224-8484, 11 a.m.–11 p.m. Sun.–Thurs., 11 a.m.–midnight Fri.–Sat., $15). This eatery on the river boasts a crafty menu, fancy drinks, fine wines, and high-caliber service. And what about that crafty menu? Try lamb T-bone with basil-lemon-mint sauce, grilled Gulf Coast yellow-fin tuna, or whiskey-soaked bread pudding and you'll know what I mean.

Carmen's de la Calle Café (720 E. Mistletoe Ave., 210/737-8272, 6 p.m.–midnight Thurs.–Sat., $10) is a little eatery north of downtown that specializes in tapas and folkloric dancing, all in a quaint environment in an old house. The house specialty is sangria. Weekend nights expect dancing, acoustic guitar playing, jazz, and all kinds of action. Carmen's is only open Thursday, Friday, and Saturday nights.

Locals love how **El Mirador** (722 S. St. Mary's St., 210/225-9444, 6:30 a.m.–9 p.m. Sun.–Fri., 9 a.m.–2 p.m. Sun., $9) cooks up traditional Mexican dishes with flair. Although the whole menu is above par, the main dish people rave about here is *sopa Azteca* (Aztec soup). Tables fill up quickly here so either arrive before the mealtime rush or prepare to wait. Believe me, the wait is well worth it.

One of San Antonio's most time-tested Mexican institutions is **La Fonda on Main** (2415 N. Main Ave., 210/733-0621, 11 a.m.–3 p.m. and 5 p.m.–9:30 p.m. Mon.–Thurs., 11 a.m.–10:30 p.m. Fri.–Sat., $9). Since 1932, lively Mexican food and ambience has been the

Rosario's

Mexican food is served up 24 hours a day at Mi Tierra.

reason people flock here. Today the menu is a combination of regional Mexican and Tex-Mex, offering the standards such as chicken enchiladas and new creations such as spinach enchiladas, shrimp with butter squash, and smoky tenderloin. The bright and cheerful environment with outdoor patio seating makes La Fonda a popular meeting place for lunch and dinner.

◖ Mi Tierra (218 Produce Row, 210/225-1262, 24 hours, $9) is the local institution that serves great Mexican food 24 hours a day. All dishes are made up of beans, meats, sauces, and handmade tortillas—the staples of Mexican food. The food is okay but gets better at around 3 A.M., when you're desperate and hungry. The old building is festively decorated with strings of lights and tinsel, and a mariachi band often strolls around the tables. Sit beneath masterfully executed murals telling the story of Mexico and Texas (notice that the

breasts and noses are strangely three dimensional), and lose yourself in enchilada sauce.

The best Mexican restaurant is **◖ Rosario's** (910 S. Alamo St., 210/223-1806, 11 A.M.–10 P.M. Mon.–Thurs., 11 A.M.–11 P.M. Fri.–Sat., 11 A.M.–9 P.M. Sun., $10). The proprietor has combined Mexican food with a chic, semi-retro, totally colorful dining space that makes a frequent customer out of everyone. On weekend nights chairs are removed from a portion of the dining area to make way for the dance floor, and the small stage is fired up with live salsa music. Favorite menu items are *pollo a la maria, chile relleno,* and prickly-pear margaritas.

The zest of the Southwest is to be found on the River Walk at **Zuni Grill** (232 Losoya, 210/227-0864, 7:30 A.M.–10 P.M. Sun.–Thurs., 7:30 A.M.–11 P.M. Fri.–Sat., $18). Sure it's pricey, but that's what you get for blue-corn enchiladas, apple-smoked salmon, herb-seared ahi tuna, and barbecue shrimp pizza, all on the beautiful River Walk. Zuni is a great place to meet up with friends for breakfast as their cinnamon buttermilk pancakes and Southwestern breakfast tacos are superb.

OTHER INTERNATIONAL FOOD

If you're not quite sure what you want, but you're sure you want a drink to go with it, there's **Cappyccino's** (5003 Broadway, 210/828-6860, 11 A.M.–11 P.M. Mon.–Thurs., 11 A.M.–midnight Fri.–Sat., $10). Both the food and drink menus are diverse and very enticing. Food items include brick-oven pizza with feta cheese and thick golden crust, Italian-style deli sandwiches, pita wraps, and crepes. As for liquor, this place is a fan of anything fermented; from a huge selection of scotches, to brews, to martinis, you're sure to find just the right beverage to accompany your meal.

Texas and sushi don't sound like they go together but **Koi Kawa** (4051 Broadway, 210/805-8111, 11 A.M.–10 P.M. Mon.–Fri., noon–10 P.M. Sat., $12) has proved all logic wrong. Two great things about this place: The chef is considered the best sushi chef in town, and the dining room affords spectacular views of Brackenridge Park and the San Antonio River. Artfully prepared black-widow rolls, devil rolls, and udon all scream healthy and tasty, and the wasabi just screams.

Housed in a converted gas station in Southtown is **La Focaccia** (800 S. Alamo St., 210/223-5353, 11 A.M.–2:30 P.M. and 5–10 P.M. Mon.–Fri., noon–11 P.M. Sat., noon–10 P.M. Sun., $13). The Italian food here is family-style, with blue blood heritage. The owner was born in Rome, and brought family recipes cooked for Italian royals to San Antonio. Italian favorites such as calzones, lasagna, spaghetti, and pizzas are all worthy of a religious procession around the block.

Asian food in Alamo Heights is best eaten at **Van's** (3214 Broadway, 210/828-8449, 11 A.M.–10 P.M. daily, $10). The combination of sushi and Chinese is tastefully set forth in a menu that can bring even the most terrified sushi disdainer to their senses, literally.

Rounding out the experience is a great wine list. Wine and sushi at a good price make this a great low-key pick for dinner with friends.

HEALTHY AND VEGETARIAN

San Antonio is a carnivore town. However there is one safe spot for vegans and vegetarians, and that's **Twin Sisters** (124 Broadway, 210/354-1559, 8 A.M.–3 P.M. Mon.–Fri., $7). Its location just a few blocks from the Alamo makes this a great lunch spot for everyone. Most everything is organic, healthy, and tasty. Meat lovers will be pleased to know this deli does have some meat choices on the menu. There's good reason why the place fills up midday, so plan to wrestle with the crows at lunch.

FINE DINING

Located inside innovative Hotel Valencia is swank **Citrus** (150 E. Houston St., 210/230-8412, 6:30 A.M.–2 P.M. and 6–10 P.M. daily, $30–50). For an amazing evening with friends, with a romantic date, or even alone, Citrus proves impeccable and divine. As soon as you are seated the knowledgeable staff makes you feel comfortable with your experience. From the brilliant selection of wines, to the creative but down-to-earth entrées, to the minimalist decor, anyone can feel like a million bucks. Of course you have to have some cash to back it up, because it is expensive. Reservations are recommended.

If you're a geek about flavor but fancy yourself a refined individual I recommend fine dining at **Tre Trattoria** (401 S Alamo. inside the Fairmount Hotel, 210/223-0401, and 4003 Broadway near Brackenridge Park, 210/805-0333, $45–65). Eating here is a serious matter—as serious as Lent is to Catholics. Men should look dapper and women should primp so as to look marvelous, and everyone has to be on time and follow the lead of the wait staff. Although classy it's still a personable place. However, if you're irritated by pomp you won't enjoy this. But if you're out to enjoy fine wines and masterfully designed entrées in the company of the crème de la crème of society, you will have one of the best fine-dining experiences San Antonio has to offer.

Popular among locals with refined style and taste, **Silo** (1133 Austin Hwy., 210/824-8686, 11 A.M.–2:30 P.M. and 5:30–10 P.M. Sun.–Thurs., 11 A.M.–2:30 P.M. and 5:30–10:30 P.M. Fri.–Sat., $22) is the eatery that can do no wrong. This converted farmers market has a swank martini bar on the ground floor and a dining room accessed only by elevator that smacks of Manhattan. The short but upscale menu includes chicken-fried oysters, seared yellowfin tuna, and chocolate soufflé cake, to name a few. Reservations are recommended.

Shopping

San Antonio isn't necessarily a shopping town, but it does have a few interesting shops with local flavor that are worth checking out. Mexican markets, massive malls, funky galleries, and a few boutique shops are what's to be expected here. The markets are particularly interesting, especially for the first-time visitor to Texas and/or San Antonio. Although there are some shops downtown and on the River Walk, most of the interesting shops are spread out throughout town. Just south of downtown is the burgeoning San Antonio Arts District, also known as Southtown. A few boutiques and art galleries can be found on South Alamo Street. Shops are generally open 10 A.M.–6 P.M.

The majority of major chain retail shops in downtown are located in **Rivercenter Mall** (849 E. Commerce, 210/225-0000, www.shoprivercenter.com, 10 A.M.–9 P.M. Mon.–Sat., noon–6 P.M. Sun.). This four-level shopping complex has over 125 shops, restaurants, and an AMC movie theater, all under one roof. The scene inside is stunning as there are picturesque views of the River Walk below.

The most interesting, smaller independently owned shops are located in historic **La Villita** (418 Villita St., 210/207-8610, www.lavillita.com, shops open 10 A.M.–6 P.M. daily). Here you'll find arts and crafts, souvenirs, upscale gifts and home decor, and art from all genres and mediums. Many of these shops are inside historic buildings from San Antonio's early days.

The largest Mexican marketplace outside of Mexico is at **Market Square** (between Dolorosa and Commerce just west of downtown, 210/207-8600, 10 A.M.–8 P.M. daily June–Aug., 10 A.M.–6 P.M. daily Sept.–May).

This entire city block of all things Mexico was originally an open-air market founded in 1840. Today Market Square is a little city unto itself, with great restaurants like Mi Terra and La Margarita, outdoor courtyards, and covered malls that feature unique retail shops and purveyors of imports such as tin lamps, jewelry, knickknacks, Mexican papier-mâché, sombreros, handmade Mexican dolls, religious kitsch, and the popular Davy Crockett 'coonskin hats. Outside the market in the beautiful courtyards, local musicians perform and celebrations take place.

CLOTHES, SHOES, AND ACCESSORIES

The craft, tradition, and art form of bootmaking has been upheld by two legendary boot companies based in San Antonio. In **Little's Boots** (110 Division St., 210/923-2221, 9 A.M.–5 P.M. Tues.–Fri., 9 A.M.–1 P.M. Sat.), a one-of-a-kind shop since 1915, prepare to stomp your feet with excitement over all the beautiful and ornate boots. Western footwear made from crocodile, alligator, kangaroo, eel, ostrich, and even lizard is sure to impress the imagination. Be sure to check out the custom and handcrafted boots here. They are great works of art in their own right.

The other bootmaker in town is **Lucchese** (255 E. Basse Rd., 210/828-9419, 10 A.M.–7 P.M. Mon.–Fri., 10 A.M.–6 P.M. Sat., noon–5 P.M. Sun.). Here you'll find high quality, precision craftsmanship, and class for the cowboy and cowgirl that enjoys getting gussied up.

Paris Hatters (119 N. Broadway, 210/223-3453, 9:30 A.M.–6:30 P.M. Mon.–Sat.,

SAN ANTONIO

COUNCIL HOUSE FIGHT

As you stroll around Market Square in downtown San Antonio and admire San Fernando Cathedral, keep in mind that in March of 1840 a major Native American battle known as the Council House Fight took place here. A group of 65 Comanches (including 12 chiefs) came to town to negotiate a peace treaty with the Texans. The Native Americans had promised to bring with them all of their white captives as a sign of good faith. Unfortunately for them, they only brought one white captive, a 15-year-old girl named Matilda Lockhart. The Texans were put in a bad mood when they saw that Matilda's nose had been burned off by the Comanches. Then Matilda informed the Texans that there were numerous other captives and that it was the Comanches' intention to bargain for their release separately.

The meeting took place in a one-story stone building on the east side of the square at Market Street. Colonel William Fisher was in charge of the Texan forces and marched a company of troops into the council room. He informed the Indians that their chiefs would be held hostage until they brought in all of the white prisoners. The Comanche chiefs refused to be held prisoner and fighting erupted. A bloody fight to the death occurred inside the council house with knives, guns, and bows and arrows. At the end of the struggle, all of the Comanche chiefs and warriors were killed. Seven Texans died in the struggle and eight were wounded. Twenty-seven Comanche women and children were captured and held hostage. Seven white captives were finally returned to the Texans in exchange for the Comanche hostages.

The aftermath of the council house fight led to the greatest Comanche raid in the history of Texas. Late in May of 1840, over 600 Comanches (encouraged and guided by representatives of the Mexican government) raided the towns of Victoria and Linnvill on the Gulf Coast. Linnville was burned to the ground and much plunder and many captives were taken by the Comanches. As the Native Americans tried to retreat to their Hill Country campgrounds, they were attacked by Texan forces at the Battle of Plum Creek, near present-day Lockhart. The Comanches suffered a stunning defeat. Subsequent attacks by the Texan forces followed the Comanches into the upper reaches of the Colorado River valley. There the Comanches suffered a string of defeats that weakened their power such that they never again made such an attack in force against a Texas town.

11 A.M.–5 P.M. Sun.) is yet another historic business in San Antonio. Family owned and operated since 1917, this headgear shop has a large variety of new hats ranging from the iconic Stetson, to Kangol, to cowhide baseball caps. Although there is a large collection of hats in the store, this boutique specializes in custom headwear for those who have the money.

MUSIC

Swim through a vast sea of new and used CDs at the **CD Exchange** (3703 Broadway St., 210/828-5525, 10 A.M.–9 P.M. Mon.–Sat., noon–7 P.M. Sun.). Everything is relatively cheap and in abundance. Here you can also find those rare 1980s movies you've been searching for on DVD and VHS.

For the vinyl aficionado, music purist, and counterculture hipster, **Hogwild Records, Tapes and CDs** (1824 N. Main Ave., 210/733-5354, 10 A.M.–9 P.M. Mon.–Sat., noon–8 P.M. Sun.) has an astounding collection of great records and tapes. This is also an outlet in town for underground press and literature.

Finally, if you just prefer a good selection of popular music at high prices there's **Borders Books and Music** (255 E. Basse Rd., No. 350, 210/828-9496, 9 A.M.–10 P.M. Mon.–Sat., 11 A.M.–9 P.M. Sun.).

BOOKSTORES

If you're in the mood for strolling around a bookstore you'll have to take a short trip north from downtown to the Alamo Heights area.

If you desire the tried and true methods of a mega–book peddler, the closet one is **Borders Books and Music** (255 E. Basse Rd., No. 350, 210/828-9496).

For cheap new and used books, and a strange array of records, there's **Half Price Books** (3207 Broadway, 210/822-4597, www.half-pricebooks.com).

A great resource for Texana and regional books and literature is **The Twig Book Shop** (200 E. Grayson St., Suite 124, 210/826-6411). Inside the Twig is a great children's bookstore called **The Red Balloon.** Books for all ages, from babies, to tots, to teens, are here. They also have children's book readings, which is great for parents and children.

ART GALLERIES

Perhaps the most innovative and noteworthy gallery in town is **ArtPace** (445 N. Main Ave., 210/212-4900). Hours vary depending on the ever-revolving door of artists and exhibits. This purely conceptual gallery puts a fresh twist on the idea of the art gallery, as it brings in artists from around the world, gives them a place to live above the gallery space, provides art supplies and lets them go crazy. The stuff produced here is generally wildly bizarre, but always amusing and thought provoking.

The beating heart of contemporary Southtown is the **Blue Star Arts Complex** (between the San Antonio River and S. Alamo St., www.bluestarart.org). This abandoned industrial warehouse was brilliantly converted into spaces and galleries for local artists, and has become San Antonio's repository for contemporary arts. If you're in the market for cutting-edge and bizarre art in all media—painting, sculpture, and performing arts—you'll find it here. Gallery spaces and showings are at random times, but chances are, if you show up sometime in the afternoon something will be open. Galleries include **San Angel Folk Art,** and **Joan Grona Gallery.**

Art is to be appreciated and sometimes even worn. At the Gallery Shop of the **Southwest School of Art and Craft** (on the Ursuline Campus at 300 Augusta St., 210/224-1848,, 10 A.M.–5 P.M. Mon.–Sat.) you'll find an interesting collection of one-of-a-kind works of art made by students. Expect to find color, innovation, and flat-out bizarre stuff in here.

Information and Services

TOURIST INFORMATION

The **City of San Antonio Visitor Information Center** (317 Alamo Plaza, 210/207-6748) is conveniently located right across the street from the Alamo. The helpful staff here can provide you with maps, brochures about the city's attractions, and lodging information, and are pleased to answer any questions you may have. The center is open 9 A.M.–5:30 P.M. daily except on major holidays.

EMERGENCY INFORMATION

In the event of an emergency involving injury or danger dial **911.** For non-emergency police needs there's the **San Antonio Sheriff's Department** (210/335-6000). The main hospital downtown is **Baptist Medical Center** (111 Dallas St., 210/297-7000). For information on other medical facilities call the **San Antonio Medical Foundation** (210/614-3724).

PUBLICATIONS

The best resource for all things hip such as live music, art gallery openings, events, and festivals is the local alternative rag, *San Antonio Current.* This free newsprint periodical is free and can be found all over town. New editions hit the streets every Thursday. The paper with a local news focus is the *San Antonio Express-News.* Nothing special here, just politics, sport pages, funnies, and the usual *Citizen Kane* stuff. The full-color glossy magazine, *Texas Monthly,* is the best state magazine in the country. It can be purchased at most supermarkets and corner stores. This is a great resource for state news, politics, and celebrity gossip, and offers a great listings section in the back with restaurant reviews.

INTERNET

If you have a laptop with a wireless card you can access the Internet through hot spots in cafés. If you're staying in a hotel chances are they have wireless or connections in rooms available to guests. For everyone else there's a **FedEx Office** (4418 Broadway, 210/821-6911) way up near Brackenridge Park. At $0.20 per minute this can get costly unless you just want to check email. For free Internet access downtown there's the **San Antonio Public Library** (600 Soledad St., 210/207-2500, 9 A.M.–9 P.M. Mon.–Thurs., 9 A.M.–5 P.M. Fri.–Sat., 11 A.M.–5 P.M. Sun.).

LAUNDRY

For coin-operated laundry machines there's **Kwik Wash Laundry** (1100 S. Presa St., 210/532-6677). While your laundry is tumbling head across the street to Taco Haven for some great Mexican grub. Check the phone book for more listings.

POST OFFICE

Just across from the Alamo is the most conveniently located post office (615 E. Houston St.) downtown. For other locations call 800/275-8777. You'll need a zip code to get a location using this toll-free number. If you prefer paying slightly higher prices for your postal needs, **UPS Store** (200 E. Market St. near HemisFair Park, 210/258-8950) has mailers, envelopes, copy machines, and even maps.

MONEY

ATM kiosks are everywhere, but beware—the ATMs you find on the street all charge extraordinarily high fees. It's always best to get money from your own banking institution, but if your bank isn't to be found, at least use a national bank's ATM. You may still incur a fee but it's much less than at kiosk ATMs.

Getting There and Around

GETTING THERE

Getting to San Antonio is a cinch. All you need is money for an airline, train, or bus ticket, or gas for a road trip. Being the eighth-largest city in the United States, San Antonio has lots of travel and commerce, by highway and by air. Since it's sort of in the middle of nowhere, with respect to the greater United States, the easiest way to get here is by air.

By Air

Located about eight miles north of downtown is **San Antonio International Airport** (9800 Airport Blvd., 210/207-3433, www.sanantonio.gov/airport). This is the region's largest airport and is an international hub with both direct flights and domestic connections that can get you to anywhere in the world. Nonstop flights are offered to 41 destinations, mostly major U.S. cities and a couple cities in Mexico. Passenger airlines that service the airport include: Aerolitoral (800/237-6639), America West (800/235-9292), American Airlines (800/433-7300), Continental Airlines (800/525-0280), Delta (800/221-1212), Mexicana (800/534-7921), Midwest (800/452-2022), Northwest (800/225-2525), Southwest (800/435-9792), and United (800/241-6522).

The airport provides hourly, daily, and economy parking. For hourly parking the first 30 minutes are free, and after that it's $1 every hour. Daily rate is $22, long-term $10, and economy is $5. For hourly and long-term parking covered garages are available.

There are several ways to get from the airport to town. The most economical way is by taking the **VIA Metropolitan Transit** bus No. 2. Buses run about every hour 8 A.M.–9:30 P.M., and it takes about an hour to get to downtown. The fastest and easiest way to get to downtown, especially if you have lots of luggage, is by taking one of two shuttle buses: **San Antonio Trans** (210/281-9900) or **SATRANS** (210/281-9900). One-way shuttle service to downtown costs $18 per passenger. For groups there's **Star Shuttle** (210/341-6000). Taking a cab costs about $20, but this may go up since gas prices have been so high. Most hotels offer shuttle service free of charge. Be sure to ask your hotel about this before traveling.

By Bus and Train

The bus station for **Greyhound** (500 N. St. Mary's St., 210/270-5824 or 800/229-9424) is conveniently located downtown near hotels, restaurants, and attractions. On Greyhound you can get to San Antonio from just about anywhere in the contiguous United States, provided you don't mind a long ride. For travel to and from many of the smaller Texas towns, including many in the Hill Country, there's **Kerrville Bus Company** (800/335-3733). The station for this bus line is shared with Greyhound. As for train access to San Antonio there's always the old American staple, **Amtrak** (350 Hoefden, 210/223-3226 or 800/872-7245). Service is provided only three times a week, so it's important to plan train travel in advance.

By Car

San Antonio has been a crossroads for centuries, and this becomes apparent when you look at a current map of the state. Major highways fan out from the metropolitan area, and shoot to all parts of the United States and Mexico. The main interstate highways that connect San Antonio to the world are I-35, I-10, I-37, and I-410. It's imperative to have both a regional map and a good city map to successfully get around. Signage is good, for the most part, but exits and exchanges can happen fast the closer you get to downtown.

GETTING AROUND

Deciding which mode of transportation you will need while in San Antonio entirely depends

on what you plan on achieving while in town. The downtown area is a self-contained tourist world chock-full of things to see and do. If you can walk, it's entirely feasible to have an enjoyable experience without ever thinking about transportation. However, the city is sprawling and some attractions are way out there.

By Car

For the fist-time visitor, getting around the city via automobile can be confusing and frustrating. There are many major freeways in the metropolitan area, and in the suburban sprawl. The city is best navigated and understood when compared to a wagon wheel. There are two rings of highways that circumnavigate the city, one in the center of downtown and the other at the outer rim of the city. Highways fan out from the center of town and shoot off into all parts of the state. The downtown area is inside the inner ring, which is defined by I-35, I-37, and I-10. Beyond this is greater San Antonio, which is circumnavigated by the outer ring, defined by I-410, also known as Loop 410.

Parking can be frustrating in the downtown area. Metered parking is available on many streets, but spots are always hard to find. If you plan on tooling around the sights downtown you might as well plan on leaving your car at a parking garage, and touring by foot. Centrally located parking garages are: **LAZ Parking** (122 N. Main Ave., 210/224-2468, and 151 Soledad St., 210/224-2468) and **Market Street Parking Garage** (421 W Market St., 210/212-4011). Most attractions outside of downtown offer parking free of charge.

All the usual rental car companies are represented at **San Antonio International Airport,** as well as around town. Car rental agencies include **Advantage Rent-A-Car** (800/777-5500), **Alamo Rent-A-Car** (800/327-9633), **Avis Car Rental** (800/831-2847), **Budget** (800/527-0700), **Dollar Rent-A-Car** (800/800-4000), **Enterprise** (800/736-8222), **Hertz Rent-A-Car** (800/654-3131), **National Car Rental** (800/227-7368), and **Thrifty** (800/847-4389). My hunch is Alamo Rent-A-Car gets the most business in this town.

SAN ANTONIO

By Bus

San Antonio's public transportation system, **VIA Metropolitan Transit** (210/362-2020, www.viainfo.net), is the cheapest way to get around, and fairly easy to get the hang of. VIA has both buses and touristy streetcars. VIA's hub-and-spoke system offers over 85 routes, with major hubs downtown fanning out into the metropolitan area. A ride costs $0.80 a trip, and transfers are $0.15. Buses and streetcars are in operation 5 A.M.–midnight. If you plan on using VIA as your primary form of transportation, I highly recommend getting a day pass for $3, which provides unlimited rides on both the buses and streetcars for a day.

Taxi

Although taxi cabs can be hailed on the streets, you'll probably save time picking one up at the bus station downtown, by catching one at a hotel, or by simply calling in advance. **Yellow Cab** (210/222-2222) has the San Antonio cab monopoly. Cab rates starts at $1.70, plus $1.80 per mile, and there's a minimum of $3 for rides in downtown. The one-way fare from San Antonio International Airport to downtown is an estimated $20.

BACKGROUND

The Land

GEOGRAPHY

The impression most people have of Texas is that it's a dry, flat, and arid land fraught with twisters, dust bowls, and cactus. That may be true for the western part of the state, but that's far from what Austin, San Antonio, and the Hill Country are like. The region at the heart of the state known as Central Texas, or the Texas Hill Country, is a lush, green land with rolling hills, crystal clear rivers and lakes, giant outcroppings of granite rock, and plentiful wildlife. Geologists claim this remarkably beautiful landscape was formed over the course of billions of years. Geological records tell a dynamic story of activity such as inundation by inland seas, volcanic eruptions, the erosion process of rivers, and earthquakes. Thanks to this extraordinary process the region is filled with great beauty both on the surface and beneath the surface. Visitors can see Central Texas geography and geology at its best by visiting any of the many parks such as Enchanted Rock State Natural Area, or by visiting some of the many caves throughout the region.

CLIMATE

Some people say Central Texas has three seasons: fixin' to be summer, summer, and just been summer. More-informed folks say there are four seasons: flood, hurricane, drought,

© JUSTIN MARLER

INTERVIEW WITH THE WEATHERMAN

With freak hail storms, flash floods, lightning, and thunder year-round, 90° Novembers, 60° Decembers, and 110° summers, this type of climate needs a professional explanation. Local weatherman **Mark Murray,** chief meteorologist of KVUE News, has the answers.

Q: At any given moment throughout the year freak storms can envelop Austin. Flash floods, thunder and lightning, and even softball-size hail in the middle of summer. Why does Central Texas have such dramatic freak storms all year-round?
A: We do get our share of severe storms, especially in the spring, and it has to do with our location. We're close enough to the Gulf of Mexico to get plenty of moisture, but we're also not too far from that dry desert air of West Texas. When that moist air from the Gulf meets the dry air from Texas, it creates something called a "dry line." When two different air masses come together—moist and dry in this case—that's what makes the fireworks. The dramatic storms that we get here often fire up along what's called the "West Texas Dry Line" and march into Austin, San Antonio, and the Hill Country. The dry line runs north and south, from West Texas all the way up to Nebraska.

Q: I've heard people say there's no spring or fall in Central Texas—it's all summer and winter. Can you explain the seasons here?
A: Seasons can change rapidly here, it's true. Fall is beautiful, but short. It's generally mid-September through late October. It's still warm but the humidity drops quite a bit, and it becomes sunny and mild. Winter is mild. On average it freezes about 19 days a year. Every couple years we get just enough snow to cover the ground but it melts pretty quickly. Only two times has the temperature dropped below zero. Spring, which is mid-March through mid-June, is a great time because temperatures are mild and the wildflowers are in full bloom. This makes it a very pretty time of the year. Wildflower festivals are happening in the Hill Country, and people are outdoors all day. Summer, which is from mid-June to mid-September, is very hot and humid. If you're in Central Texas during the summer heat, you may want to plan your day a little differently. If you want to walk around Town Lake's hike and bike trail you may want to do this in the morning or the evening.

Q: When is the best time of year to visit Austin and Central Texas?
A: You can do things outdoors in Austin pretty much year-round. Festivals and outdoor events are scheduled throughout the year here. However spring and fall are the best times of year to visit. The weather is moderate and it's beautiful.

Q: When is the least desirable time of year to visit Austin and Central Texas?
A: I think a lot of people would say the middle of summer, which is August and September. It's very hot and humid.

Q: What are the greatest meteorological threats to Central Texas?
A: There are three main threats we're faced with. Flash flooding is our biggest threat. Weak tropical depressions can dump lots of rain very quickly. Lightning is the second biggest threat. After these two, another threat we have is tornadoes. They generally don't last long and aren't that big, but they have caused damage. Central Texas has seen only two F5-class tornadoes. Hurricanes from the Gulf of Mexico aren't a threat here as they rarely hold their strength this far inland. However hurricanes can create a tornado outbreak, and can bring heavy, flooding rains.

Q: Why do you love Austin's climate?
A: I love the weather here. When people ask me what kind of weather I like, I always say I like weather that changes. Being a meteorologist, I love to forecast the changes.

Q: What's the first thing you do every morning?
A: Look outside to see if I was right.

and tornado. Combining these two theories provides an accurate, albeit unorthodox, description of the climate in this hot and meteorologically dramatic part of North America.

When it comes to crazy weather, Austin and the Hill Country seem to be particularly prone to the drama of the Greek gods above. At any given moment the sky can go from meek and mild to a violent, spectacular show of lights, thunder, and hail. Although there are more tornadoes in Texas than any other state, they rarely rip their way through Austin. As for hurricanes, they generally downgrade to a tropical storm by the time they make it this far inland.

The climates of Austin, San Antonio, and the Hill Country are very similar, with some slight variation. The Hill Country is often a few degrees cooler, San Antonio is always more humid, and Austin is somewhere in between.

Average temperatures for all of Central Texas are: summer 85°F, fall 70°F, winter 50°F, and spring 70°F. Remember this is an average—don't be fooled by these numbers. In summer months expect average highs of 90–100°F. As for the rest of the year, the temperature can range anywhere from 40–70°F.

Expect dramatic and crazy weather in the spring, late arrival of fall, moderate winters, and hot summers. Spring is a time when flash flooding is commonplace, hail can be the size of baseballs, and lightning starts fires. The summers are all that they're advertised to be. They're hot, and they're humid, and usually last about three months. The spring and the fall are the best time of year in terms of temperature and beauty. In the winter the weather is rarely the same for two days in a row. On occasion it will drop below freezing, and on the very rare occasion it will snow.

Flora and Fauna

FLORA
The climate in Central Texas has created a diverse plant ecosystem that includes everything from cactus, to maple trees, to an astounding array of wildflowers. All of the flora that exists here has the ability to survive drought conditions and extended periods of hot weather. The most common forms of plant life are oak trees, juniper (often mistakenly called cedar), and numerous varieties of wildflowers. Every spring the Hill Country explodes with wildflower color. The most prolific and popular of all Texas wildflowers are bluebonnets. When they're in full bloom it's common to see families scrunched down in fields of bluebonnets along roads and highways taking photos. If you're tempted to pick these gorgeous flowers, be aware that this is frowned upon. Most people think it's illegal to pick bluebonnets because they are the state flower, but this is a Texas myth. Other common wildflowers include Texas paintbrush, the bright and delicate fuchsia-colored winecups, greenthreads (which

are actually yellow), and the shockingly radiant Indian blanket flowers. The best way to experience wildflower season is by driving the Willow City Loop in the Hill Country, or by visiting the Lady Bird Johnson Wildflower Center just east of Austin.

FAUNA
There are thousands of species of wildlife in Central Texas, but the ones that get the most press are bats, armadillos, and the longhorn steer. These have become larger-than-life icons that represent the region as virtual ambassadors. Of the three, bats are the most popular. There are over two dozen species of bats in Texas, the most popular and well known being the Mexican free-tailed bat. The largest colony of Mexican free-tailed bats in North America happens to be beneath Congress Avenue Bridge in Austin. These little mammals have helped put Austin on the map, as they have been drawing tourists and the curious to Austin for decades.

© JUSTIN MARLER

Come spring, folks can be seen on the side of the highways taking family photos in the bluebonnets.

The prehistoric-looking armadillo is the most curious of Texas's creatures. Unfortunately these armored mammals are known most for being roadkill. These low-key residents of the state feed on insects and vegetation. Although the ones we have today are about the size of a cat, in prehistoric times they could get as big as a VW Bug. The skeletal remains of one of these monsters are at the Texas Memorial Museum in Austin.

Perhaps the most iconic of all Central Texas animals is the longhorn steer. Once the symbol of Texas pioneer ranching, the longhorn steer is now best known as the logo for University of Texas sporting teams. These majestic-looking beasts can be seen fenced in on ranches all throughout the Hill Country, grazing in fields, and resting beneath ancient oak trees. Longhorn steer are raised primarily for beef, but their unwieldy horns are also desirable. On occasion you'll see them fixed to the front of a Cadillac.

Besides bats, armadillos, and longhorn steers, Texas is also known to have more bird species than any other state in the United States. With over 600 documented bird species, and some rare birds that only live in this region, Texas has become one of the top bird-watching destinations in North America. This extraordinary number of birds is due primarily to the fact that Central Texas is a popular stopoff point for migratory birds flying the Central Flyway which runs from Canada to Mexico.

History

A history of Austin, San Antonio, and the Hill Country has to be told properly—it has to happen through the prism of Texas history. After the prehistory, the state's story unfolds in and around San Antonio, and makes its way toward Austin being named the capital. Everything in between is pure drama.

PREHISTORY

Texas must have been a popular place for prehistoric creatures to congregate. Fossils and footprints of at least 16 types of dinosaurs have been discovered all around the state. According to current paleontology the following dinosaurs ruled the state: the huge and fierce *acrocanthosaurus,* the big-toothed meat-eating *tyrannosaurus rex,* the plant-eating *ornithischian,* the giant crocodile-like *deinosuchus,* and the *tenontosaurus,* among many others. Artifacts found include bones of mammoths, horses, camels, ancient bison, giant short-faced bears and giant armadillos.

Most of the evidence of earliest human inhabitants dates back 10,000–13,000 years. These early "Texans" are believed to be of Asian origin, having come to the North American continent by way of the land bridge at the Bering Strait in Siberia and Alaska. They are believed to have been completely modern Homo sapiens, as no evidence has been found in the New World that indicates evolutionary change. Archaeologists have determined four stages in development of early inhabitants: Paleo-Indian, Archaic, Woodland, and Neo-American.

Perhaps one of the earliest tribes of indigenous peoples is the Caddoes. They were highly civilized, agricultural, had a highly defined social structure, and even participated in trade.

NATIVE AMERICANS OF TEXAS

Long before Europeans arrived in the area known today as Texas, various tribes of Native

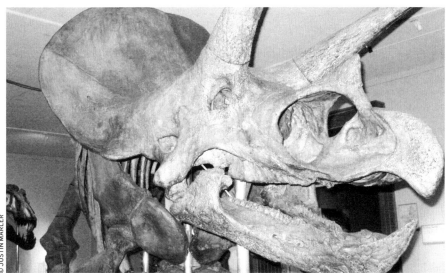

© JUSTIN MARLER

The shadows of Texas' dinosaur past can be explored at the Witte Museum in San Antonio and at the Texas Memorial Museum in Austin.

ORIGIN OF THE WORD "TEXAS"

One of the indigenous Native American tribes present in eastern Texas when Cabeza de Vaca arrived was the Caddo tribe. Their word *techas*, which means "friend," turned into "Tejas," which eventually became "Texas." The Spanish began to use "Texas" as the name for that entire group of Native Americans – records show the word appearing as early as 1689. The transition from Tejas to Texas came easily since the letters x and j have the same pronunciation in Spanish, the "h" sound in English. Thus, the Texas name is derived from a Caddo word, and the state's motto of "Friendship" still reflects that heritage.

encounter with the Karankawans, they didn't encounter Europeans for another 150 years. In 1685, the French explorer LaSalle established a fort near what is now Matagorda Bay in the heart of Karankawa country. The Karankawans eventually killed all of those settlers except for six children who were taken captive; two survived and returned to France and told of their life with the Karankawans.

During the Spanish mission period an attempt was made to civilize and Christianize the Karankawans and to make them loyal Spanish subjects. La Bahía mission and presidio complex near present-day Goliad was established in 1749 for that purpose. However, the Spanish attempts to Christianize the Karankawans met with little success. The Karankawans were hostile towards everyone: the Spanish, the French, the Comanches, and Anglo Texans. Because of this the Karankawans were exterminated. In 1858, a Texan force attacked and annihilated the last organized bands of Karankawans near Rio Grande City. The last reported Karankawan, named Indian Tom, was raised from infancy by Anglo settlers in Matagorda County. Later he enlisted as a Confederate soldier in the Civil War. He was killed by a union soldier as a rebel prisoner of war when he refused to obey his killer's commands.

The Tonkawa

The Tonkawa occupied the majority of the Central Texas Hill Country, from Llano to San Antonio. They were very mobile and hunted buffalo, deer, and smaller game. Upon the arrival of the Apache and Comanche Indians, the Tonkawa were forced into the region between Austin and San Antonio, where they existed through the Spanish period and the subsequent Texan and American periods of history. It's believed they were the friendliest of the Native American tribes in the region. They shared living space, as well as water and food sources, with the Karankawa, as well other tribes that passed through the region.

The Comanches

No tribe had more impact on Texas than the

Americans occupied the region. Some migrated here from other parts of North America, while others are believed to be indigenous. The history of present Texas is inextricably linked to these native populations who were in the region when Cabeza de Vaca landed in 1528, and those who later swept down from the plains on horseback. Regrettably, the story of the indigenous natives is not a pleasant one. Tribes were either wiped out by the Spanish, French, Mexican, and Anglo settlers, or simply merged into, and became part of the Mexican and Hispanic populations, losing their tribal identities.

Karankawans

Karankawa was the designation for several bands of coastal tribes who shared a common language and culture. They were perhaps the most successful and long lived of the indigenous tribes encountered by Cabeza de Vaca when he shipwrecked off Galveston Island. The Karankawa people were known for their distinctive physical appearance. The men were described as tall and muscular unlike the other natives. They practiced ritualistic cannibalism but were repulsed by the fact that some of Cabeza de Vaca's companions ate their dead to avoid starvation. After Cabeza de Vaca's

THE COMANCHE WARRIORS

From the early 1700s to the late 1800s, a period of approximately 200 years, the Comanches' warrior culture changed the face and destiny of what is now Texas. The Apaches, who had previously dominated the region, were forced south by the Comanches and became their mortal enemies. The Comanches completely halted Spanish and Mexican efforts to colonize Texas during the mission period. In 1758, a force of approximately 2,000 Comanches attacked a Spanish mission built for the Apaches on the San Saba River in Central Texas near present-day Menard. They sacked and burned the mission and killed most of its inhabitants, including two priests. A Spanish expedition was mounted the following year to punish the Comanches but it also met defeat. The Spanish were never able to successfully colonize Texas because of the Comanches' continued raids on their settlements for horses and captives.

In 1821, Mexico won independence from Spain but the armed, mounted, and aggressive Comanche warriors remained dominant. A series of unstable governments from Mexico City had no more success than their Spanish forefathers in projecting their power and presence in Texas.

The dominance of the Comanche warriors in Texas, probably more than any other factor, was the reason the weak Spanish and Mexican governments enacted laws to encourage foreign immigration to Texas. They were seeking to create a buffer between them and the Comanches and seeking someone who could match the Comanches in aggressiveness and warrior mentality. The new tribe that was invited into the Texas territory to battle the Comanches and ultimately defeat them was the Anglo-Americans. The interdependence of the fate of Comanches and Europeans in Texas is clear. Without the horses brought by Europeans, the Comanches never would have risen to dominance, and without the Comanches, Anglo-Americans never would have come to the Republic of Texas, which evolved into the State of Texas.

The Comanches still spread terror over much of Texas when Texans won their independence from Mexico in 1836. Sam Houston, the first elected President of the Republic of Texas, had lived with and was an adopted Cherokee. He wanted to institute a policy of peaceful coexistence with all the Native American tribes, including the Comanches. That policy was not favored by most Texans, including Sam Houston's successor in office, Mirabeau B. Lamar. Texans and Comanches remained enemies committing brutal atrocities against each other until the Comanches were almost exterminated and permanently removed from Texas to Indian Territory, now Oklahoma. Even after the Civil War, and after the Comanches entered into various peace treaties with the U.S. government, hostilities continued between them and the Texans. In reality, the Comanches and the Texans never considered themselves bound by such treaties. For them, it was a war until death or total subjugation – a war the Comanches could not win – which is why there is no Comanche presence in Texas today.

Comanches. The Comanches didn't exist when Cabeza de Vaca journeyed through Texas. In fact, the arrival of the Europeans was the genesis of the Comanche. Prior to that, anthropological evidence and linguistic studies indicate they were a branch of the Northern Shoshones. Originally, the Shoshones were typical pedestrian hunters and gatherers. When they obtained the horse in the late 1600s, a revolution occurred. This obscure branch of the Northern Shoshones evolved into a mounted and aggressive warrior culture that left their mountain home for the great plains of eastern Colorado and western Kansas where game was plentiful. They eventually migrated south, attracted most likely by the warm climate and abundant buffalo, and the presence of less-aggressive indigenous tribes they could dominate. By the 18th century, much of north, central, and west Texas was Comanche country, also known as Comanchería. This is when they became known as Comanches, a name derived from a Ute word literally meaning "anyone who wants to fight me all the time." And fight they did.

Lipan-Apaches

The Apaches are believed to be descended from Athapaskan ancestors who migrated from the forests of western Canada into the southern Great Plains. When the Apaches came to the lands of what is today known as Texas and Mexico, they were constantly forced to move due to the pressure of the Comanches. In Texas they came into contact with the new Spanish settlements. By the 1600s, the Spaniards enslaved many Apaches to work ranches and mines, and the Apaches often retaliated by stealing horses. The Apaches found themselves under pressure from Anglo-American settlers from the north and east, the Mexican-Spaniards to the south, and the Comanches from every direction. By the 1740s, pressure from the Comanches prompted the Apaches to migrate toward the Rio Grande. Eventually settlements such as San Antonio encroached upon the Apache's hunting grounds. This was a period of much violence between the Apaches, the Spanish missions, and the settlers. Avoiding the encroachment of these other groups, and conversion to Catholicism, Apaches eventually retreated to the Rio Grande.

SPANISH AND FRENCH EXPLORATIONS (1519-1685)

As early as 1519 the coast of Texas was mapped. Under the service of the governor of Jamaica, Captain Alonso Alvarez de Pineda sailed the Gulf of Mexico and became the first person in recorded history to explore the region. Just a few years later, in 1528, exploration in Texas was resumed by Spanish explorer Álvar Núñez Cabeza de Vaca. *Cabeza* is Spanish for head and *vaca* is Spanish for cow. How appropriate that the written history of Texas begins with the fascinating adventure of a man with the name of "Cow's Head."

Cabeza de Vaca was shipwrecked on the coast of Texas and washed up on the beach

DISCOVERY OF LA BELLE

One of LaSalle's ships, *La Belle*, sank in Matagorda Bay in 1686. Over 300 years later, in 1995, Texas Historical Commission archaeologists discovered its resting place and erected a cofferdam around it to salvage its contents. They eventually recovered its hull, over one million artifacts, and the skeleton of one of the crewmembers. It is one of the most important shipwrecks ever discovered in North America. Many of its artifacts are on display at the Bob Bullock Texas History Museum in Austin.

literally naked. He spent the next seven years wandering through what is now Texas. He lived with the native inhabitants until he arrived at a Mexican outpost near the Pacific Coast in early 1536. Cabeza de Vaca arrived as a conquistador but during the course of travels became a merchant, a slave, and a healer to the various small family bands of hunter-gatherers scattered throughout the region. In his role as a healer, Cabeza de Vaca removed an arrow from the chest of an Indian, for which the Texas Surgical Society honors him today as their "patron saint." He chronicled his odyssey in what is titled *La Relación* (The Account), which was first published in Spain in 1542. In it, Cabeza de Vaca describes in detail the landscape he encountered and his observations of the native people's cultural practices, including how they ate, raised their families, made love and made war, all before the land and its people were irrevocably altered by the European culture, its diseases, and the introduction of the horse. Cabeza de Vaca advocated to the Spanish crown not to enslave the natives. His exact route through Texas has been the subject of considerable study but is not exactly known. Some scholars have Cabeza de Vaca's route taking him through what is now Central Texas and the area including Austin, San Marcos, and San Antonio. The Center for the Study of the Southwest, at Texas State University in San Marcos, houses a rare 1555 edition of Cabeza de Vaca's *La Relación*. Artifacts from the natives of this era are on display at the Witte Museum in San Antonio.

After Cabeza de Vaca's unintentional tour through Texas, Spain continued to have many contacts with Texas. Subsequent Spanish explorations of Texas were conducted by Francisco Vásquez de Coronado and Luis de Moscoso Alvadaro. Forty years later, Fray Agustín Rodríguez, a Franciscan missionary, and Francisco Sánches Chamuscado led an expedition through Texas and New Mexico. In 1681 the first permanent settlement in Texas was established in the El Paso area.

REVOLVING SOVEREIGN DOOR (1685-1690)

With Spanish exploration, the region fell under the domain of Spanish rule. However, they soon learned Texas didn't have the gold, silver, and other riches they sought, and the hostile environment of Texas wasn't providing sufficient incentive for them to wander far from the reasonable comfort of Mexico City. This left a gap for the French to try and lay claim to the New World. In 1682, French explorer René Robert Cavelier, Sieur de La Salle, attempted to create a colony in Louisiana but mistakenly landed in Texas. LaSalle's settlement was on Lavaca Bay just up the coast from present day Corpus Christi.

Hearing that France was establishing a presence with a colony, the Spanish government became very interested in Texas. In 1689 Spanish authorities sent Captain Alonso de León to confront the French and reclaim the region. When he arrived at the French colony, he found the settlement had been decimated by Indians and La Salle had been killed by his own men. Thus Spain realized they ruled the land once again.

SPANISH TEXAS, MISSIONS, AND AMERICANS (1690-1821)

In 1690 an expedition of Spanish soldiers and four Franciscan priests crossed the Rio Grande. The Spanish were coming to establish their own settlements, bring Christianity to the Indians, and, more importantly, prevent any other European powers from claiming what they believed was rightly theirs. Thus began in earnest the Spanish mission period in Texas.

Between 1682 and 1793, 26 missions were

TEXAS HISTORY THROUGH THE FLAG

Texas has had a very interesting history filled with drama, power, wars, and uprisings. From being Spanish territory, to being part of Mexico, to being its own republic, the state has worn many hats and flown banners of many different colors. In all, Texas has had eight changes in sovereignty and six different flags. The state flag that is in use today is the same flag that was used during the Republic of Texas period. This flag has become a popular iconic symbol, and indelible in its simplicity. It's just red, white, and blue, with a large "Lone Star" on the left. A great way to see this radically shifty history is through the various incarnations of the flag that have flown over the state.

- Spanish (1519-1685)
- French (1685-1690)
- Spanish (1690-1821)
- Mexican (1821-1836)
- Republic of Texas (1836-1845)
- United States (1845-1861)
- Confederate States of America (1861-1865)
- United States (1865-present)

established by Franciscan priests in Texas. The most successful were the five missions established in San Antonio: Mission San Antonio de Valero (The Alamo), Mission Concepción, Mission San José, Mission San Juan, and Mission Espada. Less successful but still with a significant presence was Mission Nuestra Senora del Rosario and its accompanying Presidio la Bahía established on the lower San Antonio River in 1749 (the Goliad mission). The five missions on the upper San Antonio River still exist, and are within a few driving miles of each other. Collectively these missions form the largest concentration of Catholic missions in North America. The goal of the missions was to convert the local native population. The buildings were first built of stone, wood, and adobe and didn't have walls. Because of tensions between tribes and missionary occupants, stone walls were erected as a form of defense.

By the late 1770s it was clear that the efforts of the Spanish to civilize and colonize Texas through the mission system had been largely unsuccessful if not an outright failure. The population of the weaker indigenous tribes who had been the mission recruits declined by reason of high infant mortality rates, epidemics introduced by the Europeans, pressure from more aggressive invading tribes, and assimilation. Texas remained thinly populated and impoverished. Between 1824 and 1830, the first years of the Republic of Mexico, all the missions still in existence in Texas were officially secularized with the exception of the ones in El Paso.

One of the greatest contributions of the mission system was the establishment of ranching in Texas. Early expeditions brought livestock to the missions and within two to three decades thousands of cattle and horses roamed the pastures and prairies from central to south Texas. The horses and cattle were the genesis of the huge cattle drives after the Civil War and were managed by the "vaqueros" (from which the term "buckaroo" is derived) that evolved into the quintessential Texas cowboy.

Around the 1800s the first Anglo-Americans appeared on the scene. Initially they were tolerated by Spanish authorities, but Spain's grip on Texas began to weaken between 1790 and 1820 as Spain focused more on Europe and Mexico. This opened the door for Anglo-Americans to continue settling in Texas, which eventually morphed into unregulated colonization by Americans.

MEXICAN TEXAS (1821-1836)

Spain's efforts to colonize and populate Texas ended in failure. When Mexico gained its independence from Spain in 1821, it inherited the results of that failure. Only three towns existed and the population was estimated at approximately 2,500. The Comanches, Apaches, and other hostile tribes ruled Texas more than the government officials in Mexico City, whether they were Spanish or Mexican.

To populate this northern frontier full of hostile natives, the Spanish and then the Mexican governments looked to Anglo-American immigration. In January 1821, the Spanish government gave Moses Austin of Missouri a contract to establish a colony with 300 families. When he died, his son Stephen F. Austin inherited the contract. The Mexican government confirmed Austin's contract after independence and Austin and other *empresarios* with contracts from the Mexican government began immigrating into Texas. By 1835, there were 21 towns and the Anglo-American population was estimated to be approximately 20,000 with the Hispanic-Texans, called Tejanos, numbering less than 5,000.

Antonio Lopez de Santa Anna was elected President of Mexico as a liberal and champion of the Constitution of 1824. However, by 1835, he replaced the existing congress with a new body controlled by centralists under his control. He then abolished the Constitution of 1824 and abolished the various state governments, including that of Coahuila y Texas. Mexico, like the United States, had then and has now a federal government and various state governments. Even today the official name for Mexico is Los Estados Unidos de Mexico (the United States of Mexico). Santa Anna had replaced the state governments with departments

Mexico's past meets present at the Instituto de Mexico in San Antonio.

run by officials he appointed. When the state of Zacatecas (Texas) rebelled, Santa Anna's forces invaded the state. After defeating his opposition, Santa Anna allowed his soldiers to murder and rape the local citizens, killing thousands of them. By October 1835, Santa Anna made himself supreme dictator of Mexico.

The people of Texas, both Anglos and Tejanos, were in conflict with the policies of the brutal dictator. They had economic interests separate and apart from Mexico City and were used to little in the way of government interference. Facing the loss of their local government and the replacement of the liberal Constitution of 1824 with the arbitrariness of a supreme dictator, the Anglo-Texans, who called themselves "Texians" at that time, decided to rebel, with the support of a significant number of Tejanos.

THE TEXAS REVOLUTION (1835-1836)
The Battle at Gonzales
The flash point that ignited the Texas Revolution occurred in October 1835 in the town of Gonzales on the Guadalupe River about 70 miles east of San Antonio. The town had a small cannon given to them by the Mexican Army to defend against the native tribes. Due to the Texians' rising frustration with Mexican dictator Santa Anna, the Mexican Army sent a contingent of 100 dragoons to retrieve it. The Texians rounded up volunteers to repulse the Mexicans under their makeshift banner with an image of the cannon on it and the words COME AND TAKE IT. On October 2, the Texians and the Mexican Army faced off. The Texians fired their cannon and charged. The Mexican Army withdrew, suffering at most two fatalities. One Texian received a bloody nose when he fell off his horse. Although not a significant battle to say the least, this skirmish marked a point of no return.

The Battle at San Antonio
Stephen F. Austin was in command of the volunteers that constituted the "Texian Army." He led his volunteers to San Antonio where General Cos, the brother-in-law of Santa Anna, had arrived and taken over the Alamo as his command center. The Texian volunteers decided to use Mission Concepción, just down the road from the Alamo, as their headquarters. The Texian Army wasn't a disciplined lot and the lack of active fighting led to boredom among the troops, which led to lots of heavy drinking. At a point when the Texian Army was in danger of collapsing in total disarray, Stephen F. Austin was called to San Felipe where a "Consultation" of the Texian colonists had been meeting. Edward Burleson, a veteran Native American fighter, was elected as the Texian Army's new commander in his absence. Burleson ordered an attack on San Antonio on December 3 but the troops refused to obey. Burleson decided to pull the troops out of San Antonio and winter in Goliad. Then one man stepped up and changed history. Benjamin Rush Milam, disgusted with the decision to withdraw, went through the remaining troops with the cry: "Who will follow old Ben Milam into San Antonio?" About 300

of the remaining volunteers joined Milam in an attack that began on December 5, 1835. The battle lasted three days with the Texians fighting house-to-house cutting holes through the adobe walls to advance and gain control of San Antonio. They inflicted 150 casualties on the Mexican forces but not without loss of their own. Ben Milam himself was shot through the head on the third day of the battle.

On December 9, General Cos retreated back to the Alamo, where he chose to surrender. The Texians were generous and allowed General Cos and the Mexican troops to leave Texas with the promise not to "oppose the re-establishment of the Federal Constitution of 1824." Interestingly, the Texians weren't fighting for total independence from Mexico. They just wanted to be free from the dictatorial government of Santa Anna.

The Battle at the Alamo

After Cos surrendered, most of the Texas Army of volunteers just went home. Approximately 100 defenders remained in the Alamo. The Consultation had previously created a Texas regular army on paper and made Sam Houston commander-in-chief. The problem was that the regular army had no soldiers and the volunteers already in the field were not under his command. The bigger problem was Santa Anna. Shortly after the new year of 1836, Santa Anna crossed the Rio Grande with an estimated 4,000 troops as well as cavalry and artillery with the goal of punishing the Texians.

The Texas Army at this time consisted of the 100 men in the Alamo and about 400 men under the command of James Fannin in Goliad, with Sam Houston as commander-in-chief. When Houston received word that Santa Anna had crossed the Rio Grande, he sent a courier to the Alamo with orders to remove the cannons, destroy the Alamo, and proceed to Gonzales. Sam Houston's order to abandon the Alamo was not carried out. Nineteen cannons that had been captured from Cos bolstered the Alamo defenses. Seeing that the Alamo could be defended, Houston's orders were overruled, and William Barret Travis was sent from San Felipe to reinforce the Alamo. In February of 1836, Travis reached the Alamo but he only had with him an additional 29 men. David Crockett arrived from Tennessee about the same time in response to the call to arms. Alamo's departing commander James Neill put Travis in charge. The men, however, were used to electing their leaders and chose the popular Bowie. Bowie and Travis compromised by agreeing to a joint command with Bowie commanding the "volunteers" and Travis the "regular" army. On February 24, Bowie ceded full command to Travis when Bowie became seriously ill to the point of being bedridden. Santa Anna's troops had already made their appearance in San Antonio and the siege of the Alamo had begun.

Santa Anna marked his arrival by raising a red flag above San Fernando Church and demanding an unconditional surrender. Santa Anna had issued a decree that anyone rebelling against his rule was a "pirate" and should be shot. Captured pirates were not entitled to the status or protection afforded prisoners of war. The red flag meant "no quarter" would be given to any prisoner. Travis responded with a shot from his 18-pound cannon, the largest in the Alamo.

The siege of the Alamo lasted 13 days and ended in the early morning hours of March 6 when Santa Anna's troops overwhelmed the Alamo's defenders. Travis was one of the first to die when shot through the head, Bowie was killed in his bed in the chapel, and Crockett most likely died while defending the wooden palisades erected just outside the entrance to the chapel. The Mexican *alcalde* (mayor) of San Antonio, Francisco Antonio Ruiz, put the death toll of the Alamo defenders at 182. The number of Mexican losses will never be known for sure but modern estimates place Santa Anna's casualties in the range of 600 dead and wounded.

The importance of the battle of the Alamo as a military feat can be debated. What cannot be debated, however, is that the Alamo let all Texians know they were in a battle to the death and it inspired them with a rallying cry and thirst for vengeance that they carried with them to victory at San Jacinto.

The Battle at San Jacinto

The Consultation that began meeting in October 1835 called for a convention to meet at Washington-on-the-Brazos on March 1, 1836. On March 2, the delegates to the convention declared Texas a "free, sovereign, and independent republic." The news of the Declaration of Independence did not reach the Alamo before it fell but the defense of the Alamo certainly gave the convention delegates the time and opportunity to meet and allowed the Republic of Texas to be born.

The real military prize for Santa Anna took place after the Alamo at Goliad. As Santa Anna marched on San Antonio he sent a smaller force under Geneneral Jose de Urrea on a southerly route through the populated areas of Texas towards Goliad.

Houston ordered Goliad to be abandoned but the 400 men under the command of James Fannin left too late. Just six miles outside of Goliad the Texians were surrounded and caught by Urrea's troops. After a brief and ferocious battle, Fannin accepted his fate and sought surrender under favorable terms. He surrendered after receiving what he thought were assurances that his men would be treated as prisoners of war. Fannin and his men were marched back to Goliad and imprisoned in the chapel at the presidio of La Bahía. Urrea reported the capture of Fannin and his men to Santa Anna and requested clemency for them. Santa Anna replied with a direct order to execute all the prisoners. At sunrise on Palm Sunday, March 27, 1836, the order was carried out and the men were marched out of the presidio and shot. After the initial volley of fire, 28 prisoners escaped to the woods and lived to tell the tale of the massacre. The dead counted 342, including Fannin. Fannin had requested only two things from his captors when he learned he would be executed: that he not be shot in the head and that his personal belongings be sent to his family. Fannin was not marched out of the presidio with his men. He was executed just outside the chapel by a shot to the head. His executioners stole his personal effects.

Texas was now virtually defenseless with no army in the field. Houston went to Gonzales and rounded up several hundred men that had gathered originally with the idea of trying to relieve the Alamo. When word reached Houston that the Alamo had fallen and Santa Anna was approaching with as many as 5,000 troops, Houston, not wanting to defend fixed positions against overwhelming odds, decided to retreat. He burned the town and sunk what few cannons were available in the Guadalupe River. Within days, he learned that the Texians at Goliad had all been executed and that his men were the only hope of survival for the fledgling Texas republic.

Houston retreated further and further to the east, passing over the Guadalupe River, the Colorado River, and the Brazos River. Many of his troops and commanders didn't like the tactic, as they wanted to fight and avenge the Alamo and Goliad. Santa Anna believed Houston and his army would not fight and were fleeing to the safety and protection afforded by United States troops at the Louisiana border. But when Houston learned that Santa Anna's force was fewer than 1,000 men, he shadowed it to Harrisburg. Santa Anna failed to capture the officials that now made up the Texas government in Harrisburg. They fled again to what was called "New Washington" on Galveston Bay. Eventually Santa Anna and his troops, and Houston and his troops, arrived on the San Jacinto River where they faced off in open prairie of several hundred yards.

On the morning of April 21, General Cos arrived with an additional 500 men. Santa Anna's forces now numbered over 1,300 while the Texas forces numbered almost 900. Santa Anna, assuming he would have to attack the Texians, would let Cos's men rest after their long march while he awaited the arrival of his remaining troops. Houston, on the other hand, held his first council of war. He and his commanders decided to take the offensive. The Texians formed their line on the prairie around 3:00 P.M. The line included two small cannons called the Twin Sisters, and a cavalry contingent under the command of Mirabeau B. Lamar. The Mexican troops were not expecting offensive operations and many were enjoying their siesta. The Mexican sentries on duty detected the advance and opened fire with muskets and a 12-pound cannon. Most of the fire was without effect. The Texians were crouching low in the grass and were advancing through a small depression in the prairie. While riding his horse, Sam Houston was hit by a musket ball that fractured his leg just above his left ankle. The Twin Sisters fired once on the Mexican breastworks and Houston led his men to within twenty yards of the Mexicans when the order to fire was given. After the one volley, the Texians did not reload but charged ahead. The Mexican line broke and ran. The battle lasted only eighteen minutes but the killing lasted until it was almost dark. The Texians, yelling "Remember the Alamo, Remember Goliad," ran down the fleeing Mexicans, clubbing and knifing them to death. Many were trapped in low wetlands where the Texians could reload and fire upon them from the dry shore as they struggled to get free from knee-deep mud. Houston tried to stop the slaughter but most of his troops ignored his pleas. In all, the Texians killed 630 Mexican soldiers and captured another 730. The Texians had only two killed on the day of the battle and six more died later from the wounds they suffered.

Santa Anna was captured the following day dressed in the clothes of a common soldier. When he was brought into camp, his true identity became known because the soldiers began addressing him as "El Presidente." He was brought before Houston. Many of the Texians wanted to kill him immediately and there was no shortage of volunteers for the job. Houston, however, knew that Santa Anna was more valuable alive than dead. The remaining Mexican Army, which had more troops than were present at San Jacinto, was only miles away. Houston forced Santa Anna to sign a treaty that called for the Mexican Army to return to the other side of the Rio Grande.

The freedom of Texas from Mexico won at the San Jacinto River led to annexation and the Mexican War, resulting in the acquisition by the United States of the states of Texas, New Mexico, Arizona, Nevada, California, Utah, and parts of Colorado, Wyoming, Kansas, and Oklahoma. Almost one-third of the present area of the American nation, nearly a million square miles, changed sovereignty.

THE REPUBLIC OF TEXAS (1836-1845)

With the defeat of Santa Anna at San Jacinto, the Texians had at last been freed from the tyranny of the oppressive Mexican government. The land of Texas was theirs. Immediately a government was put in place. Within months voters of the new republic chose their first elected official. Sam Houston was elected the president of the Republic of Texas, established his capital at his namesake city in eastern Texas, and shortly thereafter the first Congress of the Republic of Texas convened. Voters also overwhelmingly approved a referendum requesting annexation by the United States, but U.S. president Martin Van Buren refused to consider the request.

A year later The Republic of Texas was officially recognized by the United States, and later by some European countries. The new Republic of Texas faced many problems. The economy needed attention, local Native American tribes were fiercer than ever, relations with the United States had to be developed, and Mexico was itching for a war. General Santa Anna was in custody and the public demanded he be executed. Wisely, Houston kept him alive and eventually released him.

In 1838 Mirabeau B. Lamar was elected president. He was notorious for spending lavishly and exacerbating problems with Native American tribes. Since he detested Sam Houston, he refused to reside at a capital named Houston. Therefore, the need arose to find a new capital for the Republic of Texas. Many communities wanted that honor but not one was the clear favorite. As a result, Lamar decided to create a new capital where no city existed before. The site he chose was a buffalo hunting camp. In 1839, a new capital city was laid out between Waller Creek on the east, Shoal Creek on the west, and the Colorado River on the south.

All went relatively well for the original 200

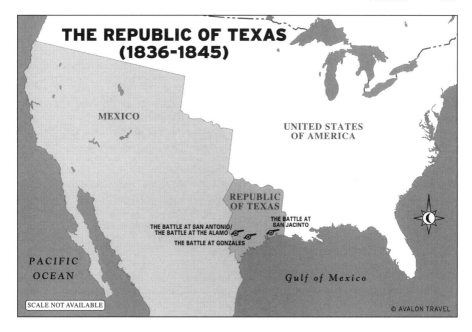

THE REPUBLIC OF TEXAS (1836-1845)

MEXICO

UNITED STATES
OF AMERICA

REPUBLIC
OF TEXAS

THE BATTLE AT SAN ANTONIO/
THE BATTLE AT THE ALAMO

THE BATTLE AT
SAN JACINTO

THE BATTLE AT GONZALES

PACIFIC
OCEAN

Gulf of Mexico

SCALE NOT AVAILABLE

© AVALON TRAVEL

residents who resided in log cabins along the street that was grandly called Congress Avenue. Unfortunately for the residents of early Austin, this part of Texas was Comanche territory (as well as buffalo territory) and thus Austin was a very dangerous place to live. The diaries of the early settlers confirm that many were killed and scalped when they strayed beyond the immediate confines of the capital city. Many times the Comanches even came into the city itself to wreak havoc and terrorize the citizens.

In 1841, Sam Houston was reelected president and quickly decided to move the capital back to Houston. Houston was pro–Native American and thought it was a ridiculous idea to stir up the Comanches by creating a capital in the middle of their territory. Furthermore, the Colorado River was not navigable that far upstream. Therefore no steamboats could travel to the capital city, leaving it quite isolated.

Houston, a savvy politician, knew that the 200 residents of Austin would not be in favor of moving the capital, so he devised a plan to move it without their knowledge. He sent some Texas Rangers with a couple of wagons down to Austin with orders to sneak into town in the middle of the night, load up the archives of the Republic, and take them back to Houston. Where the archives resided, so would reside the capital.

All went well with this plan, and the archives were loaded up and moved out of town late one night. However, one woman remained awake, Angelina Eberly. She was the proprietress of the Bullock Hotel located on the northwest corner of 6th Street and Congress. She investigated what was going on, quickly discovered that they had been robbed of their archives, and fired the cannon that the city had for protection against the Native Americans. The firing of the cannon woke up the community, and a large group mounted their horses, armed themselves, and rode out after the Rangers. They caught up with the wagons and at gunpoint turned them around. The archives headed back to Austin and the incident would forever be known as the "archives war." Thus, in spite of Sam Houston, the Hero of San Jacinto, the archives remained in Austin and so did the capital.

Houston may not have been successful in moving the capital from Austin, but he was successful at obtaining annexation. Houston courted Great Britain and France and both became interested in the idea. However, the United States was very uncomfortable with the prospect of a British or French presence in the middle of the country and quickly moved to annex Texas. In 1845 annexation to the United States took place and the Republic of Texas was dissolved.

ANNEXATION (1845-PRESENT)

The entry of Texas into the United States sparked the Mexican-American War. Mexican officials were angered at Texas's annexation because they felt the region was under negotiation. By this point, the relentless General Santa Anna had gained power in Mexico and felt it was time to take his revenge. The war lasted for two years, and came to a close in 1847 when U.S. troops gained control of Mexico City.

Settlers, Slaves, and Cowboys

In the 1850s the population almost doubled. This rapid growth of the population came about primarily because of Germans and slaves. A large majority of German immigrants pioneered their way to Texas, the largest population moving to the Hill Country. They brought with them German culture, customs, and traditions and integrated them into the Wild West. The other factor in the dramatic rise of the population came from folks migrating to Texas from the southern states, bringing with them thousands of slaves. Slavery wasn't customary in Texas until these newer, wealthy slave-owners introduced the practice.

With the Civil War (1861–1865), Texas seceded from the United States and joined forces with the Confederate States of America. Texas supplied food, supplies, and some 80,000 men. Although most of the battles took place outside of Texas, the Civil War left an indelible scar that would last for a long time. With slavery abolished, blacks did gain some rights, but they were limited.

It was at this time that Texas found its calling

in ranching. With the advent of the railway and the abundance of land, Texas's identity as ranching cowboy country quickly developed. Land barons, businesses, and money poured into the state, and small pioneer towns quickly grew into cities.

The 20th Century

In the second half of the 19th century oil had been discovered in east Texas, but it was nothing to shake a stick at. It wasn't until 1901 when a drilling site east of Houston exploded with a gusher of oil that Texas realized it was sitting on an abundant and extremely valuable natural resource. Just a few years later Henry Ford was making his automobile available to the mass public. With millions of barrels of black gold shooting out of the ground and great demand, oil made Texas rich. Although oil moguls scooped up a lot of this wealth, the tax revenues spilled into all aspects of local and state government. Schools were built, roads were paved, and homes were built. Then, with the fall of the

The architecture in modern-day Austin vividly reflects both past and present.

© JUSTIN MARLER

BIRTH OF THE CITY OF AUSTIN

Before the birth of the City of Austin, there was nothing at the location other than a low water crossing on the Colorado River, where the Congress Avenue Bridge is today. To the east was blackland prairie, and to the west of the Colorado were the limestone hills marking the beginning of the Hill Country. Immense herds of buffalo migrated south from the Panhandle region following the Colorado River through Central Texas.

In the early 1800s the Mexican government decided to allow Anglo-American settlers to immigrate to this part of Mexico in order to help populate the region and provide a buffer against Native American attacks on the town of San Antonio. Those early American settlers loved to hunt buffalo and many quickly discovered the location on the Colorado where the buffalo herds would cross. These hunters set up campsites at the crossing, which grew into a small community that was known as Waterloo. One of those early buffalo hunters was Mirabeau B. Lamar. Years later Lamar was elected the second president of the Republic of Texas and chose the buffalo campsite of Waterloo as the location of the capital.

---

stock market and the Great Depression in 1929, the state's progress and flow of money came to a screeching halt. The demand for oil hit rock bottom as the market was glutted and common people couldn't afford to fuel a car, much less own one. Thus, part of Texas became part of what was known as the Dust Bowl, an area in the Southern Plains that was afflicted with severe draught, poverty, and agricultural decline in the wake of the Great Depression.

Texas found its way out of the Great Depression during World War II as several military bases were established. With the manufacturing industry on the rise, and the federal government spending money in Texas, the state slowly regained its wealthy and influential status. Oil value increased and production followed right in step. The following two decades saw growth in the state's economy, population, and in its recognition.

Today Texas is still a major oil producer and home to several top military bases and facilities. Although ranching isn't as prevalent as it was in the past, the tradition still carries on.

Government and Economy

POLITICS

Being the capital of Texas, Austin is the hub of the state's politics. The legislature meets every other spring and consists of a 31-member senate and a 150-member house of representatives. Texas has traditionally been a democratic state, but this dramatically changed when George W. Bush became governor and later when he was elected president of the United States. Following Bush's election as president, Republican Rick Perry became the governor of Texas.

There are several problems that plague the politics of the state capital. First, the legislative process is famous for getting bogged down and for not achieving its goals. Special legislative sessions are often called to try to tackle these important issues, but the "special sessions" often end with nothing getting accomplished except taxpayer dollars being spent while the feuding legislators get nothing done. Another problem in Texas politics is big business. It should come as no surprise that politics and business are fast friends, but in Texas this is downright cultural. Texas is home to some of the nation's largest and most powerful businesses, and their agendas are consistently integrated into legislation, right under the noses of the unvigilant and unaware public.

ECONOMY

The economy of Central Texas used to be hinged on ranching and cotton, but today the main industries that contribute to the region's economy are higher education, government, and high tech. Top employers in Austin include the University of Texas, Dell Computers, City of Austin, Motorola, Seaton Healthcare Network, and IBM. The economic force that people most associate with Austin is the high-tech industry, which took root when, in the 1960s, IBM moved here. Since then Motorola, Texas Instruments, and Dell Computers have chosen Austin as their home. Today high tech is the third-largest industry in the region, and a major player on the global computer and technology scene.

In recent years an economic shot in the arm has been coming from the movie industry. This burgeoning interest in Austin is for good reason. Filming and production work in Austin is less expensive than the big cities, and the industry folks here are friendly and free of all that folks hate about Hollywood. An economic impact study conducted in 2004 estimates the total economic impact of the film industry at nearly $360 million annually. The long list of films made in and around Austin include *Dazed and Confused, The Alamo, The Faculty, Texas Chainsaw Massacre I* and *II, Miss Congeniality I* and *II, Second Hand Lions, Spy Kids, Raising Arizona, Slacker, Waiting for Guffman, Office Space,* and *How to Eat Fried Worms.*

Lastly, one can't talk about Austin's economy without mentioning the music industry. Although there's no real "industry" to speak of, such as record companies, music executives, and tall buildings where musicians sell their souls, live music is a big source of revenue for the city. It brings in an excess of 11 million per year, never mind the boost music gives the tourism industry. With high-profile festivals such as SXSW ($21 million) and Austin City Limits Festival ($26 million), live music revenue is something the city relies on.

People and Culture

Texans are bold, brash, and full of bravado. The bravado, however, is tempered with a large dose of hospitality and friendliness. The state's motto, "Friendship," has historical linguistic origins but it is also something that is reflected every day in its people. Who and what a Texan is can be summed up by two popular bumper stickers. One identifies the car's occupant as a "Native Texan" while the other boasts, "I wasn't born in Texas but I got here as fast as I could." To qualify as a true Texan you don't need established bloodlines like the Virginia planter class or the Brahmans in Boston. In fact, the founding fathers of Texas, almost to the man, came to Texas because they were running from either the law, debts, failed careers, or failed marriages. Most will agree that being Texan is open to all classes, all races, and all religions. It is a spirit and an attitude, coupled with a pride associated with a special place that was conquered and cultivated by strong-willed and independent-minded people.

Texan pride is due in no small part to the fact that Texas was created in a revolution against a brutal dictator and stood alone for almost 10 years as an independent nation. Texas joined the United States in 1845 as a result of a treaty between two sovereign nations, not because it was a conquered territory or constituted land purchased from a European power. It is understandable that the original Texans were proud of what they created and have passed on that pride to future generations and new arrivals. That is why as you travel around Texas you will see the Texas flag displayed prominently by its people at their homes and businesses.

The strongest cultural influences that have informed Central Texas character come from

Mexico and Germany. Mexico should come as no surprise, as the border is so close, and Latino heritage reaches far back into the state's history, but people are often surprised at the German heritage. Both cultures combined have shaped the cultural landscape. The Latino cultural and historical presence is especially apparent in Austin and San Antonio where most of the food, art, and music draws heavily from Latino culture, and the German heritage is strongest in the Hill Country, where folks still dance to polka and eat schnitzels. One strong reminder of both German and Mexican heritage is in the regional Latin music, which features the accordion, introduced by early German pioneers.

POPULATION

The populations of Austin, San Antonio, and the Hill Country are largely comprised of white Caucasians and Hispanics. Austin's significant demographic figures as collected during the last major census in 2010 are as follows: 49 percent white/Caucasian, 35 percent Hispanic, 16.2 percent other race, 8 percent black, 5 percent Asian, 1 percent two or more races. Primary ancestries for Austin are: 12.8 percent German, 8.7 percent English, 8.4 percent Irish, 4.3 percent United States, 2.7 percent French, 2.5 percent Italian.

San Antonio's demographics from the 2010 census are as follows: 61 percent Hispanic, 28 percent white/Caucasian, 6 percent black, 2 percent Asian, 1 percent two or more races. Primary ancestries for San Antonio are: 41 percent Mexican, 15 percent other Hispanic or Latino, 9 percent German, 9 percent black or African American, 5 percent English, 5 percent Irish, 2 percent French, 2 percent Italian, 6 percent other European, and 1 percent American Indian.

RELIGION

Religion is a major part of life in Texas. Beliefs and values are unquestionably integrated into secular culture and a church-based way of life is the acceptable norm. Texas is at the western-most reaches of the Bible Belt, the region of the United States made up of communities that are predominantly Protestant and Evangelical. There isn't a definitive boundary for this belt, but most agree that it stretches from Dallas, Texas, down to Austin, which is at the western reaches, and continues east through the South. Although only part of Texas is in what's considered the Bible Belt, the Bible is the basis for beliefs and ideologies for the majority of Texans. According to *Churches and Church Membership in the United States* Texas has the most Evangelical Protestants in the nation, with California way behind in second place. Texas rankings with other religions as compared to the rest of the United States are as follows: third-largest number of Catholics, third-largest number of Buddhist congregations, fifth-largest number of Muslims, fifth-largest number of Hindu congregations, and tenth-largest number of Jews. At least 55 percent of Texans adhere to a particular religion.

Being the most liberal piece of Texas, Austin has the most diverse representation of religions and is perhaps the most accepting and tolerant. San Antonio, on the other hand, is predominantly Catholic. This should come as no surprise due to its Mexican history and the proximity to the border.

LANGUAGE

The predominant language spoken in Central Texas is English. This may sound simple to those familiar with the language but newcomers beware—the version of English expressed here isn't always as it seems. Besides being famous for their unique accent, Texans also have a tendency to pronounce words in a creative way. The most widely known example of this is the word "y'all." Although not exclusively Texan it has become synonymous with the state. Along with this, there's a long list of weird pronunciations that first-timers will encounter. At first this approach to English is amusing and takes a little getting used to, but its charm will win you over.

Due to Central Texas's rich Mexican history and Latino and Hispanic culture, the Spanish language comes in a close second to English. Most Texans speak a little Spanish and many are fluent. The infusion of Spanish into Central Texas culture has created a unique lexicon that is to be found nowhere else. Spanish words have merged into the Texas lexicon and have taken on their own meaning. For example the Spanish word *grande* is pronounced like "grand" (i.e. Rio Grand), and Guadalupe is pronounced gwada-LOOP. In Spanish "ll" is pronounced like "y," but no one would dare pronounce Amarillo with a "y" sound. The list of weird idiosyncrasies is long and amusing. Travelers, especially those with a background in Spanish, should try to go with the vernacular flow.

MUSIC AND ART

Music is a major part of the life and culture of Central Texas. Austin is the Live Music Capital of the World and San Antonio is considered the home of Tejano and conjunto music. I won't speculate as to how music and Austin became synonymous, but I will say that Austin has been greatly blessed in its calling to live music greatness. Today Austin is compulsive about music. Throughout the year Austin's hundreds of venues, bars, and clubs are full of touring national acts, local favorites, and wannabes seeking expression and recognition. Although the city is smack dab in the middle of Texas there isn't much tractor pop (modern country) to be heard here. Austin is an independent artist, songwriter paradise that transcends all genres by offering music by the people for the people. The scene is both diverse and tolerant, and most music fans here don't subscribe to any one genre.

Austin may be known for its contribution to live music, but San Antonio and the Hill Country are known for Tejano and conjunto music. This unique form of music is the direct result of the Spanish, Mexican, Texian, and German cultures mixing over the course of two centuries in Central and South Texas. The final product is a Tex-Mex music that blends traditional Mexican forms such as the *corrido* and the western/European waltz and polka introduced by German and Czech settlers in the late 19th century. The most distinct element of this music is the accordion, which was inadvertently introduced by the German settlers. Today Tejano and conjunto music has adopted strong influences from rock, blues, and *cumbia,* and has gone from being a local and ethnic form of music to its own genre with wide appeal in North America, Latin America, and Europe. At the core of Tejano and conjunto are songs about drinking, love, heartbreak, and dancing. Popular artists that have either pioneered or popularized the Tejano sound are Narciso Martinez, Isidiro Lopez, Joe Lopez y El Groupo Mazz, and Flaco Jimenez, who can still be seen performing around Austin and San Antonio.

Folk art is second only to music in Central Texas. Although it is something that is not easily defined, it is widely accepted as simply art by and for the folk. In Austin folk art is pop paintings of Hank Williams Sr. on old fence boards, or junk from the landfill and car graveyards that are painstakingly fitted together to form a post-modern apocalyptic "sculpture," or retro-style neon signs mounted on tin with catchy statements that echo sentiments of the obscure, or a thought-provoking social/political painting of Elvis wired to light bulbs. In San Antonio a similar modern approach is taken to folk art, but with one difference—replace Elvis with the Virgin Mary. All the above expressions of folk art can be found in galleries, shops, boutiques, restaurants, on urban walls, and in people's front yards all over Austin, San Antonio, and in some Hill Country towns. You'll know it when you see it.

ESSENTIALS

Tips for Travelers

CONDUCT AND CUSTOMS
Texas Manners

In Texas chivalry, politeness, and manners are very much a part of everyday life. Men in Texas have a respect for women that harkens back to a bygone era. Opening doors for ladies, not talking vulgar in their company, and addressing women with a respectful "ma'am" are customs that are alive and well. Cursing in public isn't as prevalent as it is in many other parts of the country, so it's best to keep the sailor talk to a minimum. Also, when walking down the street people look each other in the eyes and say "Hi." Yankees and West Coasters may take this the wrong way at first. If someone starts talking to you in line at the store that doesn't mean they are mentally ill or they want your money. It's just good ol' Texas kindness.

Tipping

An important part of the income of workers in the service industry comes from tips. It's considered rude to tip too little or with spare change. With the Texas minimum wage being a measly $7.25 an hour, don't be one of those cheapskates that tips low and tries to sneak out the back door. The following workers should be tipped based on the fare, bill, or fee: cab drivers 15 percent, restaurant workers 15–20 percent, bartenders 10–15 percent, bellhops $1 per bag.

Don't Mess With Texas

UP TO $1000 FINE FOR LITTERING

QUICK FACTS FOR INTERNATIONAL TRAVELERS

Time: Central Texas is in the Central Standard Time Zone (CST), which is GMT/UTC -6; one hour behind the East Coast and two hours ahead of the West Coast.

Measurements: The metric system doesn't apply in the United States. Distances are measured in inches, feet, yards, and miles.

Weights: Dry weights are measured in ounces (oz.) and pounds (lbs.).

Temperatures: Degrees in Fahrenheit, not Celsius.

Mail: Currently domestic letters can be sent for $0.44, postcards for $0.28, and letters to most international destinations for $0.98 (except Mexico and Canada), but prices may change, so check with the post office.

Electricity: The United States uses 110V to 120V at 60 cycles. Appliances brought from Europe or Australia won't work in the United States without a 110V transformer, which can be hard to find in this country.

Liquor Laws

Liquor laws are the same throughout the United States when it comes to age and drinking and driving. However specifics regarding what can be sold vary from county to county. Some counties in Texas prohibit the sale of distilled spirits, while others are totally dry. When it comes to these varying degrees of "dry," the counties where Austin and San Antonio are located are so wet they are drenched. You have to be 21 and older to drink in the United States, and driving while intoxicated is illegal, dangerous, and flat-out stupid. It's also illegal to have an open container in a vehicle.

Smoking in Public

Just a few years ago most restaurants, bars, cafés, and music venues had ash trays on tables and a plume of smoke lingering in the rafters. Thanks to a growing concern for public health, Austin's smoking laws have been changing in favor of a smoke-free environment. Smoking is now prohibited in just about all indoor public places except for bingo parlors, pool halls, and bowling alleys. It was only in 2005 that voters banned smoking in music venues and bars, and only by a very narrow margin.

Don't Mess with Texas

It's highly suggested that one not mess with Texas while visiting Austin. There are two meanings behind this directive. First off, don't litter. The popular phrase "Don't mess with Texas" was created as an antilitter campaign, which has been very successful. Because of this, the Lone Star State is beautiful and clean. The other meaning behind "Don't mess with Texas" is this: Don't slight, mock, diss, or make fun of the state in any way. Texans are very proud of their state and take great offense at people who come in from out of town and talk trash about Texas.

WOMEN TRAVELING ALONE

When traveling in Texas women should apply all common-sense safety precautions. It is no worse or better than other U.S. destinations in terms of risk. However, women who travel to Texas should be prepared for the duality of chivalry and chauvinism that can be found in Texan men. Women will find the "little darlin'" culture of Texas either charming or oppressive. The same guy who holds the door open for you might look you up and down as you walk past. In the hot summer months you won't want to wear much more than shorts and a T-shirt, yet the less you wear the more attention you will draw.

SENIOR TRAVELERS

Nearly all attractions and many hotels and airlines offer discounts for seniors. It is highly recommended to unabashedly ask for your senior discount wherever you go and whatever you do: It can save you a lot of money over the course of a week or two. What constitutes a senior? In most places a senior is someone over 60 or 65.

TRAVELERS WITH DISABILITIES

In Austin and San Antonio most attractions are easy to access. Austin is particularly easy to get around, as most of what's great about Austin is centrally located, and most museums, restaurants, and accommodations are wheelchair accessible. Although most San Antonio attractions are accessible, sights such as the Mission Trail and the attractions in Brackenridge Park are pretty spread out. The River Walk has a few accesses for wheelchairs and the city is continually improving access. As for the Hill Country don't expect much in the way of easy access. Dirt roads, few wheelchair accesses, and just plain old rugged environs can slow you down, and even be impassable. However, the bigger towns such as Fredericksburg, Boerne, and New Braunfels do have some ADA infrastructure.

GAY AND LESBIAN TRAVELERS

Austin is the one bastion of open-mindedness in the conservative state of Texas. The city boasts a strong, vibrant gay and lesbian community and the only kind of intolerance that's acceptable is of intolerance itself. This general open-mindedness has provided an excellent atmosphere for the gay community to flourish. With a wide array of clubs and venues, popular liberal bookstores, a viable presence in the *Austin Chronicle,* and widely respectable organizations that fight for gay rights in Texas, Austin is the San Francisco of the South. However once you leave the Austin metropolitan area you're back in Texas. When it comes to safety gay and lesbian travelers in Austin, San Antonio, and the surrounding Hill Country shouldn't worry. Although in the Hill Country people aren't necessarily accepting, they leave "different" folks alone. Outside Austin public displays of affection will most certainly turn heads, and possibly solicit a rude remark.

TRAVELERS WITH CHILDREN

Family is first in Texas, and people traveling with children will find this a great advantage when visiting the state. All restaurants, businesses, and attractions are very proud to be family oriented, which makes traveling with children easy. Folks in Central Texas love to compliment others on their children, so don't be freaked out if someone in line somewhere strikes up a conversation through a flattering remark about your child. When it comes to the necessities for children such as food, bathroom, and keeping them interested in the day's activities, Austin and San Antonio are full of resources. Food is easy here as most kids like hamburgers and tacos, which can be found on every street corner; public bathrooms are easy to find and often outfitted with changing tables; and most attractions are family oriented.

Traveling with children in the Hill Country takes a little more planning but can be well worth it. With family-oriented dude ranches, underground caves to explore, great state parks to run around in, and fun festivals held throughout the year, there's much here to create a lifetime of memories. Planning comes in handy because everything is a little spread out. Things to take into account are travel time, finding the appropriate accommodations, and making sure you land in town when the kids get hungry or need to go to the bathroom.

ON THE ROAD

Folks in Central Texas drive very differently than the rest of the country. The hospitality Texans are famous for definitely carries over to the streets. They can be some of the slowest, most patient, courteous drivers in the nation. Central Texas driving philosophy is summed up on a road sign seen throughout the state that says, "Drive Texas friendly." People that are used to roadway customs such as honking, aggressive driving, and a general lack of patience should try to slow down and take their time.

Driving Courtesy

People on the roads of Central Texas are remarkably courteous. The two most important customs regarding this are waving and letting other drivers go. Locals have the hospitable custom of waving when changing lanes, when

CENTRAL TEXAS MILEAGE

	Austin	Johnson City	Fredericksburg	Kerrville	Bandera	Boerne	New Braunfels	San Marcos	Wimberly	San Antonio
Austin		47	77	101	108	85	47	30	37	79
Johnson City	47		30	54	76	52	52	50	38	61
Fredericksburg	77	30		24	50	38	72	69	58	68
Kerrville	101	54	24		25	34	75	85	79	63
Bandera	108	76	50	25		25	65	80	79	46
Boerne	85	52	38	34	25		41	57	55	30
New Braunfels	47	52	72	75	65	41		18	26	30
San Marcos	30	50	69	85	80	57	18		14	47
Wimberly	37	38	58	79	79	55	26	14		56
San Antonio	79	61	68	63	46	30	30	47	56	

passing on two lanes roads, and sometimes for no reason at all. The rule of thumb for waving is, the smaller the road the more important it is to give people a nod or a wave. This simple howdy-with-the-hand is especially crucial in the Hill Country. It's also not uncommon to see people getting into courtesy stalemates at stop signs, waving on freeways, and holding up busy traffic to let someone in.

Honking in Texas is a sign of an impending traffic accident, a friend is nearby, or a child is sitting behind the wheel of a parked car. People don't use the horn to say, "Get out of my way." Never start honking the second the light turns green; people will wonder what's wrong with you. If someone is sitting at a green light and not moving, be patient and just sit there until he or she starts moving. Road rage is a very rare occurrence here.

Traffic Police

The traffic police in Austin and the surrounding Hill Country are particularly notorious for being sticklers. Speed traps are unfairly set up all over the area, and unsuspecting folks that are good drivers are always getting tickets for going a little faster than the speed limit. Sometimes the speed cushion can be as low as four miles per hour over the speed limit. With this kind of speed enforcement it's wise to drive at the speed limit at all times. For some reason police are particularly active on Sunday mornings when people are heading to church. This stringent enforcement creates piles of paperwork and loads of headaches. My suspicion is that some of this police zealotry is to increase city revenue, but maybe I'm just bitter because I got a speeding ticket recently.

The Austin Police are also known for going to dramatic lengths to catch people committing traffic violations by setting up sting operations. My favorite is the "beggar sting," when cops dress up like homeless beggars and stand at busy intersections for the purpose of peering into cars to look for laws being violated. The moral of the story: While on Central Texas roads drive compulsively prudently.

Low Water Crossings

Central Texas is prone to flash floods and mini-deluges. For some of the roads in the Hill Country this means flooding of roads and low water crossings. In some cases these roads are designed to flood during heavy rains in order to divert water from buildings and communities. Never drive into a flooded roadway. You never have any idea how deep the water is or how fast it's moving. It doesn't take much more than a foot or two of water to sweep a car or an RV off road and down the river. Every year people drive into these and get themselves into trouble.

Freezing Conditions

People are surprised to hear that every year during winter there's an occasional freeze. When a freeze is in the forecast the city of Austin freaks out, schools close, and everyone hunkers down as if there will be nuclear fallout. Texans are the first to admit they are completely incompetent at driving on icy roadways. Although the city applies a chemical and gravel substance in order to prevent them, crashes, fender-benders, and accidents are abundant. Bridges and freeway overpasses can be especially dangerous when icy.

Health and Safety

FLOODS, LIGHTNING, AND TORNADOES

The three biggest dangers in Central Texas are flash flooding, lightning, and tornadoes—the biggest being flash flooding. People refer to the region as "Flash Flood alley" because every year there's an immense amount of water that gets dumped here. Moisture from the Gulf of Mexico, and the terrain of the Hill Country being mostly rock under a thin layer of soil, make for excellent conditions for water to pour and collect. Flash flood watches and flash flood warnings are very common, especially in the spring. Most of Austin's infrastructure was designed specifically to avoid flooding danger. For example, the city has special five-foot storm drains everywhere as well as many massive culverts strategically placed throughout town. Lake Travis, the second-largest lake in the area, was designed as a flood control lake. When all the regional rivers such as Llano River, Colorado River, and Pedernales River boil over with water they all dump it right into Lake Travis.

The second-biggest danger is lightning, and the third is tornadoes. When a lightning storm is overhead, go indoors. Twisters are far down on the list of things to be paranoid about because they don't normally pass through the region with maintained force. The time to watch out for them is during and after a coastal hurricane.

SEASONAL ALLERGIES

According to many national surveys, Austin is one of the worst places in the United States for allergies. If you are prone to allergies, come prepared with your preferred medication or time your trip to avoid the worst periods. The peak allergy times are December–January (mountain cedar), March–April (oak), and September–October (ragweed). Adding to the irritation is a wide variety of wildflowers and grasses. For day-by-day allergy levels and forecast information, check out www.kvue.com (click on the weather link, and then the allergy forecast link).

THINGS THAT BITE

There are three main critters that bite humans in Texas: mosquitoes, chiggers, and venomous snakes. Mosquitoes are the most common and can be a nuisance during the spring and summer months. Few cases of West Nile virus have been found in Central Texas. If you plan on being outdoors for any length of time during the summer months it helps to have a mosquito repellant on hand.

The most irritating of biting critters are chiggers. These common skin parasites are found throughout the central part of the United States. The scientific name for chiggers is Trombicula mites. Chiggers are usually found in the highest numbers during the spring and fall in grassy areas. They are about the size of the head of a pin and are reddish-orange in color. Their 50-day life cycle begins as an egg that's laid in soil and around vegetation. Larvae hatch from the egg and crawl onto a host animal where they attach themselves, feed on fluids in the tissue for several days, and drop off the host. Symptoms of chiggers include severe itching and irritation of skin. They prefer to attach in cozy, lower regions of the body such as underneath sock bands, behind the knees, and around ankles. As gross as it may sound, the best treatment for chiggers is to let them run their course. One method of trying to get the little suckers to dislodge is to drown them in rubbing alcohol or cooking oil.

The most deadly of all Texas creatures are venomous snakes, and the most common in Central Texas is the rattlesnake. They live under rocks, fallen trees, and in dark places in rural areas. People most often encounter snakes while hiking in parks and open spaces. Snakebites can be fatal, but if treated correctly and quickly you can survive. If you are bitten by a snake, there are a few things you should do. First of all, don't panic. Keep the area where the bite is stable, below the heart, and put a bandage over the infected area. Then quickly get to a medical facility. Antivenins are available and a full recovery is possible. If the snake that caused the bite is dead, and you have your wits enough about you to remember, bring the snake along as well. To help prevent snakebites, always be aware of your environment when in rural areas. Wearing hiking boots can help prevent contact with the venom and teeth of snakes.

Along with insect and snake bites, there's one other danger to be aware of: rabies. Animals that carry rabies are raccoons, possums, skunks, dogs, cats, and bats. It's wise to avoid contact with any wild animals, no matter how cute they may look, because rabies can be fatal.

CRIME

For its size, Austin is a very safe place. It boasts low crime rates, especially in violent crimes such as homicide, assault, and rape. The crimes most committed here are burglaries of homes and cars and bike theft. San Antonio, on the other hand, has much higher crime rates. Although crime is less than Dallas and Houston, San Antonio has enough crime to merit a gentle word of caution when exploring outside the downtown area, beyond the safety of the tourism infrastructure. When venturing into the outlying neighborhoods expect to see the seedier side of the city and be a little more careful than normal.

RESOURCES

Suggested Reading

Brands, H. W. *Lone Star Nation*. New York, NY: Doubleday, 2004. The author brings to life the epic tale of the Texians' struggle for independence. All the great figures of the Lone Star State's history are brought to life such as Santa Anna, Austin, Crockett, Bowie, and Sam Houston.

Brice, Donaly E. *The Great Comanche Raid*. Austin, TX: Eakin Press, 1987. Outlines one of the most famous Native American attacks in the Republic of Texas's brief history.

Campbell, Randolph B. *Gone to Texas*. Oxford, England: Oxford University Press, 2003. This well-written tome on Texas history covers everything from the first arrival of humans in the Panhandle some 10,000 years ago to the dawn of the 21st century, offering an interpretive account of the land and the successive waves of people who have "gone to Texas."

Favata, Martin A., and Jose B. Fernandez, eds. *The Account—Álvar Núñez Cabeza de Vaca's Relación*. Houston, TX: Arte Público Press, 1993. Perhaps one of the most insightful and historically important writings in early Texas history, this work documents the conquest of the region by both Spaniard and white man.

Friedman, Kinky. *The Great Psychedelic Armadillo Picnic: A "Walk" in Austin*. New York, NY: Crown, 2004. Famous humorist, author, and possible Texas governor takes the reader on a white-knuckle tour of Austin—poking, prodding and overturning every social, political, and cultural rock in town.

Greer, James Kimmins. *Colonel Jack Hays, Texas Frontier Leader and California Builder*. College Station, TX: Texas A&M University Press, 1952. Tells the story of Texas Ranger Colonel Jack Hays, which offers a peak into the pioneer Wild West version of Texas that has been immortalized.

Kownslar, Allan O. *European Texans*. College Station, TX: Texas A&M University Press, 2004. Considers the contributions of those who immigrated to Texas from Europe in the early days of the state's history. Readers learn about the life and culture of French, English, Scottish, Irish, Dutch, Belgian, Swiss, Danish, Norwegian, Swedish, German, Wend, Polish, Czech, Hungarian, Italian, Greek, and Slavic Texans.

Reid, Jan. *The Improbable Rise of Redneck Rock*. Austin, TX: University of Texas Press, 2004. Chronicles the days when music hit Austin, Texas, in the early 1970s at now-legendary venues such as Threadgill's, Vulcan Gas Company, and the Armadillo World Headquarters.

Smithwich, Noah. *The Evolution of a State or Recollections of Old Texas Days*. Austin, TX: University of Texas Press, 1984. Read about Texas's early period from someone who was there. It covers the early days of Austin's colony to the aftermath of the Civil War. Some of the content may not be perfectly accurate but it does offer a personable glimpse into Texas myth, legend, and folklore.

Wilbarger, J. W. *Indian Depredations in Texas*. Austin, TX: Eakin Press, 1985. A series of accounts of the turmoil on Texas soil when white men came along. The tales here are true accounts of the men involved in conquest and the desperate responses of the indigenous peoples being overrun and exterminated.

Internet Resources

The Handbook of Texas–Online
www.tsha.utexas.edu/handbook/online
Texas state history and statistical information.

Austin Chamber of Commerce
www.austin-chamber.org
Includes general information about Austin.

Austin Chronicle
www.austinchronicle.com
Comprehensive resource for music, arts, entertainment, classifieds, restaurant reviews, festivals and calendar of events, and weather for Austin.

Austin 360
www.austin360.com
Online magazine with music, arts, entertainment listings, restaurant reviews, festivals and calendar of events.

Austin Convention and Visitors Bureau
www.austintexas.org
Premier website for tourism in Austin.

Texas Tourism
www.traveltexas.com
Official site of Texas Tourism that includes maps, guidebooks, highway information, and all tourism-related information about the Lone Star State.

Texas Parks & Wildlife
www.tpwd.state.tx.us
Official Texas Parks & Wildlife site that includes information on parks, camping, hiking, and park access and hours of operation.

San Antonio River Walk
www.thesanantonioriverwalk.com
Information about San Antonio's River Walk.

San Antonio Convention and Visitors Bureau
www.visitsanantonio.com
San Antonio's primary resource for tourism information.

Index

List of Maps

Acknowledgements

Special thanks goes to Susan Brady Marler, who introduced me to Austin and came up with the brilliant idea of moving here. Without her knowledge of the region and her continual support I couldn't have written this guidebook. A special thanks also goes to Carl Pierce and Tom Mitchell for researching and compiling the Texas history information. A grateful tip of the hat also goes to all the folks who helped out with this book in some way or another including Jane Musser, Kevin McLain, Grace Fujimoto, Shari Husain, Laura Brady, Paul Brady, Reggi and Martine Liguori, Jonathan and Kelly Davis, Sara Pierce, Tyler Porterfield, Mike and Bonnie Rose, Adam Foster, Denise Foster, Dee Dee Gonzalez, Jimmie and Lelia Naumann, Mike Dunn, Debra Guerrero, Vincent Valdez, Danielle Wilson, and Mark Murray chief meteorologist for KVUE news.

www.moon.com

DESTINATIONS | ACTIVITIES | BLOGS | MAPS | BOOKS

MOON.COM is ready to help plan your next trip! Filled with fresh trip ideas and strategies, author interviews, informative travel blogs, a detailed map library, and descriptions of all the Moon guidebooks, Moon.com is all you need to get out and explore the world—or even places in your own backyard. While at Moon.com, sign up for our monthly e-newsletter for updates on new releases, travel tips, and expert advice from our on-the-go Moon authors. As always, when you travel with Moon, expect an experience that is uncommon and truly unique.

MOON IS ON FACEBOOK—BECOME A FAN!
JOIN THE MOON PHOTO GROUP ON FLICKR

MOON AUSTIN, SAN ANTONIO,
& THE HILL COUNTRY
Avalon Travel
a member of the Perseus Books Group
1700 Fourth Street
Berkeley, CA 94710, USA
www.moon.com

Editor: Shaharazade Husain
Series Manager: Kathryn Ettinger
Copy Editor: Emily Lunceford
Graphics Coordinator: Tabitha Lahr
Production Coordinator: Tabitha Lahr
Cover Designer: Tabitha Lahr
Map Editor: Kat Bennett
Cartographer: Kaitlin Jaffe
Indexer: Jean Mooney

ISBN-13: 978-1-59880-895-7
ISSN: 1931-5252

Printing History
1st Edition – 2006
3rd Edition – September 2011
5 4 3 2 1

KEEPING CURRENT

If you have a favorite gem you'd like to see included in the next edition, or see anything
that needs updating, clarification, or correction, please drop us a line. Send your
comments via email to feedback@moon.com, or use the address above.

MAP SYMBOLS

▭▭▭ Expressway	**◖** Highlight	✈ Airport	⚲ Golf Course
▭▭▭ Primary Road	○ City/Town	✗ Airfield	**ᴾ** Parking Area
▭▭▭ Secondary Road	◉ State Capital	▲ Mountain	◢ Archaeological Site
▭ ▭ ▭ Unpaved Road	⊛ National Capital	✛ Unique Natural Feature	⚑ Church
▭ ▭ ▭ Trail	★ Point of Interest		⛽ Gas Station
▪▪▪▪ Ferry	● Accommodation	⚞ Waterfall	⬬ Glacier
▭▭▭ Railroad	▼ Restaurant/Bar	♠ Park	⬬ Mangrove
▬▬▬ Pedestrian Walkway	■ Other Location	➊ Trailhead	⬛ Reef
▬▬▬ Stairs	▲ Campground	⛷ Skiing Area	⬬ Swamp

CONVERSION TABLES

°C = (°F − 32) / 1.8
°F = (°C x 1.8) + 32
1 inch = 2.54 centimeters (cm)
1 foot = 0.304 meters (m)
1 yard = 0.914 meters
1 mile = 1.6093 kilometers (km)
1 km = 0.6214 miles
1 fathom = 1.8288 m
1 chain = 20.1168 m
1 furlong = 201.168 m
1 acre = 0.4047 hectares
1 sq km = 100 hectares
1 sq mile = 2.59 square km
1 ounce = 28.35 grams
1 pound = 0.4536 kilograms
1 short ton = 0.90718 metric ton
1 short ton = 2,000 pounds
1 long ton = 1.016 metric tons
1 long ton = 2,240 pounds
1 metric ton = 1,000 kilograms
1 quart = 0.94635 liters
1 US gallon = 3.7854 liters
1 Imperial gallon = 4.5459 liters
1 nautical mile = 1.852 km

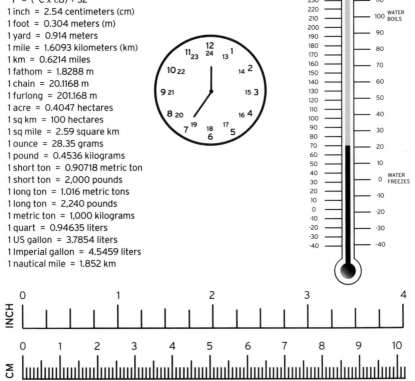